AN INTRODUCTION TO INDIAN PHILOSOPHY

AN INTRODUCTION TO INDIAN PHILOSOPHY

SATISCHANDRA CHATTERJEE
DHIRENDRAMOHAN DATTA

MOTILAL BANARSIDASS PUBLISHERS
PRIVATE LIMITED • DELHI

Reprint Edition: Delhi, 2024
7th Edition; Calcutta, 1968
1st Edition; Calcutta, 1939

ISBN : 978-81-208-3527-6 (HB)
ISBN : 978-81-208-4017-1 (PB)

Also available at:
MOTILAL BANARSIDASS
41 U.A. Bungalow Road, Jawahar Nagar, Delhi 110 007
8 Mahalaxmi Chamber, 22 Bhulabhai Desai Road, Mumbai 400 026
203 Royapettah High Road, Mylapore, Chennai 600 004
236, 9th Main III Block, Jayanagar, Bengaluru 560 011
3 Camac Street, Kolkata 700 017
Ashok Rajpath, Patna 800 004
Chowk, Varanasi 221 001

MLBD Cataloging-in-Publication Data
An Introduction to Indian Philosophy
by Satischandra Chatterjee and Dhirendramohan Datta
ISBN : 978-81-208-3527-6 (HB)
ISBN : 978-81-208-4017-1 (PB)
Includes index.
I. Philosophy/Indian II. Carvaka III Jainism
IV. Buddhism V. Nyaya VI. Vaisheshika VII. Sankhya VIII. Yoga
IX. Mimansa X. Vedanta

Printed in India
by Thomson Press, India and
published by JP Jain for Motilal Banarsidass Publishers (P) Ltd,
41 U.A. Bungalow Road, Jawahar Nagar, Delhi-110007

TO

PROFESSOR S. RADHAKRISHNAN

AND

THE LATE PROFESSOR K.C. BHATTACHARYYA

WHOSE TEACHINGS HAVE INSPIRED
THE AUTHORS

CONTENTS

CHAPTER IV

CHAPTER VI

CHAPTER X

PREFACE TO THE FIRST EDITION

The object of this book is to provide a simple introduction to the Indian systems of philosophy. Each one of these systems has had a vast and varied development and cannot be treated adequately in a brief work like this. Attempt has been made to introduce the reader to the spirit and outlook of Indian philosophy and help him to grasp thoroughly the central ideas rather than acquaint him with minute details. Modern students of philosophy feel many difficulties in understanding the Indian problems and theories. Their long experience with university students has helped the authors to realise these, and they have tried to remove them as far as possible. This accounts for most of the critical discussions which could otherwise have been dispensed with.

The book has been primarily written for beginners. The first chapter which contains the general principles and basic features of Indian philosophy, as well as a brief sketch of each system, gives the student a bird's-eye view of the entire field and prepares him for a more intensive study of the systems which are contained in the following chapters. It is hoped, therefore, that the book will suit the needs of university students at different stages, as well as of general readers interested in Indian philosophy. It will serve the needs of B.A. Pass students who may be required to have a brief general acquaintance with Indian philosophy as a whole, as well as those of Honours students who may be expected to have a more detailed knowledge of one or more systems.

It is the firm conviction of the writers that Reality is many-sided and Truth is manifold; that each system approaches Reality from one point of view or level of experience, and embodies one aspect of Truth. They have tried to approach each system with sympathy and justify it, rather than dismiss it with a customary criticism. They believe that a sympathetic insight into the great systems will enable the student to grasp their truths more easily and give him a sound philosophical outlook.

While an attempt has been made to bring out the significance of Indian views in terms of modern Western thought, care has always been exercised to preserve their distinctive marks, such as their spiritual and practical outlook, their recognition of the different levels of experience.

The authors are grateful to Dr. Syamaprasad Mookerjee, M.A., D.Litt., B.L., M.L.A., Vidyāvācaspati, Barrister-at-Law, ex-Vice-Chancellor, Calcutta University, at whose suggestion the work was undertaken, and to Sir S. Radhakrishnan, Kt., M.A., D.Litt., George V Professor of Philosophy, Calcutta University, Spalding Professor of Eastern Religions and Ethics, Oxford University, who has very kindly gone through the manuscript and made valuable suggestions. They are also indebted to Professor Krishnachandra Bhattacharyya, M.A., with whom they discussed some of the problems treated here and received much light and guidance. They are grateful also to the authorities of the Calcutta University, and especially to the Registrar, the Superintendent of the Press and his energetic colleagues, for the publication of the work.

Note to Students

The paragraphs which occur in small type in this book are meant for more advanced students and may be omitted by beginners. The attention of students is specially invited to the select bibliography given at the beginning of each chapter. Reference to it will explain the abbreviation of the names of books found in the foot-notes.

For correct pronunciation students should note that the

following scheme has been adopted for representing Sanskrit sounds in English :

अ = অ = a, आ = আ = ā, इ = ই = i, ई = ঈ = ī, उ = উ = u,
ऊ = ঊ = ū, ऋ = ঋ = ṛ, ए = এ = e, ऐ = ঐ = ai, ओ = ও = o,
औ = ঔ = au,
क् = ক্ = k, ख् = খ্ = kh, ग् = গ্ = g, घ् = ঘ্ = gh, ङ् = ঙ্ = ṅ,
च् = চ্ = c, छ् = ছ্ = ch, ज् = জ্ = j, झ् = ঝ্ = jh, ञ् = ঞ্ = ñ,
ट् = ট্ = ṭ, ठ् = ঠ্ = ṭh, ड् = ড্ = ḍ, ढ् = ঢ্ = ḍh, ण् = ণ্ = ṇ,
त् = ত্ = t, थ् = থ্ = th, द् = দ্ = d, ध् = ধ্ = dh, न् = ন্ = n,
प् = প্ = p, फ् = ফ্ = ph, ब् = ব্ = b, भ् = ভ্ = bh, म् = ম্ = m,
य् = য্ = y, र् = র্ = r, ल् = ল্ = l, व् = ব্ = v, श् = শ্ = ś,
ष् = ষ্ = ṣ, स् = স্ = s, ह् = হ্ = h, क्ष् = ক্ষ = kṣ, ङ्क = ঙ্ক্ = ṅk,
ङ्ग = ঙ্গ = ṅg, ज्ञ् = জ্ঞ = jñ, = ং = ṁ, : = : = ḥ.

PREFACE TO THE SECOND EDITION

The authors feel encouraged by the demand for a second edition of this book within such a short time. They are grateful to the many universities which have adopted this compendium as a text-book, and to the many lay readers who have intimated their appreciation of the book as a suitable introduction to Indian Philosophy. But at the same time the authors realize once more the great difficulty of compressing into such a volume all that is important in the arguments and theories of schools which have evolved through nearly two thousand years, and developed intricacies which defy easy exposition. They are, therefore, painfully aware of the many shortcomings of the book, and very eagerly avail themselves of this opportunity of a second edition to remove defects, as far as possible, by addition, alteration, omission and rearrangement of topics. In this work of improvement they have received great help from teachers and scholars who have favoured them with detailed opinions and suggestion. The authors are thankful to all of them; but they are especially indebted, in this respect, to Professors Khagendranath Mitra, Haridas Bhattacharyya, Jadunath Sinha, Surendranath Goswami, Kalidas Bhattacharyya and Mr. Anilkumar Ray Chaudhury. If some of the suggestions could not be carried out, it was mainly because of the limitation of the original scope of the book, the necessity for economizing paper, and the desire for avoiding difficulties that might embarass the beginner.

The chapter on the Vedānta has been partly rewritten. Śaṅkara and Rāmānuja have been dealt with successively (and not side by side, as before). The rational of argumentative side of the Vedānta has been substantially reinforced by the addition of many new paragraphs in small print. The authors hope that this will be useful to the advanced reader, while the simplicity of the original treatment, and the interest of the beginner, will remain unaffected.

It is necessary to mention that instead of following the ordinary translation practice of rendering 'Īśvara' into 'God' and 'Brahman' into 'Absolute', the authors have used the word 'God' also for 'Brahman'. Just as 'Brahman' (without adjectives) is used, even by the Upaniṣads and Śaṅkara, for both the immanent, personal aspect, and also for the transcendent, impersonal aspect, similarly 'God' also has been used in English in this wide sense, and, therefore, sometimes for the Absolute (e.g. of Hegel), the Indeterminate Substance (e.g. of Spinoza), the Primordial Principle (e.g. of Whitehead). The exact sense in which 'God' has been used in this book will be clear from the context. Confinement of 'God' only to the Deity of Religion, and of 'Absolute' to the ultimate philosophical principle, while convenient in one respect, suffers from the disadvantage of suggesting as though they stand for two distinct realities, and not for two aspects of the same reality, as is the case in the Vedānta.

PREFACE TO THE SIXTH EDITION

The authors feel highly gratified that the book is now being widely used in India, America, Great Britain and other countries, and that another edition has been called for so soon. This gives an opportunity for further revision and improvement. The authors are grateful to Professor Charles A. Moore of the University of Hawaii and all other teachers of Philosophy who favoured them with their opinions and suggestions for some improvements in the previous editions. They also express their thanks to Sri S. Kanjilal, Superintendent of the Calcutta University Press, and his colleagues for their help in bringing out this edition in time.

PREFACE TO THE SEVENTH EDITION

This seventh edition offered further opportunities for revision. We are much obliged to Professor Pradyotkumar Mukhopadhyay of Visva-Bharati for some suggestions, and to Sri S. Kanjilal and his colleagues for bringing out the book under very difficult circumstances.

S.C. Chatterjee
59-B, Hindusthan Park
Calcutta - 29.

D.M. Datta
Purvapalli, Santiniketan
West Bengal.

CHAPTER I
GENERAL INTRODUCTION

I. The Basic Features of Indian Philosophy

1. The Nature of Philosophy

Like all other living beings man struggles for existence. But while the lower beings struggle more or less blindly without any conscious plan and purpose, and work by instinct, man uses the superior gift of his intellect to understand the conditions and meaning of the struggle and to devise plans and instruments to ensure success. He wishes to lead his life in the light of his knowledge of himself and the world, taking into consideration not merely the immediate results of his actions, but even their far-reaching consequences. Desire for knowledge springs, therefore, from the rational nature of man. Philosophy is an attempt to satisfy this very reasonable desire. It is not, therefore, a mere luxury, but a necessity. As an eminent English writer puts its : "Men live in accordance with their philosophy of life, their conception of the world. This is true even of the most thoughless. It is impossible to live without a metaphysic. The choice that is given us is not between some kind of metaphysic and no metaphysic ; it is always between a good metaphysic and a bad metaphysic."[1]

The necessity of Philosophy.

Philosophy in its widest etymological sense means 'love of knowledge'. It tries to know things that immediately and remotely concern man. What is the real nature of man ? What is the end of this life ? What is the nature of this world in which he lives ? Is there any creator of this world ? How should man live in the light of his knowledge of himself, the world and God ? These are some of the many problems, taken at

Its meaning and scope.

---

1. Aldous Huxley, *Ends and Means*, p. 252.

random, which we find agitating the human mind in every land, from the very dawn of civilization. Philosophy deals with problems of this nature. As philosophy aims at knowledge of truth it is termed in Indian literature, 'the vision of truth' (darśana). Every Indian school holds, in its own way, that there can be a direct realization of truth (tattva-darśana). A man of realization becomes free ; one who lacks it is entangled in the world.[1]

Darśana or vision of truth.

In the history of Western philosophy we find that as human knowledge about each of the different problems mentioned above began to grow, it became impossible for the same man to study everything about every problem. Division of labour or specialization became necessary and a group of men devoted themselves to a particular problem or a few connected problems. There came into existence in this way the different special sciences. Physics, Chemistry, Botany, Astronomy, Geology and similar sciences took up each a part or aspect of the world of nature. Physiology, Anatomy and the other medical sciences devoted themselves to the different problems of the human body. Psychology began to study the problems of the human mind. The *detailed* study of many of the particular problems with which philosophical speculation originally started became thus the subject-matter of the *special* sciences. Philosophy then began to depend on the reports of the investigation made by the different sciences, tried to understand their meanings and implications critically, and utilized these results for understanding the *general nature* of the universe—man, nature and God.

The development of Western philosophy.

Western philosophy at the present day has for its main branches (a) Metaphysics, which discuss the general problems regarding reality — man, nature and

The branches of Western philosophy.

1. Vide *Manu-Saṁhitā*, 6.74 : "Samyag-darśana-sampannaḥ karmabhirna nibadhyate ; darśanena vihīnastu saṁsāram pratipadyate."

God, (b) Epistemology or theory of knowledge, which enquires into the nature of human knowledge, as to how it develops and how far it is able to grasp reality, (c) Logic, which discusses the laws of valid reasoning and other incidental problems, (d) Ethics, which investigates the problems of morality, such as the standard of moral judgment, the highest goal of human life and other cognate problems, and (e) Aesthetics, which deals with the problems of beauty. Another recent development of philosophy in the West, called Axiology, is devoted to the discussion of the problem of values. Social Philosophy is also regarded as a branch of philosophy and often discussed along with Ethics. Psychology had been for long a very important branch of philosophy, but the tendency now is to treat it as one of the special sciences like Physics and Chemistry and give it a place independent of philosophy.

The problems and methods of Indian philosophy.

Though the basic problems of philosophy have been the same in the East as in the West and the chief solutions have striking similarities, yet the methods of philosophical enquiry differ in certain respects and the process of the development of philosophical thought also vary. Indian philosophy discusses the different problems of Metaphysics, Ethics, Logic, Psychology and Epistemology, but generally it does not discuss them separately. Every problem is discussed by the Indian philosopher from all possible approaches, metaphysical, ethical, logical, psychological and epistemological. This tendency has been called by some thinkers, like Sir B.N. Seal, the synthetic outlook of Indian philosophy.

2. The Meaning and Scope of Indian Philosophy

Indian philosophy is not Hindu philosophy.

Indian philosophy denotes the philosophical speculations of all Indian thinkers, ancient or modern, Hindus or non-Hindus, theists or atheists. 'Indian philosophy' is supposed by some to be synonymous with 'Hindu philosophy'. This would be true only if the word 'Hindu' were taken in the geographical sense of 'Indian'. But if 'Hindu' means the followers of a particular religious faith known as Hinduism, the supposition would be wrong and misleading. Even in the ancient writings of the orthodox Hindu philosophers, like the *Sarva-darśana-saṅgraha* of Mādhavācārya which tries to present in one place the views of *all* (sarva) schools of philosophy, we find in the list of philosophies (darśanas) the views of atheists and materialists like the Cārvākas, and unorthodox thinkers like the Bauddhas and the Jainas, along with those of the orthodox Hindu thinkers.

The broad outlook of Indian philosophy.

Indian philosophy is marked, in this respect, by a striking breadth of outlook which only testifies to its unflinching devotion to the search for truth. Though there were many different schools and their views differed sometimes very widely, yet each school took care to learn the views of all the others and did not come to any conclusion before considering thoroughly what others had to say and how their points could be met. This spirit led to the formation of a method of philosophical discussion. A philosopher had first to state the views of his opponents before he formulated his own theory. This statement of the opponent's case came to be known as the prior view (pūrvapakṣa). Then followed the refutation (khaṇḍana) of this view. Last of all came the statement and proof of the philosopher's own position, which, therefore, was known as the subsequent view (uttarapakṣa) or the conclusion (siddhānta).

The consequent thoroughness of the Indian systems.

This catholic spirit of treating rival positions with consideration was more than rewarded by the thoroughness and perfection that most of the Indian schools attained. If we open a comprehensive work on the Vedānta, we will find in it the statement of the views of all other schools, Cārvāka, Bauddha, Jaina, Sāṅkhya, Yoga, Mīmāṁsā, Nyāyā and Vaiśeṣika, discussed and weighed with all care ; similarly any good work on the Bauddha or Jaina philosophy discusses the other views. The systems thus became encyclopaedic in their grasp of ideas. Naturally we find that many of the problems of contemporary Western philosophy are discussed in Indian systems of philosophy. Besides, we find that indigenous scholars with a thorough training, exclusively in Indian philosophy, are able to deal even with abstruse problems of Western philosophy with surprising skill.

Its moral for the future of Indian philosophy.

If the openness of mind—the willingness to listen to what others have to say—has been one of the chief causes of the wealth and greatness of Indian philosophy in the past, it has a definite moral for the future. If Indian philosophy is once more to revive and continue its great career, it can do so only by taking into consideration the new ideas of life and reality which have been flowing into India from the West and the East, from the Aryan, the Semitic, the Mongolian and other sources.

3. The Schools of Indian Philosophy

Classification of the Indian schools : orthodox and heterodox.

According to a traditional principle of classification, most likely adopted by orthodox Hindu thinkers, the schools or systems of Indian philosophy are divided into two broad classes, namely, orthodox (ā stika) and heterodox (nāstika). To the first group belong the six chief philosophical systems (popularly known as ṣaḍ-darśana), namely Mīmāṁsā, Vedānta, Sāṅkhya, Yoga, Nyāya and Vaiśeṣika. These are regarded as orthodox (āstika), not because they believe in God, but because they accept the authority of the Vedas.[1] The Mīmāṁsā and the Sāṅkhya do not believe in God as the creator of the world, yet they are called orthodox (āstika), because they believe in the authoritativeness of the Vedas. The six systems

1. In modern Indian languages, 'āstika' and 'nāstika' generally mean 'theist' and 'atheist', respectively. But in Sanskrit philosophical literature, 'ā stika' means 'one who believes in the authority of the Vedas' or 'one who belives in life after death'. ('Nāstika' means the opposite of these). The word is used here in the first sense. In the second sense, even the Jaina and Bauddha schools are 'āstika', as they believe in life after death. The six orthodox schools are 'āstika', and the Cārvāka is 'nāstika' in both the senses.

mentioned here are not the only orthodox systems; they are the chief ones, and there are some other less important orthodox schools, such as the Grammarian school, the medical school, etc., also noticed by Mādhavācārya. Under the other class of heterodox systems, the chief three are the schools of the Materialists like the Cārvākas, the Bauddhas and the Jainas. They are called heterodox (nāstika) because they do not believe in the authority of the Vedas.

The place of the Vedas in Indian philosophy.

To understand this more clearly, we should know something regarding the place of the Vedas in the evolution of Indian thought. The Vedas are the earliest available records of Indian literature, and subsequent Indian thought, specially philosophical speculation, is greatly influenced by the Vedas, either positively or negatively. Some of the philosophical systems accepted Vedic authority, while others opposed it. The Mīmāṁsā and the Vedānta may be regarded as the direct continuation of the Vedic culture. The Vedic tradition had two sides, ritualistic and speculative (karma and Jñāna). The Mīmāṁsā emphasised the ritualistic aspect and evolved a philosophy to justify and help the continuation of the Vedic rites and rituals. The Vedānta emphasised the speculative aspect of the Vedas and developed an elaborate philosophy out of Vedic speculations. As both these schools were direct continuation of Vedic culture, both are sometimes called by the common name, Mīmāṁsā ; and for the sake of distinction the first is called Pūrva-Mīmāṁsā (or Karma-Mīmāṁsā) and the second Uttara-Mīmāṁsā (or Jñāna-Mīmāṁsā). But the more usual names of these two are Mīmāṁsā and Vedānta respectively, and we shall follow this common usage here. Though the Sāṅkhya, Yoga, Nyāya and Vaiśeṣika based their theories on ordinary human experience and reasoning, they did not challenge the authority of the Vedas, but tried to show that the testimony of the Vedas was quite in harmony with their rationally established theories. The Cārvāka, Bauddha and Jaina schools arose mainly by opposition to the Vedic culture and, therefore, they rejected the authority of the Vedas. These facts may be summed up in a tabular form as follows :

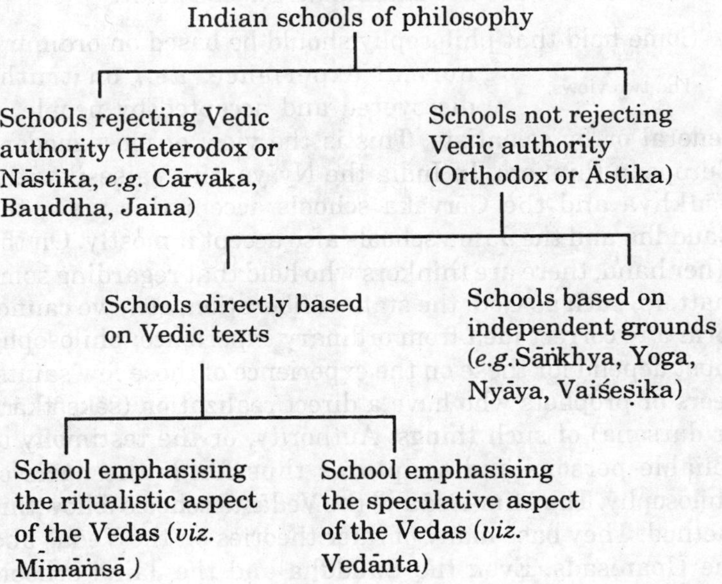

4. The Places of Authority and Reasoning in Indian Philosophy

The grounds of philosophy.

The distinctions discussed above can be ultimately traced to distinctions in the methods of speculation, adopted by the different schools.

Should philosophy always depend on ordinary experience or should it sometimes depend on the experience of the wise few ?

Solutions of philosophical problems, like 'What is the ultimate cause of the world ?', 'Does God exist ?', 'What is the nature of God ?', cannot be obtained by observation. The philosopher must employ his imagination and reasoning, and find out answers consistent with truths already established by experience. Like most other branches of knowledge, philosophy proceeds, therefore, from the known to the unknown. The foundation of philosophy is experience, and the chief tool used is reason. But the question arises here : "What experience should form the basis of philosophy ?" Indian thinkers are not unanimous on this point.

The two views.

Some hold that philosophy should be based on ordinary, normal experience, *i.e.*, on truths discovered and accepted by people in general or by scientists. This is the view of most modern European thinkers. In India the Nyāya, the Vaiśeṣika, the Sāṅkhya and the Cārvāka schools accept this view; the Bauddha and the Jaina schools also accept it mostly. On the other hand, there are thinkers who hold that regarding some matters, such as God, the state of liberation, etc., we cannot form any correct idea from ordinary experience; philosophy must depend for these on the experience of those few saints, seers or prophets who have a direct realization (sākṣātkāra or darśana) of such things. Authority, or the testimony of reliable persons and scriptures thus forms the basis of philosophy. The Mimāṁsāand the Vedānta schools follow this method. They base many of thier theories on the Vedas and the Upanisads. Even the Bauddha and the Jaina schools depend sometimes on the teachings of Bauddha and Jainas who are regarded as perfect and omniscient. In Europe the scholastic philosophy of the middle ages was based similarly on the authority of the Christian scriptures.

Whatever be the grounds, reason is the instrument of philosophical speculation.

Reasoning is the chief instrument of speculation for philosophers of both these classes. The difference is that while by the former reasoning is made always to follow the lead of ordinary experience, by the latter reasoning is made to follow in some matters the lead of authority, as well.

The charge is often heard against Indian Philosophy that its theories are not based on independent reasoning but on authority and, therefore, they are dogmatic, rather than critical. This charge is clearly not true of the majority of Indian systems which are as much based on free thinking as any we can find in the West even in this modern age of critical speculation. The criticism may be chiefly levelled against the two systems of the Mīmāṁsā and the Vedānta which, we have found, give an important place to authority. Though these systems start from authority, the theories they develop are supported also by such strong independent arguments that even if we withdraw the support of authority, the theories can stand well and compare favourably with any theory established elsewhere on independent reasoning alone. Man, as a rational creature, cannot of course be satisfied unless his reason is satisfied. But if arguments in favour of a philosophy are sufficient to satisfy his reason, the additional fact of its being based on the experiences of persons of clearer minds and purer hearts would only add to its value.

5. *How the Indian Systems Gradually Developed*

The parallel growths of the Indian schools and their persistence through the lives and teachings of active followers.

In the history of Western philosophy we usually find the different schools coming into existence successively. Each school predominates till another comes in and replaces it. In India, on the other hand, we find that the different schools, though not originating simultaneously, flourish together during many centuries, and pursue parallel courses of growth. The reason is to be sought perhaps in the fact that in India philosophy was a part of life. As each system of thought came into existence it was adopted as a philosophy of life by a band of followers who formed a school of that philosophy. They *lived* the philosophy and handed it down to succeeding generations of followers who were attracted to them through their lives and thoughts. The different systems of thought thus continued to exist through unbroken chains of successive adherents for centuries. Even to-day, we find the active followers of some of the chief philosophical schools in different parts of India, though development of indigenous philosophy has been much retarded now, owing to social and political vicissitudes.

Each school criticizes and influences every other school.

It should not be supposed, however, that the different systems developed within their respective circles of active followers, without mutually influencing one another. On the contrary, as we have pointed out previously, each philosophy regarded it as its duty to consider and satisfy all possible objections that might be raised against its views. In fact, it is by constant mutual criticism that the huge philosophical literature has come into existence. Owing to this again, there developed a passion for clear and precise enunciation of ideas and for guarding statements against objections. Mutual criticism further makes Indian philosophy its own best critic.

Indian philosophy is its own best critic.

Bearing this fact of mutual influence in mind we may try to understand the general process by which the systems originated and developed. The Vedas, we have said, are directly or indirectly responsible for most of the philosophical speculations. In the orthodox schools, next to the Vedas and the Upaniṣads, we find the sūtra literature marking the definite beginning of systematic philosophical thinking 'Sūtra' etymologically means 'thread' and in this context it means a brief mnemonic statement. As philosophical discussions took place mostly orally, and as they were passed down through oral traditions handed down by teachers to students, it was perhaps felt necessary to link up or *thread* together the main thoughts in the minds of students by brief statements of problems, answers, possible objections and replies to them. A sūtra-work consists of a collection of many sūtras or aphorisms of this kind, arranged into different chapters and sections according to different topics. The *Brahmasūtra* of Bādarāyaṇa, for example, contains the aphorisms that sum up and *systematize* the philosophical teachings of different Vedic works, chiefly the Upaniṣads, and also briefly mention and answer actual and possible objections to these views. This work is the first *systematic* treaties on the Vedānta. Similarly, we have for the Mīmāṁsā, the sūtras of Jaimini, for the Nyāya, the sūtras of Gotama, for the Vaiśeṣika, the sūtras of Kaṇāda, for the Yoga, the sutras of Patañjali. According to tradition, for the Sāṅkhya

How philosophical literature developed.

The sūtra works of the orthodox schools.

also there were the sūtras of Kapila, who is regarded as the founder of the system. But the sūtras now available are not recognized by all as the original sūtras. The earliest systematic work available now is the *Sāṅkhya-kārikā* of Iśvara Kṛṣṇa.

Commentaries on the sūtras.

The sūtras were brief and, therefore, their meanings were not always clear. There arose thus the necessity for elaborate explanation and interpretation through commentaries. These chief commentaries on the respective sūtras were called the Bhāṣyas, the names and further particulars about which will be found later in the chapters on the different schools. But it should be noted that, in some cases, on the same sūtra-work different authors wrote different major commentaries (bhāṣyas) and interpreted the sūtras to justify their respective stand-points. Thus came into existence, for example, the different Bhāṣyas on the *Brahma-sūtra* by Śankara, Rāmānuja, Madhva, Vallabha, Nimbārka, Baladeva and others. The followers of each interpretation formed into a school of the Vedānta and there arose the many schools of the Vedānta itself.

Sub-commentaries and independent works.

As time went on, commentaries on commentaries arose and sometimes independent works also were written to supply hand-books or to justify elaborate or criticize existing doctrines. The philosophical literature of the orthodox schools developed in this way. The history of the development of the heterodox schools is also more or less the same. They do not start, however, from any sūtra-work of the above kind. The accounts of these will be given in the chapters dealing with those schools.

The harmony among the schools. The gradation of the schools according to the fitness of followers.

Though the different schools were opposed to one another in their teachings, a sort of harmony among them was also conceived by the Indian thinkers. They believed that all persons were not fit for all things and that in religious, philosophical and social matters we should take into consideration these differences and recognize consequent distinctions of natural aptitudes (adhikārabheda). The different philosophical disciplines, as already pointed out, were taken in India as the different ways of shaping practical lives. Consequently, it was all the more necessary to discriminate the fitness of their followers. The many systems of philosophy beginning from the materialism of the Cārvāka school and ending with the Vedānta of Śaṇkara were thus conceived to offer different paths for philosophical thinking and living to persons of differing qualifications and temperaments. But even apart from this pragmatic explanation, we can discover in these schools, outwardly opposed, many positive points of agreement, which may be regarded as the common marks of Indian culture.

6. The Common Characters of the Indian Systems

The unity of moral and spiritual outlook among the systems.

The philosophy of a country is the cream of its culture and civilisation. It springs from ideas that prevail in its atmosphere and bears its unconscious stamp. Though the different schools of Indian philosophy present a diversity of views, we can discern even in them the common stamp of an Indian culture. We may briefly describe this unity as the unity of moral and spiritual outlook. To understand this, let us consider its main aspects and illustrate points of agreement among the different schools.

Its chief factors.

(1) The practical motive present in all systems.

The most striking and fundamental point of agreement, which we have already discussed partly, is that all the systems regard philosophy as a practical necessity and cultivate it in order to understand how life can be best led. The aim of philosophical wisdom is not merely the satisfaction of intellectual curiosity, but mainly an enlightened life led with far-sight, foresight and insight. It became a custom, therefore, with an Indian writer to explain, at the beginning of his work, how it serves human ends (puruṣārtha).

This does not aflect their theoretical development.

But it should also be remembered that the presence of a practical motive did not narrow the scope of Indian philosophy to Ethics and Theology alone as some. Western critics[1] imagine. Its scope is as wide as any philosophy springing only from theoretic motives ; and even on theoretical grounds

1. *E.g.*, Thilly, *A History of Philosophy*, p. 3;
Stace, *A Critical History of Greek Philosophy*, p. 14.

some branches of Indian philosophy, like Metaphysics, Epistemology and Logic can easily hold their own against any system of the West.

(2) Philosophy springs from spiritual disquiet at the existing order of things.

The reason why the practical motive prevails in Indian philosophy lies in the fact that every system, pro-Vedic or anti-Vedic, is moved to speculation by a spiritual disquiet at the sight of the evils that cast a gloom over life in this world and it wants to understand the source of these evils and incidentally the nature of the universe and the meaning of human life, in order to find out some means for completely overcoming life's miseries.

Pessimism in Indian philosophy is initial, not final.

The attitude of mind which looks at the dark side of things is known as pessimism. Indian philosophy has often been criticized as pessimistic and, therefore, pernicious in its influence on practical life. How far this criticism is justified will be seen in the course of this book. But one general point should be noted here. Indian philosophy is pessimistic in the sense that it works under a sense of discomfort and disquiet at the existing order of things. It discovers and strongly asserts that life, as it is being thoughtlessly led, is a mere sport of blind impulses and unquenchable desires; it inevitably ends in and prolongs misery. But no Indian system stops with this picture of life as a tragedy. It perhaps possesses more than a literary significance that even an ancient Indian drama rarely ends as a tragedy. If Indian philosophy points relentlessly to the miseries that we suffer through short-sightedness, it also discovers a message of hope. The essence of Buddha's enlightenment—the four noble truths—sums up and voices the real view of every Indian school in this respect; namely : There *is* suffering.—There is a *cause* of suffering.— There is *cessation* of suffering.—There is a *way* to attain it. Pessimism in the Indian systems is only initial and not final.[1] The influence of such pessimism on life

1. For a full discussion of this point, see Introduction to Prof. Radha Krishnan's *Indian Philosophy*, Vol. I. pp. 49-50.

is more wholesome than that of uncritical optimism. An eminent American teacher rightly points out : "Optimism seems to be more immoral than Pessimism, for Pessimism warns us of danger, while Optimism lulls into false security."[1]

(3) The belief in an 'eternal moral order' in the universe.

The outlook which prevents the Indian mind from ending in despair and guarantees its final optimism is what may be described as spiritualism after William James. "Spiritualism," says James, "means the affirmation of an eternal moral order and letting loose of hope." "This need of an eternal moral order is one of the deepest needs of our breast. And those poets, like Dante and Wordsworth, who live on the conviction of such an order, owe to that fact the extraordinary tonic and consoling power of their verse."[2] The firm faith in "an eternal moral order" dominates the enitre history of Indian philosophy, barring the solitary exception of the Cārvāka materialists. It is the common atmosphere of faith in which all these systems, Vedic and non-Vedic, theistic and atheistic, move and breathe. The faith in an order—a law that makes for regularity and righteousness and works in the gods, the heavenly bodies and all creatures—pervades the poetic imagination of the seers of *Ṛg-veda* which calls this inviolable moral order Ṛta.[3] This idea gradually shapes itself (*a*) into the Mīmāṁsā conception of apūrva, the law that guarantees the future enjoyment of the fruits of rituals performed now, (*b*) into the Nyāya-Vaiśeṣika theory of adṛṣta, the unseen principle which sways even over the material atoms and brings about objects and events in accordance with moral principles, and (*c*) into the general conception of karma, which is accepted by all Indian systems. The law of karma in its different aspects may be regarded as the law of the conservation of moral values, merits and demerits of actions.

The different forms of this faith.

1. George Herbert Palmer, *Contemporary American Philosophy,* Vol. 1. p. 51.
2. *Pragmatism,* pp. 106-107.
3. *Cf. Ṛg-veda,* 1.1.8, 1.23.5, 1.24.9, 1.123.13, passim.

This law of conservation means that there is no loss of the effect of work done (kṛtapraṇāśa) and that there is no happening of events to a persòn except as the result of his own work (akṛtābhyupagama). The law of karma is accepted by the six orthodox schools, as well as the Jainas and the Bauddhas. It will be more fully explained when we come to these systems.

The law of Karma.

In general the law of *karma* (action) means that all actions, good or bad, produce their proper consequences in the life of the individual who acts, provided they are performed with a desire for the fruits thereof. This law helps us to explain certain differences in individual beings, which cannot be explained by the known circumstances of their lives. It is not infrequently that we find that men who are born and brought up under the same or similar circumstances differ very much in respect of their achievements and enjoyments in life. Some men are happy and some miserable, some wise and some ignorant. We see also how some virtuous men suffer and many wicked people prosper in this world. How are we to explain these variations and anomalies in our wordly life ? Some of them, we find, are obviously due to the different actions performed by us in this present life. But many of them cannot be explained by reference to the deeds of this life. Now if some good or bad actions are thus found to produce certain good or bad effects in the present life, it is quite reasonable to maintain that all actions — past, present and future — will produce their proper effects in this or another life of the individuals who act. The law of karma is this general moral law which governs not only the life and destiny of all individual beings, but even the order and arrangement of the physical world.

Kinds of karma.

The word *karma* means both this law and also the force generated by an action and having the potency of bearing fruit. *Karma* in the second sense is variously classified. According to one principle, karmas are broadly divided into (*a*) those which have not yet begun to bear fruits (ana¯rabdha karma), and (*b*) those which have already begun to bear fruits like the present body and its accompaniments (ārabdha or prārabdha karma). Anārabdha karma again can be subdivided into two classes, according as it is accumulated from past lives (prā ktana or sañcita karma) or is being gathered in this life (kriyamāṇa or sañcīyamāna karma).[1]

The status of the law of karma.

Some systems of Indian philosophy like the Nyāya-Vaiśeṣika believe that the law of karma is under the guidance and control of God, the Supreme Being who creates the world in accordance with the law. It is here held that the adṛṣṭa or the stock of merits and demerits of karmas of the individual souls, cannot by itself lead to their proper effects, because it is an unintelligent and unconscious principle. It is God who controls our adṛṣṭa and dispenses all the joys and sorrows of our life in accordance with our karma. In some other systems, *e.g.* the Jaina, the Bauddha, the Sāṁkhya and the Mīmāṁ sā, the law of karma is autonomous and works independently of the will of God. These systems hold that the origin and order of the world may be explained by the law of karma without the supposition of God. But it should be noted here that whatever may be the status of the law of karma it has a limited application to the world of actions done under the influence of the ordinary passions and desires of the worldly life. All actions, of which the motives are desires for certain gains here or hereafter, are governed by this law. Disinterested and passionless actions, if any, do not produce any fettering effect or bondage just as a fried seed does not germinate. The law, therefore, holds good for individuals who work with selfish motives and are swayed by the ordinary passions and impulses of life and hanker after worldly or other-worldly gains. The performance of disinterested actions not only

The sphere of its operation.

1. Vide *Prakaraṇapañcikā*, p. 156 (Chowkhamba ed.)

produces no fettering consequences but helps us to exhaust and destroy the accumulated effects of our past deeds done under the influence of attachment, hatred and infatuation, or of interested hopes and fears, and thereby leads to liberation. With the attainment of liberation from bondage, the self rises above the law of karma and lives and act in an atmosphere of freedom. The liberated one may act for the good of mankind, but is not bound by his karma, since it is free from all attachment and self-interest.

A distinguished Danish philosopher, Harald Höffding, defines religion as "the belief in the conservation of values."[1] It is mainly such belief that raises Indian systems like Jainism and Buddhism to the status of religion in spite of the absence of a belief in God.

Optimism is generated by this faith in the moral order.

It is again this faith in 'an eternal moral order,' which inspires optimism and makes man the master of his own destiny. It enables the Indian thinker to take present evil as consequence of his own action, and hope for a better future by improving himself now. There is room, therefore, for free will and personal endeavour (puruṣakāra). Fatalism or determinism, therefore, a misrepresentation of the theory of karma. Fate or destiny (*daiva*) is nothing but the collective force of one's own actions performed in past live (pūrva-janma-kṛtaṁkarma). It can be overcome by efforts of this life, if they are sufficiently strong just as the force of old habits of this life can be counteracted

1. Vide *Perry, Philosophy of the Recent Past*, p. 206 f.n. *Cf.* Höffding, *The Philosophy of Religion*, pp. 1-13.

by the cultivation of new and opposite habits.[1]

(4) The universe as the moral stage.

Intimately connected with this outlook is the general tendency to regard the universe as the moral stage, where all living beings get the dress and the part that befit them and are to act well to deserve well in future. The body, the senses and the motor organs that an individual gets and the environment in which he finds himself are the endowments of nature or God in accordance with the inviolable law of karma.

(5) Ignorance is the cause of bondage and knowledge is necessary for liberation.

Another common view, held by all Indian thinkers, is that ignorance of reality is the cause of our bondage and sufferings, and liberation from these cannot be achieved without knowledge of reality, *i.e.* the real nature of the world, and the self. By 'bondage' is commonly meant the process of birth and rebirth and the consequent miseries to which an individual is subject. 'Liberation' (mukti or mokṣa) means, therefore, the stoppage of this process. Liberation is the state of perfection; and according to some Indian thinkers like the Jainas, the Bauddhas, the Sāṅkhyas and the Advaita Vedāntins, this state can be attained even in this life. Perfection and real happiness can, therefore, be realized even here, at least according to these chief Indian thinkers. The teachings of these masters need not make us wholly unworldly and other-worldly. They are meant only to correct the one-sided emphasis on 'the here' and 'the now'— the short-sightedness that worldliness involves.

But while ignorance was regarded as the root cause of the individual's trouble and knowledge, therefore, as essential,

---

1. Vide *Yoga-vāśiṣṭha-rāmāyana,* Prak. 2, Sar. 4-9, for discussion. Also in *Mahābhārata* (śāntiparva), Bhīṣma says, "I consider personal effort to be above all; belief in fate makes man dull." (*Pauruṣam hi param manye; daivam niścitya muhyate.)* Among the conditions responsible for the success of any work Bhagavad-Gītā (18.14) mentions both ceṣṭā and daiva. *Pañcadaśī* (6.158) says : "God in man is transformed into effort." So also *Yājñavalkya-Smṛti*(1.351) says :"Just a chariot cannot move on one wheel, so fate (daiva) without personal endeavour (puruṣakāra) cannot lead to success."

the Indian thinkers never believed that a mere acquaintance with truth would at once remove imperfection. Two types of discipline were thought necessary for making such understanding permanent as well as effective in life, namely, continued meditation on the accepted truths and practical life of self-control.

But mere theoretical knowledge is not sufficient.

The necessity of concentration and meditation led to the development of an elaborate technique, fully explained in the Yoga system. But *yoga*, in the sense of concentration through self-control, is not confined to that system only. It is found in some form or other in Buddhism, Jainism, the Sāṅkhya, the Vedānta, and even in the Nyāya-Vaiśesika systems. The followers of these various views believed, in common, that the philosophic truths momentarily established and understood through arguments were not enough to dispel the effects of opposite beliefs which have become a part of our being. Our ordinary wrong beliefs have become deeply rooted in us by repeated use in the different daily situations of life. Our habits of thought, speech and action have been shaped and coloured by these beliefs which in turn have been more and more strengthened by those habits. To replace these beliefs by correct ones, it is necessary to meditate on the latter constantly and think over their various implications for life. In short, to instil right beliefs into our minds, we have to go through the same long and tedious process, though of a reverse kind, by which wrong beliefs were established in us. This requires a long intellectual concentration on the truths learned. Without prolonged meditation the opposite beliefs cannot be removed and the belief in these truths cannot be steadied and established in life.

(6) Continued meditation on truths learnt is needed to remove deep-rooted false beliefs.

Self-control (samyama) also is necessary for concentration of the mind on these truths and for making them effective in

(7) Self-control is needed to remove passions that obstruct concentration and good conduct.

life.[1] Socrates used to say, 'Virtue is knowledge'. His followers pointed out that mere knowledge of what is right does not always lead to right actions, because our actions are guided as much by reason as by blind animal impulses. Unless these impulses are controlled, action cannot fully follow the dictates of reason. This truth is recognised by all the Indian systems, except perhaps the Cārvāka. It is neatly expressed by an oft-quoted Sanskrit saying which means : 'I know what is right, but feel no inclination to follow it; I know what is wrong but cannot desist from it.'[2]

Our speech and action cannot always follow our intellectual convictions because of the contrary impulses deeply rooted in our character owing to past misconceptions about things and their values. These impulses are variously described by different Indian thinkers; but there is a sort of unanimity that the chief impulses are likes and dislikes—love and hate (rāga and dveṣa). These are the automatic springs of action; we move under their influence when we act habitually without forethought. Our indriyas, *i.e.* the instruments of knowledge and action (namely, the mind, the senses of sight, touch, smell, taste, sound, and the motor organs for movement, holding things, speaking, excretion and reproduction), have always been in the service of these blind impulses of love and hate and they have acquired some fixed bad habits. When philosophic knowledge about the real nature of things makes us give up our previous wrong beliefs regarding objects, our previous likes and dislikes for those objects, have also to be given up. Our indriyas have to be weaned from past habits and broken to the reign of reason. This task is as difficult as it is important. It can be performed only through long, sustained practice and formation of new good habits. All Indian thinkers lay much stress on such practice which chiefly consists of repeated efforts in the right direction (abhyāsa).

---

1. In the *Mahābhārata* (śantiparva) Bhīṣma teaches that self-control (dama) is the sum (samudaya) of all virtues and the secret (upaniṣad) of truth (satya).

2. Vide *Pañcadaśī*, 6. 176.

Self-control, then, means the control of the lower self, the blind, animal tendencies—love and hate—as well as the instruments of knowledge and action (the indriyas). From what has been said above it will be clear that self-control was not a mere negative practice, it was not simply checking the indriyas, but checking their bad tendencies and habits in order to employ them for a better purpose, and make them obey the dictates of reason.

Self-control implies the bringing of the lower self under the control of the higher.

It is a mistake, therefore, to think, as some do, that Indian ethics taught a rigorism or asceticism which consists in killing the natural impulses in man. As early as the Upaniṣads, we find Indian thinkers recognizing that though the most valuable thing in man is his spirit (ātman), his existence as a man depends on non-spiritual factors as well; that even his thinking power depends on the food he takes.[1] This conviction never left the Indian thinkers; the lower elements, for them, were not for destruction but for reformation and subjugation to the higher. Cessation from bad activities was coupled with performance of good ones. This we find even in the most rigoristic systems, like the Yoga, where, as *aids to the attainment of perfect concentration* (yogāṅga), we find mentioned not simply the negative practice of the 'don'ts' (yamas), but also positive cultivation of good habits (niyamas). The yamas consist of the five great efforts for abstinence from injury to life, falsehood, stealing, sensuous appetite and greed for wealth (ahimsā, satya, asteya, brahmacarya and aparigraha). These are to be cultivated along with the niyamas, namely, purity of body and mind, contentment, fortitude, study and resignation to God. Essentially similar teachings we find as much in the other orthodox schools as in Buddhism and Jainism which, like the Yoga, recommended, for example, the cultivation of love (maitrī) and kindness (karuṇā) along with non-violence (ahiṁsā). That

It does not kill the natural impulses, but trains them to the yoke of reason.

Morality is not merely negative, but needs the cultivation of positive virtues.

1. *Chāndogya Up.*, 6.7.

the action of the indriyas is not to be suppressed but only to be turned to the service of the higher self, is also the teaching of the Gītā, as would appear from the following : "One who has controlled himself attains contentment by *enjoying objects through the indriyas which have been freed* from the influence of love and hate."[1]

Lastly, all Indian systems, except the Cārvāka, accept the idea of liberation as the highest end of life. The conception of liberation received, of course, slightly different meanings. All negatively agreed that the state of liberation is a total destruction of sufferings which life in this world brings about. A few went a little beyond this to hold that liberation or the state of perfection is not simply negation of pain, but is a state of positive bliss. The Vedānta and Jaina thinkers belong to this latter group, and even some Bauddhas, later Naiyāikas and Mīmāṁsakas.

(8) Belief in the possibility of liberation is common to the systems. Liberation is regarded as the highest good.

7. *The Space-Time Background*

In addition to the unity of moral and spiritual outlook described above, we may also note the prevailing sense of the vastness of the space-time world, which formed the common background of Indian thought and influenced its moral and metaphysical outlook.

The idea of the vastness of the world of space and Time formed the common background of Indian thought.

The Western belief that the world was created six thousand and odd years ago and all for the purpose of man constituted a narrowness of outlook and exaggerated the importance of man. This belief has been shaken by the biological discoveries of Darwin and others who show that the evolution of living beings has to be conceived in terms of millions of years, not thousands. The science of astronomy, again, is gradually generating the belief

Modern scientific conception of Time and Space as inconceivably vast entities.

1. *Bhagavadgītā, 2. 64.*

in the vastness of the universe, the diameter of which is "at least hundreds of millions of light-years."[1] The sun in this calculation is a mere speck in the universe, and the earth is less than one-millionth part of this speck. And we are reminded that each faint speck of nebula observable in the sky contains "matter enough for the creation of perhaps a thousand million suns like ours."[2]

Similar ideas in Indian literature.

Our imagination feels staggered in its attempt to grasp the vastness of the space-time universe revealed by science. A similar feeling is caused by the accounts of creation given in some of the Purāṇas, which would, but for modern discoveries, be laughed at as pure fantasy. In the *Viṣṇu-Purāṇa,*[3] for example, we come across the popular Indian conception of the world (brahmāṇḍa) which contains the fourteen regions (lokas) of which the earth (bhūtala) is only one and which are separated from one another by tens of millions (koṭis) of yojanas, and again the infinite universe is conceived as containing thousands of millions of such worlds (brahmāṇḍas).

As to the description of the vastness of time, we find that the Indian thinker, like the modern scientist, feels unable to describe it by common human units. The unit adopted for the measurement of cosmic time is a day of the creator Brahmā. Each day of the creator is equal to 1,000 yugas or 432 million years of men. This is the duration of the period of each creation of cosmos. The night of the creator is cessation of creative activity and means destruction or chaos. Such alternating days and nights, creation and destruction (sṛṣṭi and pralaya), form a beginningless series.

It is not possible to ascertain the first beginning of creation. It would be arbitrary to think that creation began *at first at*

---

1. Sir J.H. Jeans, in *Nature,* 26-2-27. A light-year = the distance travelled by light in a year, at the rate of 186,325 miles per second = 60 x 60 x 24 x 365 x 186,325 miles = 5,875,945,200,000 miles.
2. *Ibid.* (quoted in *Everyday Science*, by L.M. Parsons, pp. 14-15).
3. Part 2, Chap. 7.

some particular time and not earlier. As there are no data for fixing the *first* beginning of the universe, Indian thinkers, in general, look upon the universe as beginningless (anādi). They try to explain the beginning of the present creation by reference to previous states of dissolution and creation and think it idle and meaningless to enquire about the *first* creation. Any term of a beginningless series can only be siad to be earlier or later in *relation* to others; there is nothing like an *absolute first* in such a series.

With this overwhelming idea of the vast universe as its background, Indian thought naturally harped on the extreme smallness of the earth, the transitoriness of earthly existence and the insignificance of earthly possessions. If the earth was a mere point in the vast space, life was a mere ripple in the ocean of time. Myriads of them come and go, and matter very little to the universe as a whole. Even the best civilization evolved through centuries is nothing very unique : there is not one golden age only in the life of the earth. In the beginningless cycles of creation and dissolution there have been numberless golden ages as well as iron ones. Prosperity and adversity, civilization and barbarity, rise and fall, as the wheel of time turns and moves on.

The general influence of this outlook on metaphysics has been to regard the present world as the outcome of a past one and explain the former partly by reference to the latter. Besides, it sets metaphysics on the search for the eternal. On the ethical and religious side it helped the Indian mind to take a wider and detached view of life, prevented it from the morbid desire to cling to the fleeting as the everlasting and persuaded it always to have an eye on what was of lasting, rather than of momentary, value. While man's body is limited in space and time, his spirit is eternal. Human life is a rare opportunity.[1] It can be utilized for realizing the immoral spirit and for transcending thereby the limitations of space and time.

1. Vide *Bhāgavata,* 11.2.29, and *Dhammapada, 14.4.*

II. A Brief Sketch of the Systems

1. The Cārvāka System

In Indian philosophy the word 'Cārvāka' means a materialist. The Cārvākas hold that perception is the only valid source of knowledge. They point out that all non-perceptual or indirect sources of knowledge like inference, the testimony of other persons, etc., are unreliable and often prove misleading. We should not, therefore, believe in anything except what is immediately known through perception.

Perception reveals to us only the material world, composed of the four bhutas or elements of matter, *viz.* air, fire, water and earth, the existence of which we can directly know through the senses. All objects of this perceptible world are composed of these elements. There is no evidence that there is anything like an immaterial soul in man. Man too is made wholly of matter. We say 'I am stout,' 'I am lean,' 'I am lame'. These judgments also tend to show that the individual is identical with the body. There is of course consciousness in man, but consciousness is the quality of the living body which is a product of matter. It should not be thought that because the elements of matter are unconscious, there can be no consciousness in objects made of them. There are many examples in which qualities originally absent in the component parts are developed when the parts are combined together in a particular way. There are examples even of the same substance acquiring new qualities under different conditions. Betel leaf, nut and lime chewed together acquire a red tinge originally absent in any of the constituents : molasses acquires by fermentation the power of intoxication originally absent. Similarly, the elements of matter combined together in a particular way give rise to the living body having consciousness. Consciousness ceases apparently with the body. When man dies nothing is left of him to enjoy or suffer the consequences of his actions hereafter.

The survival of man in any form after death is, therefore, unproved. The existence of God also is a myth. God cannot be perceived. The world is made by the automatic combination of the maternal elements and not by God. It is foolish, therefore, to perform any religious rite either for enjoying happiness after this life in heaven or for pleasing God. No faith should be put in the Vedas or in the cunning priests who earn their livelihood by exploiting the credulity of men.

The highest end of life, for a rational man, should, therefore, be the enjoyment of the greatest amount of pleasure here in this life, of which alone we are sure. It is foolish to forgo the pleasure of life simply because they happen to be mixed with pain. It would be as though one were to reject the kernel because of its husk or cease sowing crops for fear of cattle. We should try to get the best out of this life by enjoying it as best as we can and avoiding as far as possible the chances of pain.

2. The Jaina System

The origin of the Jaina faith lies far back in the prehistoric times. The long line of teachers through whom the faith was handed down consists of twenty-four Tīrthaṅkaras or liberated propagators of the faith, the last of whom was Vardhamāna (also styled Mahāvīra), a contemporary of Gautama Buddha.

The Jainas reject the Carvaka view that perception is the only valid source of knowledge. They point out that if we are to reject altogether the possibility of obtaining correct knowledge through inference and the testimony of other persons because sometimes they prove misleading, we should doubt the validity of perception also, because even perception sometimes proves illusory. In fact, the Cārvākas themselves take the help of inference when by observing *some* cases of inference to be misleading they come to hold that *all* inference is invalid, and also when they deny the existence of objects *because* they are not perceived. The Jainas admit, in addition to perception, inference and testimony as sources of valid knowledge. Inference yields valid knowledge when it obeys the logical rules of correctness. Testimony is valid when it is the report of a reliable authority. In fact, the Jainas hold that it is on the authority of the teachings of the omniscient liberated saints (Jainas or Tīrthaṅkaras) that we can have unerring knowledge about certain spiritual matters, which our limited sense-perception and reasoning cannot reveal to us.

On the basis of these three kinds of knowledge, the Jainas form their view of the universe. Perception reveals the reality of material substances, composed of the four kinds of elements, as the Cārvākas hold. By inference they come to believe in space (ākā śa), because material substances must exist somewhere, believe in time (kāla), because changes of succession of the states of substances cannot be understood without it and believe also in the two causes of motion and rest respectively, for without them movement and cessation of movement in things cannot be explained. These last two are called respectively dharma and adharma which should not be taken here in their ordinary moral sense, but in the technical sense of the causes of motion and rest. But the physical world, consisting of the four elements of matter, space, time, dharma and adharma, is not all. Perception, as well as inference, proves the existence of souls in all living bodies. When we perceive the qualities of an orange such as its colour, shape, smell we say we perceive the existence of the orange. On similar grounds, when we internally perceive pleasure, pain and other qualities of the soul, we should admit that the soul also is directly known through perception. Consciousness cannot be said to be the product of matter; the Cārvākas cannot point out any case where the combination of material substances is *perceived* to generate consciousness. The existence of the soul can also be inferred on the ground that if there had been no conscious agent to guide them, material substances could not be formed into living bodies by themselves. Without a conscious substance to regulate them, the body and the senses could not do their work so systematically.

There are, then, as many souls as there are living bodies. There are souls, the Jainas hold, not only in animals, but also in plants and even in particles of dust. The existence of very minute living beings (such as germs) in dust and other apparently non-living material things is also admitted by modern science. All souls are not equally conscious. Some, like those in plants or dust-bodies, have only the sense of touch and have tactual consciousness alone. Some lower animals have two senses, others three, still others four. Man and some higher animals have five senses through all of which they know things. But, however developed the senses may be, the soul in bondage is limited in knowledge; it is limited in power also and is subject to all kinds of miseries.

But every soul is capable of attaining infinite consciousness, power and happiness. These qualities are inherent in the very nature of the soul. They are obstructed by karmas, just as the natural light of the sun is obstructed by clouds. The karmas or the forces of passions and desires in the soul attract to it particles of matter which permeate the soul just as particles of dust permeate the light of any flame or the sun. In a word the karmas lead to the bondage of the soul by matter. By removing karmas a soul can remove bondage and regain its natural perfections.

The teachings and lives of the liberated saints (Tīrthaṅkaras) prove the possibility of liberation and show also the path to be followed for the purpose. Three things are necessary for the removal of bondage, *viz.* perfect faith in the teachings of the Jaina teachers, correct knowledge of the teachings, and right conduct. Right conduct consists in the practice of abstinence from all injury to life, from falsehood, from stealing, from sensuality and from attachment to sense objects. By the joint culture of right faith, right knowledge and right conduct the passions are controlled and the karmas that fetter the soul to matter are removed. The obstacles being removed, the soul attains its natural perfection — infinite faith, infinite knowledge, infinite power and infinite bliss. This is the state of liberation.

The Jainas do not believe in God. The Tīrthaṅkaras, to whom all the godly powers like omniscience and omnipotence belong, take the place of God. They are adored as ideals of life.

Sympathy for all living beings is one of the chief features of the Jaina faith. Coupled with this there is, in Jaina philosophy, respect for all opinions. The Jaina philosophers point out that every object has infinite aspects, judged by what it is and what it is not from different points of view. Every judgment that we ordinarily pass about a thing is, therefore, true only in relation to a particular aspect of the thing seen from a particular point of view. We should remember, therefore, the limited nature of our knowledge and judgment and should refrain from thinking that any view is the whole truth about any thing. We should guard and qualify our own statements and also learn to appreciate the possibility of the correctness of others' views.

The Jaina philosophy is a kind of realism, because it asserts the reality of the external world, and it is pluralism, because it believes in many ultimate realities. It is atheism as it rejects the existence of God.

3. The Bauddha System

The Bauddha system of philosophy arose out of the teachings of Gautama Buddha, the well-known founder of Buddhism. Gautama was awakened to a consciousness of human suffering by the sight of disease, old age, death and other miseries, to which man is subject. He spent years in study, penance and meditation to discover the origin of human sufferings and the means to overcome them. At last he received enlightenment, the result of which was set forth by him in the form of what has come to be known as 'the four noble truths' (catvāri ārya-satyāni). These are — the truth that there is misery, the truth that there is a cause of misery, the truth that there is cessation of misery and the truth that there is a path leading to the cessation of misery.

The first truth about the existence of misery is admitted by all in some form or other. But with his penetrating insight Buddha saw that misery is not simply casual; it is ordinarily present in all forms of existence and in all kinds of experience. Even what appears as pleasant is really a source of pain at bottom.

Regarding the second truth, Buddha's conclusion is deduced from his analysis of causation. He points out that the existence of everything in the world, material and mental, is caused by some other thing. There is nothing which is unconditional and self-existent. Nothing is, therefore, permanent in the world. All things are subject to change. Our sufferings are similarly caused by some conditions. Sufferings depend on birth in this world, Birth again is caused by our desire (taṇhā and tṛṣṇā) for the worldly objects. The force of desires drags us down to the world. But our desires can be traced ultimately to our ignorance. If we had a correct knowledge of the things of the world, understood their transitory and painful nature, there would be no desire for them ; birth would then cease and along with it also misery.

As suffering, like other things, depends on some conditions, it must cease when these conditions are removed. This is the third truth about cessation of misery.

The fourth truth about the path that leads to the cessation of misery concerns the control of the conditions that cuase misery. This path is known as the eight-fold noble path as it consists of eight steps, namely, right views, right determination, right speech, right conduct, right livelihood, right endeavour, right mindfulness and right concentration. These eight steps remove ignorance and desire, enlighten the mind and bring about perfect equanimity and tranquillity. Thus misery ceases completely and the chance of rebirth also is stopped. The attainment of this state of perfection is nirvāṇa.

The teachings of Buddha are contained in the four noble truths described above. It will appear from this that Buddha himself was not concerned so much with the problems of philosophy as with the practical problem how human misery can be removed. He regarded it as a waste of time to discuss metaphysical problems, while man is writhing in misery. But though averse to theoretical speculation he could not avoid philosophical discussions altogether. Thus we find from early literature the following theories among his teachings : (a) All things are conditional; there is nothing that exists by itself. (b) All things are, therefore, subject to change owing to the change of the conditions on which they depend; nothing is permanent. (c) There is, therefore, neither any soul nor God nor any other permanent substance. (d) There is, however, continuity of the present life which generates another life, by the law of karma, just as a tree generates another tree through its seed, and the second continues while the first withers away.

The later followers of Buddha, in India and outside, developed the germs of philosophical theories contained in Buddha's teachings, and many schools thus came into existence. Of these the four schools that became well known in Indian philosophy may be mentioned here.

The Mādhyamika or Śūnyavāda School. — According to this, the world is unreal (śūnya); mental and non-mental phenomena are all illusory. This view is known as nihilism (śūnyavāda).

The Yogācāra or Vijñānavāda School.— This holds that external objects are unreal. What appears as external is really an idea in the mind. But mind must be admitted to be real. It is self-contradictory to say that the mind is unreal; for, then, the very thought that mind is unreal stands self-condemned, thought being an activity of the mind. This view is called subjective idealism (vijñānavāda).

The Sautrāntika School. — This holds that both the mental and non-mental are real. If everything that we perceive as external were unreal, then our perception of an object would not depend on anything outside the mind but absolutely on the mind. But we find that the mind cannot perceive any object, like a tiger, at any place it likes. This proves that the idea of the tiger, when we perceive it, depends on a non-mental reality, the tiger. From the perceptual idea or representation of a tiger in the mind we can infer the existence of its cause, the tiger, outside the mind. Thus external objects can be *inferred* to exist outside the mind. This view may be called representationism, or theory of the inferability of external objects (bāhyānumeya-vāda).

The Vaibhāṣika School. — This school agrees with the last on the point that both internal and external objects are real. But it differs from it regarding the way external objects are known. External objects, according to the Vaibhāṣikas, are *directly perceived* and not inferred from their ideas or representation in the mind. For, if no external object were ever *perceived* corresponding to any idea it would not be possible to infer the existence of an external object from any idea. This view may be called direct realism, because it holds that external objects are perceived directly (bāhya-pratyakṣa-vāda).

Buddhism is divided, on religious matters, into the two well-known schools, Hīnayāna, flourishing now in the south, in Ceylon, Burma and Siam, and Mahāyāna, found now in the north, in Tibet, China and Japan. The first two of the four philosophical schools mentioned above come under the Mahāyāna and the last two under the Hīnayāna. The most important religious question on which these two schools differ is : What is the object of nirvāṇa ? The Hīnayāna holds that nirvāṇa should be sought in order that the individual may put an end to his own misery. The Mahāyāna thinks, on the other hand, that the object of nirvāṇa is not to put an end to one's own misery, but to obtain perfect wisdom with which the liberated can work for the salvation of all beings in misery.

4. The Nyāya System

The Nyāya system is the work of the great sage Gautama. It is a realistic philosophy based mainly on logical grounds. It admits four separate sources of true knowledge, *viz.* perception (pratyakṣa), inference (anumāna), comparison (upamāna) and testimony (sabda). Perception is the direct knowledge of objects produced by their relation to our senses. It may be external (bāhya) or internal (āntara), according as the sense concerned is external, like the eye and the ear, or internal, like the mind (manas). Inference is the knowledge of objects, not through perception, but through the apprehension of some mark (liṅga) which is invariably related to the inferred objects (sādhya). The invariable relation between the two is called vyāpti. In inference there are at least three propositions and at most three terms, *viz.* the pakṣa or minor term about which we infer something, the sādhya or major term which is the inferred object, and the liṅga or sādhana or middle term which is invariably related to the major, and is present in the minor. To illustrate : "The hill is fiery, because it smokes; and whatever smokes is fiery." Comparison is the knowledge of the relation between a name and things so named on the basis of a given description of their similarity to some familiar object. A man is told that a *gavaya* is like a cow. Then he finds an animal in the forest, which strikingly resembles the cow, and comes to know that the animal must be a *gavaya*. Such knowledge is derived from upamana or comparison. Śabda or verbal testimony is the knowledge about anything derived from the statements of authoritative persons. A scientist tells us that water is a compound of hydrogen and oxygen in a certain proportion. Although we may not have verified the truth ourselves, we know it on the authority of the scientist. Here our knowledge is derived from Śabda or testimony. All other sources of knowledge have been reduced by the Naiyāyikas to these four.

The objects of knowledge, according to the Nyāya, are the self, the body, the senses and their objects, cognition (buddhi), mind (manas), activity (pravṛtti), mental defects (doṣa), rebirth (pretyabhāva), the feelings of pleasure and pain (phala), suffering (duḥkha), and freedom from suffering (apavarga). The Nyāya, like many other systems of Indian philosophy, seeks to deliver the self from its bondage to the body, the senses and their objects. According to it, the self is distinct from the body and the mind. The body is only a composite substance made of matter. The mind (manas) is a subtle, indivisible and eternal substance (aṇu). It serves the soul as an instrument for the perception of psychic qualities like pleasure, pain, etc. It is, therefore, called an internal sense. The self (ātman) is another substance which is quite distinct from the mind and the body. It acquires the attribute of consciousness when it is related to any object through the senses. But consciousness is not an essential quality of the self. It is an accidental or adventitious quality which ceases to qualify the self in the state of mukti or liberation. While the mind (manas) is infinitesimal like an atom, the self is all-pervading (vibhu), indestructible and eternal. It is an agent which likes and dislikes objects and tries to obtain or avoid them and enjoys or suffers the consequences of its actions. It is ignorance of the truth (mithyā-jñāna) and the consequent faults of desire, aversion and infatuation (rāga, dveṣa and moha) that impel the self to act for good and bad ends and plunge it into the world of sin and suffering, birth and death. Liberation (apavarga) means the absolute cessation of all pain and suffering brought about by the right knowledge of reality (tattva-jñāna). Some people think that it is a state of happiness. But this is entirely wrong, for there is no pleasure without pain, just as there is no light without shade. So liberation is only release from pain and not pleasure or happiness.

The existence of God is proved by the Naiyāyikas by several arguments. God is the ultimate cause of the creation, maintenance and destruction of the world. He did not create the world out of nothing, but out of eternal atoms, space, time, ether, minds and souls. This world has been created in order that individual souls (jīvas) might enjoy pleasure or suffer pain according to the merit or demerit of their actions in other lives and in other worlds. The most popular argument for God's existence is : "All things of the world like mountains and seas, the sun and the moon, are effects, because they are made up of parts. Therefore, they must have a maker (kartā)." The individual selves cannot be the maker or creator of the world, because they are limited in power and knowledge, and so cannot deal with such subtle and imperceptible entities as atoms, of which all physuical things are composed. The creator of the world must be an intelligent spirit with unlimited power and wisdom, and capable of maintaining the moral order of the universe. God created the world not for any end of His own, but for the good of all living beings. This, however, does not mean that there must be only happiness and no misery in the world. If individual selves have any freedom of will in them, they would act for good or bad ends and thereby bring happiness or misery on themselves. But under the loving care and wise guidance of the Divine Being, all individuals can sooner or later attain right knowledge about themselves and the world, and thereby final release from all suffering (mukti).

5. The Vaiśeṣika System

The Vaiśeṣika system was founded by the sage Kaṇāda also named Ulūka. It is allied to the Nyāya system and has the same end in view, namely, the liberation of the individual self. It brings all objects of knowledge, *i.e.* the whole world, under the seven categories of substance (dravya), quality (guṇa), action (karma), generality (sāmānya), particularity (viśeṣa), the relation of inherence (samavāya), and non-existence (abhāva).

A substance is the substratum of qualities and activities, but is different from both. There are nine kinds of substances, *viz.* earth, water, fire, air, ether (ākāśa), time, space, soul and mind (manas). Of these, the first five are called the physical elements (bhūtas) and have respectively the specific qualities of smell, taste, colour, touch and sound. The first four are composed of the four kinds of atoms (of earth, water, fire and air) which are invisible and indestructible particles of matter. The atoms are uncreated and eternal entities which we get by resolving any material object into smaller and smaller parts till we come to such as cannot be further divided. Ākāśa, space and time are imperceptible substances, each of which is one, eternal and all-pervading. The mind (manas) is an eternal substance which is not all-pervading, but infinitely small like an atom. It is the internal sense which is directly or indirectly concerned in all psychical functions like cognition, feeling and willing. The mind being atomic we cannot have more than one experience at one instant of time. The soul is an eternal and all-pervading substance which is the substratum of the phenomena of consciousness. The individual soul is perceived internally by the mind of the individual, as when one says 'I am happy'. The supreme soul or God is inferred as the creator of the world of effects. God creates the world out of eternal atoms. The composition and decomposition of atoms explain the origin and destruction of the composite objects of the world. But the atoms cannot move and act by themselves. The ultimate source of their actions is to be found in the will of God, who directs their operations according to the law of karma. The atoms are made to compose a world that befits the unseen moral deserts (adṛṣṭa) of individual souls and serves the purpose of moral dispensation. This is the atomic theory of the Vaiśeṣikas. It is rather teleological than mechanistic and materialistic like other atomic theories.

A quality is that which exists in a substance and has itself no quality or activity. While a substance can exist by itself, a quality cannot exist unless it be in some substance. There is no activity or movement in the qualities of things. There are altogether twenty-four kinds of qualities, *viz.* colour, taste, smell, touch, sound, number, magnitude, distinctness (pṛthaktva), conjunction (saṁyoga), disjunction (vibhāga), remoteness (paratva), nearness (aparatva), fluidity (dravatva), viscidity (sneha), cognition (buddhi), pleasure, pain, desire, aversion, striving (prayatna), heaviness (gurutva), tendency (saṁskāra), merit (dharma) and demerit (adharma).[1]

An action is a movement. Like quality, it belongs only to substances. There are five kinds of action, *viz.* throwing upward (utkṣepaṇa), throwing downward (avakṣepaṇa), contraction (ākuñcana), expansion (prāsaraṇa) and going (gamana).

1. 'Paratva' stands for both remoteness in space and remoteness in time and 'aparatva' for nearness both in space and time. 'Saṁskāra' really stands for three qualities. *viz.* velocity, elasticity and memory-impression.

All cows have in them a certain common nature for which they are grouped into one class and excluded from other classes. This is called 'gotva' or cowness and is the sāmā nya or universal in them. Since cowness is not generated by the birth of any cow nor destroyed by the death of any, it is eternal. A universal is thus the eternal essence common to all the individuals of a class.

Particularly (viśeṣa) is the ground of the ultimate differences of things. Ordinarily, we distinguish one thing from another by the peculiarities of its parts and other qualities. But how are we to distinguish the ultimate simple and eternal substances of the world, like two atoms of earth? There must be some ultimate difference or peculiarity in each of them, otherwise they would not be different, both having all the qualities of earth. Particularity stands for the peculiarity or individuality of the eternal entities of the world. It is the special treatment of this category of viśeṣa that explains the name 'Vaiśeṣika' given to this system of philosophy.

Inherence (samavāya) is the permanent or eternal relation by which a whole is in its parts, a quality or an action is in a substance, the universal is in the particulars. The cloth as one whole always exists in the threads, qualities like 'green,' 'sweet' and 'fragrant,' and motions of different kinds abide in some substances. Cowness as a universal is in all cows. This permanent relation between the whole and its parts, between the universal and its individuals, and between qualities or actions and their substances, is known as samavāya or inherence.

Non-existence (abhāva) stands for all negative facts. 'There is no snake here,' 'that rose is not red,' 'there is no smell in pure water' are propositions which express respectively the non-existence of the snake, redness and smell in certain things. All such cases of non-existence are brought under the category of abhāva. It is of four kinds, namely, prāgabhāva, dhvaṁsābhāva, atyantābhāva (these three being put together under saṁsargābhāva or the absence of one thing in another thing), and anyonyābhāva.

The first means the non-existence of a thing before (prior to) its production, *e.g.* the non-existence of pot in clay before it is produced by the potter. The second is the non-existence of a thing after its destruction (dhvaṁsa), *e.g.* the non-existence of the pot in its broken parts. The third is the absence of a thing in another thing for all time—past, present and future, *e.g.* the non-existence of colour in the air. The last kind represents the difference of one thing from another. When two things (say a jar and a cloth) differ from each other, there is the non-existence of either *as* the other. The jar is not the cloth, nor is the cloth the jar. This mutual non-existence of two different things is called anyonyābhāva.

With regard to God and liberation of the individual soul the Vaiśeṣika theory is substantially the same as that of the Nyāya.

6. The Sāṅkhya System

The Sāṅkhya is a philosophy of dualistic realism, attributed to the sage Kapila. It admits two ultimate realities, namely, puruṣa and prakṛti, which are independent of each other in respect of their existence. The puruṣa is an intelligent principle, of which consciousness (caitanya) is not an attribute, but the very essence. It is the self which is quite distinct from the body, the senses and the mind (manas). It is beyond the whole world of objects, and is the eternal consciousness which witnesses the changes and activities going on in the world, but does not itself act and change in any way. Physical things like chairs, beds, etc. exist for the enjoyment of beings other than themselves. Therefore, there must be the puruṣa or the self which is distinct from prakṛti or primary matter, but is the enjoyer (bhoktā) of the products of prakṛti. There are many different selves related to different bodies, for when some men are happy, others are unhappy, some die but others live.

Prakṛti is the ultimate cause of the world. It is an eternal unconscious principle (jaḍa) which is always changing and has no other end than the satisfaction of the selves. Sattva, rajas and tamas are three constituents of prakṛti which holds them together in a state of rest or equilibrium (sāmyāvasthā). The three are called guṇas. But they are not qualities or attributes in any sense. Rather, they are three substantial elements which constitute prakṛti like three cords making up a rope. The existence of the guṇas is inferred from the qualities of pleasure, pain and indifference which we find in all things of the world. The same sweet is liked or disliked or treated with indifference by the same man in different conditions. The same salad is tasteful to some person, distasteful to another and insipid to a third. Now the cause and the effect are essentially identical. The effect is the manifested condition of the cause, *e.g.* oil as an effect manifests what is already contained in the seeds. The things of the world are effects which have the qualities of pleasure, pain and indifference. Therefore, prakṛit or pradhāna which is their ultimate cause must have the three elements of sattva, rajas and tamas which respectively possess the natures of pleasure, pain and indifference, and cause manifestation, activiity and passivity.

The evolution of the world has its starting point in the association (saṁyoga) of the purusa with prakṛti, which disturbs the original equilibrium of the latter and moves it to action. The course of evolution is as follows : From prakṛti arises the great germ of this vast universe which is called, therefore, the great one (mahat). The consciousness of the self is reflected on this and makes it appear as conscious. It represents the awakening of nature from her cosmic slumber and the first appearance of thought; and, therefore, it is also called the Intellect (buddhi). It is the creative thought of the world to be evolved. Ahaṅkāra, the second product, arises by a further transformation of the Intellect. The function of ahaṅkāra is the feeling of 'I and mine' (abhimāna). Owing to its identification with this principle, the self considers itself to be an agent (kartā) which it really is not. From ahaṅkāra, with an excess of the element of sattva, arise the five organs of knowledge (jñānendriya), the five organs of action (karmendriya) and the mind (manas) which is at once an organ of knowledge and activity (ubhayendriya). With an increase of tamas, ahaṇkāra produces, on the other hand, the five subtle elements (tanmātra) which are the potentialities of sound, touch, colour, taste and smell. From the five subtle elements come the five gross elements of ākāsa or ether, air, fire, water and earth in the same order. Thus we have altogether twenty-five principles in the Sāṅkhya. Of these all but the puruṣa is comprised by prakṛti which is the cause or the ultimate source of all other physical objects including mind, matter and life. Prakṛit is the uncaused cause of all objects. The seven principles of mahat, ahaṅkāra and the five tanmātras are causes of certain effects and themselves effects of certain causes. The eleven senses and the five gross elements are only the effects of certain causes and not themselves the cuases of anything which is substantially different from them. The puruṣa or the self is neither the cause (prakṛti) nor the effect (vikṛti) of anything.

Although the self is in itself free and immortal, yet such is the influence of avidyā or ignorance that it confuses itself with the body, the senses and the mind (manas). It is the want of discrimination (aviveka) between the self and the not-self that is responsible for all our sorrows and sufferings. We feel injured and unhappy when our *body* is injured or indisposed, because we fail to realize the distinction between the self and the body. Similarly, pleasure and pain in the mind seem to affect the self only because the self's distinction from the mind is not clearly perceived by us. Once we realize the distinction between the self and the not-self including the body and the senses, the mind, the intellect and the ego (vivekajñāna), our self ceases to be affected by the joys and sorrows, the ups and downs of life. It rests in itself as the dispassionate observer of the show of events in the world without being implicated in them. This is the state of liberation or freedom from suffering which has been variously described as mukti, apavarga, kaivalya, etc. It is possible for us to attain this state while alive in this world (jīvanmukti) or after this life in the other world (videhamukti). But mere knowledge or intellectual understanding of the truth will not help one to realize one's self and thereby attain final release from sin and suffering. For this we require to go through a long course of spiritual training with deep devotion to, and constant meditation on, the truth that the self is the pure eternal consciousness which is beyond the mind-body complex and above the space-time and cause-effect order of existence. It is the unborn and undying spirit, of which the essence is freedom, immortality and life eternal. The nature and methods of the spiritual training necessary for self-realization have been elaborated in the Yoga philosophy.

With regard to the problem of God, we find that the main tendency of the Sāṅkhya is to do away with the theistic belief. According to it, the existence of God cannot be proved in any way. We need not admit God to explain the world; for prakṛti is the adequate cause of the world as a whole. God as eternal and unchanging spirit cannot be the creator of the world; for to produce an effect the cause must change and transform itself into the effect. Some Sāṅkhya commentators and writers, however, try to show that the system admits the existence of God as the supreme person who is the witness but not the creator of the world.

7. The Yoga System

The sage Patañjali is the founder of the Yoga philosophy. The Yoga is closely allied to the Sāṅkhya. It mostly accepts the epistemology and the metaphysics of the Sāṅkhya with its twenty-five principles, but admits also the existence of God. The special interest of this system is in the practice of yoga as the means to the attainment of vivekajñāna or discriminative knowledge which is held in the Sāṅkhya to be the essential condition of liberation. According to it, yoga consists in the cessation of all mental functions (cittavṛttinirodha). There are five levels of mental functions (cittabhūmi). The first is called kṣipta or the dissipated condition in which the mind flits among objects. The second is mūḍha or the stupefied condition as in sleep. The third is called vikṣipta or the relatively pacified condition. Yoga is not possible in any of these conditions. The fourth and the fifth levels are called ekāgra and niruddha. The one is a state of concentration of the mind on some object of contemplation. The other is the cessation of even the act or function of contemplation. The last two levels of the mind (cittabhūmi) are conducive to yoga. There are two kinds of yoga or samādhi, *viz.* saṁprajñāta and asaṁprajñāta. In the first we have yoga in the form of the mind's perfect concentration on the object of contemplation, and, therefore, involving a clear apprehension of that object. In the second, there is the complete cessation of all mental modifications and, consequently, the entire absence of all knowledge including that of the contemplated object.

There are eight steps in the practice of yoga (yogāṅga). These are : yama or restraint, niyama or moral culture, āsana or posture, prāṇāyāma or breath-control, pratyāhāra or withdrawal of the senses, dhārāṇa or attention, dhyāna or meditation and samādhi or concentration. Yama or restraint consists in abstaining from injury to any life, from falsehood, theft, incontinence and avarice. Niyama or moral culture is the cultivation of good habits like purification, contentment, penance, study of the Vedas and contemplation of God. Āsana is the adoption of steady and comfortable postures. Prāṇāyāma or breath-control is regulated inhalation, exhalation and retention of breath. Pratyāhāra or sense-control consists in withdrawing the senses from their objects. Dhāraṇā or attention is fixing the mind on some intra-organic or extra-organic objects like the nose-tip or the moon. Dhyāna or meditation is the steady contemplation of the object without any break. Samā dhi or concentration is that state in which the contemplative consciousness is lost in the contemplated object and has no awareness of itself.

The Yoga system is called the theistic (seśvara) Sāṅkhya as distinguished from the Kapila Sāṅkhya which is generally regarded as atheistic (nirīśvara). It holds that God is the highest object of contemplation for concentration and self-realization. He is the perfect Being who is eternal, all-pervading, omniscient and completely free from all defects. The Yoga argues for the existence of God on the following grounds : Whatever has degrees must have a maximum. There are degrees of knowledge; therefore, there must be such a thing as perfect knowledge or omniscience. He who has omniscience is God. The association of puruṣa with prakṛti is what initiates the evolution of the world, and the cessation of this leads to dissolution. Neither the association nor the dissociation is natural to prakṛti and puruṣa. Therefore, there must be a supreme being who is able to bring about these relations between prakṛti and puruṣa according to the moral deserts of individual souls.

8. The Mīmāṁsā System

The Mīmāṁsā (or Pūrva-Mīmāṁsā) school was founded by Jaimini. Its primary object is to defend and justify Vedic ritualism. In course of this attempt it had to find a philosophy supporting the world-view on which ritualism depends.

The authority of the Vedas is the basis of ritualism, and the Mīmāṁsā formulates the theory that the Vedas are not the works of any person and are, therefore, free from errors that human authors commit. The Vedas are eternal and self-existing; the written or pronounced Vedas are only their temporary manifestations through particular seers. For establishing the validity of the Vedas, the Mīmāṁsā discusses very elaborately the theory of knowledge, the chief object of which is to show that the validity of every knowledge is self-evident. When there are sufficient conditions, knowledge arises. When the senses are sound, objects are present to them and other auxiliary conditions also prevail, there is perception. When there are sufficient data, there is inference. When we read a book on geography, we have knowledge of the lands described, through authority. In each of these cases the knowledge that arises claims to be true and we accept it without further argument. If there is any cause for doubt, then knowledge does not arise at all, because belief is absent. Similarly, by reading the Vedas we have at once knowledge and belief in what they say. The validity of Vedic knowledge is self-evident like that of every other knowledge. If any doubts arise, they are removed with the help of Mīmāṁsā arguments; and the obstacles being removed, the Vedas themselves reveal their contents to the reader. The authority of the Vedas thus becomes unquestionable.

What the Vedas command one to perform is right (dharma). What they forbid is wrong. Duty consists in doing what is right and desisting from forbidden acts. Duty must be done in the spirit of duty. The rituals enjoined by the Vedas should be performed not with the hope of any reward but just becuase they are so enjoined. The disinterested performance of the obligatory rites, which is possible only through knowledge and self-control, gradually destroys the karmas and brings about liberation after death. The state of liberation is conceived in the early Mīmāṁsā as one of unalloyed bliss or heaven. But the later Mīmāṁsā conceives liberation only negatively as the cessation of birth and, therefore, of all pains.

The soul must be admitted as an immortal eternal substance, for if the soul perished on death, the Vedic injunctions that certain rites should be performed for the attainment of heaven would be meaningless. The Mīmāṁsā writers also adduce independent arguments, like the Jainas, to prove the existence of the immortal soul, and refute the materialistic view that it is nothing other than the body. But they do not admit consciousness as intrinsic to the soul. Consciousness arises in it only when it is associated with the body and then also only when an object is presented to the organs of knowledge (the five outer senses and the inner organ called manas). The liberated soul, which is disembodied, has no actual consciousness, though it has the potentiality for it.

The soul in the body has different kinds of knowledge. One school of the Mīmāṁsā founded by Prabhākara admits five different sources of knowledge (pramāṇas), namely perception (pratyakṣa), inference (anumāna), comparison (upamāna), testimony (śabda) and postulation (arthāpatti). The first four are admitted as in the Nyāya system. There is, however, one notable difference regarding comparison. According to the Mīmāṁsā, knowledge by comparison arises in a case like the following : A man who has seen a monkey goes to a forest, sees an ape and judges, 'this ape is like a monkey.' From this judgment of perception he passes to the judgment 'the monkey I saw before is like this ape.' This last knowledge is obtained by comparison and not by perception, because the monkey is not present then. Knowledge by postulation arises when we have to postulate something as the only explanation of an apparent conflict. When we find that a man does not eat anything in the day, but increases in weight, we postulate that he must be eating at night. When a man is known to be alive and yet not found at home, it is known by postulation that he exists somewhere out. Another school of the Mīmāṁsā founded by Kumārila Bhaṭṭa admits another source of valid cognition, in addition to the above five. This sixth pramāṇa is called non-cognition (anupalabdhi). It is pointed out that when on entering a room, and looking round one says, 'There is no fan in this room,' the non-existence of the fan cannot be said to be known by perception. Perception of an object arises when our sense is stimulated by the object, and non-existence, which is the object known here, cannot be admitted to stimulate sense. Such knowledge of non-existence takes place by non-cognition. We judge the absence of the fan not because other things are perceived, but because the fan is *not perceived*.

The Mīmāṁsā believes in the reality of the physical world on the strength of perception. It is, therefore, realistic. It believes, as we have seen, in the reality of souls, as well. But it does not believe that there is a supreme soul, or God who has created the world. It does not hold like other orthodox systems that there is a cycle of creation and dissolution. The world has always been as it is. It has neither a beginning nor an end. The world's objects are formed out of matter in accordance with the karmas of the souls. The law of karma is an autonomous natural and moral law that rules the world. The Mīmāṁsā also admits that when any man performs any ritual, there arises in his soul a potency (apūrva) which produces in future the fruit of the action at an opportune moment. On account of this potency generated in the soul by rites performed here, one can enjoy their fruits hereafter.

9. The Vedānta System

This system arises out of the Upaniṣads which mark the culmination of the Vedic speculation and are fittingly called the Vedānta or the end of the Vedas. As we have seen previously, it develops through the Upaniṣads in which its basic truths are first grasped, the *Brahma-sūtra* of Bādarāyaṇa which systematizes the Upaniṣadic teachings, and the commentaries written on these sūtras by many subsequent writers among whom Śaṅkara and Rāmānuja are well known. Of all the systems, the Vedānta, especially as interpreted by Śankara, has exerted the greatest influence on Indian life and it still persists in some form or other in different parts of India.

The idea of one Supreme Person (puruṣa), who pervades the whole universe and yet remains beyond it, is found in a hymn of the *Ṛg-veda.* All objects of the universe, animate and inanimate, men and gods, are poetically conceived here as parts of that Person. In the Upaniṣads this unity of all existence is found developed into the conception of One impersonal Reality (sat), or the conception of One Soul, One Brahman, all of which are used synonymously. The world is said to originate from this Reality, rest in it and return into it when dissolved. The reality of the many particular objects perceived in the universe is denied and their unity in the One Reality is asserted ever and again : All is God (sarvam khalu idam Brahma). The soul is God (ayam Ātmā, Brahma). There is no multiplicity here (neha nānāsti kiñcana). This Soul or God is the Reality (satya). It is infinite consciousness (jñāna) and Bliss (ānanda).

Śaṅkara interprets the Upaniṣads and the *Brahma-sūtra* to show that pure and unqualified monism is taught therein. God is the only Reality, not simply in the sense that there is nothing except God, but also in the sense that there is no multiplicity even within God. The denial of plurality, the unity of the soul and God, the assertion that when God is known, all is known, and similar views found in the Upaniṣads, in fact the general tone that pervades their teachings, cannot be explained consistently if we believe even in the existence of many realities within God.

Creation of the many things by God (Brahman) or the Soul (Ātman) is, of course, related in some Upaniṣads. But in others, and even in the Vedas, creation is compared to magic or jugglery; God is spoken of as the Juggler who creates the world by the magical power called Māyā.

Śaṅkara, therefore, holds that, in consistency with the emphatic teaching that there is only One Reality, we have to explain the world not as a real creation, but as an *appearance* which God conjures up with his inscrutable power, Māyā. To make the conception of Māyā more intelligible to ordinary experience, he interprets it in the light of ordinary illusions that we have in daily life, when a rope appears, for example, as a snake or a glittering shell appears as silver. In all such cases of illusion there is a substratum or a reality (*e.g.* rope, shell) on which something else (*e.g.*, snake, silver) is imagined or superimposed owing to the ignorance of the substratum. This ignorance not only conceals the underlying reality or substratum, but also makes it appear as something else. Our perception of the world's objects can be similarly explained. We perceive the many objects in the One Brahman on account of our ignorance (avidyā or ajñāna) which conceals the real Brahman from us and makes it appear as the many objects. When the juggler produces an illusory show, makes one coin appear as many, the cause of it from *his* point of view is his magical *power*; from our point of view the reason why *we* perceive the many coins, is our *ignorance* of the one real coin. Applying this analogy to the world-appearance, we can say that this appearance is due to the magical power of Māyā in God and we can also say that it is due to our ignorance. Māyā and ignorance are then the two sides of the same fact looked at from two different points of view. Hence Māyā is also said to be of the nature of Ignorance (Avidyā or Ajñāna). Lest one should think that Śaṅkara's position also fails to maintain pure monism, because two realities—God and Māyā — are admitted, Śaṅkara points out that Māyā as a power of God is no more different from God than the power of burning is from fire. There is then no dualism but pure monism (advaita).

But is not even then God really possessed of creative power ? Śaṅkara replies that so long as one believes in the world-appearance, he looks at God through the world, as the creator of it. But when he realizes that the world is apparent, that nothing is really created, he ceases to think of God as a Creator. To one who is not deceived by the magician's art and sees through his trick, the magician fails to be a magician; he is not credited with any magical power. Similarly, to the few who see nothing but God in the world, God ceases to have Māyā or the power of creating appearances.

In view of this Śaṅkara finds it necessary to distinguish two different points of view the ordinary or empirical (vyāvahārika) and the transcendental or real (pāramā rthika). The first is the standpoint of unenlightened persons who regard the world as real : our life of practice depends on this; it is rightly called, therefore, the vyāvahārika or practical point of view. From this point of view the world appears as real; God is thought to be its omnipotent and omniscient creator, sustainer and destroyer. Thus God appears as qualified (saguṇa) by many qualities. God in this aspect is called by Śaṅkara Saguṇa Brahman or Īśvara. From this point of view the self also appears as though limited by the body, it behaves like a finite ego (aham). The second or the real (pāramārthika) standpoint is that of the enlightened who have realized that the world is an appearance and that there is nothing but God. From this point of view, the world being thought unreal, God ceases to be regarded as any real creator, or as possessed of any qualities like omniscience, omnipotence. God is realized as One without any internal distinction, without any quality. God from this transcendental standpoint (pāramā rthikadṛṣṭi) is indeterminate, and characterless; it is Nirguṇa Brahman. The body also is known to be apparent and there is nothing to distinguish the soul from God.

The attainment of this real standpoint is possible only by the removal of ignorance (avidyā) to which the cosmic illusion is due. And this can be effected only by the knowledge that is imparted by the Vedānta. One must control the senses and the mind, give up all attachment to objects, realizing their transitory nature, and have an earnest desire for liberation. He should then study the

Vedānta under an elightened teacher and try to realize its truths by constant reasoning and meditation. When he is thus fit, the teacher would tell him at last : "Thou art Brahman". He would meditate on this till he has a direct and permanent realization of the truth, 'I am Brahman'. This is perfect wisdom or liberation from bondage. Though such a liberated soul still persists in the body and in the world, these no longer fetter him as he does not regard them as real. He is *in* the world, but not *of* the world. No attachment, no illusion can affect his wisdom. The soul then being free from the illusory ideas that divided it from God, is free from all misery. As God is Bliss, so also is the liberated soul.

The teachings of the Vedānta are interpreted and developed by Rāmānuja in a different way, as follows : God is the only Reality. Within Him there exist as parts the different unconscious (acit) material objects as well as the many conscious souls (cit). God is possessed of all supremely good qualities like omniscience, omnipotence. Just as a spider spins the cobweb out of his own body, so God creates the world of material objects out of matter (acit) which eternally exists in Him. The souls are conceived as infinitely small (aṇu) substances which also exist eternally. They are, by their very nature, conscious and self-luminous. Every soul is endowed with a material body in accordance with its karma. Bondage of the soul means its confinement to this body. Liberation is the complete dissociation of the soul from the body. The cause of bondange is karma which springs from ignorance. The soul identifies itself with the body, through ignorance of its real nature and behaves as though it were the body. It hankers after sensuous pleasures. Thus it becomes attached to the world and the force of this attachment causes its repeated rebirth. Ignorance is removed by the study of the Vedānta. Man comes to know that his soul is distinct from the body, that it is really a part of God or Brahman, on whom his existence depends. The disinterested performance of the obligatory duties enjoined by the Vedas destroys the accumulated forces of attachment or karmas and helps the perfection of knowledge. God is known as the only object worthy of love. Such knowledge leads to constant meditation on God and resignation to His will. God is pleased by devotion and releases the devotee from bondage. He is never born again after death. The liberated soul becomes *similar* to God, because like God it has pure consciousness free from imperfections. But it does *not* become *identical* with God, as the finite can never become infinite.

According to Rāmānuja, though God is the only Reality and there is nothing outside God, yet within God there are many other realities. Creation of the world and the objects created are all as real as God. It is, therefore, not unqualified monism (advaita), but a monism of the One qualified by the presence of many parts (viśiṣṭādvait). God *possessed* of the conscious souls and unconscious matter is the only Reality.

THE CĀRVĀKA PHILOSOPHY

A SELECT BIBLIOGRAPHY

Dakshinaranjan Shastri ... *A Short History of Indian Materialism* (Book Company, Calcutta, 1930.)

... *Chārvāka-shashti* (Book Company, 1928).

Mādhavācārya ... *Sarva-darśana-saṅgraha* (Bhandarkar Institute, Poona, 1924).

Eng. trans. by Cowell and Gough, (Chowkhamba, Varanasi, 1961), Ch. on Cārvāka.

Haribhadra ... *Ṣaḍ-darśana-samuccaya* (Asiatic Soc., Calcutta, 1905).

Vātsyāyana ... *Kāma-sūtra* (Chowkhamba, 1929), Chs. I-II.

Jayarāśi ... *Tattvopaplava-siṁha* (Gaekwad's Oriental Series, Baroda, 1940).

Radhakrishnan ... *Indian Philosophy* (George Allen & Unwin Ltd., London, 1923), Vol. I, Ch. V.

Radhakrishnan and Charles A. Moore ... *A Source Book in Indian Philosophy* (Princeton University Press, 1957), Ch. VII.

CHAPTER II

THE CĀRVĀKA PHILOSOPHY

I. Its Origin And Scope

The meaning of materialism.

Materialism is the name given to the metaphysical doctrine which holds that matter is the only reality. This doctrine tries to explain mind and consciousness as the products of matter. In general outlook materialism represents the tendency that seeks to reduce the higher to the lower or explain the higher phenomena in the light of the lower ones. In this respect it is opposed to spiritual interpretations of the universe.

No systematic work of Indian materialists is available.

Though materialism in some form or other has always been present in India, and occasional references are found in the Vedas, the Buddhistic literature, the Epics, as well as in the later philosophical works we do not find any systematic work on materialism, nor any organised school of followers as the other philosophical schools possess. But almost every work of the other schools states, for reputation, the materialistic views. Our knowledge of Indian materialism is chiefly based on these.

'Cārvāka' is the word that generally stands for 'materialist'. But the original meaning of this word is shrouded in mystery. According to one view, 'Cārvāka' was originally the name of a sage who propounded materialism. The common name 'Cārvāka' is derived from this proper name and means the follower of that sage, *i.e.,* a materialist. According to another view, 'Cārvāka' was even originally a common descriptive name given to a materialist, either because he preaches the doctrine of 'eat, drink and be merry'[1] (carv—eat, chew), or because his words are pleasant

---

1. *Cf.* 'Piva Khāda ca varalocane', *Sad-darśana-samuccaya,* Lokāyatamatam.

and nice (cāru—nice, vāk—word). Some writers[1] again regard Brahaspati as the founder of materialism. This view is based on the facts *(a)* that some Vedic hymns ascribed by tradition to Brhaspati, son of Loka, are marked by a spirit of revolt and free-thinking, *(b)* that in the Mahābhārata and elsewhere materialistic views are put in the mouth of Bṛhaspati and *(c)* that about a dozen sūtras and verses are found quoted or reffered to by different authors as the materialistic teachings of Bṛhaspati. Some even go a little further and say that Bṛhaspati, the teacher of the gods, propagated the materialistic views among the giants (the enemies of the gods) so that by following these attractive teachings they might come to ruin !

A materialist is called 'Cārvāka' or Lokāyatika.

But whoever be the founder of Indian materialism, 'Cārvāka' has become synonymous with 'materialist'. The word used for materialism is also lokāyatanata, *i.e.*, the view of common people. A materialist is accordingly called also lokāyatika.

Though the materialistic ideas are scattered here and there, they may be systematized and conveniently presented under three chief heads, namely, Epistemology, Metaphysics and Ethics.

II. The Cārvāka Epistemology

Preception is the only source of knowledge.

The entire philosophy of the Cārvākas may be said to depend logically on their epistemology of the theory of knowledge. The main problems of epistemology are : How far can we know reality? How does knowledge originate and develop? This last question involves the problem : What are the different sources of knowledge? This problem forms one of the chief topics of Indian epistemology. Knowledge of reality or valid cognition is called pramā and the source of such knowledge is called pramāṇa. The Cārvāka holds that perception is the only pramāṇa or dependable source of knowledge. For

1. *Ibid.* and *Sarva-darśana-saṅgraha.*

establishing this position he criticizes the possibility of other sources of knowledge like inference and testimony which are regarded as valid pramāṇas by many philosophers.

1. Inference is not Certain

If inference is to be regarded as a pramāṇa, it must yield knowledge about which we can have no doubt and which must be true to reality. But inference cannot fulfil these conditions, because when we infer, for example, the existence of fire in a mountain from the perception of smoke in it, we take a leap in the dark, from the perceived smoke to the unperceived fire. A logician, like the Naiyāyika, will perhaps point out that such a leap is justified by the previous knowledge of the invariable concomitance between smoke and fire and that the inference stated more fully would be : All cases of smoke are cases of fire, this (mountain) is a case of smoke, therefore, this is a case of fire.

Inference is an uncertain leap from the known to the unknown.

For, it depends on a universal relation between the middle and the major term, and

The Cārvāka points out that this contention would be acceptable only if the major premise, stating the invariable relation between the middle term (smoke) and the major (fire), were beyond doubt. But this invariable relation (vyāpti) can be established only if we have a knowledge of *all* cases of smoke and presence of fire. This, however, is not possible, as we cannot perceive even all the cases of smoke and fire existing now in different parts of the world, to speak nothing of those which existed in the past or will exist in the future. No invariable, universal relation (vyāpti) can, therefore, be established by perception. Neither can it be said to be based on another inference, because it will involve a *petitio principii,* since the validity of that inference again has to be similarly prove. Nor can

No such universal relation can be ascertained.

this vyāpti be based on the testimony (śabda) of reliable persons (who state that all cases of smoke are cases of fire). For, the validity of testimony itself requires to be proved by inference. Besides, if inference always depended on testimony, no one could infer anything by himself.

But it may be asked : Though it is not possible to perceive all individual cases of smoke and fire, is it not possible to perceive the constant class-characters (sāmānya) like 'smokeness' and 'fireness' which must be invariably present in all instance of smoke and fire respectively ? If so, then can we not say that we at least perceive a relation between smokeness and fireness and with its help infer the presence of fire, wherever we perceive smoke. The Cārvāka replies that even if we grant the perception of a relation between smokeness and fireness, we cannot know therefrom any invariable relation between all *individual* cases of smoke and fire. To be able to infer a *particular* fire, we must know that it is inseparably related to the *particular* smoke perceived. In fact, it is not possible even to know by perception what 'smokeness' or the class-character universally present in *all* particular instances of smoke is, because we do not perceive *all* cases of smoke. What is found to be universally present in the *perceived* cases of smoke, may not be present in the *unperceived* ones. The difficulty of passing from particulars to the universal, therefore, remains here as before.

Uniformities of experience are explained by the inherent nature of things which also may change in future.

But it may be asked : If we do not believe in any fixed universal law underlying the phenomena of the world, how would we explain the uniformities that experienced objects possess ? Why is fire always experienced to be hot and water to be cool ? The Cārvāka reply is that it is due to the inherent natures (svabhāva) of things that they possess particular characters. No supernatural principle need be supposed to account for the properties of experienced objects of nature. There is neither any guarantee that uniformity perceived in the past would continue in future.

Causal relation is not ascertainable.

A modern student of inductive logic would be tempted to ask the Cārvāka : "But can we not base our knowledge of the invariable relation between smoke and fire on a *causal relation* between them?" The Cārvāka reply would be that a causal relation, being only a kind of invariable relation, cannot be established by perception owing to the same difficulties.

The Cārvāka would further point out that a causal or any other invariable relation cannot be established merely by repeated perception of two things occuring together. For one must be certain that there is no other unperceived condition (upādhi) on which this relation depends. For example, if a man perceives a number of times fire accompanied by smoke and on another occasion he infers the existence of smoke on the perception of fire, he would be liable to error, because be failed to notice a condition (upādhi), namely, wetness of fuel, on the presence of which alone fire is attended with smoke. So long as the relation between two phenomena is not proved to be unconditional, it is an uncertain ground for inference. And unconditionality or absence of conditions cannot be established beyond doubt by perception, as some conditions may always remain hidden and escape notice. Inference or testimony cannot be used for proving this unconditionality without a *petitio principii* because its validity also is being questioned here.

Some inferences accidentally turn out to be true.

It is true that in life we very often act unsuspectingly on inference. But that only shows that we act uncritically on the wrong belief that our inference is true. It is a fact that sometimes our inference comes true and leads to successful results. But it is also a fact that sometimes inference leads to error as well. Truth is not then an unfailing character of all inferences; it is only an accident, and a separable one, that we find only in *some* inferences.

Inference cannot be regarded, therefore, as a pramāṇa—a sure source of valid cognition.

2. *Testimony is not a Safe Source of Knowledge*

Testimony relating to unperceived objects is not reliable.

But can we not regard the testimony of competent persons as a valid and safe source of knowledge? Do we not very often act on knowledge received from authority? The Cārvāka replies that testimony consists of words (śabda). So far as words are heard through our ears, they are perceived. Knowledge of words is, therefore, knowledge through perception and is quite valid. But in so far as these words suggest or mean things not within our perception, and aim at giving us knowledge of those unperceived objects, they are not free from error and doubt. Very often we are misled by so-called authority. The authority of the Vedas, for example, is held in high esteem by many. But in reality the Vedas are the works of some cunning priests who earned their living by duping the ignorant and the credulous. With false hopes and promises the Vedas persuade men to perform Vedic rites, the only tangible benefit of which goes to the priests who officiate and enjoy the emoluments.

Even the Vedas are not reliable.

Testimony supported by inference is as uncertain as inference.

But will not our knowledge be extremely limited and practical life sometimes impossible, if we do not accept the words of the experienced and do not depend on expert advice? The Cārvāka reply is that in so far as we depend on any anthority, *because* we think it to be reliable, the knowledge obtained is really based on inference; because our belief is generated by a mental process like this : This authority should be accepted because it is reliable, and all reliable authority should be accepted. Being based on inference, knowledge derived from verbal testimony or authority is as precarious as inference. And as in the case of inference, so here we often act on knowledge derived from authority on the wrong belief that it is reliable. Sometimes this belief accidentally leads to successful results, sometimes it does not. Therefore, authority or testimony cannot be ragarded as a safe and valid source of knowledge.

As neither inference nor authority can be proved to be reliable, preception must be regarded as the only valid source of knowledge (pramāṇa).

III. Metaphysics

Matter is the only reality because it alone is perceived.

Meṭaphysics is the theory of reality. The Cārvāka theory of reality follows from the epistemological conclusion just dicussed. If perception is the only reliable source of knowledge, we can rationally assert only the reality of perceptible objects. God, soul, heaven, life before birth or after death, and any unperceived law (like adṛṣṭa) cannot be believed in, because they are all beyond perception. Material objects are the only objects whose existence can be received and whose reality can be asserted. The Cārvākas, thus, come to establish materialism or the theory that matter is the only reality.

1. The World is made of Four Elements

Matter is composed of four elements.

Regarding the nature of the mateial world most other Indian thinkers hold that it is composed of five kinds of elements (pañcabhūta), namely, ether (ākāśa), air (vāyu), fire (agni), water (ap) and earth (Kṣiti). But the Cārvākas reject ether, because its existance cannot be perceived; it has to be inferred. The material world is, therefore, held to be composed of the four perceptible elements. Not only non-living material objects but also living organisms, like plants and animal bodies, are composed of these four elements, by the combinition of which they are produced and to which they are reduced on death.

2. There is no Soul

The soul is nothing but the living body, with this quality of consciousness.

But it may be asked, even if perception is the only source of knowledge, do we not have a kind of preception, called internal, which gives an immediate knowledge of our mental states? And do we not perceive in these consciousness which is nowhere to be perceive in the external material objects? If so, does it not compel us to believe that there is in us some non-material substance whose quality is conciousness—the substance which is called soul or spirit (ātmā)?

The Cārvākas admit that the existence of consciousness is proved by perception. But they deny that consciousness is the quality of any unperceived non-material or spiritual entity. As consciousness is preceived to exist in the perceptible living body composed of the material elements, it must be a quality of this body itself. What people mean by a soul is nothing more than this concious living body (caitanya-viśiṣta deha eva ātmā). The non-material soul is never perceived. On the contrary, we have direct evidence of the identity of the self with the body in our daily experiences and judgements like, 'I am fat,' 'I am lame', 'I am blind'. If the 'I', the self, were different from the body, these would be meaningless.

But the objection may be raised : We do not perceive consciousness in any of the four material elements. How can it then come to qualify their product, the body? In reply the Cārvāka points out that qualities not present originally in any of the component factors may emerge subsequently when the factors are combined together. For example, betel leaf, lime and nut, none of which is originally red, come to acquire a reddish tinge when chewed together. Or, even the same thing placed under a different condition may develop qualities originally absent. For example, molasses (guḍa), originally non-intoxicant, becomes intoxicant when allowed to ferment. In a similar way it is possible to think that the material elements combined in a particular way give rise to the conscious living body. Consciousness is an epiphenomenon or bye-product of matter ; there is no evidence of its existence independent of the body.

If the existence of a soul apart from the body is not proved, there is no possibility of proving its immortality. On the contrary, death of the body means the end of the individual. All questions about previous life, after-life, rebirth, enjoyment of the fruits of actions in heaven or hell, therefore, become meaningless.

3. *There is no God*

God, whose existence cannot be perceived, fares no better than the soul. The material elements produce the world, and the supposition of a creator is unnecessary. The objection may be raised : Can the material elements by themselves give rise to this wonderful world? We find that even the production of an object like an earthen jar requires, in addition to clay which is its material cause, a potter who is the efficient cause, that shapes the material into the desired form. The four elements supply only the material cause of the world. Do we not require an efficient cause, like God as the shaper and designer who turns the material elements into this wonderful world? In reply, the Cārvāka states that the material elements themselves have got each its fixed nature (svabhāva). It is by the natures and laws inherent in them that they combine together to form this world. There is thus no necessity for God. There is no proof that the objects of the world are the products of any design. They can be explained more resonably as the fortuitous products of the elements. The Cārvākas, therefore, prefer atheism.

The supposition of God as creator is unnecessary. The world comes into existence by the spontaneous combination of material elements.

In so far as this Cārvāka theory tries to explain the world only by nature, it is sometimes called naturalism (svabhāvavāda). It is also called mechanism (yadṛcchā-vāda), because it denies the existence of conscious purpose behind the world and explains it as a mere mechanical or fortuitous combination of elements. The Cārvāka theory on the whole may also be called positivism, because it believes only in positive facts or observable phenomena.

IV. Ethics

Ethics is the science of morality. It discusses problems like : What is highest goal or *summum bonum* man can achieve? What should be the end of human conduct? What is the standard of moral judgement? The Cārvākas discuss these ethical problems in conformity with their metaphysical theories.

Some Indian philosophers like the Mīmāṁsakas believe that the highest goal of human life is heaven (svarga) which is a state of unalloyed bliss that can be attained hereafter by performing here the Vedic rites. The Cārvāka rejects this view, because it is based on the unproved existence of a life after death. 'Heaven' and 'hell' are the inventions of the priests whose professional interest lies in coaxing threatening and making people perform the rituals. Enlightened men will always refuse to be duped by them.

Heaven is a myth and cannot be the goal of life.

Many other philosophers regard liberation as the highest goal of human life. Liberation, again, is conceived as the total destruction of all sufferings. Some think that it can be attained only after death, when the soul is free from the body; and others believe that it can be attained even in this life. But the Cārvāka hold that none of these views stands to reason. If liberation is freedom of the soul from its bondage to physical existence, it is absurd because there is no soul. But if liberation means the attainment of a state free from all pain, in this very life, it is also an impossible ideal. Existence in this body is bound up with pleasure as

Liberation as freedom from all pain, is an impossible ideal.

well as pain. We can only try to minimise pain and enjoy as much pleasure as we can. Liberation in the sense of complete cessation of sufferings can only mean death.[1] Those who try to attain in life a state free from pleasures and pains by rigorously suppressing the natural appetites, thinking that all pleasures arising out of their gratification are mixed with pain, act like fools. For no wise man would 'reject the kernel because of its husk,' nor 'give up eating fish because there are bones,' nor 'cease to grow crops because there are animals to destroy them,' nor 'stop cooking his food because beggars might ask for a share.' If we remember that our existence is confined to the existence of the body and to this life, we must regard the pleasure arising in the body as the only good thing we can obtain. We should not throw away the opportunities of enjoying *this* life, in the futile hope of enjoyment hereafter. 'Rather a pigeon today than a peacock tomorrow.' 'A sure shell (courie) is better than a doubtful golden coin.' 'Who is that fool who would entrust the money in hand to the custody of others ?'[2] The goal of human life is, therefore, to attain the maximum amount of pleasure in *this* life, avoiding pain as far as possible. A good life is a life of maximum enjoyment. A good action is one which leads to a balance of pleasure and a bad action is one which brings about more pain than pleasure. This Cārvāka ethics may be called, therefore, hedonism or the theory that pleasure is the highest goal.

Pleasure, though mixed with pain, is the only possible good.

Pleasure is the ideal of life.

Some Indian thinkers speak of the four ends of human activity (puruṣārtha), namely, wealth (artha), enjoyment (kāma), virtue (dharma) and liberation (mokṣa). Of these four, the Cārvāka rejects the last two. Liberation in the sense of destruction of all sufferings can be obtained

And neither virtue (dharma) nor liberation (mokṣa)

1. 'Maraṇam eva apavargaḥ,' *Bṛhaspati-sūtra.*
2. *Kāma-sūtra,* Chap. 2.

only by death and no wise man would willingly work for that end. Virtue and vice are distinctions made by the scriptures, whose authority cannot be rationally accepted.

Wealth is good only as a means to enjoyment.

Therefore neither liberation nor virtue should be our end. Wealth and enjoyment are the only rational ends that a wise man can toil to achieve. But enjoyment is the ultimate end; wealth is not an end in itself, it is good only as a means to enjoyment.

Vedic rites are all useless.

Having rejected the authority of the scriptures, the notions of virtue and vice and belief in life after death, the Cārvākas are naturally opposed to the performance of religious ceremonies with the object of either attaining heaven or avoiding hell or propitiating departed souls. They raise cheap laughter at the customary rites. If the food offered during funeral ceremony (śrāddha) for the departed soul can appease his hunger, what is the use of a traveller's taking food with him? Why should not his people make some offerings in his name at home to satisfy his hunger? Similarly, food offered on the ground floor should satisfy a person living upstairs. If the priests really believe, as they say, that the animals killed at a sacrifice (yajña) are sure to reach heaven, why do they not rather sacrifice their old parents instead of animals and make heaven sure for them?

Religion is thus reduced to morality and morality to the search of pleasure. The ethics of the Cārvāka is only the logical outcome of his materialistic metaphysics.

V. Conclusion

The contribution of the Cārvāka to Indian philosophy.

Like the Epicureans of Greece, the Cārvākas in India have been more hated than understood. 'Cārvāka' in the mind of people at large is a term of reproach. But it is useful for a student of philosophy to remember as well what Indian philosophy owes to the Cārvāka. Scepticism or agnosticism is only the expression of a free mind that refuses to accept traditional wisdom without a thorough criticism. Philosophy, as critical speculation, claims to live chiefly on free thought and the more it can satisfy the sceptic, the sounder can it hope to be. By questioning the soundness of popular notions, the sceptic sets new problems, by the solution of which philosophy becomes richer. Kant, one of the greatest philosophers of the West, recognised his debt to scepticism when he declared : "The scepticism of Hume roused me from my dogmatic slumber." And we may say that the Cārvāka similarly saved Indian philosophy from dogmatism to a great extent. As noted already, every system of Indian thought tried to meet the Cārvāka objections and made the Cārvāka a touchstone of its theories. The value of the Cārvāka philosophy, therefore, lies directly in supplying fresh philosophical problems and indirectly in compelling other thinkers to give up dogmatism, and become critical and cautious in speculation as well as in statement of views. Finally, it may be noted that the contribution of Cārvāka epistemology is not insignificant. The criticism of inference put in the mouth of the Cārvāka by his opponents reminds us of similar criticism made in modern times against the soundness of deductive logic. The Cārvāka view that no inference can yield certain knowledge is the view of many contemporary. Western thinkers like the pragmatists and logical positivists.

What has made the Cārvāka most disreputable to people is perhaps their ethics of pleasure. Pursuit of pleasure is not by itself an object of condemnation : pleasure, in some form is recognized as desirable by other philosophers as well. It is condemned only when the nature of pleasure is coarse and the pleasure is wanted only for one's own self. It is true that some Cārvākas advocate a life of gross sensual pleasures. But a distinction found sometimes between the cunning (dhūrta) and cultured (suśikṣita) Cārvākas make it likely that the Cārvāka were not all of the same gross, uncultured type. There is evidence that the materialists devoted themselves also to the pursuit of more refined pleasures by cultivating, for example, the fine arts, the number of which is as large as sixty-four (catuḥ-ṣaṣṭi-kalāḥ), according to Vātsyāyana, a recognized headonist and author of the famous *Kāma-sūtra*. All materialists were not egoistic hedonists. Egoistic hedonism in its gross form is not compatible with social discipline. Life in society is impossible if man does not sacrifice a part of his pleasures for others. Some Cārvākas, we are told, regard the king as God. This implies their great faith in the necessity of society and its head. This view is further strengthened when we find that political philosophy and economy (daṇḍanīti and vārttā) came to be incorporated at some stage in the philosophy of the Lokāyatikas. It would appear from these facts that there were among the materialists of ancient India as cultured thinkers as we find among the positivists of modern Europe or the followers of Democritus in ancient Greece.

The best positive evidence of refined hedonism is found in the ethical philosophy propounded by Vātsyāyana in the second chapter of the *Kāma-sūtra*. It is here that we find a great hedonist himself stating and defending his own views.[1] Though Vātsyāyana believes in God and in life after death and, therefore, is not a materialist in the ordinary sense, yet he may be regarded as one, according to a wider sense of the term, namely, one who tries to explain 'higher phenomena by lower ones'.[2] Vātsyāyana admits three desirable ends of human life (purusārtha), namely, dharma, artha and kāma (virtue, wealth and enjoyment) which should be cultivated harmoniously.[3] His materialist tendency consists in holding that dharma and artha are to be treated only as means to enjoyment, which is, therefore,

1. The date of Vātsyāyana, according to some, is near about the beginning of the Christian era, and Vātsyāyana tells us that he is only summarising the views of a long line of previous writers, about a dozen in number, whose works are not available now. This shows the great antiquity of his line of thought.

2. Vide James, *Pragmatism*. p. 93

3. 'Parasparasya anupaghātakaṁ, trivargaṁ seveta,' *Kāma-sūtra*. 1.2.1.

the supreme end. The element of refinement in his hedonism consists in his emphasis on self control (brahmacarya) and spiritual discipline (dharma), as well as urbanity (nāgarikavṛtti), without which human enjoyment of pleasure is reduced to the level of beastly enjoyment. He shows that all physical enjoyment (kāma) is ultimately reducible to the gratification of the five sense. He further asserts that the satisfaction of the sense is necessary for the very existence of the body (śarirasthiti), like the satisfcation of hunger.[1] But he also maintains that the senses must be educated, disciplined and cultured through a training in the sixty-four fine arts. This training should be given only after a person has devoted the earlier part of his life to absolute self-continence and study of the Vedas and the other subsidiary branches of learning. He points out that without culture human enjoyment would be indistinguishable from beastly pleasures. To the impatient hedonist who would not forgo present comfort and would not undergo any toil for future enjoyment in this life, Vātsyāyana points out that such attitude would be suicidal. For, this would prevent a man even from the toil of cultivation and sowing seeds in the hope of the future enjoyment of a crop. In favour of regulation of the desire for enjoyment, he points out, with historical examples, that inordinate desire, inconsistent with the principles of dharma and wealth, leads to ruin and annihilates the chances of all enjoyment. In support of scientific study of the conditions and means of enjoyment, he urges, like a modern scientific man, that some science is at the root of every successful practice; and that though all persons may not study science, they are benefited by the ideas which unconsciously and indirectly filter down to the masses, among which the few scientists live. We find then, that Vātsyāyana represents Indian hedonism at its best. It is

1. Yaśodhara, the commentator on *Kāma-sūtra*., explanning this mentions that non-satisfaction of the senses might lead to disease like insanity (unmāda). *Vide* commentary on 1.2.46.

perhaps to thinkers of this kind that the name 'cultured hedonists' (susikṣita-cārvāka) was applied.

In the early Buddhist scriptures also we come across short references to some sceptics, agnostics, sophists and materialsts whom Buddha had to confront, and who may be regarded as cunning (dhūrta) Cārvāka. In the Sāmaññaphala-sutta are mentioned : (a) one Purṇa Kassapa who denies moral responsibility, virtue and vice; (b) one Makkhali Gosāla who denies free will, and the possibility of moral effort; (c) one Ajita Kesakamball who teaches the material origin and destructibility of man, the futility of good action and the impossibility of knowledge and (d) one Sañjaya Belaṭṭhiputta who would neither affirm, nor deny, nor affirm and deny at the same time, nor even admit that he neither affirms nor denies, anything.

In a recently discovered manuscript called *Tattvopaplavasiṁha* (now available in print in Gaekwad's Oriental Series) we have an interesting specimen of Indian absolute scepticism. The author, Jayarāśi, probably of the 8th century A. D., is believed to be a Cārvāka (or Lokāyatika) of an extreme type. He carries the scepticism of the ordinary Cārvāka to its logical conclusion by challenging the validity of even perceptual knowledge and refusing to accept the existence of even the physical elements. With a relentless destructive dialectic he exposes the defects of all the usually accepted sources of knowledge. He concludes, like an anti-intellectualist pragmatist, that even on the denial of all theoretical principles and doctrines practical life will go on as ever with unreflective case.[1]

1. "Tadevam upapluteṣu tattveṣu avicārita-ramaṇīyāḥ sarve vyavahārā ghaṭante." — Op., Cit., p. 125.

THE JAINA PHILOSOPHY

A SELECT BIBLIOGRAPHY

Umāsvamī ... *Tattvārthādhigama-sūtra* (Eng. trans. by J. L. Jaini. The central Jaina Publishing House, Arrah, India, 1920).

Siddhasena Divākara ... *Nyāyāvatāra* (Eng. trans. and Introduction by S. C. Vidyābhūṣana. The Indian Research Society, Calcutta, 1909).

Malliṣeṇa ... *Syādvāda-mañjari* (Commentary by Hemachandra. Chowkhamba Sanskrit series, Benares, India, 1900).

Haribhadra ... *Ṣaḍ darśana-samuccaya*, Com. by Guṇaratna (Asiatic Society Cal. 1905), Com. of Manibhadra (Chowkhamba, 1905) Chap. on Jaina.

Hermann Jacobi ... *The Jaina Sūtras* (Eng. trans. Sacred Books of the East series, Oxford, 1884).

Nemichandra ... *Dravya-Saṅgraha* (Ed. with Eng. trans. by S. C. Ghoshal. The Central Jaina Publishing House, Arrah, C 1917).

S. Stevenson ... *The Heart of Jainism* (Oxford University Press, 1915).

J. L. Jaini ... *Outlines of Jainism* Cambridge University Press, 1916).

Mohanlal Mehta ... *Outlines of Jaina Philosophy* (Jaina Mission Society, Bangalore, 1954).

CHAPTER III

THE JAINA PHILOSOPHY

I. Introduction

The founders of Jainism.

The Jainas recount the names of twenty-four teachers (tīrthaṅkaras) through whom their faith is believed to have come down from unknown antiquity. The first of these teachers was Ṛṣabhadeva.[1] The last was Vardhamāna, also styled Mahā vīra ('the great hero'). He is said to have lived in the sixth century B. C. during the time of Gotama Buddha. The teacher who immediately preceded Vardhamāna was Pārśvanātha, who lived in the ninth century B.C. The other twenty-two teachers belong to pre-historic ages.[2] The word "Jina" etymologically means a conqueror. It is the common name applied to the twenty-four teachers, because they have conquered all passions (rāga and dveṣa) and have attained liberation.

Their place in Jaina faith.

The Jainas do not believe in God. They adore the Tīrthaṅkaras or the founders of the faith. These are the liberated souls who were once in bondage, but became, through their own efforts, free, perfect, omniscient, omnipotent and all-blissful. The Jainas believe that every spirit (jīva), that is in bondage now can follow the example set by the Jainas and attain, like them, perfect knowledge, power and joy. This is the great element of optimism that inspires every true Jaina

---

1. In the Bhāgavata (5. 3-6) there is the story of a great saint-king, Ṛṣabha, who gave up all possessions, even clothes, and attained liberation (kaivalya) and loved all beings.

2. For a complete account, *vide* The Kalpa-sūtra of Bhadrabāhu (Jacobi, *Jaina Sūtras*, Part I) and Mrs. Stevenson's *The Heart of Jainism*, Chap. IV.

with absolute self-confidence. The possibility of the realization of absolute perfection, through personal effort, is for him not a mere speculation but a promise repeated by the life of every liberated saint.

The two sects of Jainism — Śvetāmbara and Digambara.

In course of time the followers of Jainism were divided into two sects well-known now as the Śvetāmbaras and the Digambaras. The difference between them lies, however, not so much in the basic philosophical doctrines as in some minor details of faith and practice. The teachings of the Jinas are accepted by both the sects. But the Digambaras are more rigorous and puritanic, while the Śetāmbaras are more accommodating to the common frailties of men. The Digambaras hold, for example, that ascetics should give up all possessions, even clothes, whereas the Śvetāmbaras hold that they should put on white clothes.[1] Again, according to the Digambaras, a saint who has obtained perfect knowledge needs no food, and women cannot obtain liberation (without being born once more as men). The Śvetāmbaras do not accept these views.

Jaina Literature.

Jainism possesses a vast literature, mostly in Prākṛta. The canonical or authoritative works accepted by all sects are said to contain the teachings of the last Tīrthaṅkara, Mahāvīra. They are too many to be mentioned here. Much of the early literature has been lost. When Jainism had to defend itself against the criticism of other schools, it adopted, for this purpose, the technical philosophical terminology of Sanskrit and thus developed its literature in Sanskrit as well.

The philosophical outlook of Jainism is common-sense realism and pluralism. The objects perceived by us are real, and they are many. The world consists of two kinds of reality,

1. 'Digambara' means space-clad or nude and 'Śvetāmbara' whiterobed.

living and non-living. Every living being has a spirit or a soul (jīva), however imperfect its body may be. Avoidance of all injury to life (ahiṁsā) plays, therefore, an important role in Jaina ethics. Along with this respect for life there is in Jainism another great element, namely, respect for the opinion of others. This last attitude is justified by a metaphysical theory of reality as many-faced (anekāntavāda) and a consequent logical doctrine (syādvāda) that every judgment is subject to some condition and limitation, and various judgments about the same reality may, therefore be true, each in its own sense, subject to its own condition.

The philosophical outlook of Jainism.

The philosophy of the Jainas may be conveniently discussed under three topics, *viz*. Epistemology (or theory of knowledge including Logic), Metaphysics, and Ethics and Religion.

II. The Jaina Theory Of Knowledge

1. The Nature and Kinds of Knowledge

Consciousness is the inseparable *essence* of every soul according to the Jainas ; it is not, as the Cārvākas hold, a mere accidental property, arising only under *some* conditions. Moreover, consciousness is conceived like the sun's light, capable of mainfesting itself and every thing else unless some obstruction prevents it from reaching its object.[1] Had there been no obstacles, the soul would have been omniscient. Omniscience is a potentiality inherent in every soul. As it is, however, we find that ordinary souls are all more or less ignorant, their knowledge is limited. The Jainas hold that this limitation is due to the obstacles created by different karmas which obstruct in different degrees the natural consciousness of the soul and

Consciousness is the essence of the soul.

It manifests itself and other objects.

1. 'Jñānaṁ sva-para-bhāsi.'

thus deprive it of its omniscience. The body, the senses and the mind (manas) are all constituted by karmas and the soul's power is limited by them.

Immediate and mediate knowledge.

Like other thinkers, the Jainas admit the twofold classification of knowledge into immediate and mediate (aparokṣa and parokṣa). But they point out that what is ordinarily regarded as immediate knowledge is only *relatively* immediate. Perception of external or internal objects through the senses (indriya) or mind (manas) is immediate as compared with inference. Still such knowledge cannot be said to be absolutely immediate, because even here the soul knows through the *medium* of something *else*, the senses or manas. In addition to such ordinary or empirical (vyāvahārika) immediate knowledge, there is also a really or absolutely (pāramārthika) immediate knowledge, which a soul attains, by removing its karma obstacles. In such knowledge the soul's consciousness becomes immediately related to objects, without the medium of senses, etc., simply by the removal of the karmas that prevented it from reaching those objects.[1] Three different kinds of such *really* immediate knowledge are distinguished.

Two kinds of immediate knowledge—ordinary immediate and really immediate.

Three kinds of really immediate knowledge—avadhi, manaḥ-paryāya and kevala.

When a person has partially destroyed and allayed the influences of karmas, he acquires the power of knowing objects which have forms, but are too distant or minute or obscure to be observed by the senses or manas. Such immediate knowledge by the unaided soul is, however, *limited* as its objects are limited and therefore, it is called *avadhijñāna* (limited knowledge). Again, when a

1. Early Jaina writers like Umāsvāmī confine 'aparokṣa' only to the soul's immediate knowledge without any medium. Later writers like Hemachandra extend it to ordinary sense perception as well, as most other Indian logicians do. To justify the narrower sense 'akṣa' is interpreted as 'jīva' and not 'indriya' as ordinarily explained (*vide* Guṇaratna's Com. on *Ṣaḍ-darsana, verse 55).*

person has overcome hatred, jealousy, etc. (which create obstacles that stand in the way of knowing other minds), he can have direct access to the present and past thoughts of others. This knowledge is called manaḥ-paryāya (entering a mind). But when *all* karmas that obstruct knowledge are completely removed from the soul, there arises in it absolute knowledge or omniscience. This is called kevalajñāna. Only the liberated souls have such knowledge.[1]

These are, then, the three kinds of extraordinary or extra-sensory perceptions which are immediate *par excellence*. But in addition to these, there are the two kinds of ordinary knowledge possessed by an average person. These are called mati and śruta. There are differences of opinion among Jaina writers regarding the exact meanings of these terms. But ordinarily mati is taken to mean any kind of knowledge which we can obtain through the senses or through manas.[2] Thus understood, mati includes *ordinary* immediate knowledge (or internal and external perception), memory recognition and inference.[3] Śruta is knowledge obtained from authority.

Ordinary immediate and mediate knowledge.

The Jainas give an account of the process by which ordinary perception takes place and is retained.[4] At first there is only a distinct sensation, say of a sound. It is not yet known what it means. This primary state of consciousness is called *avagraha* (i. e., grasping the object). Then arises the query : "What is this sound ?" This questioning state of the mind is called īhā(*i.e.*, query). Then comes a difinite judgment like "This is the sound of a car." This is called āvāya (removal of doubt). Then what is ascertained is retained in the mind. This retention is called dhāraṇā *(i.e.,* holding in the mind).

---

1. Vide *Tattvārthādhigama-sūtra*, Chap. I, sūtras 9, 12, 21-29.

2. *Ibid.*, 1.14.3. 3. *Ibid.*,1.13.4. 4. *Ibid.*, 1.15.

Śruta, the second kind of ordinary knowledge is mostly interpreted as knowledge obtained from what is *heard* from others.[1] This includes all kinds of knowledge derived from spoken or written authority. As the understanding of any authority is dependent on the perception of sounds or written letters, śurta is said to be preceded by mati.

It is pointed out, further, that these two kinds of ordinary knowledge (namely, mati and śruta), as well as the lowest kind of immediate extraordinary knowledge (namely, avadhi), are not absolutely free from chances of error. But the two higher kinds of immediate extra-sensory knowledge (manḥbparyāya and kevala) are never liable to any error.

For ordinary purposes, the Jainas accept the general view that there are three pramāṇas, namely, perception, inference and testimony (*i. e.*, authority).[2]

2. The Cārvāka View Criticised

In accepting non-perceptual sources of knowledge like inference and testimony, the Jaina writers feel it necessary to justify their view by refuting the Cārvāka theory that perception is the only source of valid knowledge.[3] They ask : If a Cārvāka were called upon to show why even perception should not be rejected as an invalid source of knowledge, what would he say? He would either remain silent and thus confess that he has no reason to support his view, or hold that perception is valid *because* it is not misleading. If he

Inference is not invalid. Even the Cārvāka theory presupposes inference.

1. Vide *Tattvārthādhigama-sūtra,* 1.20

2. Vide *Nyāyāvatāra vivṛti* (p. 4, S. C. Vidyābhuṣaṇa's ed.): pramāṇāni pratyakṣānumāna - śabdāni.

3. *Prameya-kamala-mārtaṇḍa,* Chap. 2. (Nirṇaya-Sāgara, 2nd ed. 1941): *Syādrā-domañjarī*, Verse 20 and Hemchandra's Com. thereon.

adopts the first course, his view is a mere *ipse dixit,* an opinion unsupported by reason and, therefore, not acceptable. If he adopts the second alternative, then he supports his view by a reason, and therefore, he is himself taking the help of inference. Besides, if the Cārvāka admits that perception is valid because it is uncontradicted and not misleading, for similar reasons inference and testimony also should be accepted. If the Cārvāka says to this, that inference and testimony are sometimes misleading, then it is possible to point out that even perception is sometimes misleading. So the only reasonable conclusion is that any source of knowledge, be it perception or inference or testimony, should be regarded as valid in so far as it yields a knowledge that does not prove misleading. The criterion of validity should be the harmony (saṁvāda) of knowledge with the practical consequences to which it leads.

Moreover, when the Cārvāka denies the existence of non-perceptible objects like life after-death, he goes beyond perception and infers the non-existence of the objects from the fact of their non-perception. Even when the Cārvāka says about perception in general that it is valid, he goes beyond the perceived cases of perception found to be valid in the past and infers, from general similarity, something about the future unperceived cases of perception as well. Similarly, when the Cārvāka argues with his critics, he infers their thoughts from their expression : for otherwise the Cārvāka could not take part in any discussion. Hence the Cārvāka view that perception is the only valid source of knowledge is not correct.

3. *The Jaina Theory of Judgment*

(*i*) Syādvāda or the Theory that Every Judgment is Relative

Every judgment expressess one aspect of reality and is therefore relative and subject to some condition.

The Jainas point out that the different kinds of immediate and mediate knowledge that we possess about objects show that every object has innumerable characters.[1] An omniscient being can obtain (through kevala-jñāna) an immediate knowledge of an object in all its innumerable aspects. But imperfect beings look at objects from one particular point of view at a time and have consequently the knowledge of only one aspect or character of the thing. Such partial knowledge about some one of the innumerable aspects of an object is called by the Jainal writers 'naya'.[2] Judgment (parāmarsa) basesd on such partial knowledge is also called a 'naya'.[3] Every judgement that we pass in daily life about any object is, therefore, true only in reference to the standpoint occupied and the aspect of the object considered. It is because we forget this limitation and regard our judgments as unconditionally true, that we come to quarrel and disagree very often in life. The story of the blind men who formed their ideas of an elephant by touching its legs, ears, tail and trunk respectively and thus came to quarrel about the real shape of the animal, illustrates this truth. They quarrelled because each thought that his knowledge was the *only* true and complete knowledge and should be accepted unconditionally. The quarrel was over as soon as each of them realized that his knowledge was only of *one* of the many parts of the animal.

1. Vide *Ṣaḍ-darśana-samuccaya,* 55 : "anantadharmakaṁ vastu, etc. and Gunaratna's Com.

2. Vide *Nyāyāvatāra,* verse 29 ; "Ekadeśa-viśiṣṭo'rtha nayasya viṣayo mataḥ;"

3. "nayati prāpayati saṁvedanam arohayati. iti nayaḥ pramāṇapravṛtte-ruttarakālabhāvi- parāmarśaḥ," *Nyāyāvatāra-viv.,* 29.

The various systems of philosophy which give different accounts of the universe similarly occupy different points of view and discover the different aspects of the many-sided universe. They quarrel because they do not bear in mind that each account is true only from its own standpoint, and is subject to certain conditions. They fail to realize, therefore, that the different views may be true like the different descriptions of the elephant.

Different systems of philosophy represent different partial aspect of reality.

In view of these facts, the Jainas insist that every judgment (naya) should be qualified by some word like 'somehow' (syāt, *i. e.*, in some respect), so that the limitation of this judgment and the possibility of other alternative judgments from other points of view may be always clearly borne in mind. For example, instead of a judgment like "the elephant is like a pillar", it should be said, to remove the chance of confusion. "Somehow (*i. e.*, in respect of its legs) the elephant is like a pillar". Similarly, on perceiving a black earthen jug existing in a room at a particular time, we should not assert unconditionally, "The jug exist", but should rather say, "*Some how*, the jug exists", which would remind us that the judgment is true only with regard to the many conditions of space, time, quality, etc., under which the jug exists. The qualified judgment, "Somehow, the jug exists" (syād ghaṭaḥ asti) would prevent the possibility of the misapprehension that the pot exists at all times or in every place, or that a pot of any other colour, shape etc., exists. The unqualified judgment, "The jug exists", leaves the possibility of such misapprehension.

Every judgment should be qualified by some word like 'somehow' (syāt), expressing conditionality.

The theory of the Jainas has come to be known as syādvāda. It is the view that every ordinary judgment (passed by imperfect minds like ours) holds good only of the particular aspect of the object judged and of the point of view from which the judgment is passed.

This view is called syādvāda.

This view is called in keeping with the Western view that every judgment relates to a particular universe of discourse whose constituents are too many to be mentioned.

This Jaina view is quite in keeping with the view accepted by Western logicians generally, namely, that every judgment is passed in a particular universe of discourse or contest and must be understood only in reference thereto. The universe of discourse is constituted by different factors like space, time, degree, quality, etc., which are left unmentioned partly because they are obvious and partly because they are too many to be stated exhaustively. Now, if these conditions cnanot be exhaustively enumerated, as some modern logicians like Schiller also admit, it is good for the sake of precision to qualify the judgment explicity by a word like 'somehow' (syāt).[1]

This view makes Jaina philosophy catholic and tolerant.

The principle underlying 'syādvāda' makes Jaina thinkers catholic in their outlook. They entertain and accept the views of other philosophers as different possible versions of the universe from different points of view. The only thing that the jainas dislike in other thinkers is the dogmatic claim of each that he alone is in the right. This claim amounts to the fallacy of exclusive predication (ekānta-vāda). Against such a fallacy of philosophical speculation a protest has been raised recently in America by the Neo-realists who have called it the fallacy of exclusive particularity.[2] But no Western or Eastern philosopher has so earnestly tried to avoid this error in practice as the Jainas have done.

(*ii*) Saptabhaṅginaya or the Seven Forms of Judgment:

The seven forms of conditional predication :

Ordinarily, logic distinguishes two kinds of judgment, affirmative and negative. The Jainas distinguish seven kinds of judgment including these two. Any object may be described affirmatively by a judgment which predicates of

1. 'Syāt' (='kathaficit') means 'in some respect'.
2. *The New Realism*, PP. 14-15.

it any of the characters it possesses, or it may be described negatively by a judgment which denies of it characters belonging to other objects but absent in this.[1] These two are the affirmative and negative judgments ordinarily recognized; but the Jainas qualify each with 'somehow' (syāt) to emphasize its conditional or relative character. Affirmative judgments about a jug, for example, would be like '*somehow* the jug is in the room' (*i.e.*, in the room at a particular place and particular time, and as a jug of a particular description): '*somehow* the jug is red (*i.e.,* not always red but only during a particular time or under particular circumstances and the red is of a specific shade, etc.). The general form of all affirmative judgments can then be symbolically represented as '*somehow* S is P' (syāt asti). Again, negative judgments about an object would be like '*somehow* the jar is *not* outside the room' meaning that the jar of that particular kind, at that particular time, etc., is not outside); '*somehow* the jar is *not* black (*i.e.,* not black at that particular space and time and under those conditions, etc.). We find then that the general form of all negative judgments in '*somehow* S *is not* P' (syāt nāsti).

(1) 'Somehow S is P' (syāt asti).

(2) 'Somehow S is not P' (syāt nāsti).

When, however, we have to describe the complex fact that the jar is sometimes red and sometimes not, we must have a compound judgment like '*somehow* the jar is and also is not red'. The general form of this judgement would, therefore, be '*somehow* S *is and also is not* P' (syāt asti ca nāsti ca). This is the third form of judgment recognized by Jaina logic. This form is obtained by combining *successively* the points of view of the first two judgments into one composite points of view. The necessity of such compound judgment lies in the need of a comprehensive view of the positive and the negative character of an object.

(3) 'Somehow S is and also is not P' (syāt - asti ca nāsti ca).

1. Vide Gunaratna's Com., *op. cit.* (pp, 219-20, Asiatic Soc. ed,); "The dvidhā saṁbandho'stitvena nāstitvena ca, Tatra svaparyāyairastitvena saṁbandhah .... paraparyāyaistu nāstitvena."

(4) 'Somehow S is indescribable' (syāt avaktavyaṁ).

A jar is black when raw, and red when it is baked. But if we are asked, what is the real colour of the jar always or under all conditions, the only honest reply would be that the jar cannot be described then, *i.e.*, under the conditions of the question. Under such circumstances when we are forced to predicate simultaneously, of any object, characters which are incompatible, being contrary or contradictory, our judgment, according to the Jainas, would be of the general form '*somehow* S *is* indescribable' (syāt avaktavyaṁ). This is the fourth kind of judgment recognized by Jaina logic.

Recognition of this fourth form of judgment is of great philosophical value. It points out, first, that though an object can be described from different standpoints, in different aspects separately or successively, it cannot be described at all, if no such distinction of standpoint and aspect is made. An object in general is an indescribable entity. Secondly, this also points out that philosophical wisdom does not always consist in the ability to answer a question by a straight affirmative or negative, but also in realising that some questions, by their very nature, are unanswerable. Thirdly, the recognition of this form of judgment shows that the Jaina logic does not violate the principle of contradiction. On the contrary, it shows that obedience to this law makes the Jaina confess that incompatible characters cannot be simultaneously predicated of any subject in the same aspect.

(5) 'Somehow S is P and is also indescribable' (syāt asti ca avaktavyaṁ

The other three, of the seven forms of judgment, are obtained by combining successively each of the first three standpoints with the fourth. Thus by combining the first and the fourth *successively,* we get the fifth form of judgment, '*somehow* S *is* P and is also indescribable' (syāt asti ca, avaktavyaṁ ca). When we consider together, from a comprehensive point of view, the fact that a jug is sometimes red, but also that without reference to any particular time or state it cannot be described as having any predicable character, our judgment is of the form, 'The jug is somehow red but is also somehow indescribable.' Similarly, combining again the second and the fourth standpoint *successively* we have the sixth judgment of the general form, *'Somehow'* S *is not* P *and is* also indescribable, (syāt nāsti ca, avaktavyaṁ ca). Lastly, combining *successively* the third with the fourth point of view, we get the seventh form of judgment *'somehow* S *is* P, also *is not* P, *and is* indescribable too' (syāt asti ca, nāsti ca, avaktavyaṁ ca).

(6) 'Somehow S is not P and is also indescribable' (syāt nāsti ca, avaktavyaṁ ca).

(7) 'Somehow S is P, also is not P and is indescribable too' (sy āt nāstica, avaktavyaṁ ca).

If we combine *simultaneously* any of the first three points of view with the fourth, instead of doing so successively, we shall have in each case the simultaneous predication of incompatible characters (like 'is and is indescribable'; or 'is, is not and is indescribable'. or 'is, is not and is indescribable'. Hence in each case the judgment would be the same in form as in the fourth case, namely, 'Somehow S is indescribable' (syāt avaktavyaṁ). Therefore, though there are innumerable aspects of every thing, the forms of judgment would be only seven, neither more nor less.

No other form is possible.

To sum up, Jaina logic recognizes the following seven kinds of conditional judgment (saptabhaṅgīnaya) :

(1) Somehow, S is P (syāt asti).

(2) Somehow, S is not P (ṣyāt nāsti).

(3) Somehow, S is P, and is also not P (syāt asti ca, nāsti ca).

(4) Somehow, S is indescribable (syāt avaktavyaṁ).

(5) Somehow, S is P, and is also indescribable (syāt asti ca, avaktavyaṁ ca).

(6) Somehow, S is not P, and is also indescribable (syāt nāsti ca, avaktavyaṁ ca).

(7) Somehow, S is P, and is also not P, and also indescribable (syāt asti ca, nāsti ca, avaktavyaṁ ca).

Syādvāda is realistic and, therefore, not pragmatic.

The Jaina doctrine of syādvāda is sometimes compared with the pragmatism of some Western thinkers. It is true that a pragmatic logician , like Schiller, also recognizes the truth that no judgment is true or false without particular reference to its context and purpose. Even a so-called self-evident judgment, like 'A square is not a circle', or 'Two and two are four', is true only in a specific sense, according to Schiller. This is a striking point of resemblance. But there is a very great difference also which should not be forgotten. The Jainas are *realists*, but the pragmatist have a distinct *idealistic* bias. According to the Jainas, the different judgments about an object are not simply different *real* aspects of the object. The Jainas would accept, therefore, a realistic view of truth which is rejected by all thorough going pragmatists.

It is a kind of relativism, but is realistic and not idealistic.

The Jaina syādvāda is sometimes compared with the Western theory of relativity. There are two kinds of relativity, idealistic (as of Protagoras Berkely, Schiller), and realistic (as of Whitehead or Boodin). And if the Jaina is to be called a relativist, he must be understood to be of the realistic type. Our judgments about things are relative – but relative to or dependent upon not simply the mood of judging mind, but upon the relational characters of the many-sided reality itself.

It is not scepticism.

Another misunderstanding often found is the interpretation of the Jaina word 'syāt' as 'may be'. This would impart a sceptical or agnostic form to the Jaina theory, and make it look like the view of the Greek sceptic Pyrrho who also recommended the qualification of every judgment with a phrase like 'may be'. But it should be noted that the Jaina is not a sceptic. It is not the uncertainty of a judgment, but its conditional or relative character, that is expressed by the addition of the qualifying particle 'syāt'. Subject to the conditions or the universe of discourse under which any judgment is made, the judgment is valid beyond all doubt. There is, therefore, no room for scepticism.[2]

1. 'Yathāvasthitārthavyavasāyarūpaṁ hi saṁvedanaṁ pramāṇam' *Prameyakamalam rtaṇḍa*, p. 164

2. For the statistical implication of Syādvāda *vide* P.C. Mahalanobis's article, 'The Foundations of Statistics', *Dialectica*, International Review of Philosophy of Knowledge, 15-6-54, Switzerland.

III. The Jaina Metaphysics

Every object is found to possess innumerable characters, positive and negative.

The Jainas hold that every object known by us has innumerable characters (anantadharmakam vastu). Let us try to understand a little more clearly the implication of this view. Every object is what it is because of its positive and negative characters. The positive characters which determine, for example, an object like a man, are his size, colour, shape, weight, constitution, heredity, family, race, nationality, education, employment, place of birth, date of birth, habitation, age, etc., and the numberless relations he bears to the uncountable other objects of the world. The negative characters which determine the man consist of what he is not. To know him fully, we should know how he is distinguished from everything else; we should know, for example, that he is not a European, nor a Chinese, nor a Negro, etc., that he is not a Christian, nor a Mohammedan, nor a Zoroastrian, etc., not dishonest, not foolish, not selfish etc. As the negative characters of the man consist in his distinctions from *all* other objects in the universe, the number of these would, therefore, be far greater than that of the positive characters.[1]

Moreover, it acquires new character with changes in time.

If we consider, then, an object in the light of its own positive characters and also in the light of the characters of all other objects which are absent in it, the object would no longer appear to be a simple thing having only a limited number of qualities, as we ordinarily take it to be. The object, on the contrary, turns out to be one possessed of unlimited characters. But when, moreover, the element of time is taken into consideration, and it is remembered that the object takes

1. "stokāḥ svaparyāyā ḥ paraparyāvāstu vyāvṛttirūpā anantā. anante. Abyo dravyebhyo vyāvṛttivāt," Guṇaratna on *Ṣaḍ,*verse 55, p.214.

on new characters with the change of time, the object is found really to possess infinite characters (anantadharma).

Hence an object has infinite characters.

Jaina writers, therefore, remark that he who knows *one* object fully, knows every thing. Only an omniscient person (kevalī) can have such complete knowledge of an object. For practical purposes (vyavahāra) a partial knowledge of what an object is or is not is of course, quite sufficient. But this should not make us think, as we do, that a finite object is really possessed of limited characters. Nor should we think that our ordinary knowledge about it is complete and perfect.

Only the omniscient can, therefore, know an object fully.

1. The Jaina Conception of Substance

We have just seen that objects have many characters. As in common conversaton so also in philosophy a distinction is made between the characters (dharma) and that which possesses the characters (dharmī). The latter is generally called a substance (dravya). The Jainas accept this common philosophical view of substance. But they point out that there are two kinds of characters found in every substance, essential and accidental. The essential characters of a substance remain in the substance as long as the substance remains. Without these the substance will cease to be what it is. Consciousness, for example, is an essential character of the soul. Again, the accidental characters of a substance come and go; they succeed one another. Desires, volitions, pleasure and pain are such accidental characters possessed by the soul-substance. It is through such characters that a substance undergoes change or modification. They may also be called, therefore, modes. The Jainas call an essential unchanging

A. substance is possessed of some unchanging essential characters (gunas) and changing modes (paryāyas).

character guṇa, and an accidental, changing paryāya or paryaya. A substance is defined therefore; as that which possesses qualities (guṇas), as well as modes (paryāyas).[1]

Change and permanence are, therefore, both real.

The world is composed of substances of different kinds. In so far as the essential characters of the ultimate substances are abiding, the world is permanent, and in so far as the accidental characters undergo modification, the world also changes. The Jainas, therefore, hold that those philosophers like the Bauddhas, who say that there is nothing really permanent in the universe, and that everything changes from moment to moment (kṣaṇika-vāda), are one-sided and dogmatic. Equally mistaken also are philosophers like the monistic Vedāntins, who declare that change is unreal and that Reality is absolutely unchanging (nitya-vāda).[2] Each of them looks at one side (ekānta) of reality only and thus commits the fallacy of exclusive predication. Change and permanence are both real. It should not be thought contradictory to say that a particular substance (or the universe as a whole) is both subject to change and free from it. Change is true of the substance in one respect (syāt), whereas permanence is true in another one respect (syāt). The contradiction vanishes when we remember that each predication is relative and not absolute, as taught by syād-vāda.

There are the three factors present in reality, *viz.* permanence, origination and decay.

A substance is real (sat). Reality consists of three factors: permanence, origination, and decay.[3] In substance there is its unchanging essence and, therefore, it is permanent, there are again the origin and decay of its changing modes (paryāya). Hence all the three elements that characterize reality are there in a substance.

---

1. Guṇa-paryāyavad dravyam, *Tat. sūt.*, 5.38.
2. *Syādvādamañjarī*, verse 26.
3. 'Utpāda-vyaya-dhrauvyayuktaṁ sat, – *Tat. sūt.*, 5.30.

Causal efficiency cannot be a mark of reality, as Bauddhas think.

By accepting this criterion of reality the Jainas reject the Bauddha view that reality consists in causal efficiency, *i.e.,* that an object is real if it is capable of causing any effect.The Bauddha criterion is faulty, because according to it even an illusory snake must be called real as it can cause effects like fear, flight, etc. From this

The Bauddha theory of momentariness is also untenable.

faulty criterion of reality the Bauddhas deduce the theory of the momentariness of things, which, therefore, turns out to be fallacious. Against the one-sided theory of momentariness the Jainas also adduce the following arguments :[1]

Refutation of momentariness.

(1) If every thing be momentary, the soul also would be so, and then we could not explain memory, recognition, the immediate feeling of personal identity, etc. (2) Liberation would then be meaningless, because there would be no permanent soul to be liberated. (3) No moral life would be possible then, because a momentary person could not attempt to attain any end. The work of the person who would begin an effort would bring about a fruit that would be enjoyed by the person succeeding him. (4) Consequently there would be no moral law; the consequences of one's own action would be lost to him (kṛtapraṇāśa) and the consequences of another man's action would befall him (akṛtābhyupagama). (5) Mere momentary states would not even constitute any individual series, because without something permanent running through the changing modes, the different changing states cannot be held to gether to form a continuous individual. (6) Neither perception nor inference reveals the existence of any thing in the world in which there is only change and no element of continuity.

2. Classification of Substances

Substances, extended and non-extended.

The broadest classification of substances, according to the Jaina, is into the extended and the non-extended. There is only one substance, namely, time (kāla), which is devoid of extension. All other substances possess

1. *Sarva-dariana-saṅgraha*, Ch. on Jaina, and Guṇaratna's Com. on *Ṣaḍ*, 52.

extension. They are called by the general name *astikāya* because every substance of this kind exists (asti) like a body (kāya), possessing extension.[1]

Substances possessing extension (astikāyas) are subdivided into two kinds, namely, the living (jīva) and the non-living (ajīva). Living substances (jīvas) are identical with souls or spirits. The souls againg can be classified into those that are emancipated or perfect (mukta) and those that are in bondage (baddha). The souls in bondage are again of two kinds, those that are capable of movement (trasa) and those that are immobile (sthāvara). The immobile living substances have the most imperfect kinds of bodies. They live in the five kinds of bodies made of earth, water, fire, air or plants respectively. They have only the sense of touch; they possess, therefore, tactual consciousness. The mobile living substances have bodies of different degrees of perfection and variously possess two, three, four or five senses. Souls or living substances like worms have two senses, namely those of touch and taste ; those like ants have three senses, namely, those of touch, taste and smell ; those like bees possess four senses, namely, those of touch, taste, smell and sight. Higher animals like beasts, birds and men have five senses, namely, those of touch, taste, smell, sight and hearing.

The living and the non-living.

The fettered and the liberated.

The moving and the non-moving.

The five kinds of immobile living substances having only one sense.

The mobile living substances having two to five senses.

Non-living substances possessing extension are dharma, adharma, ākāśa and pudgala.

---

1. *Vide Dravyasaṅgraha*, 24. According to Guṇaratna, however, astikāya' means a collection of indivisible parts of space.

2. *Syādvāda*, 22, and also Guṇaratna's Com. on *Ṣaḍ*, 49.

The following table will clearly show the above scheme of classification :

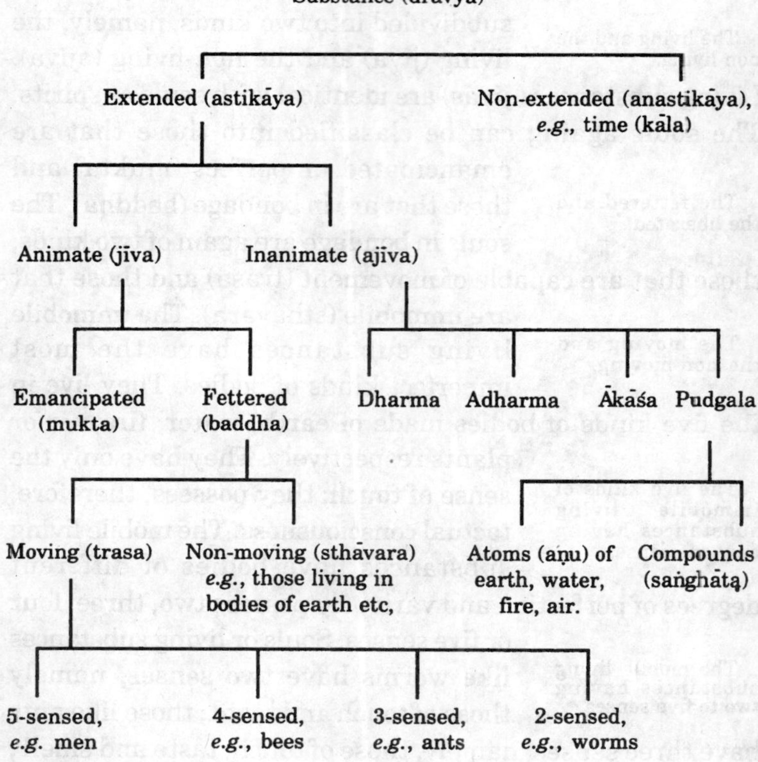

3. *The Soul or Jiva*

Jīva is a soul

A jīva or a soul is a conscious substance. Consciousness is the essence of the soul.[1] It is always present in the soul, though its nature and degree may vary. Souls may be theoretically arranged in a continuous series according to the degrees of

1. Cetanā -lakṣaṇo jīvaḥ, Guṇaratna oṇ *Ṣaḍ*, 47. 'Upayogo lakṣaṇam *Tat. Sut.*,2.8

consciousness. At the highest end of the scale would be perfect souls that have overcome all karmas and attained omniscience. At the lowest end would stand the most imperfect souls which inhabit bodies of earth, water, fire, air or vegetable.[1] In them life and consciousness appear to be absent. But really even here consciousness of a tactual kind is present : only consciousness is in a dormant form owing to the overpowering influence of karma obstacles.[2] Midway between would lie souls having two to five senses, like worms, ants, bees and men.[3]

Souls have varying degrees and kinds of knowledge.

It is the soul that knows things, performs activities, enjoys pleasures, suffers pains, and illumines itself and other objects. The soul is eternal, but it also undergoes, change of states. It is different from the body and its existence is directly proved by its consciousness of itself.[4]

The soul manifests itself and others. It is eternal.

Owing to the inclinations generated by its past actions a jīva comes to inhabit different bodies successively. Like a light it illuminates or renders conscious the entire body in which it lives. Though it has no form (mūrti), it acquires like a light the size and form of the body wherein it lives. It is in this sense that a jīva, though formless, is said to occupy space or possess extension. The jīva is not infinite but co-extensive with the body, as it can immediately know objects only within the body. Consciousness is not present everywhere but only in the body.[5]

Like a light the soul pervades the entire body in which it lives.

Students of Western philosophy find it difficult to understand how a soul can possess both consciousness and extension – qualities which are diamerically opposed, according to Descartes.

How can the soul occupy space?

1. Vanaṣpatyantānām ekam. *Tat.*, *Sūt.*, 2.22.

2. Vide Guṇaratna (*Ṣad.*, 49) for elaborate arguments supporting the existence of life in plants and minerals.

3. Kṛmi-pipīlikā-bhramara-manuṣyādinām ekaikavṛdhāni, *Tat.*, *Sūt.*, 2.23.

4. *Nyā yācatā ra,* verse 31 and *Dravya-saṅgraha,* verse 2.

5. Vide *Syā d.*, 8, and *Tat.*, *Sūt.*, 5.16: "Pradeśa-saṁhāra-visurpā bhyā m pradipavat."

Extension, Descartes thinks, is the exclusive quality of material substances, and consciousness is the exclusive quality of the soul. But the soul, as proved by Descartes, is essentially 'a *thinking* being'; and 'thought' seems to have no connection with space or matter. But the Jainas conceive the soul primarily as a *living* being (jīva). Consciousness is found in every part of living body, and if consciousness be the character of the soul, the soul should be admitted to be present in every part of the body and, therefore, to occupy space. The soul's ability to pervade space is admitted by other Indian thinkers as also by many Greek philosophers like Plato, and even by some modern realistic philosophers like Alexander. It should be borne in mind, however, that a soul's occupying space simply means its *presence* in the different parts of space and *not filling* space like a material body. A material body fills a part of space in such a way that while it is there, no other matter can occupy it. But a soul's presence in a particular space does not prevent another soul's presence there ; two souls may be present at the same place, the Jainas point out, just as two lights can illumine the same area.

The soul does not fill space like matter.

It is present in space like light.

The Jaina philosophers feel it necessary to meet the Cārvāka views regarding the soul. Guṇaratna, a great Jaina thinker, gives elaborate arguments to meet Cārvāka sceptism and proves the existence of the soul. We may state here the purport of his arguments.

The existence of the soul is directly proved by such uncontradicted immediate experience as 'I feel pleasure'. When we perceive the quality of a substance, we say, we perceive the substance. For example, on seeming a rosy colour we hold that we perceive the substance rose to which the colour belongs. On similar grounds we can hold that the soul is directly perceived, because we immediately perceive such characters of the soul as pleasure, pain, remembrance, volition, doubts, knowledge, etc. The existence of the soul may also be indirectly proved by inferences like the following : The body can be moved and controlled at will like a car, and therefore, there must be *some one* that moves and controls it. The senses of sight, hearing, etc., are only instruments, and there must be *some*

Proofs for the existence of the soul.

The soul is immediately known in the perception of its qualities like pleasure.

It is also knowable mediately through many inferences.

agent who employs them. Again, there must be *some efficient cause* or producer of the body, because material objects which have a beginning are found to require some agent for shaping their material cause. Thus in different ways the existence of a substance like the soul can also be inferred.

The Cārvāka view that unconscious material elements can produce consciousness is not verified by perception.

The Cārvāka holds that consciousness is the product of the material elements. But we never *perceive* anywhere the generation of consciousness by the unconscious material elements. The Cārvāka believes that perception is the only valid source of knowledge. How can he then believe in what perception fails to show? Even if inference were accepted as valid by the Cārvāka, it would not prove that consciousness is the effect of matter or the material body. Because, if the body were the cause of consciousness, there would be no absence of consciousness so long as the body existed, and consequently, loss of consciousness in sleep, swoon, or in a dead body would be impossible. Besides,we find that there is no relation of concomitant variation between the body and sonsciousness, the development and decay of the body are not invariably followed by corresponding changes of consciousness. So no casual connection between matter and consciouness can be proved even by inference. The Cārvāka would perhaps say that,though every kind of matter does not produce consciousness, yet when matter is organized into a living body, it produces consciousness. In reply to this it is pointed out that but for some organizer, matter would not be formed into a living body, and that this organizer is the soul itself. Judgments like 'I am stout', 'I am thin', on which the Cārvāka tries to prove that the soul is identical with the body, must be understood figuratively and not literally. The soul sometimes treats the body as itself, because it is intimately interested in the body. Again, if the soul were absolutely unreal, the negative judgment 'there is no soul in the body' would be unintelligible. Denial of something in any place implies the knowledge of its existence somewhere in some form.[1] Apart from all other arguments, to say that 'my self does not exist' is as absurd as to say 'my mother is barren' or 'this sun, the giver of light, does not exist'.

Nor by inference.

---

1. 'Yannisidhyate tat sāmānyena vidyate eva,' Guṇaratna on *Ṣaḍ*, 48-49.

4. The Inanimate Substances or Ajīvas

The five inanimate substances : matter time, space, dharma and adharma.

The physical world in which souls live is constituted by the material bodies that the souls occupy and the other material objects that form their environment. But in addition to these material substances, there are space, time and the conditions of motion and rest, without which the world and its events cannot be fully explained. Let us consider these different substances one by one.

(*i*) Matter or Pudgala

Material substances are capable of combination and separation.

Matter in Jaina Philosophy is called pudgala, which etymologically means 'that which is liable to integration and disintegration'. Material substances can combine together to form larger and larger wholes, and can also break up into smaller and smaller parts. The smallest parts of matter which cannot be further divided, being partless, are called atoms (aṇu). Two or more such atoms may combine together to form compounds (saṅghāta or skandha). Our bodies and the objects of nature are such compounds of material atoms. Mind (manas), speech and breath are also the products of matter.[2]

They have the qualities of touch, taste, smell and colour.

A material substance (pudgala) possesses the four qualities of touch, taste, smell and colour.[3] These qualities are possessed by atoms and also by their products, the compounds. Sound is not an original quality like these four, as most other Indian philosophers hold. The Jaina points out that sound along with light, heat, shadow, darkness, union, disunion, fineness, grossness, shape is produced later by the accidental modifications of matter.[4]

---

1. 'pūrayanti galanti ca,' Sarvadarśana, III.

2. *Tat. sūt.* 5.19. 3. *Ibid.* 5.23 4. *Ibid.* 5.24

(*ii*) Space or Ākāśa

The function of space is to afford room for the existence of all extended substances. Soul, matter, dharma and adharma all exist in space. Though space is imperceptible, its existence is known by an inference like the following : Substances which are extended can have extension only in some place, and that is called ākāśa. Though to be extended is the very nature of some substances, and no substance which lacks that nature can be made extended by space, yet it is also true that, to be extended, a substance requires space, as a necessary condition.

Space given room for extension.

It should not be thought that extension is explained fully by substances extended, without the supposition of some other condition like space. For, substances are those that occupy or pervade, and space is that which is occupied or pervaded.[1] Space is not the same as extension, as Descartes thought, but it is the locus of extension, or of extended things, as Locke held.

Without space, substances could not be extended.

The Jaina distinguishes two kinds of space, the space containing the world where souls and the other substances live (lokākāśa), and empty space beyond such world (alokākāśa).

Filled space and empty space.

(*iii*) Time or Kāla

Time (kāla), as Umāsvāmī states, makes possible the continuity, modification, movement, newness and oldness of substances.[2] Like space, time also is inferred, though not perceived. It is inferred as the condition without which substances could not have the characters just mentioned, though it is true that time alone cannot cause a thing to have the characters. without time

Time is the necessary condition of duration, change, motion, newness and oldness.

1. Guṇaratna on *Ṣaḍ.*, 49.

2. *Tat. sūt.*, 5.22: 'vartanā-parināma-kriyāḥ paratvāparatve ca kālasya.

a thing cannot endure or *continue* to exist; duration implies moments of time in which existence is prolonged. Modification or change of states also cannot be conceived without time. A mango can be green and ripe only successively, *i.e.*, at different moments of time; and without the supposition of time-distinctions we cannot understand how a thing can possess such incompatible characters. Similarly, movement which implies the assumption of successive states by an object can be conceived only with the supposition of time. Lastly, the distinction between the old and the new, the earlier and the later cannot be explained without time. These are, therefore, the grounds on which the existence of time can be inferred.

Time is not extended in space.

The reason why time is not regarded as an astikāya is that time is one indivisible substance. One and the same time is present every where in the world.[1] Unlike all other substances called astikā yas,time is devoid of extension in space.

Real time and empirical time.

Jaina writers sometimes distinguished between real time (pāramārthika kāla) and empirical or conventional time (vyāvahārika kāla, also called samaya). Continuity or duration (vartanā) is the mark of real time. It is this latter (samaya) which is conventionally divided into moments, hours, etc., and is limited by a beginning and an end. But real time is formless and eternal. By imposing conventional limitations and distinctions on real time, empirical time is produced.[2]

Some Jaina teachers, Guṇaratna observes, do not admit time as a separate substance, but regard it as a mode (paryāya) of the other substances.[3]

1. Guṇaratna on *Ṣaḍ* p. 163.
2 *Dra vyasaṅgraha* 21.
3. *Ṣad.*, p. 162.

(*iv*) Dharma and Adharma

Dharma and Adharma are the conditions of movement and rest.

Like space and time, these two substances also are inferentially proved to exist. Mobility and immobility — motion and rest — are the grounds of such inference. The Jaina argues that just as the movement of a fish in the river, though initiated by the fish itself, would not be possible without the *medium* of water, which is therefore, a necessary condition, similarly the movement of a soul or a material thing requires some auxiliary condition, whithout which its motion would not be possible. Such a condition is the substance called dharma. Dharma can only favour or help the motion of moving objects; it cannot make a non-moving object move, just as water cannot make a fish move. Adharma, on the contrary, is the substance that helps the restful state or immobility of objects, just as the shade of a tree helps a traveller to rest, or the earth supports things that rest on it. It cannot, however, arrest the movement of any moving object. Dharma and adharma, though thus opposed, are also similar in so far as both are eternal, formless, nonmoving, and both pervade the entire world-space (lokākāśa). As conditions of motion and rest, both are passive,[1] and not active. Dharma and adhrma are used here in these technical senses, and not in their ordinary moral senses (*i.e.* merit and demerit).[2]

They are formless passive substances.

Space, time, dharma and adharma are remote and passive instrumental conditions.

Regarding all tha four substances – space, time, dharma and adharma – it should be noted that as causal conditions they all have a peculiar status. The causal conditions (kāranas) may be distinguished into three chief kinds, agent (as potter is of the pot), instrument (as the potter's wheel is of the pot) and material (as clay is of the pot). Space, time, etc., come under the category of instrumental conditions, but they should be distinguished

---

1. 'Udāsīnakāraṇa' (Guṇaratna, *Ṣaḍ*, p. 172).

2. *Cf.* "Dharmādayaḥ sañjñḥ sāmayikāḥ" etc. (*Tattvārtharājazārttika*, 5. 1. 17. 18.)

from ordinary conditions of that kind, being more indirect and passive than ordinary instrumental conditions. Guṇaratna gives them, therefore, a special name, apekṣākāraṇa.[1] The stone on which the potter's wheel rests may be cited as a condition of this kind in relation to the pot. Space, time, etc. are similar conditions.

IV. The Jaina Ethics and Religion

The most important part of Jaina philosophy is its Ethics. Metaphysics or epistemology – in fact, knowledge of any kind – is useful for the Jaina in so far as it helps him to right conduct. The goal of right conduct again is salvation (mokṣa), which means negatively removal of all bondage of the soul and positively the attainment of perfection.

1. Bondage of the Soul

The soul in itself is possessed of infinite potentiality.

Bondage means, in Indian philosophy in general, the liability of the individual to birth an all consequent sufferings. This general conception of bondage is differently interpreted by the different systems in the light of their ideas of the individual and the world. The suffering individual, for the Jaina, is a Jīva or a living, conscious substance called the soul. This soul is inherently perfect. It has infinite potentiality within. Infinite knowledge, infinite faith, infinite power and infinite bliss, can all be attained by the soul if it can only remove from within itself all obstacles that stand in the way. Just as the sun shines forth to illuminate the entire world as soon as the atmosphere is freed of cloud and fog, similarly the soul attains omniscience and the other perfections inherent in it as soon as the

1. *Ṣaḍ*, p. 162.

obstacles are removed. But what then are these obstacles, and how do they come to rob the soul of its native perfections ? The obstacles, the Jaina asserts, are constituted by matter-particles which infect the soul and overpower its natural qualities. In other words, the limitations that we find in any individual soul are due to the material body with which the soul has identified itself. The body is made of particles of matter (pudgala), and for the formation of a particular kind of body, particular kinds of matter-particles are to be arranged and organized in a particular way. In the formation of this body the guiding force is the soul's own passions. Roughly speaking, a soul acquires the body that it inwardly craves for. The karma or the sum of the past life of a soul – its past thought, speech and activity — generates in it certain blind cravings and passions that seek satisfaction. These cravings in a soul attract to it particular sorts of matter-particles and organize them into the body unconsciously desired. The soul with its passions or karma-forces is, therefore, regarded by the Jaina as the organizer of the body, the efficient cause of it, whereas matter (pudgala) is said to be its material cause. The organism which the soul thus acquires, consists not simply of the gross perceptible body, but also the senses, manas, the vital forces and all the other elements which curb and limit the soul's potentialities.

Owing to karma it is associated with matter and thus its limitation or bondage occurs.

Passions attract matter to the soul.

The body that we have inherited from our parents is not a mere chance acquisition. Our past karma determines the family in which we are born as well as the nature of the body–its colour, stature, shape, longevity, the number and nature of sense organs and motor organs which it possesses. While all these, taken collectively, may be said to be due to karma, taken also in the collective sense (of the sum total of all tendencies generated by past life), each of these taken separately may be said to be due to a particular kind of karma. The Jaina, therefore, speaks of the many karmas, and names each after the effect it produces. For example,

The body and other conditions of an individual are all due to karma.

gotra-karma is the karma that determines the family into which one is born, āyus-karma is the karma determining the length of life, and so on. similarly, we are told of the karma that clouds knowledge jñānāvaraṇīya), that which clouds faith (darśanāvaraṇīya), that which produces delusion (mohanīya), that which produces emotions of pleasure and pain (vedanīya), and so on.

The passions causing bondage are anger, pride, infatuation and greed.

The passions which cause bondage are anger, pride, infatuation and greed (krodha, mānā, māyā, lobha).[1] These are called kaṣāya (*i. e.* sticky substances), because the presence of these in the soul makes matter-particles stick to it.

The influx of karma-matter into the soul.

As the nature and number of material particles attracted by the soul depend on its karma, these particles themselves come to be called karma-matter (karma-pudgala) or even simply karma. The flow of such karma-matter into the soul is called, therfore, influx (āsrava) of karma.

Bondage of the soul to matter is due to its bondage to bad dispositions or passions.

Bondage, in Jaina philosophy, comes, therefore, to mean the fact that jīva, infected with passions, takes up matter in accordance with its karma.[2] As passion or bad disposition (bhāva) of the soul is the internal and primary cause of bondage, and the *influx of matter (āsrava)* into the soul is only the effect of it, the Jaina writers point out that bondage or fall of the soul begins in thought. They, therefore, speak sometimes of two kinds of bondage : (1) internal or ideal bondage, *i. e.* the soul's bondage to bad disposition (bhāva-bandha), and (2) its effect, material bondage *i. e.* the soul's actual association with matter (dravya-bandha).

1. *Tat. sūt.*, 8. 9.
2. *Tat. sūt.*, 8. 2. : "sakaṣāyatvāj-jīvaḥ karmaṇo yogyān pudgalānādatte sa bandhaḥ"

The interpenetration of matter and soul (which, accoridng to the nature of bondage) would appear to be crude to some. But we should bear in mind that the soul, for the Jaina, is not devoid of extension, but co-extensive with the living body. The soul is the *jīva*, the living being; and in every part of the living body we find matter as well as consicousness and, therefore, the compresence or interpenetration of matter and the conscious living substance (*i.e.*, the soul) is as good a fact of experience as the interpenetration of milk and water in a mixture of the two, or of fire and iron in a red-hot iron ball.[1]

Interpenetration of the soul and matter is proved by the presence of consciousness in every part of the body.

2. *Liberation*

If bondage of the soul is its association with matter, liberation must mean the complete dissociation of the soul from matter. This can be attained by *stopping the influx* of new matter into the soul as well as by *complete elimination* of the matter with which the soul has become already mingled. The first process is called saṁvara (*i.e.* the stoppage of influx) and the second nirjarā (*i.e.* exhaustion or wearing out of karma in the soul).

Liberation is expulsion of matter from the soul.

We have seen that the passions or cravings of the soul lead to the association of the soul with matter. Looking into the cause of the passions themselves, we find that they ultimately spring from our ignorance. Our ignorance about the real nature of our souls and other things leads to anger, vanity, infatuation and greed. Knowledge along can remove ignorance. The Jainas, therefore, stress the necessity of right knowledge (samyag-jñāna) or the knowledge of reality. Right knowledge can be obtained only by studying carefully the teachings of the omniscient

Ignorance is the cause of Passions.

Knowledge alone can remove ignorance.

Right knowledge is obtainable from the teachings of the omniscient tīrthaṅkaras.

1. Guṇaratna. Com. on *Ṣaḍ.*, p. 181.

tīrthankaras or teachers who have already attained liberation and are, therefore, fit to lead others out of bondage. But before we feel inclined to study their teachings, we must have a general acquaintance with the essentials of the teachings and consequent faith in the competence of these teachers. This right sort of faith based on general preliminary acquaintance (called samyag-darśana) paves the way for right knowledge (samyag-jñāna) and is, therefore regarded as indispensable. But mere knowledge is useless unless it is put to practice. Right conduct (samyak-cāritra) is, therefore, regarded by the Jaina as the third indispensable condition of liberation. In right conduct, a man has to control his passions, his senses, his thought, speech and action, in the light of right knowledge. This enables him to stop the influx of new karma and eradicate old karmas securing gradually thereby the elimination of matter which ties the soul into bondage.

Therefore faith in them is necessary.

knowledge is perfected in right conduct

Right faith, right knowledge, and right conduct have, therefore, come to be known in Jaina ethics as the three gems (triratna) that shine in a good life. In the very first sūtra of *Tattvārthādhigama sūtra.* Umāsvāmī states this cardinal teaching of Jainism; The path to liberation lies through right faith, knowledge and conduct.[1] Liberation is the joint effect of these three.

Hence, right faith, right knowledge and right conduct constitute the three gems of a good life.

They jointly produce liberation.

Right faith samyag darśana. – Umāsvāmī defines right faith as the attitude of respect (śraddhā) towards truth. This faith may be inborn and spontaneous in some; by others it may be acquired by learning or culture.[2] In any case faith can arise only when the karmas that stand in its way (*i.e.* the tendencies that cause disbelief) are allayed or worn out.

Right faith is respect for truth.

1. 'Samyag-darśana-jñāna-cāritrāṇi mokṣa mārgaḥ'.
2. *Tat.sut.*, 1. 2-3,

It is not blind faith

It should not be thought that Jainism wants its followers to accept blindly what is taught by the *tīrthaṅkaras*. As Maṇibhadra, a Jaina. writer, states, the attitude of the Jaina is rationalistic, rather than dogmatic, and it is summed up in the following dictum : I have no bias for Mahāvīra, and none *against* Kapila and others. *Reasonable words alone are acceptable* to me, whose-ever they might be.[1]

It is the minimum will to believe, without which no study can rationally begin.

The initial faith is a reasonable attitude, first, because it is based on some initial acquaintance and is proportionate to this, and secondly, because without such faith there would be no incentive to further study. Even a sceptical philosopher, who begins to study something rationally, must possess some faith in the utility of his method and the subject he studies.

Perfect faith can result only from perfect knowledge.

Starting with a partial faith and studying further, if the beginner finds that the Jaina teachings are reasonable, his faith increases. The Jaina claims that the more one studies these views, the greater would faith grow, would cause, therefore, perfect faith (samyagdarśana).

Right knowledge consists in the detailed knowledge of all truths.

Right knowledge (samyag-jñāna).— While faith is initially based on knowledge of only the essentials of the Jaina teachings, right knowledge is, as *Dravya-saṅgraha* states, the "detailed cognition of the real nature of the ego and non-ego, and is free from doubt, error and uncertainty" (verse 42). We have already seen in connection with jaina epistemology the different ways in which correct cognition can be obtained. As in the case of faith, so in the case of knowledge the existence of certain innate tendencies (karmas) stands in the way of correct knowledge. For the attainment of perfect knowledge the removal of these karmas should be attempted. Perfection of this process ends in the attainment of absolute omniscience (kevalajñāna).

Removal of karma in necessary for this.

1. Com. on *Ṣaḍ* , 44 (Chowkhamba ed., p. 39).

Right conduct (samyak cāritra).– Good conduct is briefly described in *Drabya-saṅgraha* (verse 45) as refraining from what is harmful and doing what is beneficial. In a word, it is what helps the self to get rid of the karmas that lead him to bondage and suffering. for the stoppage of the influx of new karmas, and eradication of the old, one must (1) take the five great vows (pañca-mahāvrata), (2) practise extreme carefulness (samiti) in walking, speaking, receiving alms and other things, and answering calls of nature so as to avoid doing any harm to any life, (3) practise restraint (gupti) of thought, speech and bodily movements, (4) practise dharma of ten different kinds, namely, forgiveness, humility, straightforwardness, truthfulness, cleanliness, self-restraint, austerity (internal and external), sacrifice, non-attachment and celibacy, (5) meditate on the cardinal truths taught regarding the self and the world, (6) conquer, through fortitude, all pains and discomforts that arise from hunger, thirst, heat, cold, etc., and (7) attain equanimity, purity, absolute greedlessness and perfect conduct.[1]

Right conduct is refraining from wrong and performing what is right

But Jaina writers are not unanimous regarding the necessity of all the above steps. Some of them select the first, namely, the five great vows as sufficient for perfection of conduct. Many of the other steps recommended are found to repeat in different ways the basis principles of these five.

The five great vows form the basis of right conduct.

The value of the five great vows (pañca-mahāvrata) is recognized by the Upaniṣadic thinkers as well as the Bauddhas (who teach the Pañca-sīla). The principles of most of these are recognized also in the commandments of the Bible. But the Jainas try to practise these with a rigour scarcely found elsewhere. These vows consist of the following :

The principles underlying these accepted by many other faiths.

1. *Dravya-saṅgraha, 35.*

(1) The vow of ahiṁsā of non-injury to life.

Ahiṁsā : Abstinence from all injury to life. – Life, as we have seen, exists not simply in the moving beings (trasa), but also in some non-moving ones (sthāvara) such as plants and beings inhabiting bodies of earth. The ideal of tha Jaina is, therefore, to avoid molesting life not only of the moving creatures but also of the non-moving ones. The Jaina saints who try to follow this ideal are, therefore, found even to breathe through a piece of cloth tied over their noses lest they inhale and destroy the life of any organism floating in the air. Ordinary laymen would find this ideal too high. They are advised, therefore, to begin with the partial observance of ahiṁsā by abstaining from injury to moving beings which are endowed with at least two senses.

It is based on the idea of potential equality of all souls.

The Jaina attitude of ahiṁsā is the logical outcome of their metaphysical theory of the potential equality of all souls and recognition of the principle of reciprocity *i.e.*, we should do to others as we would be done by. It is unfair to think that ahiṁsā is the remnant of the savages primitive awe for life, as some critics have thought.[1] If every soul, however lowly now, *can* become as great as any other soul, then one should recognize the value and the claims of every life, as his own. 'Respect for life wherever found' becomes then an irresistible duty.

Ahiṁsā must be practised in thought, speech and action.

The Jaina tries to perform this duty in every minute act in life, because he wants to be thoroughly consistent with the basic principle he has accepted. The Jaina also thinks, therefore, that it is not sufficient simply not to take life; one should not even *think* and *speak* of taking life, nor even *permit, nor encourage* others to take life. Otherwise the vow of ahiṁsā cannot be fully maintained.

(2) The vow of satya or truthfulness consists in speaking what is true, as well as pleasant and good.

Satyam : Abstinence from falsehood. – This vow also is taken very rigorously. Truthfulness is not speaking what is only true, but speaking what is true as well as good and pleasant. Without these

1. *Vide* McKenzie, *Hindu Ethics*, p. 112 : "The root idea of the doctrine ahiṁsā..... is the awe with which the savage regards life in all its forms." But even the early Jaina teachers make it clear that it is the sense of fellow-feeling and equity on which ahiṁsā is based, *Vide Acārāṅgasūtra*, 1. 4, 2. (Jacobi, *Jainasūtras*, Part I, pp. 38-39), and *Sūtra kṛtāṅga. 1. 1. 4* (*op cit.*, Part II, pp. 247-48), which speak of ahiṁsā as 'the legitimate conclusion from the principle of reciprocity".

qualifications the practice of truthfulness would be of little use as an aid to moral progress. Because, merely speaking what is true may sometimes descend into garrulity, vulgarity, frivolity, vilification, etc. Truth set as the ideal of this vow is sometimes called, therefore, *sūnrta,* to suggest the fuller meaning of truth which is also wholesome and pleasant. It is also pointed out that for the perfect maintenance of this vow, one must conquer greed, fear and anger and even restrain the habit of jesting.

(3) The vow of asteya or non-stealing is based on the idea of the sanctity of property.

Asteyam : Abstinence from stealing. – This vow consists in not taking what is not given. The sanctity of the property of others, like that of their lives, is recognized by the Jainas. A Jaina writer wittily remarks the wealth is but the outer life of man and to rob wealth is to rob life. If human life is impossible without wealth in some form or other there is no exaggeration in the Jaina thought that depriving a man of his wealth is virtually to deprive him of an essential condition on which his life depends. This vow, therefore, may be said to be logically inseparable from the vow of ahiṁsā, the sanctity of property being a logical sequence of the sanctity of life.

(4) The vow of brahmacarya consists in abstaining from all forms of self-indulgence.

Brahmacaryam : Abstinence from self-indulgence.– This vow is generally interpreted as that of celibacy. But the Jaina attaches to this also a deeper meaning that raises the standard of this vow far above mere sexual self-continence. It is interpreted as the vow to give up self-indulgence (kāma) of every form. The Jaina, bent on self-criticism, discerns that though outwardly indulgence may stop, it may continue still in subtle forms — in speech, in thought, in the hopes of enjoyment hereafter in heaven, even in asking or permitting others to indulge themselves. For the complete maintenance of this vow one must, therefore, desist from all forms of self-indulgence –external and internal, subtle and gross, mundane and extra-mundane, direct and indirect.

(5) The vow of aparigraha consists in abstaining from all attachment to sense objects.

Aparigraha : Abstinence from all attachment.– This is explained as the vow to give up all attachment for the objects of the five senses - pleasant sound, touch, colour, taste and smell.[1] As attachment to the world's objects means bondage to the world, and the force

1. *Ācārāṅga-sūtra*, Jacobi, E.T. p. 208.

of this causes rebirth, liberation is impossible without the withdrawal of attachment.

(5) The vow of aparigraha consists in abstaining from all attachment to sense objects.

Knowledge, faith and conduct are inseparably bound up ; and the progress and degeneration of the one react on the other two. Perfection of conduct goes hand in hand with the perfection of knowledge and faith. When a person, through the harmonious development of these three, succeeds in overcoming the forces of all passions and karmas, old and new, the soul becomes free from its bondage to matter and attains liberation. Being free from the obstacles of matter, the soul realizes its inherent potentiality. It attains the fourfold perfection (ananta catuṣṭaya), namely, infinite knowledge, infinite faith, infinite power and infinite bliss.

3. *Jainism as a Religion without God*

The grounds of Jaina atheism :

Jainism presents, along with Buddhism, a religion without belief in God. The atheism of the Jainas is based on the following chief grounds[1] :

(1) Neither perception nor inference can prove God.

(i) God is not perceived, but sought to be proved through inference. The Nyāya holds, for example, that as every product, like a house, is the work of an agent (kartā), the world which is a product must also have an agent or creator who is called God. But this inference is inconclusive, because one of the premises, 'the world is a product,' is doubtful. How is it proved that the world is a product? It cannot be said that the world is a product because it has parts. Though ākāśa has parts, it is not admitted by the Nyāya to be a product ; it is said to be an eternal substance not produced by anything else. Again, wherever we perceive anything being produced, the producer or the agent is found to work on the material with his limbs. God is said to be

1. *Vide Prameya-kamala-mārtaṇḍa.* Chap, II. and *Syādvādamañjarī* verse 6 and com. for elaborate arguments in support of atheism.

bodiless. How can He, then, work on matter to produce the world ?

(*ii*) Like the existence of God, the qualities of omnipotence, unity, eternity and perfection, generally attributed to Him, are also doubtful. If God is omnipotent, He should be supposed to be the cause of all things. But this is not ture, because we perceive daily that many objects like houses, pots, etc. are not produced by God. God is held to be one on the ground that if there were many gods, they would act with different plans and purposes, and consequently a harmonious world, as we have, would not have been possible. But this argument is not sound, because we observe that many human beings like masons, and even lower animals like palaces, ant-hills, and hives. God, again, is said to be eternally perfect. But eternal perfection is a meaningless epithet. Perfection is only a removal of imperfection, and it is meaningless to call a being perfect who was never imperfect.

(2) The qualities attributed to God are not reasonable.

Though the Jainas thus come to reject God, as the creator of the world, they think it necessary to meditate on and worship the liberated, perfect souls (siddhas). The liberated souls possessing the God like perfections, mentioned already, easily take the place of God. Prayers are offered to them for guidance and inspiration. The offering of prayers to five kinds of pure souls (pañcaparameṣṭi)[1] also forms a part of the daily routine of the devout Jainas. In spite of the absence of a creator-God, the religious spirit of the Jaina lacks neither in internal fervour nor in external ceremonial expressions. By meditating on the pure qualities of the liberated and those who are advanced on the path to liberation, the Jaina reminds himself daily of the possibility of attaining the high destiny. He purifies his mind by the contemplation of the pure and

The Jainas worship the liberated souls possessing God-like qualities instead of God.

The religious fervour of the Jainas does not, therefore, suffer.

1. These are the Arhats, the Siddhas, the Ācāryas, the Upādhyāyas, the Sādhus, *vide Dravya-saṅgraha. 49.*

strengthens his heart for the uphill journey to liberation. Worship, for the Jaina, is not seeking for mercy and pardon. The Jaina belives in the inexorable moral law of karma which no mercy can bend. The consequences of the past misdeeds can only be counteracted by generating within the soul strong opposite forces of good thought, good speech and good action. Every one must work out his own salvation. The liberated souls serve only as beacon lights. The religion of the Jaina is, therefore, a religion of the strong and the brave. It is a religion of self-help. This is why the liberated soul is called a victor (jina) and a hero (vīra). In this respect it has some other parallels in India, in Buddhism, the Sāṅkhya and the Advaita-Vedānta.

Jainism is a religion of self-help.

THE BAUDDHA PHILOSOPHY

A SELECT BIBLIOGRAPHY

T. W. Rhys Davids ... *Dialogues of the Buddha* (Eng. trans. Sacred Books of the Buddhists series, Luzac & Co. Ltd., London, 1950), Parts I & II.

Mokṣākaragupta ... *Tarkabhāṣā*, 2nd edn. (ed. by H. R. R. Iyenger, Hindusthan Press, Mysore, 1952).

Jitāripāda ... *Vādasthāna* (ed. by H.R.R. Iyenger, Hindusthan Press, Mysore, 1952).

Christmas Humphreys ... *Buddhism* (Penguin Books, 1951).

H.C. Warren ... *Buddhism in Translations* (Harvard University Press, 1922).

Yamakami Sogen ... *Systems of Buddhistic Thought* (Calcutta University, 1912).

D.T. Suzuki ... *Outlines of Mahayana Buddhism* (Luzac & Co., 1907).

Mrs. Beatrice L. Suzuki *Mahayana Buddhism* (George Allen & Unwin, 1959).

Th. Stcherbatsky ... *The Central Conception of Buddhism* (Royal Asiatic Society, London, 1923).

Junjiro Takakusu ... *The Essentials of Buddhist Philosophy* (University of Hawaii, 1949).

S. Radhakrishnan ... *The Dhammapada* (Eng. trans., Oxford University Press, 1950).

History of Philosophy : Eastern and Western (G. Allen & Unwin Ltd.), Chaps. IX and XXI-XXV.

E. J. Thomas ... *History of Buddhist Thought* (Kegan Paul, London, 1953).

T.R.V. Murti ... *The Central Philosophy of Buddhism* (G. Allen & Unwin, 1955).

CHAPTER IV

THE BAUDDHA PHILOSOPHY

I. Introduction

The life of Gautama Buddha.

The life of Siddhārtha or Gautama Buddha, the Light of Asia and the founder of Buddhism, is fairly well-known. Born in a Royal family of Kapilavastu (on the foot-hills of the Himālayas, north of India) in the sixth century B.C., Siddhārtha renounced the world early in life. The sights of disease, old age and death impressed the young prince with the idea that the world was full of suffering, and the life of a care-free mendicant suggested to him a possible way of escape. As an ascetic, he was restless in search of the real source of all sufferings and of the means of complete deliverance. He sought light from many religious teachers and learned scholars of the day and practised great austerities; but nothing satisfied him. This threw him back on his own resources. With an iron will and a mind free from all disturbing throughts and passions, he endeavoured to unravel, through continued intense meditation, the mystery of the world's miseries, till at last his ambition was crowned with success. Siddhārtha became Buddha or the Enlightened. The message of his enlightenment laid the foundation of both Buddhistic religion and philosophy which, in course of time, spread far and wide—to Ceylon, Burma and Siam in the south, and to Tibet, China, Japan and Korea in the north.

The teachings of Buddha were oral.

Like all great teachers of ancient times Buddha taught by conversation, and his teachings were also handed down for a long time through oral instruction imparted by his disciples to successive generations. Our knowledge about

Buddha's teachings depends to-day cheifly on the *Tripiṭakas* or the three baskets of teachings which are claimed to contain his views as reported by his most intimate disciples.

They were recorded later by his followers.

These three canonical works are named *Vianayapiṭaka Suttapiṭaka* and *Abhidhammapiṭaka*. Of these, the first deals chiefly with rules of conduct for the congregation (saṅgha), the second contains Buddha's sermons and dialogues, and the third contains expositions of philosophical theories. All these three contain information regarding early Buddhist philosophy. These works are in the Pāli dialect.

The three accepted works—the Tripiṭakas.

In course of time, as his followers increased in number, they were divided into different schools. The most important division of Buddhism on religious principles was into the Hīnayāna or Theravāda and the Mahāyāna. The first flourished in the south and its present stronghold is in Ceylon, Burma and Siam. Its literature is vast and is written in Pāli. It is claimed to be more orthodox and faithful to the teachings of Buddha. Mahāyāna flourished mostly in the north and its adherents are to be found in Tibet, China and Japan. It adopted Sanskrit for philosophical discussion and thus the enormous Buddhist literature in Sanskrit came to be developed. Most of this literature was translated into Tibetan and Chinese and thus became naturalized in the lands in which Buddhism flourished. Many such valuable Sanskrit works lost in India are now being recovered from those translations and restored to Sanskrit.

The Hīnayāna and the Mahāyāna schools of Buddhism.

As Buddhism flourished in different lands, it became coloured and changed by the original faiths and ideas of the converts. The different schools[1] of Buddhism which thus arose are so numerous and the total output of

The vast literature of Buddhism.

1. *Vide* Humphreys, *Buddhism*, for a good account of the spread and present position of Buddhism in different parts of the world.

philosophical works in the different languages is so vast that a thorough acquaintance with Buddhist philosophy requires the talents of a versatile linguist, as well as the insight of a philosopher—and yet one life-time may be found all too short for the purpose. Our account of Bauddha philosophy will necessarily be very brief and so inadequate. We shall first try to give the chief teachings of Buddha as found in the dialogues attributed to him, and next deal with some aspects of Bauddha philosophy developed in India by his followers in the different schools, and conclude with a short account of the main religious tendencies of the Hīnayāna and the Mahāyāna schools.

II. The Teachings of Buddha: The Four Noble Truths

1. *The Anti-speculative Attitude*

Buddha was primaly an ethical teacher and reformer, not a metaphysician. The message of his enlightenment points to man the way of life that leads beyond suffering. When any one asked Buddha metaphysical questions as to whether the soul was different from the body, whether it survived death, whether the world was finite or infinite, eternal or non-eternal, etc., he avoided discussing them. Discussion of problemes for the solution of which there is not sufficient evidence leads only to different partial views like the conflicting one-sided accounts of an elephant given by different blind persons who touch its different parts.[1] Buddha referred to scores of such metaphysical views advanced by earlier thinkers and showed that all of them were inadequate, since they were based on uncertain sense-experiences, cravings, hopes and

Buddha disliked metaphysical discussions devoid of practical utility.

1. For this parable *vide* Rhys Davids, *Dialogues of Buddha*, I, pp. 187-88; *Udāna*, VI. 4.

fears.[1] Such speculation should be avoided, Buddha repeatedly pointed out, also because it does not take man nearer to his goal, *viz.* Arhatship or Vimutti, the state of freedom from all suffering. On the contrary, a man who indulges in such speculation remains all the more entangled in the net of theories he himself has woven.[2] The most urgent problem is to end misery. One who indulges in theoretical speculation on the soul and the world, while he is writhing in pain, behaves like the foolish man, with a poisonous arrow plunged into his flank, whiling away time on idle speculation regarding the origin, the maker and the thrower of the arrow, instead of trying to pull it cut immediately.[3]

The unprofitable and unanswerable questions.

Ten questions are often mentioned by Buddha (vide *Poṭṭhapada Sutta, Dialogues,* I., R.Davids, pp. 254-57) as uncertain, ethically unprofitable and so not discussed (vyākata) by him : (1) Is the world eternal ? (2) Is it non-eternal? (3) Is it finite? (4) Is it infinite? (5) Is the sould the same as the body? (6) Is it different from the body? (7) Does one who has known the truth (Tathāgata) live again after death? (8) Does he not live again after death? (9) Does he both live again and not live again after death? (10) Does he neither live nor not-live again after dealth? These have come to be known as the 'indeterminate questions' (in Pāli *avyākatāni)* in Buddhist literature and made the subject of discourses in Saṁyutta Nikāya[4] and Majjhima Nikāya.[5]

The useful question about misery.

Instead of discussing metaphysical questions, which are ethically useless and intellectually uncertain, Buddha always tried to enlighten persons on the most important questions of

1. *Brahma-Jāla-Sutta.* op. cit., pp. 52-55.
2. *Ibid.*, p. 44.
3. *Majjhima-nikāya-sutta*. 63 (Warren. p. 120).
4. Vide *Dialogues*, I. P. 187. These questions become sixteen by putting for *each* of the four problems, four alternatives as in the case of the last problem.
5. Suttas 63 and 72 (Avyākata-pañhā).

sorrow, its origin, its cessation and the path leading to its cessation. Because, as he puts it : "This does profit, has to do with fundamentals of religion, and tends to aversion, absence of passion, cessation, quiescence, knowledge, supreme wisdom and nirvāṇa."[1]

The answers to the four questions noted above constitute, as we know, the essence of Buddha's enlightment which he is eager to share with all fellow-beings. These have come to be known as the four noble truths (catvāri āryasatyāni). They are : (1) Life in the world is full of suffering. (2) There is a cause of this suffering. (3) It is possible to stop suffering. (4) There is a path which leads to the cessation of suffering (duḥkha, duḥkha-samudaya, duḥkha-nirodha-mārga). All the teachings of Gautama centre round these four.

The four noble truths concerning suffering.

2. *The First Noble Truth about Suffering*

The sights of suffering which upset the mind of young Siddhārtha were of disease, old age and death. But to the enlightened mind of Buddha not simply these, but the very essential conditions of life, human and sub-human, appeared, without exception, to be fraught with misery. Birth, old age, disease, death, sorrow, grief, wish, despair, in short, all that is born of attachment, is misery.[2] We have mentioned in the *General Introduction* that pessimism of this type is common to all the Indian schools; and in emphasizing the first noble truth Buddha has the support of all important Indian thinkers. The Cārvāka materialists would, of course, take exception to Buddha's wholesale condemnation of life in the world, and point out the different sources of pleasure that exist in life among with those of

Life is full of suffering.

Even apparent pleasures are fraught with pain.

1. *Majjhima-nikāya-sutta*. 63 (Warren. p. 122).
2. *Digha-nikāya-sutta*, 22 (Warren, p. 368).

pain. But Buddha and many other Indian thinkers would reply that worldly pleasures appear as such only to short-sighted people. Their transitoriness, the pains felt on their loss and the fears felt lest they should be lost, and other evil consequences, make pleasures lose their charm and turn them into positive sources of fear and anxiety.

To the far-sighted worldly pleasures are sources of fear.

3. *The Second Noble Truth about the Cause of Suffering : the Chain of Twelve Links*

Suffering, like every other thing, depends on some conditions.

Though the fact of suffering is recognized by all Indian thinkers, the diagnosis of this malady is not always unanimous. The origin of life's evil is explained by Buddha in the lights of his special conception of natural causation (known as Pratītyasamutpāda). According to it, nothing is unconditional; the existence of everything depends on some conditions. As the existence of every event depends on some conditions, there must be something *which being there* our misery comes into existence. Life's *suffering* (old age, death, despair, grief and the like, briefly denoted by the phrase *jarā-maraṇa)* is there, says, Buddha, because there is *birth* (jāti). If a man were not born, he would not have been subject to these miserable states. Birth again has its condition. It is the *will* to *become* (bhava),[1] the force of the blind tendency or predisposition to be born, which causes our birth. But what is the cause of this tendency? Our mental clinging to cr *grasping* (upādāna) the objects of the world is the condition responsible for our desire to be born. This clinging again is due to our *thirst* (tṛṣṇā) or craving to enjoy objects—sights, sounds, etc. But wherefrom does this desire originate? We

The chain of causes and effects that leads to suffering in the world.

---

1. Mrs. Rhys Davids' rendering 'the disposition for becoming' (*Buddhism*, Home, U.L., p. 91) is better than its ordinary rendering as 'existence,' which is nearly meaningless in this context. 'Bhāva is used' in the meaning of 'disposition,' in the Sāṅkhya and other Indian systems.

would not have any desire for objects, had we not tasted or experienced them before. Previous *sense-experience*, tinged with some pleasant feelings (vedanā), is, therefore the cause of our thirst or craving. But sense-experience could not arise but for *contact* (sparśa) *i.e.* contact of sense-organs with objects. This contact again would not arise had there not been the *six organs of cognition,* the five sense and manas (ṣaḍā-yatana). These six again deped for their existence on the *mind-body* organism (nāma-rūpa), which constitutes the perceptible being of man. But this organism could not develop in the mother's womb and come into existence, if it were dead or devoid of *consciousness* (vijñāna). But the consciousness that descends into the embryo in the mother's womb is only the effect of the *impressions* (saṁskāra) of our past existence. The last state of the past life, which intiates our present existence, contains in a concentrated manner the impressions of effects or all our past deeds. The impressions which make for rebirth are due to *ignorance* (avidyā) about truth. If the transitory, painful nature of the wordly existence were perfectly realized, there would not arise in us any karma resulting in rebirth. Ignorance, therefore, is the *root cause* of impressions or tendencies that cause rebirth.

The twelve links in the chain of suffering.

Briefly speaking, then (1) *suffering* in life is due to (2) *birth*, which is due to (3) *the will to be born,* which is due to (4) our mental *clinging* to objects. Clinging again is due to (5) *thirst* or desire for objects. This again is due to (6) *sense-experience* which is due to (7) *sense-object-contact,* which again is due to (8) the *six organs of* cognition; these organs are dependent on (9) the *embryonic organism* (composed of mind and body), which again could not develop without (10) some *initial consciousness*, which again hails from (11) the *impressions* of the experience of past life, which lastly are due to (12) *ignorances* of truth.

These constitute the wheel of existence : birth and re-birth.

Thus we have the *twelve links* in the chain of causation. The order and number of the links are not always the same in all the sermons; but the above has come to be regarded as the full and standard account of the matter. It has been popularized among Buddhists by various epithets, such as the twelve sources (dvādaśa nidāna), the wheel of rebirth (bhava-cakra). Some devout Buddhists remind themselves even to-day, of this teaching of Buddha by turning wheels which are made to symbolize the wheel of causation. Like the telling of beads, this forms a part of their daily prayers.

The present life is the effect of the past and the cause of the future.

The twelve links are sometimes interpreted to cover the past, the present and the future life which are casually connected, so that present life can be conveniently explained with reference to its past condition and its future effect. The twelve links are, therefore, arranged with reference to the three periods[1] in the following way proceeding from cause to effect :

(1) Ignorance (avidyā) (2) Impressions (saṁskāra)	Past Life
(3) The initial consciousness of the embryo (vijñāna) (4) Mind and body, the embryonic organism (nāma-rūpa) (5) Six organs of knowledge (ṣaḍā-yatana) (6) Sense contact (sparśa) (7) Sense-experience (vedanā) (8) Thirst (tṛṣṇā) (9) Clinging (upādāna) (10) Tendency to be born (bhava)	Present Life
(11) Rebirth (jāti) (12) Old age, death, etc. (jarā-maraṇa)	Future Life

An important contribution of Buddha.

Before we close this topic, we may note one very important contribution made by Indian thinkers in general and Buddha in particular; namely, the conception that the external phenomenon of life or the living or organism is due to an internal impetus of desire, conscious or unconscious. The evolution of life is sought to be explained

1. Vide *Abhidhammattha-saṅgha*, 8. 6.

mechanically by modern biologists—both Darwinians and anti-Darwinians—with the help of material conditions, inherited and environmental. The first appearance of a horn on the cow's head, or the formation of an eye, is to them nothing more than an accidental variation, slow or sudden. The famous contemporary French, philosopher, Bergson, shows that the development of life cannot be satisfactorily explained as merely accidental, but that it must be thought to be the outward expression of an internal urge or life-impetus (*élan vital).* Buddha's basic principle of the explanation of life, namely that bhava (internal predisposition, the tendency to be) leads to birth existence of the body or that consciousness is the condition of the development of the embryo, anticipates the Bergsonian contention, that the living body is not caused simply by collection of pieces of matter, but is the outward manifestation or explosion of an internal urge. Incidentally we may note also that Bergson's philosophy of reality as change resembles the Buddhistic doctrine of impermanence.

Life is not the product of a mechanical combination of material conditions.

It is the expression of inner forces as Bergson holds.

4. *The Third Noble Truth about the Cessation of Suffering*

The third noble truth that there is cessation of suffering, follows from the second truth that misery depends on some conditions. If these conditions are removed, misery would cease. But we should try to understand clearly the exact nature of the state called cessation (nirodha) of misery.

Suffering must cease if its cause is stopped.

First of all it should be noted that liberation from misery is a state attainable here in this very life, if certain conditions are fulfilled. When the perfect control of passions and constant contemplation of truth lead a person through the four stages of concentration to perfect

Cessation of suffering, *i.e.*, nirvāṇa, is attainable here, in this very life.

wisdom (as will be described hereafter), he is no longer under the sway of worldly attachment. He has broken the fetters that bound him to the world. He is, therefore, free, liberated. He is said then to have become an Arhat—a venerable person. The state is more popularly known now as nirvāṇa—the extinction of passions and, therefore, also of misery.

Nirvāṇa is not inactivity.

We should remember next that the attainment of this state is not necessarily a state of inactivity, as it is ordinarily misunderstood to be. It is true that for the attainment of perfect, clear and steady knowledge of the fourfold truth one has to withdraw all his attention from outside and even from other ideas within, and concentrate it wholly on repeated reasoning and contemplation of the truths in all their aspects. But once wisdom has been permanently obtained, through concentrated thought, the liberated person should neither always remain rapt in meditation nor wholly withdraw from active life. We know what an active life of travelling, preaching, founding brotherhood, Buddha himself led during the long forty-five years that he lived after enlightenment, and even to the last days of his eightieth year when he passed away! Liberation then was not incompatible with activity in the life of the founder himself.

Buddha's life was full of activity, even after his enlightenment.

Work without attachment, hatred and infatuation does not cause bondage.

As he clearly pointed out once, there are two kinds of action, one that is done under the influence of attachment, hatred, infatuation (rāga, dveṣa, moha), another that is done without these. It is only the first that strengthens our desire to cling to the world and generates the seeds of karma causing rebirth. The second kind of action, done with perfect insight into the real nature of the universe and without attachment, does not create a karma producing rebirth. The difference between the two kinds of karma, Buddha points out, is like that between the sowing of ordinary productive seeds and the sowing of seeds which have been fried and made barren.[1] This lesson he teaches also in the story of his enlighrenment.[2] After he had attained nirvāṇa, he was at first reluctant to work. But soon his enlightened heart began to beat with sympathy for the countless beings who were still writhing in pain.

Buddha set the example of such selfless service of fellow beings.

He thought it proper, therefore, that the raft which he constructed with toil and with which he got across the flood of misery, should be left for others and not allowed to perish.[3] Nirvāṇa he thus shows by his own example and precept, does not require the Arhat to shun activity; on the contrary, love and sympathy for all beings increase with enlightenment and persuade the perfect man to share his wisdom with them and work for their moral uplift.

Nirvāṇa does not mean extinction of existence.

If this be a correct interpretation of Buddha's life and teaching, it is wrong to think, as it is very often done, that nirvāna means total extiction of existence. The etymological meaning of 'nirvāṇa' is 'blown out'. The metaphor of a 'blown out light' is there; and the liberated one is sometimes compared to it. Depending on such etymological meaning and the negative description of nivā ṇa as the absence of all physical and mental states known to us, some interpreters of Buddhism—Buddhists and non-Buddhists—have explained nirvāṇa as complete cessation of existence. But against this view we have to remember, first, that if nirvāṇa or liberation be extinction of all existence, then Buddha cannot be said to have been liberated till he died; his attainment of perfect wisdom and freedom for which we have his own words, turns then into a myth. It is difficult to hold, therefore, that nirvāṇa as taught by Buddha means cessation of all existence.[4] Secondly, we are to remember that though nirvāṇa, according to Buddha, stops rebirth and, therefore, means the extinction of all misery and of the conditions that cause future existence in this world after death, it does not mean necessarily that after death the liberated saint does not

But the extinction of misery and of the causes of rebirth.

1. *Aṅguttara-nikāya* III, 33 (Warrent. pp. 215 f.).
2. *Majjhima-nikāya,* 26 (*Ibid.,* pp. 339 f.).
3. *Majjhima-nikāya* (vide Sīlācāra's trans., P. 170, German Pali Society).
4. Rhys Davids shows that the Pali word for 'liberated,' 'Parinibbuto' is used of living persons and scarcely of dead Arhants. (*Vide Dialogues,* II. P. 132, f. n.).

continue in any form. This last point, as we mentioned previously, is one of the ten points on which Buddha repeatedly refused to express any opinion. So that even the view that, after death, the person who attains nirvāṇa ceases to exist altogether is one which Buddha cannot be said to have held. Buddha's silence might just mean that the state of liberation cannot be described in terms of ordinary experience.[1]

Buddha's silence about the condition of the liberated after death does not mean his denial of the existence of such a person after death.

The important question that arises here then is : If Buddha is not explicit about the fate of a liberated person after death, what according to him is gained by nirvāṇa? The gain is double, negative and positive. Nirvāṇa is a guarantee that rebirth whose conditions have been destroyed, will not occur. Nirvāṇa also positively means that one who has attained it enjoys perfect peace even in this life so long as he lives after enlightenment. This peace is not, of course, like any of the pleasures born of the fulfilment of desires. It is, therefore, said to be beyond worldly pleasures and pains. But it is a state of serenity, equanimity and passionless self-possession. It cannot be described in terms of ordinary experiences; the best way of understanding it in the light of our imperfect experience is to think of it as a relief from all painful experience from which we suffer. We can understand this because all of us have experience at least of temporary feelings of relief from some pain or other, such as freedom from disease, debt, slavery, imprisonment.[2] Besides, the advantages of nirvāṇa can be enjoyed in part, even before it has been obtained, by the partial fulfilment of its conditions. As Buddha explains to King Ajātaśatru in a discourse on the advantages of the life of a recluse every bit of ignorance removed, and passion conquered, brings about palpable benefit, such as purity, good-will, self-possession, courage, unperplexed mind, unruffled temper.[3] This heartens him

The double gain of Nirvāṇa : stopping of rebirth and future misery, and attainment of perfect peace in this life.

Even the partial fulfilment of the conditions of nirvāṇa cause palpable benefits.

1. *Vide* Prof. Radhakrishnan's article, 'The Teaching of Buddha by speech and silence,' *Hibberi, Journal,* April, 1934. Also his *Dhammapada* pp. 52 f.

2. *Vide Sāmañña-phala-sutta (Dialogues,* 1, p. 84).

3. *Ibid.*

and gives him the strength to pursue the difficult goal of nirvāna till it is fully obtained.

We know that a later Buddhist teacher of great eminence Nāgasena, while instructing the Greek King Menander (Milinda) who accepted his discipleship, tried to convey to him the idea of the blissful character of nirvāṇna with a series of metaphors; Nirvāṇa is profound like an ocean, lofty like a mountain peak, sweet like honey; etc.[1] But all these, as Nāgasena points out, can scarcely convey to the imperfect man the idea of what that thing is Reasoning and metaphor ares of little avail for convincing a blind man what colour is like.

The real nature of nirvāṇa can only be realized and not described in terms of ordinary experience.

5. The Fourth Noble Truth about the Path to Liberation

The fourth noble truth, as seen already, lays down that there is a path (mārga)—which Buddha followed and others can similarly follow—to reachs a state free from misery. Clues regarding this path are derived from the knowledge of the chief conditions that cause misery. The path recommended by Buddha consists of eight steps or rules and is, therefore, called the eightfold noble path (aṣṭāṅgika-mārga).[2] This gives in a nutshell the essentials of Bauddha Ethics. This path is open to all, monks as well as laymen.[3] The noble path consists in the acquisition of the following eight good things :

The path consists of eight steps :

Right views (sammādiṭṭhi or samyagdṛṣṭi)—As ignorance, with its consequences, namely, wrong views (mithyādṛṣṭi) about the self and the world, is the roots cause of our sufferings, it is natural that the first step to moral reformation should be the acquisition of right views or the knowledge of truth. Right view is defined as the correct

(1) Right views or knowledge of the four noble truths.

1. *Vide Milinda-pañha.*

2. Full discussion occurs in *Dīgha-nikāya-sutta,* 22 (Warren, pp. 372-74). *Majjhima-nikāya* (quoted by Sogen. *Systems, pp. 169-71); Dhammapada,* Magga-vagga.

3. *Vide* Rhys Davids, *Dialogues*, I, pp. 62-63.

knowledge about the four noble truths. It is the knowledge of these truths alone, and not any theoretical speculation regarding nature and self, which, according to Buddha, helps moral reformation, and leads us towards the goal—nirvāṇa.

(2) Right resolve, or firm determination to reform life in the light of truth.

Right resolve (sammāsaṅkappa or samyaksaṇkalpa).—A mere knowledge of the truths would be useless unless one resolves to reform life in their light. The moral aspirant is asked, therefore, to renounce worldliness (all attachment to the world) to give up ill-feeling towards others and desist from doing any harm to them. These three constitute the contents of right determination.

(3) Right speech, or control of speech.

Right speech (sammāvācā or samyagvāk).—Right determination should not remain a mere 'pious wish' but must issue forth into action. Right determination should be able to guide and control our speech, to begin with. The result would be right speech consisting in abstention from lying, slander, unkind words and frivolous talk.

(4) Right conduct or abstention from wrong action.

Right conduct (sammākammanta or samyakkarmā nta).—Right determination should end in right action or good conduct and not stop merely with good speech. Right conduct includes the Pañca-Sīla, the five vows for desisting from killing, stealing, sensuality, lying and intoxication.[1]

(5) Right livelihood or maintaining life by honest means.

Right livelihood (sammā-ājīva or samyagājiva).—Renouncing bad speech and bad actions, one should earn his livelihood by honest means. The necessity of this rule lies in showing that even for the sake of maintaining one's life, one should not take to forbidden means but work in consistency with good determination.

1. For a discussion see Humphreys, *Buddism*, pp. 111f.

Right effort (sammāvāyāma or samyagvyāyāma). While a person tries to live a reformed life, through right views, resolution, speech, action and livelihood, he is constantly knocked off the right path by old evil ideas which were deep-rooted in the mind as also by fresh ones which constantly arise. One cannot progress steadily unless he maintains a constant effort to root out old evil thoughts and prevent evil thoughts from arising anew. Moreover, as the mind cannot be kept empty, he should constantly endeavour also to fill the mind with good ideas, and retain such ideas in the mind. This fourfold constant endeavour, negative and positive, is called right effort. This rule points out that even one high up on the path cannot afford to take a moral holiday without running the risk of slipping down.

(6) Right effort, or constant endeavour to maintain moral progress by banishing evil thoughts and entertaining good ones.

Right mindfullness (sammāsati or samyaksmrti)—The necessity of constant vigilance is further stressed in this rule, which lays down that the aspirant should constantly bear in mind the things he has already learnt. He sould constantly remember and contemplate the body as body, sensations as sensations, mind as mind, mental states as mental states. About any of these he should not think, "This am I," or "This is mine."[1] This advice sounds no better than asking one to think of a spade as a spade. But ludicrously superfluous as it might appear to be, it is not easy to remember always what things really are. It is all the more difficult to practise it when false ideas about the body, etc. have become so deep-rooted in us and our behaviours based on these false notions have become instinctive. If we are not mindful, we behave as though the body, the mind, sensations and mental states are permanent and valuable. Hence there arise attachment to such things and grief over their loss, and we become subject to bondage and misery. But contemplation on the frail, perishable, loathsome nature of these, helps us to

(7) Right mindfulness of constant remembrance of the perishable nature of thing.

This is necessary for keeping off attachment to things, and grief over their loss.

1. *Vide Majjhima-nikāya*, i, p. 171 (E. T. by Silācāra).

remain free from attachement and grief. This is the necessity of constant mindfulness about truth.

In *Digha-nikāya*, sutta 22, Buddha gives very detailed instructions as to how such contemplation is to be practised. For example, regarding the body, one should remember and contemplate that the body is only a combination of the four elements (earth, water, fire, air), that it is filled with all sorts of loathsome matter, flesh, bone, skin, entrails, dirt, bile, phlegm, blood, pus, etc. Going to a cemetery one should observe further how the dead body rots, decays is eaten by dogs and vultures and after wardsgradually becomes reduced to and mixed up with the elements. By such intense contemplation he is able to remember what the body really is : how loathsome, how perishable, how transitory ! "He gives up all false emotions and affection for the body, his own and others." By similar intense comtemplation about sensation, mind and harmful mental states, he becomes free from attachment and grief regarding all these. The net result of this fourfold intense contemplations is detachment from all objects that bind man to the world.[1]

The practice of such thought is recommended by Buddha in minute details in Dīgha-nikāya.

Right concentration (sammāsamādhi or samyaksamādhi)—One who has successfully guided his life in the light of the last seven rules and thereby freed himself from all passions and evil thoughts is fit to enter step by step into the four deeper and deeper stages of concentration that gradually take him to the goal of his long and arduous journey—cessation of suffering. He concentrates his pure and unruffled mind on reasoning (vitarka) and investigation (vicāra) regarding the truths, and enjoys in this state, joy and ease born of detachment and pure thought. This is the first stage of intent meditation (dhyāna or jhāna).

(8) Right concentration, through four stages, is the last step in the path that leads to the goal—nirvāṇa.

(a) The first stage of concentration is on reasoning and investigation regarding the truths. There is then a joy of pure thinking.

1. *Vide* Warren, *Buddhism in Trans.*, p. 354.

When this concentration is succeful, belief in the fourtfold truth arises dispelling all doubts and, therfore, making resoning and investigation unnecessary. From this results the second stage of concentration, in which there are joy, peace and internal tranquility born of intense, unruffled contemplation. There is in this stage a consciousness of this joy and peace too.

(b) The second stage of concentration is unfulfiled meditation, free from reasoning, etc. There is then a joy of tranquility.

In the next stage attempt is made by him to initiate an attitude of indifference, to be able to detach himself even from the joy of concentration. From this results the third deeper kind of concentration, in which one experiences perfect equanimity, coupled with an experience of bodily ease. He is yet conscious of this ease and equanimity, though indifferent to the joy of concentration.

(c) The third stage of concentration is detachment from even the joy of tranquility. There is then indifference even to such joy but a feeling of bodily ease still persists.

Lastly, he tries to put away even this consciousness of ease and equanimity and all the sense of joy and elation he previously had. He attains thereby the fourth state of concentration, a state of perfect equanimity, indifference and self-possession—without pain, without ease. Thus he attains the desired goal of cessation of all suffering, he attains to arhatship or nirvāṇa.[1] There are then perfect wisdom (prajñā) and perfect righteousness (śīla).

(d) The fourth stage of concentration is detachment from this bodily ease too. There are then perfect equanimity and indifference. This is the state of nirvāṇa or perfect wisdom.

To sum up the essential points of the eightfold path (or, what is the same, Buddha's ethical teachings), it may be noted first that the path consists of three main things—conduct (śīla), concentration (samādhi) and knowledge (prajñā) harmoniously cultivated. In Indian

Knowledge, conduct and concentration from the essentials of the path.

1. *Vide Poṭṭhapāda-sutta*, and *Sāmaññaphala-sutta* for the detailed treatment of the Jhānas (*Dialogues*. I. pp. 84 f, and 245 f.).

philosophy knowledge and morality are thought inseparable—not simply because morality, or doing of good, depends on the knowledge of what is good, about which all philosophers would agree, but also because perfection of knowledge is regarded as impossible without morality, perfect control of passions and prejudices. Buddha explicitly states in one of his discourses that virtue and wisdom purify each other and the two are inseparable.[1] In the eightfold path one starts with 'right views' — a mere intellectual apprehension of the fourfold truth. The mind is not yet purged of the previous wrong ideas and the passions or wrong emotions arising therefrom; moreover, old habits of thinking, speaking and acting also continue still. In a word, conflicting forces—the new good ones and the old bad ones—create, in terms of modern psychology, a divided personality. The seven steps beginning with right resolve furnish a continuous discipline for resolving this conflict by reforming the old personality. Repeated contemplation of what is true and good, training of the will and emotion accordingly, through steadfast determination and passionless behaviour, gradually achieve the harmonious personality in which thought and will and emotion are all thoroughly cultured and purified in the light of truth. The last step of perfect concentration is thus made possible by the removal of all obstacles. The result of this unhampered concentration on truth is perfect insight or wisdom, to which the riddle of existence stands clearly revealed once for all. Ignorance and desire are cut at their roots and the source of misery vanishes. Perfect wisdom, perfect goodness and perfect equanimity—complete relief from suffering—are

Perfect knowledge is impossible without morality.

"Virtue and wisdom purify each other," says Buddha.

Reformation of life—ideas, will and emotion—in the light of truth forms a major part of the eightfold path.

Concentration is possible only after such reform.

1. *Soṇadaṇḍa-sutta* (*ibid*., p. 156).

simultaneously attained, therefore, in nirvāṇa.[1]

6. *The Philosophical Implications of Buddha's Ethical Teachings*

We may discuss here briefly some of the more important ideas about man and the world underlying Buddha's ethical teachings. Some of these are explicitly stated by Buddha himself. We shall mention four of these views, on which his ethics mainly depends, namely, (1) the theory of dependent origination, (2) the theory of karma, (3) the theory of change, and (4) the theory of the non-existence of the soul.

(i) The Theory of Dependent Origination or Conditional Existence of Things

Everything depends on some condition.

There is a spontaneous and universal law of causation which conditions the appearance of all events, mental and physical. This law (dharma or dhamma) works automatically without the help of any conscious guide. In accordance with it, whenever a particular event (the cause) appears, it is followed by another particular event (the effect). "On getting the cause, the effect arises." The existence of *everything* is *conditional,* dependent on a cause. Nothing happens fortuitously or by chance. This is called the theory of dependent origination (Pratītyasamutpāda in Sanskrit and

1. Four stages, progressively attained by the initiate, on the path or stream leading to nirvāṇa are distinguished *viz.* the stages of a Srotapānna (one who has entered the stream, the path) a Sakrdāgāmin (one who will return only once again to this world), an Anāgāmin (one who will not return) and an Arhat (liberated in this very life).

Paṭiccasamuppāda in Pāli).[1] This view, as Buddha himself makes clear, avoids two extreme views : On the hand, eternarlism or the theory that some reality eternally exists independently of any condition and, on the other hand, nihilism or the theory that something existing can be annihilated or can cease to be. Buddha claims, therefore, to hold the middle view,[2] namely, that everything that we perceive possesses an existence but is dependent on something else, and that thing in turn does not perish without leaving some effect.

Nothing exists without a cause, nor does it perish without leaving some effect.

This is the middle view avoiding the two extremes of eternalism and nihilism.

Buddha attaches so much importance to the understanding of this theory that he calls this the Dhamma. "Let us put aside questions of the Beginning and the End." he says, "I will teach you the Dhamma : That being thus, this comes to be. From the coming to be of that, this arises. That being absent, this does not happen. From the cessation of that, this ceases." "He who sees the paṭiccasamuppāda sees the Dhamma, and he who sees the Dhamma, sees the paṭiccasamuppāda." It is again compared to a staircase, by mounting which one can look round on the world and see it with the eye of a Buddha.[3] It is the failure to grasp this standpoint which, Buddha asserts, is the cause of all our troubles.[4] Later Buddhism, as Rhys Davids notes, does not pay much heed to this theory. But Buddha himself says that this

Buddha regards this theory as indispensable for understanding his teachings.

The failure to grasp this principle of causation is the cause of all troubles.

1. *Visudhimagga,* Chap. xvii (Warren, pp. 168 f.) Etymologically pratitay = getting (something), samutpāda-crigination (of something else).

2. *Saṃyutta-nikāya,* xxii (*ibid.,* p. 165.).

3. *Dialogues.* II. p. 44.

4. *Mahānidāna-sutta* (Warren, p. 203).

theory is very profound.[1] We have seen already how this theory is applied to the solution of the question regarding the origin of misery, as well as to that regarding the removal of misery. We shall see just now how profound in its many sided implications this theory is in some other respects as well.

(ii) The Theory of Karma

The law of karma is an aspect of this principle of causation.

The belief in the theory of karma, it will be seen, is only as aspect of this doctrine. The present existence of an individual is, according to this doctrine, as according to that of karma, the effect of its past; and its future would be the effect of its present existence. This has been seen very clearly already in connection with the explanation of the origin of suffering in the light of the theory of dependent origination. The law of karma is only a special form of the more general law of causation as conceived by Buddha.

(iii) The Doctrine of Universal Change and Impermanence

Whatever exists, arises from some condition and is, therefore, impermanent.

The Doctrine of dependent origination also yields the Buddhist theory of the transitory nature of things. All things, Buddha repeatedly teaches, are subjcet to change and decay. As everything originates from some condition, it disappears when the condition ceases to be. Whatever has a beginning has also an end. Buddha, therefore, says, "Know that whatever exists arises from causes and conditions and is in every respect impermanent."[2] "That which seems ever lasting will

1. *Ibid.*

2. *Mahāparinirvāṇa-sūtra* (quoted in Sogen's *Systems,* p. 9).

perish, that which is high will be laid low; where meeting is, parting will be; where birth is, death will come."[1]

Subsequent Bauddha thinkers further develop the theory of impermanence into that of momentariness.

Transitoriness of life and wordly things is spoken of many other poets and philosophers. Buddha logically perfects this view into the doctrine of *impermanence*. His later followers develop this further into a theory of *momentariness* (kṣaṇika-vāda), which, means not only that *everything* has conditional and, therefore, non-permanent existence, but also that things last not even for short *periods* of time, but exist for *one partless moment only*. This doctrine of momentariness of all things is supported by later writers with elaborate arguments, one of which may be briefly noticed here : The criterion of the existence (sattā) of a thing is its capacity to producce some effect (arthakriyā-karitvā-lakṣaṇam sat). A non-existent thing, like a hare's horn, cannot produce any effect. Now, from this criterion of existence, it may be deduced that a thing having existence must be momentary. If, for example, a thing like a seed be not accepted to be momentary, but thought to be lasting for more than one moment, then we have to show that it is capable of producing an effect during each moment it exists. Again, if it really remains the same unchanging thing during these moments, then it should be able to produce the *same effect* at every one of those moments. But we find that this is not the case. The seed in the house does not produce the seedling which is generated by a seed sown in the field. The seed in the house cannot then be the same as that in the field. But it may be said that though the seed does not *actually* produce the same effect always, it always has the *potentiality* to produce it, and this potentiality becomes kinetic in the presence of suitable auxiliary conditions like earth, water, etc. Therefore, the seed is always the same. But this defence is weak; because then it is virtually confessed that the seed

The view is deduced from the criterion of existence as casual efficiency.

1. *Dhammapada* (Chinese and Tibetan), Sogen *loe. cit.*

of the first moment is not the causes of the seedling, but that the seed modified by the other conditions really causes the effect. Hence the seed must be admitted to have changed. In this way it may be shown regarding everything that it does not stay unchanged during any two moments, because it does not produce the indentical effect during both moments. Hence everything lasts only for a moment.

Nothing exists for more than one moment.

(iv) The Theory of the Non-existence of the Soul

The law of change is universal; neither man, nor any other being, animate or inanimate, is exempt from it. It is commonly believed that in man there is an abiding substance called the soul (ātmā), which persists through changes that overcome the body, exists before birth and after death, and migrates from one body to another. Consistently with his theories of conditional existence and universal change, Buddha denies the existence of such soul. But how, it may be asked, does he then explain the continuity of a person through different births, or even through the different states of childhood, youth and old age? Though denying the continuity of an identical substance in man, Buddha does not deny the *continuity of the stream* of successive states that compose his life. Life is an unbroken series of states : each of these states depends on the condition just preceding and gives rise to the one just succeeding it. The continuity of the life-series is, therefore, base on a causal connection running through the different states. This continuity is often explained with the example of a lamp burning throughout the night. The flame of each moment is dependent on its own conditions and different from that of another moment which is dependent on other conditions. Yet there is an unbroken succession of the different flames. Again, as from one flame another may

The common belief is that there is a permament substance in man, namely, the soul. But this belief is untenable because of the law of universal change and imperma-nence.

Life is an unbroken stream of successive states which are caus-ally connected.

be lighted, and though the two are different, they are connected causally, similarly, the end-state of this life may cause the beginning of the next. Rebirth is, therefore, not transmigration, *i.e.* the migration of the same soul into another body; it is the causation of the next life by the present.[1] The conception of a soul is thus replaced here by that of an unbroken stream of consciousness as in the philosophy of William James. As the present state of consciousness inherits its characters from pervious ones, the past in a way continues in the present, through its effect. Memory thus becomes explicable even without a soul. This theory of the non-existence of soul (Anattā-vāda) plays a very important part in understanding the teachings of Buddha. He, therefore, repeatedly exhorts his disciples to give up the false view about the self. Buddha points out that people who suffer from the illusion of the self, do not know its nature clearly; still they strongly protest that they love the soul; they want to make the soul happy by obtaining salvation. This, he, wittily remarks, is like falling in love with the most beautiful maiden in the land though she has never been seen nor known.[2] Or, it is like building a stair-case for mounting a palace which has never been seen.[3]

This stream extends backward and forward and makes the past, present and future lives continuous.

The soul is thus replaced by a continuous stream of states.

The illusion of a permanent soul causes attachment and misery.

Man is only a conventional name for a collection of different constituents,[4] the material body (kāya), the immaterial mind (manas or citta), the formless consciousness (vijñāna), just as a chariot is a collection of wheels, axles, shafts, etc.[5] The existence of man depends on this collection and it dissolves when the collection breaks

Man is an unstable collection of body, manas and consciousness.

1. *Vide* Warren, pp. 234 f.
2. *Potthapāda-sutta (Dialogues,* I. p. 258).
3. *Ibid.*, p. 261.
4. *Ibid.*, pp. 259-61.
5. *Milinda-pañha,* Warren, pp. 129-33.

up. The soul or the ego denotes nothing more than this collection.

Man may also be regarded as a combination of five kinds of changing states—pañca—skandhas.

From a psychological point of view, man, as perceived from without and within, is analysable also into a collection of five groups (pañca-skandhas) of changing elements, namely, (1) form (rūpa) consisting of the different factors which we perceive in this body having form, (2) feelings (vedanā) of pleasure, pain and indifference, (3) perception including understanding and naming (sañjñā), (4) predispositions or tendencies generated by the impressions of past experience (saṁśkāras), and (5) consciousness itself (vijñāna).[1] The last four are together called nāma.

The essence of Buddha's teachings : suffering and cessation of suffering.

In summing up his teachings Buddha himself once said: "Both in the past and even now do I set forth just this : suffering (duḥkha) and cessation of suffering." Rhys Davids, quoting this authority, observes that the theory of dependent origination (in its double aspect of explaining the world and explaining the origin of suffering), together with the formula of the eightfold path, gives us "not only the whole of early Buddhism in a nutshell, but also just those points concerning which we find the most emphatic affirmations of Dhamma as Dhamma ascribed to Gautama."[2] And this is the substance of what we have learnt in the above accounts of Buddha's teachings.

III. The Schools of Bauddha Philosphy

Buddha's attempt to avoid metaphysics gives rise to a new kind of metaphysics.

It has been found again and again in the history of human thought that every reasoned attempt to avoid philosophy lands a thinker into a new kind of philosophy.

In spite of Buddha's aversion to theoretical speculation,

1. *Saṁyutta-nikāya, Ibid.*, pp. 138-45. *Vide* also Mrs. Rhys Davids : *Buddhist Psychology,* Chap. III; Suzuki : *Outlines*, pp. 150-53.

2. *Dialogues*, II, p. 44.

he never wanted to accept, nor did he encourage his followers to accept, any course of action without reasoning and criticism. He was extremely rational and contemplative, and wanted to penetrate into the very roots of human existence, and tried to supply the full justification of the ethical principles he followed and taught. It was no wonder, therefore, that he himself incidentally laid down the foundation of a philosophical system. His philosophy, partly expressed and partly implicit, may be called positivism in so far as he taught that our thoughts should be confined to this world and to the improvement of our existence here. It may be called phenomenalism in so far as he taught that we were sure only of the phenomena we experienced. It is, therefore, a kind of empiricism in method because experience, according to him, was the source of knowledge.

His teachings contained the germs of positivism, phenomenalism and empiricism.

These different aspects of his philosophy came to be developed by his followers along different lines as they were required to justify Buddha's teaching, to defend it from the severe criticism it had to face in India and outside, and to convert other thinkers to their faith. Buddha's reluctance to discuss the ten metaphysical questions concerning things beyond our experience and his silence about them came to be interpreted by his followers in different lights. Some took this attitude as only the sign of a throughgoing empiricism which must frankly admit the inability of mind to decide non-empirical questions. According to this explanation, Buddha's attitude would be regarded as scepticism. Some other followers, mostly the Mahāyānists, interpreted Buddha's view neither as a denial of reality beyond objects of ordinary experience, nor as a denial of any means of knowing the non-empirical reality, but only as signifying the indescribability of that transcendental experience and reality. The justification of this last interpretation can be obtained from some facts of Buddha's

These are developed by his diverse followers along different lines.

Empiricism and scepticism.

life and techings. Ordinary empiricists believe that our sense-experience is the only basis of all our knowledge; they do not admit the possibility of any non-sensuous experience. Buddha, however, taught the possibility of man's attaining in nirvāṇa an experience of consciousness which was not generated by the activity of the sense. The supreme value and importance that he attached to this non-empirical consciousness, justify his followers in supposing that the regarded this as the supreme reality, as well. The fact that very often Buddha used to say[1] that he had a profound experience of things 'far beyond', which is 'comprehended only by the wise' and 'not grasped by mere logic', may be taken to mean that his non-empirical experience can neither be logically proved with arguments nor be expressed in empirical ideas and language. These grounds lead some followers, as we shall see, to raise a philosophy of mysticism and transcendentalism out of the very silence of Buddha. The nemesis of neglected metaphysics thus overtakes Buddhism soon after the founder's passing away.

Mysticism and transcendentalism.

Buddhism, though primarily an ethical-religious movement, thus came to give birth to about thirty schools, not counting the minor one.[2] And some of these get into the deep waters of metaphysical speculation, heedless of the founder's warning. Of these many schools we shall first notice the four distinguished in India by Buddhist[3] and non-Buddhist writers. In this account, (1) some Bauddha philosophers are nihilists (śūnya-vādī or Mādhyamika),

There are about thirty chief schools of later Buddhism.

1. *Vide Brahmajāla-sutta.*
2. *Vide Sogen Systems*, p. 3.
3. *e.g., Mokṣākaragupta in Tarkabhāṣā*, pp. 60-71.

(2) others are subjective idealists (Vijñānavādī or Yogācāra),(3) others again are representationists or critical realists (Bāhyānumeya-vādī or Sautrāntika), and (4) the rest are direct realists (Bāhyapratyakṣa-vādī or Vaibhāṣika). The first two of the above four schools come under Mahāyāna and the last two under Hīnayāna. It should be noted, however, that under both Mahāyāna and Hīnayāna there are many other schools.[1]

Four schools of Bauddha philosophy distinguished by Indian philosophers.

The fourfold classification of Bauddha philosophy is based upon two cheif questions, one metaphysical or concerning reality and the other epistemological or concerning the knowing of reality. To the metaphysical question "Is there at all any reality, mental or non-mental?" Three different replies are given : *(a)* the Mādhyamikas hold[2] that there is no reality, mental or non-mental; that all is void (śūnya). Therefore, they have been known as the nihilists (śūnya-vādins). *(b)* The Yogācāras hold that only the mental is real, the non-mental or the material world is all void of reality. They are, therefore, called subjective idealists (vijñānavādins). *(c)* Still another class of Bauddhas hold that both the mental and the non-mental are real. They may, therefore, be called realists. Sometimes they are styled Sarvāstivādins (*i.e.* those who hold the reality of all things), though this term is often used in a narrower sense by some

This fourfold division is based on two problems : (1) Is there any reality ? Three replies to this question.

1. *Ibid.*, Sogen mentions 21 schools of Hīnayāna and eight of Mahāyāna, which are said to have many other less known schools.

2. According to non-Buddhist Indian critics. This interpretation is not supported by the Mahāyanist writers as will be shown later.

Buddhist writers.[1] But when the further epistemological question is asked : "How is external reality known to exist?" This third group of thinkers, who believe in external reality, give to different answers. Some of them, called Sautrāntikas, hold that external objects are not perceived but known by *inference*. Others, known as Vaibhāṣikas, hold that the external world is directly *perceived*. Thus we have the four schools, representing the four important standpoints. This classification has much philosophical importance, even in the light of contemporary Western thought, where we find some of these different views advocated with great force. Let us consider these four schools.

(2) How is external reality known ? Two replies to this question.

1. The Mādhyamika School of Sūnya-vāda

The founder of this school is said to be Nāgārjuna, who was a Brahmin born in South India about the second century A.D.[2] Aśvaghoṣa, the author of *Buddhacarita*, is also regarded as a pioneer. In his famous work, *Mā dhyamikaśāstra*, Nāgārjuna states, with great dialectical skill and scholarship, the philosophy of the Mādhyamika school.[3]

Nāgārjuna, the founder of this school of Sūnya-vāda

The doctrine of Śūnya-vāda has been understood in India, by non-Buddhist philosophers in general, to mean that the universe is totally devoid of reality, that everything is śūnya or void. In setting forth this doctrine in his *Sarvadarśanasangraha*, Mādhavācārya has mentioned the following as an argument in its support. The self (or the knower), the object (or the known) and

Sūnya-vāda is understood as nihilism by Indian writers.

A proof of nihilism or the unreality of all things:objects,knowledge and knower.

1. *Vide* Stcherbatsky, *The Central Conception of Buddhism*, pp. 63-76 (where Sarvāstivādin=Vaibhāṣika) ; also *Hist of Phil. E. W.*, Vol. I. pp. 174f. 190, 196, 200.
2. *Vide*, Sogen, *Systems*, Chap. V. p. 187.
3. This work, under the title, *mūlamadhyamaka-Kārikā* (Mādhyamika sūtras of Nāgārjuna with the *Prasannapadā* com. of Chandrakīrti) was published by Poussin in 1903, in St. Petersbourg.

knowledge are mutually interdependent. The reality of one depends on each of the other two, and if one be false, the others also must be so (just as the fatherhood of any person will be proved false if the existence of his children be proved to be false). But it must be admitted by all that when we perceive a snake, in a rope, the object perceived, namely, the snake is absolutely false. Hence the mind or the subject which knows such an object turns out to be false and its knowledge also becomes false. Thus it may be concluded that all that we perceive within or without, along with their perception and the percipient mind, are illusory like dream-objects. There is, therefore, nothing, mental or non-mental, which is real. The universe is śūnya or void of reality.

Sūnya-vāda really denies only the phenomenal world, and not all reality.

From such arguments it would appear that, according to the Mādhyamika view, everything is unreal. Hence it is that such a view came to be known as nihilism in Europe as well as in India (where it has also been termed Sarvavaināśika-vāda by some writers). The word *śūnya*, used by the Mādhyamikas themselves, is cheifly responsible for this notion—because śūnya means ordinarily void or empty. But when we study this philosphy more closely, we come to realize that the Mādhyamika view is not really nihilism, as ordinaily supposed; and that it does not deny all reality, but only the apparent phenomenal world perceived by us. Behind this phenomenal world there is a reality which is not describable by any character, mental or non-mental, that we perceive. Being devoid of phenomenal characters, it is called śūnya. But this is only the negative aspect of the ultimate reality : it is only a description of what it is not. In the *Laṅkavātāra-sūtra* (sagāthaka, 167) it is stated that the real nature of objects cannot be ascertained by the intellect and cannot, therefore, be described. That which is real must be independent and should not depend on anything else for its existence and origination. But everything we know of is dependent on some condition. Hence it cannot be real. Again, it cannot be said to be unreal. Because an unreal

Sūnya means the indescribable nature of phenomena.

A thing cannot be said to be either real or unreal, or both real and unreal, or neither real nor unreal.

thing, like a castle in the air, can never come into existence. To say that it is both real and unreal or that it is neither real nor unreal, would be unintelligible jargon.[1] Śūnyatā or voidness is the name for this indeterminable, indescribable real nature of things. Things appear to exist, but when we try to understand the real nature of their existence our intellect is baffled. It cannot be called either real or unreal, or both real and unreal, or neither real nor unreal.

Śūnyatā is this indeterminable nature.

It will be seen that in the above arguments, the indescribable nature of things is deduced from the fact of their being dependent on other things or conditions, Nāgārjuna says, therfore, "The fact of dependent origination is called by us śūnyatā."[2] "There is no dharma (character) of things which is not dependent on some other condition regarding its origin. Therefore, there is no dharma which is not śūnya."[3] It would appear, therefore, that śūnya only means the conditional character of things, and their consequent constant changeability and indeterminability or indescribability.[4]

Śūnyatā is only an aspect of the dependent nature of things.

This view is called the middle (madhyama) path, because it avoids extreme views by denying, for example, both absolute reality and absolute unreality of things and asserting their conditional existence. This was the reason why Buddha, as we saw, called the theory of dependent origination—the middle path.[5] And so Nāgārjuna says[6] that śūnya-vāda is called the middle path because it implies the theory of dependent origination.

This view avoids the two extreme views of the absolute reality and the absolute unreality of things. Hence it is known as the middle (madhyama) view.

---

1. *Sarvadarśana-sangraha*, Chap. II.
2. *Mādhyamika-śāstra*, Chap. 24. *Kārikā*, 18.
3. *Ibid.*, *Kārikā*, 19.
4. Sogen. *Systems*, P. 14 and pp. 194-98; *Suzuki, outlines*.
5. *Vide ante* p. 134.
6. *Kārikā* 18 quoted above.

Śūnya-vāda is a kind of relativity.

The conditionality of things which makes their own nature (svabhāva) unascertainable, either as real or unreal, etc., may be also regarded as a kind of relativity. Every character of a thing is conditioned by something else and therefore its existence is relative to that condition. Śūnya-vāda can therefore, also be interpreted as a theory of relativity which declares that no thing, no phenomenon experienced, has a fixed, absolute, independent character of its *own* (svabhāva) and, therefore, no description of any phenomenon can be said to be unconditionally true.

The positive side of the Mādhyamika doctrine; there is reality behind phenomena; it is unconditional and free from change.

To this philosophy of phenomena (or things as they appear to us), the Mādhyamikas add a philosophy of noumenon (or reality in itself). Buddha's teachings regarding dependent origination impermanence, etc., apply, they hold, only to the phenomenal world, to things commonly observed by us in ordinary experience. But when nirvāna is attained and the conditions of sense-experience and the appearance of phenomena are controlled, what would be the nature of the resultant experience? To this we cannot apply the conditional characters true of phenomena. the Mādhyamikas, therefore, hold that there is a transcedental reality (noumenon) behind the phenomenal one and it is free from change, conditionality and all other phenomenal characters. As Nāgārjuna says : "There are two truths, on which Buddha's teaching of Dharma depends, one is empirical (saṁvṛti-satya) and meant for the ordinary people, another is the transcendental or the absolutely true one (paramārtha-satya). Those who do not know the distinction between these two kinds of truth, cannot understand the profound mystery of Buddh's teachings."[1]

Nāgārjuna speaks, therefore, of two truths, empirical or phenomenal and transcendental or noumenal.

---

1. *Mādhyamika-śāstra*, Chap. 24, *Kārikas* 8-9.

The truth of the order is only a stepping-stone to the attainment of the higher. The nature of nirvāṇa-experience which takes one beyond ordinary experience cannot be described, it can only be suggested negatively with the help of words which describe our common experience. Nāgārjuna, therefore, describes nirvāṇa with a series of negatives, thus : "That which is not known (ordinarily), not acquired anew, not destroyed, not eternal, not suppressed, not generated is called nirvāṇa."[1] As with nirvāṇa so also with the Tathāgata or one who has realized nirvāṇa. His nature also cannot be described. That is why, when Buddha was asked what becomes of the Tathāgata after nirvāṇa is attained, he declined to discuss the question.

The higher truth realized in nirvāṇa, can be described only as negation of what is known in ordanary experience.

No positive description of it is possible.

In the same light the silence of Buddha regarding all metaphysical questions about non-empirical things can be interpreted to mean that he believed in a transcendental experience and reality, the truths about which cannot be descrinebed in terms of common experience. Buddha's frequent statements that he had realized some profound truth which resoning cannot grasp, can be cited also to support this Mādhyamika contention about the transcendental.[2]

This accounts for Buddha's silence on matters beyond ordinary experience.

It may be noted here that in its conception of twofold truth, its denial of the phenomenal world, its negative description of the transcendental, and its conception of nirvāṇa as the attainment of unity with the transcendetal self, the Mādhyamika approaches very close to Advaita Vedānta as taught in some Upaniṣads and elaborated later by Gauḍapāda and Saṅkarācārya.

The points of agreement between Buddha's teaching (as interpreted by the Madhyamikas) and that of the Upaniṣads.

1. *Ibid.*, Chap. 25, *Kārikā* 3.

2. *Vide* Prof. Radhakrishnan's article, "The teaching of Buddha by speech and silence," *Hibbert Journal*, April, 1934 for a fuller discussion.

2. *The Yogācāra School of Subjective Idealism*

Denial of the reality of the mental is self-contradictory.

While agreeing with the Mādhyamikas, as to the unreality of external objects, the Yogācāra school differs from them in holding that the mind (citta) cannot be regarded as unreal. For then all resoning and thinking would be false and the Mādhyamikas could not even established that their own arguments were correct. To say that everything, mental or non-mental, is unreal is suicidal. The reality of the mind should at least be admitted in order to make correct thinking possible.

Mind must, therefore, be admitted.

The objects perceivad are all ideas in the mind.

The mind, consisting of a stream of different kinds of ideas, is the only reality. Things that appear to be outside the mind, our body as well as other objects, are merely ideas of the mind. Just as in cases of dreams and hallucinations a man fancies to perceive things outside, though they do not really exist there, similarly the objects which appear to be out there, are really ideas in the mind. The existence of any external object cannot be proved, because it cannot be shown that the object is different from the consciousness of the object. As Dharmakīrti states, the blue colour and the consciousness of the blue colour are identical, because they are never perceived to exist separately. Though really one, they appear as two owing to illusion, just as the moon appears as two owing to defective vision. As an object is never known without the consciousness of it, the object cannot be proved to have an existence independent of consciousness.

The mind alone is real.

There is no external reality.

If any external reality is admitted, many difficulties arise.

The Yogācāras also point out the following absurdities which arise from the admission of an object external to the mind. An external object, if admitted, must be either partless (*i.e.*, atomic) or composite (*i.e.*, composed of many parts). But atoms are too small to be perceived. A composite thing (like a pot) also cannot be perceived, because it is not possible to perceive *simultaneously* all the sides and parts of the object. Nor can it be said to be perceived *part by part,* because, if those parts are atomic they are too small to be perceived, and if they are composite, the original objection again arises. so if one admits extramental objects, the perception of these objects cannot be explained. These objections do not arise if the object be nothing other than conciousness, because the question of parts and whole does not arise with regard to consciousness.

(1) An external object cannot be perceived.

(2) How a *momentary* object cause, perception is unexplained.

Another difficulty is that the consciousness of the object cannot arise before the object has come into existence. Neither can it arise afterwards, because the object, being momentary, vanishes as soon as it arises. The external object, according to those who admit it, being the cause of conciousness cannot be simultaneous with conciousness. Nor can it be said that the object may be known by consciousness after it has ceased to exist. For in that case the object being in the *past* there cannot be any *immediate* knowledge or *perception* of it. Perception of *present* objects, as we must admit always to have, remains, therefore, unexplained if objects are supposed to be external to the mind. This difficulty does not arise, if the object be supposed to be nothing other than consciousness.

The Yogācāra view is called Vijñāna-vāda or idealism because it admits that there is only one kind of reality which is of the nature of consciousness (vijñāna) and objects which appear to be material or external to consciousness are really ideas or states of consciousness. This theory may be described further as *subjective idealism*, because according to it the existence of an object perceived is not different from the *subject* or the perceving mind.

The Yogācāra view is called Vijñāna-vāda because it admits vijñāna or consciousness as the only reality. It is *subjective* idealism.

One of the chief difficulties of subjective idealism is : If an object depends for its existence solely on the subject, then, how is it that the mind cannot create at will any object at any time? How is it explained that objects do not change, appear or disappear at the will of the perceiver? To explain this difficulty, the Vijñāna-vādin says that the mind is a stream

The ideas of objects are all latent in the mind. The conditions of a particular moment make a particular idea mature or become conscious and vivid.

of momentary conscious states and within the stream there lie, buried the impressions (samskāra) of all past experience. At a particular moment that latent impression comes to the surface of consciousness for which the circumstances of the moment are the most favourable. At that moment that impression attains maturity (paripāka), so to say, and develops into immediate consciousness or perception. It is thus that at that particular moment *only that object*, whose latent impression can, under the circumstances, reveal itself becomes perceived; just as in the case of the revival of past impressions in memory, though all the impressions are in the mind, only some are remembered at a particular time. This is why only some objects can be perceived at a time and not any at will.

Hence a particular object is perceived at a particular time.

The mind considered in its aspect of being a store-house or home of all impressions is called by the Vijñāna-vādins Ālaya Vijñāna.[1] It may be regarded as the potential mind and answers, to the soul or ātman of other systems, with the difference that it is not one unchanging substance like the soul, but is a stream of continuously changing states. Through culture and self-control this Ālaya-vijñāna or the potential mind can gradually stop the arising of undesirable mental states and develop into the ideal state of nirvāṇa. Otherwise, it only gives rise to thoughts, desires, attachment which bind one more and more to the fictitious extermal world. The mind, the only reality according to this school, is truly its own place, it can make heaven of hell and hell of heaven.[2]

The mind as the home of all Intent ideas, is called Ālaya - vijñāna.

Culture and control of the mind can stop the illusions of external objects and attachment to them.

The Yogācarās are so called either because they used to practise yoga[3] by which they came to realize the sole reality of mind (as Ālaya-vijñāna) dispelling all belief in the external world, or because they combined in them both critical inquisitiveness (yoga) and good conduct (ācāra).[4] Asaṅga, Vasubandhu, Diṅnāga are the famous leaders of the Yogācāra school. Laṅkāvatāra-sūtra is one of its most important works.[5]

The meaning of Yogācāra.

1. *Vide* Sogen, *Systems*, p. 258.
2. *Ibid.*, p. 259.
3. *Vide* Sogen, *Systems*, p. 213.
4. *Sarvadarśana-sangraha, p. 213.* Ch. II.
5. *Vasubhandhu's Vijñaptimātrasiddhi* and *Trisvabhavanirdeśa* and Diṅnāga's *Alambanaparikṣā* are the other source books.

3. The Sautrāntika School of Representationism

The mental and the external are both real.

The Sautrāntikas believe in the reality not only of the mind, but also of external objects. They point out that without the supposition of some external objects, it is not possible to explain even the illusory appearance of external objects. If one never perceived anywhere any external object, he could not say, as a Vijñāna-vādin does, that, through illusion, consciousness appears *like* an external object. The phrase 'like an external object' is as meaning less as 'like the son of a barren mother' because an external object is said by the Vijñāna-vādin to be wholly unreal and never perceived. Again, the argument from the simultaneity of consciousness and object to their identity is also defective. Whenever we have the preception of an object like a pot, the pot is felt as external and consciousness of it as internal (*i.e.* to be in the mind). So the object, from the very beginning, is known to be different from and not identical with consciousness. If the pot perceived were identical with the subject, the perceiver would have said, "I am the pot." Besides, if there were no external objects, the distinction between the 'consciousness of a pot' and 'the consciousness of a cloth' could not be explained, because as consciousness both are identical; it is not only regarding the objects that they differ.

Proofs for the reality of external objects (1) If there were *no* external object, it would be meaningless to say 'consciousness appears as the external objects'.

(2) Objects are felt directly as being outside the self.

(3) If a pot were perceived as identical with the self, then one would say, 'I am the pot' and not, 'There is the pot.'

Hence we must admit the existence of different external objects outside consciousness. These objects give particular forms to the different states of consciousness. From these forms or representations of the objects in the mind we can infer the existence of their causes, *i.e.* the objects outside the mind.

Ideas are not objects, but only copies of them. Hence objects outside *can be inferred* from their mental pictures or ideas.

The reason why we cannot perceive at will any object

at anytime and place, lies in the fact that a perception depends on four different conditions[1] and not simply on the mind. There must be the object to impart its *form* to consciousness, there must be the conscious mind (or the state of the mind at the just previous moment) to cause the *consciousness* of the form, there must be the sense to *determine* the kind of the consciousness, that is, whether the consciousness of that object would be visual, tactual or of any other kind. Lastly, there must be some favourable *auxiliary* condition, such as light, convenient position, perceptible magnitude, etc. All these combined together bring about the perception of the object. The form of the object thus generated in the mind, is the effect of the object, among other things. The existence of the objects is not of course perceived, because what mind immediately knows is the copy or representation of the object in its own consciousness. But from this it can *infer* the object without which the copy would not arise.

Perception of external objects depends on four factors : object, mind, sense and auxilary conditions.

The effect of these conditions is the copy or idea of the object produced in the mind. We infer the object from this idea.

The Sautrāntika theory is, therefore, called also the theory of the inferability of external objects (Bāhyānumeya-vāda). The name 'Sautrāntika' is given to this school because it attaches exclusive importance to the authority of the *Sūtra-piṭaka*.[2] The arguments used by this school for the refutation of subjective idealism anticipated long ago some of the most important arguments which modern. Western realists like Moore use to refute the subjective idealism of Berkely. The Sautrāntika position in epistemology resembles 'representationism' or the 'copy theory of ideas' which was common among Western philosophers like Locke. This exists even now in a modified form among some critical realists.

The meaning of Sautrāntika.

---

1. These are called respectively, the ālambana, the samanantara, the adhipati and the sahakāri pratyayas (conditions).

2. Many works of this class are named suttānta.' *Vide* Sogen *Systems*, p. 5, for this interpretation of 'sautrāntika.

4. *The Vaibhāṣika School*

Vaibhāṣikas admit, like sautrāntikas, the reality of both mind an external objects.

While agreeing with the Sautrāntikas regarding the reality of both the mental and the non-mental, the Vaibhāṣikas, like many modern neo realists, point out that unless we admit that external objects are *perceived* by us, their existence cannot be known in any other way. Inference of fire from the perception of smoke is possible, because in the past we have perceived both smoke and fire together. One who has never pereceived fire previously cannot infer its existence from the perception of smoke. If external objects were *never perceived*, as the Sautrāntikas hold, then they *could not even be inferred*, simply from their mental forms. To one unacquainted with an external object, the mental form would not appear to be the *copy* or the *sign* of the existence of an extra-mental object, but as an original thing which does not owe its existence to anything outside the mind. Either, therefore, we have to accept subjective idealism (vijñāna-vāda) or, if that has been found unsatisfactory, we must admit that the external object is directly known. The Vaibhāṣikas thus come to hold a theory of direct realism' (bāhya.pratyakṣa-vāda).

But unlike Sautrā tikas they hold that external objects are directly known inperception and not inferrd.

Meaning of 'Vaibhāsika'.

The Abhidhamma treatises formed the general foundation of the philosophy of the realists. The Vaibhāṣikas followed exclusively a particular commentary, *Vibhāṣā* (or *Abhidhamma-mahāvibhāṣā*)[1] on an Abhidhamma treatise (*Abhidharma-jñāna-praṣtnāna*).[2] Hence their name.

IV. The Religious Schools of Buddhism : Hīnayāna and Mahāyāna

In respect of religion Buddhism is divided, as we know, into the two great schools, the Hīnayāna and the Mahāyāna.

The Hīnayāna school adheres to the teaching of Buddha that everyone should work out his own salvation.

Representng faithfully the earlier form of Buddhism the Hīnayāna, like Jainism, stands as the example of a religion without God. The place of God is taken in it by the

1. *Vide*, J. E. Turner, *A Theory of Direct Realism*, p. 8.
2. *Vide* Sogen. *Systems*. pp. 102 and 106.

universal moral law of karma or dharma which governs the universe in such a way that no fruit of action is lost and every individual gets the mind, the body and the place in life that he deserves by his past deeds. The life and teachings of Buddha furnish the ideal as well as the promise or the possibility of every fettered individual's attaining liberation. The organized church (saṅgha) of his faithful followers adds strength to spiritual aspirations. So an aspirant is advised to take the threefold solemn vow (tisaraṇa) : "I take refuge in Buddha, I take refuge in Dhamma, I take refuge in the Saṅgha."

But with an unshaken confidence in his own power of achievement and a faith in the moral law that guarantees the preservation of every bit of progress made, the Hīnayānist hopes to obtain liberation in this or any other future life by following Buddha's noble path. His goal is Arhatship or Nibbāna, the state that extinguishes all his misery. Hīnayāna is, therefore, a religion of self-help. It sticks fast to Buddha's saying : Be a light unto thyself.'[1] *Everyone can and should achieve the highest goal for and by himself*. It is inspired by the last words that Buddha said before he passed away : "Decay is inherent in all things composed of parts. Work out your salvation with diligence." This path is meant only for the strong, who are all too few in this world.

Hīnayāna is the difficult path of self-help.

As the fold of Buddhism widened in course of time, it came to include not only the few select persons fit to follow this difficult ideal, but also multitudes of half-convinced nominal converts who neither understood the Path nor had the necessary moral strength to follow it. With the support of royal patrons like Aśoka. Buddhism gained in number but lost its original quality. The bulk of people who accepted Buddhism, on grounds other than moral, brought it down to their own level. They came with their own habits, beliefs

It did not suit, therefore, the multitude of ordinary converts.

1. 'ātmadīpo bhava.'

and traditions which soon became a part of the new faith they accepted. The teachers had to choose between upholding the ideal at the cost of number and upholding the number at the cost of the ideal. A few sturdy ones preferred the first. But the majority could not resist the temptation of the second. They came thus to build what they were pleased to call the Great Vehicle. Mahāyāna, contrasting it with the orthodox faith of the former, which they nicknamed the Lesser Vehicle, Hīnayāna. By the criterion of number Mahāyāna surely deserved the name, for it was designed to be a religious omnibus, with room enough to hold and suit persons of all taste and cultures.

This gives rise to Mahāyāna which tries to suit all tastes and culture.

Its accommodating spirit and missionary zeal made it possible for Mahāyāna to penetrate into the Himalayas and move across to China, Korea and Japan and absorb peoples of divers cultures. As it progressed, it assumed newer and newer forms, assimilating the beliefs of the people it admitted. Modern Mahāyānist writers are resonably proud of their faith and love to call it a living, progressive religion whose adptability is the sign of its vitality.

The accommodating spirit and the missionary zeal of Mahāyana.

The accommodating spirit of Mahāyānism can be traced back to the catholic concern which Buddha himself had for the salvation of all beings. Mahāyānism emphasizes this aspect of the founder's life and teachings. Mahāyānists point out that the long life of Buddha, after enlightenment, dedicated to the service of the suffering béings. sets an example and ideal, namely, that enlightenment should be sought *not for one's own salvation* but for being able to minister to the moral needs of others. In fact, in

Mahayana lays great stress on Buddha's anxiety for the salvation of fellow beings.

The object of enlightenment is not one's own salvation.

course of time, Mahāyānism came to look upon the Hīnayānist saint's anxiety to liberate himself, as a lower ideal which had yet an element of selfishness in it, however subtle or sublime this selfishness might be. The ideal of the salvation of all sentient beings thus came to be regarded as the higher aspect of Buddha's teachings. The greatness of their faith, Mahāyānists contend, consists in this ideal and the inferiority of the Hīnayānists in the lack of it.[1]

It is the ability to liberate all suffering being.

The greatness of Mahāyāna lies in this spirit, and the inferiority of Hīnayāna is due to the lack of it.

The new elements which Mahāyānism came to acquire or develop in its different branches were many and sometimes conflicting. We shall mention here only a few of the more important ones.

(a) The Ideal of Bodhisattva : As noted previously Mahāyāna regards even the desire for one's own salvation as selfish at bottom. In the place of personal liberation it establishes the 'liberation of all sentient beings' as the ultimate goal of every Mahāyānist spiritual aspirations. The vow that a devout Mahāyānist is expected to take is that he would try to achieve the Stae of Enlightenment, Bodhisattva (the Wisdom-State-of-Existence), not to live aloof from the world but to work with perfect wisdom and love among the multitudes of suffering beings for removing their misery and achieving their salavation. This spiritual ideal of mahāyāna has, therefore, come to be called Bodhisattva.

The ideal of Bodhisattva is attainment of perfect wisdom with a view to being able to lead all beings out of misery.

One who has attained this ideal of Enlightenment and

---

1. All these aspects of Mahāyānism are summed up by the eminent Japanese writer, D,T. Suzuki, in his *Outlines of Mahāyāna Buddhism,* thus "It (Mahāyānism) is the Buddhism which, inspired by a progressive spirit, broadened its original scope, so far as it did not contradict the inner significance of the teachings of the *Buddha*, and which assimilated other religio-philosophical beliefs within itself, whenever it felt that, by so doing, people of more widely different characters and intellectual endowments could be saved" (p. 10.)

works for the salvation of other beings is also called a Bodhisattva. Love and wisdom (karunā and prajñā) constitute the essence of his existence.[1] Speaking about such perfect persons Nāgārjuna saya in the *Bodhicitta* : "Thus the essential nature of all Bodhisattvas is a great loving heart (mahākarunā citta) and all sentient beings constitute the object of its love."[2] "Therefore, all Bodhisattavas, in order to emancipate sentient beings from misery, are inspired with great spiritual energy and mingle themselves in the filth of birth and death. Though thus they make themselves subject to the laws of birth and death, their hearts are free from sins and attachments. They are like unto those immaculate undefiled lotus flowers which grow out of mire, yet are not contaminated by it."[3] By an exchange (parivarta) of the fruits of action, a Bodhisattva relieves the miseries due to others with his own good deeds and suffers the consequences of their actions himself.

Love of all Beings, along with wisdom, marks the perfect person or Bodhisattva.

A Bodhisattva exchanges his desires with those of the fellow beings and suffers to relieve their misery.

This ideal of Bodhisattva is nartured by the Mahāyāna philosophy, which comes to think that all individuals are unreal as separate particular phenomena, and that they are all really grounded in *one* transcendental Reality (Ālaya-vijñāna according to some yogācāras, or Śūnya or Tathata, according to some Mādhyamikas), of which they are the partial or illusory manifestations. This philosophy favoured the rejection of the idea of the individual ego and acceptance of an universal absolute self (Mahātman and

The ideal of Bodhisattva is based on the philosophy of the unity of all beings.

1. *Vide,* Suzuki *Outlines,* p. 296.

2. *Ibid,* P. 292.

3. *Ibid.,* PP. 293-94.

Paramātman)[1] as the real self of man. Striving for the liberation of all and not simply for the little self (hīnātman) was, therefore, the logical outcome of this philosophy of the unity of all beings. Moreover, the idea that the trancendental Reality is not away from but within the phenomena paved the way for the belief that perfection or nirvāṇa is not to be sought away from the world but within it. Nirvāṇa, says Nāgārjuṇa, is to be found within the world by those who can see what the world really is at bottom.[2] Asceticism of the Hīnayāna is, therefore, replaced by a loving, enlightened interest in the world's affairs.

Nirvāṇa is within the world and not away from it.

(b) *Buddha as God* : The philosophy which gives the advanced followers of Mahāyāna on the one hand, the ideal of Bodhisattva, supplies the backward ones, on the other hand, with a religion of promise and hope. When an ordinary man finds himself crushed in life's struggle and fails, in spite of all his natural egoism, to avert misery, his weary spirit craves for some unfailing source of mercy and help. He turns to God. A religion of self-help, such as we have in early Buddhism, is a cold comfort to him. To such forlorn multitudes. Mahāyāna holds out the hope that Buddha's watchful eyes are on all miserable beings.

Buddha comes to be conceived as God.

Buddha is identified with the transcendenatl Reality that Mahāyāna philosophy accepted. The historical Buddha or Gautama is believed, in the common Indian way, to be the incarnation of that ultimate Reality or Buddha. Many other previous incarnations of Buddha are also believed in and described in the famous Jātakas (or stories of the different *births* of Buddha). As in Advaita Vedānta, so also here, the ultimate Reality in itself is conceived as beyond all description (like

Buddha is identified with transcendental Reality possessed of the power of incarnation.

1. *Vide* Sogen, *Systems* pp. 23-24,

2. *Vide* Nāgārjuna's saying "na saṁsārasya nirvāṇāt Kiñcidasti viśeṣanam" etc., *Mādhyamika-sāstra*, Chap. 25, *Kārikā* 19,

the Nirguna Brahma). But this reality is also thought of as manifesting itself in this world, as the Dharmakāya or the regulator of the universe. In this aspect of Dharmakāya the ultimate Reality or Buddha is anxious for the salvation of all beings, lends himself to incarnation in the different spiritual teachers and helps all beings out of misery. So, Buddha as the Dharmakāya, for all practical purpose, takes the place of God to whom the weary heart can pray for help, love and mercy. In this aspect Buddha is also called Amitābha Buddha. Thus the religious hankerings of those who accepted Buddhism are also satisfied by the Mahāyā na by identifying Buddha with God.

Buddha incarnated as teachers and helpers of beings.

(c) *The Restoration of the Self* : One of the sources of the ordinary man's dread of earlier Buddhism must have been the negation of self. If there is no self, for whom is one to work? Mahāyā na philosophy points out that it is the little individual ego which is false. But this apparent self has behind it the reality of one trancendental self (Mahātman), which is the Self of all beings. The devout Mahāyānist thus finds his self restored in a more elevating and magnified form.

Though individual selves are unreal there is one universal self, *i.e.* the Reality behind all phenomena. This last is the Real Self of all beings.

At the present day the followers of Hīnayāna and Mahāyāna often try to belittle one another. But to the discerning outsider they stand as the living examples of a fight between two equally noble motives, namely, greater purity and greater utility. Two impartial observers the mighty current of Buddhism, like every current, naturally divides itself into two parts—the narrow but pure and impetuous stream that runs through the solitary uplands near the source, and the

The Hīnayāna and the Mahayāna are inspired by two different, but equally noble motives.

gradually widening river that floods and fertilises the vast plains below, though not unmingled with the indifferent streams that increase its volume on the way and not unsoiled with the vast amount of dirt that it carries down. The first without the second would remain sublime but relatively useless; the second without the first would cease to be. It is good, therefore, to find that attempts are being made to unify the Buddhists of all countries and schools by emphasizing the basic common principles of the faith.[1]

---

1. See Humphreys, *Buddhism* (Penguin, 1951), pp. 73f and 230f for the 12 princeples of a nava-yāna (new vehicle).

THE NYĀYA PHILOSOPHY

A SELECT BIBLIOGRAPHY

Jīvānanda Vidyāsāgara, ed. ... *Nyāya-darśana* with Vātsyāyana's *Bhāṣya* and Viśvanātha's *Vṛtti* (Calcutta, 1919).

" ... *Tarkasaṅgraha* with *Tarkadīpikā and Vivṛti* (Calcutta, 1897).

Keśavamiśra ... *Tarkabhāṣā* (Original text & Eng. trans., Oriental Book Supplying Agency, Poona, 1924).

A. N. Jere, ed. ... *Kārikāvalī* (or *Bhāṣā-pariccheda*) with *Siddhāntamuktāvali, Dinkarī and Rāmarudrī* (Nirnaya Sagar, 1927).

Mādhavācārya ... *Sarva-darśana-saṅgraha.*

Udayana ... *Nyāya-kusumāñjali* (Chowkhamba, Varanasi, 1957).

Dharmarājādhvarīndra ... *Vedānta-paribhāṣā* (Cal. Univ., 1927), Chaps. I-III.

Brajendranath Seal ... *The Positive Sciences of the Ancient Hindus* (Longmans, Green & Co., 1915), Ch. VII.

S. Radhakrishnan ... *Indian Philosophy,* Vol. II, Ch. II.

Phaṇibhūṣaṇa Tarkavāgīśa ... Nyāya-paricaya (Jadavpur University, Calcutta, 1933).

CHAPTER V

THE NYĀYA PHILOSOPHY

I. Introduction

Gotama was the founder of the Nyāya system

The Nyāya philosophy was founded by the great sage Gotama who was also known as Gautama and Akṣapāda. Accordingly, the Nyāya is also known as the Akṣapāda system. This philosophy is primarily concerned with the conditions of correct thinking and the means of acquiring a true knowledge of reality. It is very useful in developing the powers of logical thinking and rigorous criticism in its students. So we have such other names for the Nyāya philosophy as Nyāyavidyā, Tarkaśāstra (*i.e.* the science of reasoning) and Ānvīkṣikī (*i.e* the science of critical study).

Its ultimate end is liberation, although its main interest is in logic.

But the logical problem as to the methods and conditions of true knowledge or the canons of logical criticism is not the sole or the ultimate end of the Nyāya philosophy. Its ultimate end, like that of the other systems of Indian philosophy, is liberation, which means the absolute cessation of all pain and suffering. It is only in order to attain this ultimate end of life that we require a philosophy for the knowledge of reality, and a logic for determining the conditions and methods of true knowledge. So we may say that the Nyāya, like other Indian systems, is a philosophy of life, although it is mainly interested in the problems of logic and epistemology.

Historical sketch of the system.

The first work of the Nyāya philosophy is the *Nyāyasūtra* of Gotama. It is divided into five adhyāyas or books, each containing two āhnikas or sections. The subsequent works of the Nyāya system, such as Vātsyā yana's *Nyāyabhāṣya, Uddyotakara's Nyāya-vārttika,* Vā caspati's *Nyāya-vārttika-tātparya-tikā,* Udayana's *Nyāya-vā rttika-tātparya-pariśuddhi* and *Kusumāñjali,* Jayanta's *Nyā yamañjari*, etc., explain and develop the ideas contained in the *Nyāya-sūtra,* and also defend them against the attacks of hostile critics. The ancient school of the Nyāya (prācīna-nyāya) is thus a development of the sūtra-philosophy of Gotama through a process of attack, counter-attack and defence among the Naiyāyikas and their hard critics. The modern school of the Nyāya (navya-nyāya) begins with the epoch-making work of Gaṅgeśa, *viz. Tattvacintāmaṇi.* This school flourished at first in Mithilābut subsequently became the glory of Bengal with Navadvīpa as the main centre of its learning and teaching. The modern school lays almost exclusive emphasis on the logical aspects of the Nyāya, and develops its theory of knowledge into a formal logic of relations between concepts, terms and propositions. With the advent of the modern Nyāya, the ancient school lost some of its popularity. The syncretist school of the Nyāya is a later development of the Nyāya philosophy into the form of a synthesis or an amalgamation between the Nyāya and the Vaiśeṣika systems.

The sixteen philosophical topics of the Nyāya.

The whole of the Nyāya philosophy may be conveniently divided into four parts, namely, the theory of knowledge, the theory of the physical world, the theory of the individual self and its liberation, and the theory of God. It should, however, be observed here that the Nyāya system is in itself an elaboration of sixteen philosophical topics (padārtha).[1] These are : pramāṇa, prameya, saṁśaya, prayojana, dṛṣṭānta, Siddhānta, avayava, tarka, nirṇaya, vāda, jalpa, vitaṇḍā, hetvābhāsa, chala, jāti and nigrahasthāna. These may be briefly explained here.

Pramāṇa is the way of knowing anything truly. It gives us true knowledge and nothing but true knowledge. It thus includes all the sources or methods of knowledge. Of the philosophical topics, pramāṇa is the most important and so it will be treated more fully in the next section.

1. *Nyāya -sūtra and Bhāṣya,* 1.1.1-1.2.23.

Prameya literally means a knowable or an object of true knowledge, *i.e.* reality. The objects of such knowledge, according to the Nyāya, are (1) the self (ātmā); (2) the body (śarīra)which is the seat of organic activities, the senses and the feelings of pleasure and pain; (3) the senses (indriya) of smell, taste, sight, touch and hearing; (4) their objects (artha), *i.e.* the sensible qualities of smell, taste, colour, touch and sound; (5) congnition (buddhi) which is the same thing as knowledge (jñāna) and apprehension (upalabdhi); (6) mind (manas) which is the internal sense concerned in the internal perceptions of pleasure, pain, etc., and limits our cognition to one at a time, the mind being like an atom and one in each body; (7) activity (pravṛtti) which may be good or bad, and is of three kinds, namely, vocal, mental and bodily; (8) mental defects (doṣa) such as attachment (rāga), hatred (devṣa) and infatuation (moha) which are at the root of our activities, good or bad; (9) rebirth after death (pretyabhāva) which is brought about by our good or bad actions; (10) the experiences of pleasure and pain (phala) which result from the activities due to mental defects; (11) suffering (duḥkha) which as a bitter and painful experience is known to everybody; (12) liberation or freedom from suffering (apavarga) which means the absolute cessation of all suffering without any possibility of its recurrence.[1] This list of twelve is not an exhaustive list of all realities. This mentions, as Vātsyāyana points out,[2] only those the knowledge of which is important for liberation.

Saṁśaya or doubt is a state of uncertainty. It represents the mind's wavering between different conflicting views with regard to the same object. Doubt arises when with regard to the same thing there is the suggestion of different alternative views but no definite cognition of any differentia to decide between them. One is said to be in doubt when, looking at a distant figure, one is led to ask: 'Is it a plant or a man?' but fails to discern any specific mark that would definitely decide which of them it really is. Doubt is not certain knowledge, nor is it the mere absence of knowledge, nor is it an error. It is a positive state of cognition of mutually exclusive characters in the same thing at the same time.[3]

1. *Nyāya -sūtra and Bhāṣya,* 1.1. 9-22.
2. *Ibid., 1.1.9*
3. *Ibid., 1.1.23*

Prayojana or an end-in-view is the object for which or to avoid which one acts. We act either to obtain desirable objects or to get rid of undesirable ones. Both these kinds of objects constitute the end of our activities and are, therefore, included within prayojana.

Dṛṣṭānta or an example is an undisputed fact which illustrates a general rule. It is a very useful and necessary part of any discussion or reasoning, and it should be such that both the parties in the discussion may accept it without dispute or difference of opinion. Thus when any one argues that there must be fire in a certain place because there is smoke in it, the kitchen may be cited as an instance (dṛṣṭānta) for in the case of a kitchen we are all agreed that some smoke is related to some fire.

Siddhānta or a doctrine is what is taught and accepted as true in a system or school. A view that a certain thing is, or is such-and-such, if accepted as true in a system, will be a doctrine of that system, e.g. the Nyāya doctrine that the soul is a substance of which consciousness is a separable attribute.

Avayava or a member of the sylogism is any of the five propositions in which sylogistic inference requires to be stated if it is to prove or demonstrate a doctrine. It may be one of the premises or the conclusion of the syllogism, but never any proposition that is not a part of any syllogism. The avayavas or constituent propositions of the syllogism will be more fuly explained under *Inference.*

Tarka or an hypothetical argument is an indirect way of justifying a certain conclusion by exposing the absurdity of its contradictory. It is a form of supposition (ūha), but is an aid to the attainment of valid knowledge. It will be explained more fully later on.

Nirṇaya is certain knowledge about anything, attained by means of any of the legitimate methods of knowledge. It is usually preceded by doubt and requires a consideration of all the arguments for and against a certain view or doctrine. But it is not always conditioned by doubt in the mind of the inquirer who ascertains the truth about something. So we may say that nirṇaya is just the ascertainment of truth about something by means of any of the recognized methods or sources of knowledge.

Vāda is a discussion which is conducted with the help of pramāṇas and tarka, and in which arguments are fully stated in the five formal steps of inference. It does not go against any accepted theory. In it each of the parties, the exponent (vādī) and the opponent (prativādī), tries to establish his own position and refute that of the other, but *both try to arrive at the truth*. This is very well illustrated by a philosophical discussion between the teacher and his student provided both of them are honest seekers after truth.

Jalpa is mere wrangling in which the parties aim only at victory over each other, but do not make an honest attempt to come to truth. It has all other characteristics of a discussion than that of aiming at truth. Here the parties aim at victory only and, therefore, make use of invalid reasons and arguments with the full consciousness that they are such. Lawyers sometimes indulge in this kind of wrangling.

Vitaṇḍā is a kind of debate in which the opponent does not establish his own position but only tries to refute that of the exponent. While in jalpa each of the parties somehow establishes his own position and tries to gain victory over the other by refuting the other position, in vitaṇḍā each of the parties tries to win simply by refuting the other's position. Otherwise, the two are the same. So vitaṇḍā may be said to be a sort of cavil in which the opponent indulges in a merely destructive criticism of the exponent's views. It is something like abusing the plaintiff's pleader when one has no case.

Hetvābhāsa literally means a hetu or reason which appears as, but really is not, a valid reason. It is generally taken to mean the fallacies of inference. We shall consider them separately in connection with the theory of inference.

Chala is a kind of unfair reply in which an attempt is made to *contradict* a statement by taking it in a sense other than the intended one. It is a questionable device for getting out of a difficulty by quibbling. Thus when an opponent cannot meet the exponent's argument fairly and squarely he may take it in a sense not intended by the latter and point out that it is fallacious. One man says 'the boy is *nava*-kambala' (possessed of a new blanket),and another unfairly objects 'he is not *nava*-kambala' (possessed of *nine* blankets) ; here the latter is using 'chala'.[1]

The word jāti is here used in a technical sense to mean an unfair reply based on false analogy. It consists in basing a futile argument on any kind of similarity or dissimilarity between two things to controvert another sound argument.Thus if one argues 'sound is non-eternal, because it is an effect like the pot,' and another objects that 'sound must be eternal, because it is incorporeal like the sky,' then the objection is a kind of jāti or futile argument, for there is no necessary of universal relation between the incorporal and the eternal, as we find in the case of many objects like pleasure and pain.

Nigrahasthāna literally means a ground of defeat in debate. There are two primary grounds of such defeat, namely, misunderstanding or wrong understanding and want of understanding. If any party in a debate misunderstands or fails to understand his own or the other party's statement and its implication, he is brought to the point at which he has to admit defeat. Thus one is defeated in a debate when one shifts the original proposition or one's ground in the argument, or uses fallacious arguments and the like.

The Nyāya philosophy is a system of logical realism. In philosophy realism means the theory or doctrine that the existence of things or objects of the world is independent of all knowledge or relation to mind. The existence of ideas

The Nyāya is a system of logical realism.

1. The Sanskrit word, nava, means 'new', and also 'nine' : and 'kambala' means 'blanket'.

and images, feelings of pleasure and pain, is dependent on some mind. These cannot exist unless they are experienced by some mind. But the existence of tables and chairs, plants and animals, does not depend on our minds. These exist and will continue to exist, whether we know them or not. Realism is a philosophical theory which holds that the existence of all things or objects of the world is quite independent of all minds, finite or infinite, human or divine.

Definitions of realism and idealism.

Idealism, on the other hand, holds that things or objects can exist only as they are related to some mind. Just as feelings and cognitions exist only as they are in some mind, so the objects of the world exist only as they are actually experienced or at least thought of by us or by God. Now the Nyāya is a realistic philosophy in so far as it holds that the objects of the world have an independent existence of their own apart from all knowledge or experience. In the Nyāya this realistic view of the world is based, not on mere faith or feeling, intuition or scriptural testimony, but on logical grounds and critical reflections. According to it, the highest end of life, *i.e.*, liberation, and be attained only through a right knowledge of reality. But a true knowledge of reality presupposes an understanding of what knowledge is, what the sources of knowledge are, how true knowledge is distinguished from wrong knowledge and so forth. In other words, a theory of reality or metaphysics presupposes a theory of knowledge or epistemology. Hence the realism of the Nyāya is based on the theory of knowledge which is the logical foundation of all philosophy. Thus we see that the Nyāya is a system of philosophy. which may be justly characterized as logical realism.

II. The Nyāya Theory of Knowledge

The Nyāya theory of reality is based on the Nyāya of knowledge. According to this, there are four distinct and separate sources of true knowledge. These are (*i*) pratyakṣa, perception ; (*ii*) anumāna, inference ; (*iii*) upamāna, comparison; and (*iv*) śabda, testimony. We shall explain them separately. But before we come to these pramāṇas or sources of valid knowledge, let us understand what knowledge is, what the different kinds of knowledge are, and how true knowledge is distinguished from false knowledge.

1. Definition and Classification of Knowledge[1]

Knowledge is the manifestation of objects.

Knowledge or cognition (jñāna or buddhi) is the manifestation of objects. Just as the light of a lamp reveals or shows physical things, so knowledge manifests all its objects. Knowledge is broadly divided into aubhava or presentative cognition and smṛti or memory, *i.e.*, representative cognition. Each of the two can be valid (yathārtha) or non-valid (ayathārtha). Valid presentative knowledge is called pramā . It is divided into perception, inference, comparison and testimony. Non-valid presentative knowledge (apramā) is divided into doubt (saṁśaya), error (bhrama or viparyyaya) and hypothetical argument (tarka). Thus valid presentative knowledge (pramā) is a definite or certain (asandigdha), faithful or unerring (yathārtha), and non-reproductive experience (anubhava) of the object. My visual perception of the table before me is such knowledge (pramā) because in it the table is presented to me directly just as it really is, and I am certain about the truth of my cognition. Though memory is not pramā, as it is non-pressentative or a mere reproduction of past knowledge, it may also be valid or nonvalid, according as it is a reproduction of some previous

There are two main kinds of knowledge, anubhava and smṛti, each of which may be valid or non valid.

Definition of pramā.

---

1. *Vide Tarkasaṅgraha,* pp. 32-35, 82-84 *Tarkabhāṣā, p.* 29 ; *Tātparyṭīkā, 1.1.1. f.*

valid or non-valid presentative knowledge.[1]

Doubtful cognition cnanot be called pramā, because it is not certain knowledge. Error is undoubted knowledge indeed, and may also be presentative, but it is not true to the nature of its object. Sometimes we perceive a snake in a rope in the twilight and have then no doubt about the reality of what we see. Still this perception is erroneous, because it is not a true cognition of the object (yathārthā nubhava). Tarka is not pramā, since it does not give us any knowledge of objects. A tarka is like this : Looking out of the window of your class-room you see a mass of smoke rising from a distant house and say that the house has caught fire. A friend contradicts you and asserts that there is no fire. Now you argue : If there is no fire there cannot be smoke. This argument, starting with an 'if,' and exposing the absurdity of your friend's position, and thereby indirectly proving your own, is tarka. It is not pamā or valid presentative knowledge, because to argue like this is not to know the fire, but to confirm your previous inference of fire from smoke. That there is fire, you know by inference. To argue that if there is no fire there cannot be smoke, is not to know the fire as a real fact either by way of perception or by that of inference.

How true knowledge is distinguished from false knoledge.

The next question is : How is true knowledge distinguished from false knowledge? Knowledge is true when it agrees with or corresponds to the nature of its object, otherwise it becomes false. Your knowledge of the rose as red is true, if the rose has really a red colour as you judge it to have tadvati tatprakāraka). On the contrary, your impression of the crow as white is false, since the white colour does not really belong to the crow ; the white colour is ascribed to the crow in which it is absent (tadabhāvavatitatprakāraka). But then it may be asked : How do we know that the first knowledge is true

1. *Vide Tarkasaṅgraha*, p. 84. Some *Mīmāṁsakas* also exclude memory from pramā, on the ground that it does not give us any new knowledge. it is only a reproduction of some past experience and not a cognition of anything not known before (anadhigata).

and the second false? In other words : How do we test the truth or falsity of knowledge? The Naiyāyikas (also the Vaiśeṣikas, Jainas and Bauddhas) explain it in the following manner : Suppose you want a little more sugar for your morning tea and take a spoonful of it from the cup before you and put it into your tea. Now the tea tastes sweeter than before and you know that your previous perception of sugar was true. Sometimes, however, it happens that while looking for sugar, you find some white powdered substance and put a pinch of it into your mouth under the impression that it is sugar. But to your utter surprise and disappointment, you find that it is salt and not sugar. Here then we see that the truth and falsity of knowledge consist respectively in its correspondence and non-correspondence to fact. But the test of its truth or falsity consists in *inference* from the success or failure of our practical activities in relation to its object (pravṛttisāmarthya or pravṛttivisaṁvāda). True knowledge leads to successful practical activity while false knowledge ends in failure and disappointment.[1]

The tests of truth and error.

2. *Perception*

In Western logic the problem of perception as a source of knowledge has not been properly discussed. The reason probably is this. We generally believe, that what is given in perception must be true. Ordinarily, no man questions the truth of what he perceives by his senses. So it is thought that it is unnecessary, if not ridiculous, to examine the validity of perception, or to determine the conditions of perception as a source of valid knowledge. Indian thinkers are more critical than dogmatic in this respect, and make a thorough examination of perception in almost the same way as Western logicians discuss the problem of inference.

1. For a detailed account of the nature and forms of knowledge, and the tests of truth and error, *vide* S. C. Chatterjee, *The Nyāya Theory of knowledge,* Chaps. II, V.

(*i*) Definition of Perception

In logic perception is to be regarded as a form of true cognition. Taking it in this sense, some Naiyāyikas define perception as a definite cognition which is produced by sense-object contact and is true or unerring.[1] The perception of the table before me is due to the contact of my eyes with the table, and I am definite that the object is a table. The perception of a distant figure as either a man or a post is a doubtful and indefinite cognition, and, therefore, not a true perception. The perception of a snake in a piece of rope is definite but false ; and so it is different from valid perception.

Perception is a definite and true cognition of objects produced by sense-object contact.

The definition of perception as a cognition due to the stimulation of our sense organs by the perceived object is generally accepted by us. It is accepted also by many systems of philosophy, Indian and Western. Some Naiyāyikas, the Vedāntins and others, however, reject on the ground that there may be perception without sense-object contact. God, we are told, perceives all things, but has no senses. When I *see* a snake in a rope, there is really no snake to come in contact with my eyes. Mental states like the feelings of pleasure and pain are directly cognised or perceived by us without the help of any sense organ. All this shows that sense-object contact is not common to, and cannot, therefore, be a defining character of, perceptions. What, however, is really common to, and distinctive of, all perceptions is a feeling of *directness or immediacy* of the knowledge given by them. We are said to perceive an object, if and when we know it directly, *i.e.,* without taking the help of previous knowledge or any reasoning process (jñānākaraṇaka). If at midday you turn your eyes overhead,

Another definition of perception is that it is immediate cognition.

1. *Nyāya -sūtra*, 1.1.4.

you see the sun directly, and not by means of any process of inference or reasoning. There is neither any necessity nor any time for you to think and reason before the perception of the sun arises in you mind. So some Indian logicians propose to define perception as immediate cognition (sākṣāt pratīti), although they admit that perception is in almost all cases conditioned by sense-object contact.[1]

(*ii*) Classification of Perception[2]

Ordinary and extraordinary perception

There are different ways of classifying perception. First, we have the distinction between *laukika* or ordinary and *alaukika* or extraordinary perceptions. This distinction depends on the way in which the senses come in contact with their objects. We have *laukika* perception when there is the usual sense-contact with objects present to sense. In *alaukika* perception, however, the object is such as is not ordinarily present to sense, but is conveyed to sense through an unusual medium. Perception, again is of two kinds, namely, external (bāhya) and internal (mānasa). The former is due to the external senses of sight hearing, touch, taste and smell. The latter is brought about by the mind's contact with psychical states and processes. Thus we have six kinds of *laukika* or ordinary perceptions, *viz.*, the visual (cākṣuṣa) auditory (śrautra), tactual (spārśana), gustatory (rāsana), olfactory (ghrāṇaja), and the internal or mental (mānasa) perception. *Alaukika* or extraordinary perception is of three kinds, *viz.*, sāmānyalakṣaṇa, and jñānalakṣaṇa and yogaja.

External and internal perceptions.

1. *Vide Tarkabhāṣā*, p. 5 ; *Siddāntamuktāvali*, pp. 235-36 ; *Tattvacintā mani i*. pp. 539-43, 552.

2. *Vide Bhāṣāpariccheda and Muktāvali*, 52.

According to the Nyāya (also the Vaiśeṣika Mīmāṁsā, and Jaina), there are six organs of knowledge. Of these five are external and one is internal. The five external senses are the organs of smell (ghrāṇa), taste (rasanā), sight (cakṣuḥ), touch (tvak), and hearing (śrotra). These perceive respectively the physical qualities of smell, taste, colour, touch and sound. They are physical in nature and each of them is constituted by that very same physical element whose qualities are sensed by it. This seems to be suggested by the fact that in many case we use the same name for both the sense organ and the physical quality sensed by it. It is probably based on the principle that only like can perceive like. Mind (manas) is the internal organ which perceives such qualities of the soul as desire (icchā), aversion (dveṣa), striving or willing (prayatna), pleasure (sukha), pain (duḥkha) and cognition. It is not made of the material elements (bhūtas) like the external senses. It is not limited to the knowledge of any particular class of things or qualities but functions as a central and common organ in all kinds of knowledge. The Nyāya view of mind as an 'internal sense' (antarindriya) is accepted by the Vaiśeṣikas, the Sāṅkhyas, the Mīmāṁsakas and others. But some Vedāntins criticize and reject the Nyāya view of mind as an 'inner sense'.

The six organs of knowledge, *viz.* the five external senses and the internal sense manas.

(*iii*) Extraordinary Perception[1]

Alaukika or extraordinary perception is of three kinds. The first is called sāmānyalakṣaṇa. When we ask whether all men are mortal, the question raised is as to whether mortality is true, not of this or that man only, nor of all men who are dead and gone, but of all men in the past, present and future. But such a query persupposes *some* knowledge of the class of men. But the question is : How do we know the whole class of men ? We cannot know it by ordinary perception, since all men cannot be physically present to our senses. Yet we must somehow know *all* men. The Naiyāyika Explains this knowledge of the class by

1. *Op. sit.*, 63–65. For a fuller account, *vide* S. C. Chatterjee, *The Nyāya Theory of Knowledge* Ch. X.

extraordinary perception, in which the class *men* is presented through the class essence or the universal "manhood". When I perceive a man *as man*, I do perceive the manhood in him ; otherwise I cannot directly recognize him as man. Now this direct knowledge or perception of the universal *manhood* is the medium through which I perceive all men or the class of men. To perceive manhood is to perceive all men so far as they are possessed of the Universal "manhood". In short, to perceive manhood is to perceive all men as the individuals in which the universal "manhood" inheres. This perception of the class of men, being due to the perception of the universal (sāmānya), is called sāmānyalakṣaṇa perception and is marked off as extraordinary (alaukika) on account of its obvious difference from our ordinary perceptions.

The second is jñānalakṣaṇa or complication.

The second kind of extraordinary perception is called jñānalakṣaṇa. We often use such expressions as "ice looks cold", "the stone looks hard", "the grass looks soft", and so forth. This means that the coldness of ice, the hardness of a stone, the softness of luxuriant grass are perceived by us with our eyes. But the question is : How can the eyes perceive touch qualities, like hardness and softness, which can ordinarily be sensed only by the sense of touch? Among Western psychologists, Wundt, Ward and Stout explain such perceptions by "complication",[1] a process by which sensations or perceptions of different senses become so closely associated as to become integral parts of a single perception. Similarly, when on *seeing* something one says, "I *see* a piece of fragrant sandalwood", one has a perception of its fragrance by means of one's eyes. How can we explain this visual perception of fragrance which can be ordinarily sensed only by the sense of smell? The Naiyāyika says that here our past *olfactory* experience of fragrance as closely associated with the visual appearance of sandalwood since every time we smelt it we

1. Vide Stout, *Manual of Psychology*, p. 102 ; Wundt, *Human* and *Animal Psychology*, pp. 285-86 ; Ward, Article "Psychology," *Encyclopaedia Britannica*, 9th ed., Vol. XX, p. 57. *Cf* Woodworth, *Psychology* 9th ed., p. 115, where perception of the smell of roses shut in a glass-case and seen through the glass is cited as an example of hallucination.

saw its colour, unless that was in a dark room)is vividly revived and brings about the present *visual* perception of fragrance simultaneously with that of its colour. This present perception of fragrance, being due to the revived past *knowledge* of fragrance *(saurabhajñāna),* has been called Jñānalakṣaṇa perception, which is also extraordinary in the sense that it is brought about by a sense organ which is not ordinarily capable of perceiving fragrance. The Naiyāyikas also explain illusion, *e.g.,* of a snake in a rope, as a case of jñānalakṣaṇa perception.

The third is yogaja or intuitive perception of yogins.

The third kind of extraordinary perception is called yogaja. It is the intuitive perception of all objects – past and future, hidden and infinitesimal–by one who possesses some supernatural power generated in the mind by devout meditation (yogābhyāsa). In the case of those who have attained spiritual perfection (yukta), such intuitive knowledge of all objects is constant and spontaneous. In the case of others who are on the way to perfection (yuñjāna), it requires the help of concentration as an auxiliary condition.

(iv) Three Modes of Ordinary Perception[1]

There are three modes of ordinary perception.

According to another classification, ordinary perception is of two kinds, namely, nirvikalpaka or the indeterminate and savikalpaka or the determinate. Here the principle of classification is the more or less developed character of perceptual knowledge. To these two we may add pratyabhijñā or recognition. Keeping in view the nature of perception, the Naiyāyikas distinguish thus between three modes of ordinary perception. Extraordinary perception is always determinate, since it is definite and explicit knowledge.

1. Vide *Nyāya-bhāṣya* and *Tātparyaṭīka*, 1.1.4 : *Tarkabhāṣā,* p. 5 : *Nyāyalilāvati*, p. 53. For a detailed account, vide S. C. Chatterjee. *The Nyāya Theory of Knowledge,* Ch. IX.

Nirvikalpaka or indeterminate perception is the primary cognition of an object and its diverse characters without any judgment to interrelate them. Suppose you look at an orange placed on the other side of your table. Immediately after the first glance, or after the first moment of contact between your eyes and the object, you apprehend *something*, its colour, shape, etc., along with a general character called orangeness. But at first sight, you do not *think* of it *as* yellow or round, or *as* an orange. This kind of primary perception is called indeterminate perception. Suppose on the first day of your examination you enter the bath room engrossed in thinking about the possible questions and their answers. It is not unlikely that you may finish your bath without thinking of the water used by you *as water, as cold,* etc. Yet it cannot be said that you did not perceive the water. But for a very real perception of it, your act of bathing cannot be explained. This perception of water and its characters, without any thought or *judgment* of it *as water, as liquid, as cold,* etc., is the nirvikalpaka or indeterminate perception of it.

The first is nirvikalpaka, which is cognition of things without any explicit interrelation or characterization.

Savikalpaka perception is the cognition of an object *as possessed* of some character. While nirvikalpaka is the cognition of the existence of a thing as such, savikalpaka may be said to be the recognition of its nature. Thus when, looking at the orange, I judge within myself "this is an orange", "this is round, red, etc". I do not only cognise the unrelated elements as such, but also explicitly relate them. Here the existent fact, *this*, becomes the subject of proposition and orangeness, etc., are related to it as predicates. Thus we may say that nirvikalpaka is an indeterminate apprehension, and savikalpaka a determinate, predicative judgment. There could not be any savikalpaka perception of an object without a previous nirvikalpaka perception of it. Unless we first knew the unrelated elements *as such*, we could not possibly know them *as* related. Unless I first perceive water, coldness, liquidity, etc., I cannot come to know it *as water* or *as cold*, or *as liquid,* etc.

The second is savikalpaka, in which the object is judged as possessed of some character.

Pratyabhijñā is recognition in its literal meaning. It is a *re-cognition* of some object, *i.e.*, a cognition of it as that which was cognised before. In it we know immediately that the thing which we now cognise is the same as that which was cognised before, as when one says : "This must be the same man who helped me into the tram-car yesterday." It should be remarked here that the distinctions of nirvikalpaka perception, savikalpaka perception, and pratyabhijñā have not been recognized, or recognized in the same way, in all the systems of Indian philosophy. While the Vaiseśika, the Sāṅkhya and the Mīmāṁsā systems accept, on the whole, the Nyāya view as explained here, the Bauddha and the Advaita Vedānta systems reject it and hold very different views.

The third is pratyabhijñā, which is the cognition of an object as what was cognised before.

3. *Inference*

(*i*) Definition of Inference

After perception comes anumāna or inference. Anumāna (anu –after, māna – knowledge) literally means a cognition or knowledge which follows someother knowledge. Take the following ilustrations : "The hill is fiery, because it smokes and whatever smokes is fiery ;" "Devadatta is mortal, because he is a man, and all men are mortal." In the first example, we pass from the perception of smoke in the hill to the knowledge of the existence of fire in it, on the ground of our previous knowledge of the universal relation between smoke and fire. In the second example we know the mortality of Devadatta which is not now perceived, from the presence of manhood in him. Thus we see that inference is a process of reasoning in which we pass from the apprehension of some mark (liṅga) to that of something else, by virtue of a relation of invariable concomitance (vyāpti) between the two. As Dr. B. N. Seal puts it : "Anumāna (inference) is the

Inference is the process of knowing something not by observation, but through the medium of a mark that is invariably related to it.

process of ascertaining, not by perception or direct observation, but through the instrumentality or medium of a mark, that a thing possesses a certain character."[1]

(*ii*) The constituents of Inference[2]

Inference has three terms and at least three propositions.

From the definition of inference it will appear that an inference must have as its constituents three terms and at least three propositions. In inference we arrive at the knowledge of some character of a thing through the knowledge of some mark and that of its universal relation to the inferred character. Thus in the above inference of fire we know the unperceived fire in the hill through the perception of smoke in it and the knowledge of an invariable relation between smoke and fire. There is, first, the knowledge or apprehension of smoke as a mark in the hill. Secondly, there is a recollection of the relation of invariable concomitance between smoke and fire, as we have observed it in the past. Thirdly, we have the resulting knowledge of the existence of the unperceived fire in the hill. Now in this inference the hill is the paksa (minor term), since it is the subject under consideration in the course of the inferential reasoning. Fire is the sādhya (major term), as that is something which we want to prove or establish in relation to the hill by means of this inference. Smoke is the liṅga (middle term), as it is the mark or sign which indicates the presence of fire. It is also called the hetu or sādhana, *i. e.* the reason or ground of inference. Thus corresponding to the minor, major and middle terms of the syllogism, inference, in Indian logic, contains three terms, namely, pakṣa, sādhya, and hetu. The pakṣa is the subject with which we are concerned in any inference. The sādhya is the object which we want to know in relation to the pakṣa or the infereable character of

Pakṣa is the minor term, sādhya the major term, and sādhana the middle term of anumāna or inference.

1. *The Positive Sciences of the Ancient Hindus*, p. 250.
2. Vide *Muktāvali*, 66-67.

the pakṣa. The hetu is the reason for our relating the sādhya to the pakṣa. It is the ground of our knowledge of the sādhya as related to the pakṣa.

The three steps and propositions in an inference.

In order of the events which take place when a certain thinker is inferring; the first step in inference is the apprehension of the hetu (smoke) in the pakṣa (hill), the second, recollection of the universal relation between hetu and sādhya (smoke and fire), and the last is the cognition of the sādhya (fire) as related to the pakṣa (hill). But as a matter of formal statemnet or verbal expression, the first step in inference is the predication of the sādhya with regard to the pakṣa, *e.g.*, "The hill is fiery." The second is the affirmation of the hetu as related to the pakṣa, *e.g.*, "Because the hill is smoky." The third is the affirmation of the hetu as invariably related to the sādhya, *e. g.*, "Wherever there is smoke, there is fire, as in the kitchen." Thus in inference we must have at least three propositions, all of which are categorical and one must be affirmative and the others may be affirmative or negative. The first proposition corresponds to the conclusion of the syllogism, the second to the minor premise, and the third to the major premise. Thus inference, in Indian logic, may be said to be a syllogism consisting of three categorical propositions. But the order of the propositions is reversed in Indian logic, in so far as it puts the conclusion of the syllogism first, and its usual major premise last, in the formal statement of an inference.

Indian and Western forms of the syllogism.

Indian logicians are agreed that so far as inference is svārtha or for oneself, it requires no formal statement by way of a number of propositions. It is only in the case of inference which is parārtha, *i.e.*, meant to prove or demonstrate some truth, that we require to state an inference in the form of a rigorous chain of argument without any gap. This is the logical form of an infernce. We may say that in Indian logic inference corresponds roughly, in respect of its form, to the categorical syllogism of Western logic. But there are certain important differences between the Indian and Western forms of the syllogism. In Western logic, the syllogism is generally stated in the form of three propositions, of which the first is the major premise, the second is the minor premise, and the last is the conclusion. According to the Naiyāyikas, however, inference, as a conclusive proof, must be stated in the form of five propositions, called its avayavas or members. These are pratijñā, hetu, udāharaṇa, upanaya, and nigamana.[1] The five-membered syllogism may be thus illustrated :

(1) Ram is mortal (pratijñā) ;

(2) Because he is a man (hetu) ;

(3) All men are mortal, *e.g.*, Socrates, Kant, Hegel (udāharaṇa) ;

(4) Ram also is a man (upanaya) ;

(5) Therefore he is mortal (nigamana).

The pratijñā is the first proposition, which asserts something. The hetu is the second proposition, which states the reason for this assertion. The udāharaṇa is the universal proposition, showing the connection between the reason and the asserted fact, as supported by known instances. Upanaya is the application of the universal proposition to the present case. Nigamana is the conclusion which follows from the preceding propositions.[2]

(*iii*) The Grounds of Inference[3]

There are two conditions of an inference.

Now we come to the consideration of vyāpti or invariable concomitance between the middle term and the major term, which is the logical ground of inference. In inference our knowledge of the sādhya (fire) as related to the pakṣa (hill) depends on the previous

1. Vide *Tarkabhāsā*, pp. 48-49. For a critical discussion of the logical form of inference, *vide* S. C. Chatterjee, *The Nyāya Theory of Knowledge* Ch. XIII.

2. The Mīmāṁsakas and Vedāntins hold that the first three or the last three propositions suffice for inference.

3. Vide *Tarkabhāsā*, pp, 7 f.; *Tarhasaṅgraha*, pp. 43 f.; *Bhāsāpariccheda* and *Muktāvali*, pp. 137-38 ; *Sarvadarsan* Ch. II ; *Paribhāṣā*, Ch. II.

knowledge of the hetu (smoke as connected with the pakṣa on the one hand, and universally related to the sādhya on the other. We infer that there is fire in the hill, because we see that there is smoke in the hill and know that smoke is always accompained by fire. It appears, therefore, that an inference has two conditions. The first is a cognition of the hetu or middle term (smoke) in the pakṣa or minor term (the hill). The second is the relation of invariable concomitance between the middle and the major term. That there is fire in the hill is a conclusion which we can justify only if we know that there is an invariable concomitance between the hill smoke and fire. This relation of invariable concomitance between the hetu and the sādhya, or the middle term and the major term of inference is technically called vyāpti, and is regarded as the logical ground of inference, since it guarantees the truth of the conclusion. So the questions we are to consider now, are; What is vyā pti? How is vyāpti known by us?

Vyāpti is the logical condition of inference.

With regard to the first question, we have to say that vyāpti literally means the state of pervasion. It implies a correlation between two facts, of which one is pervaded (vyāpya), and the other pervades (vyāpaka). A fact is said to *pervade* another when it always accompaines the other. A fact is said to be pervaded by another when it is always accompained by the other. In this sense smoke is pervaded by fire since it is always accompained by fire, or all smoky objects are fiery. But while all smoky objects are fiery, all fiery objects are not smoky, *e.g.*, the red-hot iron ball. A vyāpti between terms of unequal extension, such as smoke and fire, is called asamavyāpti or viṣamavyāpti. It is a relation of non-equipollent concomitance between two terms, from one of which we may infer the other, but not *vice versa.* We may infer fire from smoke, but not smoke from fire. As distinguished from this, a vyāpti between two terms of equal extension is called samabyāpti or equipollent concomitance. Here the vyāpti holds between two terms which are co-extensive, so that we may infer either of them

There are two kinds of vyāpti.

from the other, *e.g.*, 'nameable' and 'knowable'. Whatever is nameable is knowable, and *vice versa*.

For any inference the minimum condition is some kind of vyāpti between the middle and the major term. This satisfies the fundamental law of syllogistic inference that one of the premises must be universal. Now the vyāpti between the middle and the major term means generally a relation of co-existence (sāhacarya) between the two, *e.g.* "Wherever there is smoke, there is fire." Every case of co-existence, however, is not a case of vyāpti. In many instances fire may co-exist with smoke. Still there is no vyāpti or universal relation between fire and smoke, since there may be fire without smoke. The reason is that in such cases the relation of co-existence is dependent on certain conditions (upādhi) other than the terms related. Thus the presence of smoke in fire is conditioned by wet fuel (ārdrendhana). So we are to say that vyāpti is that relation of co-existence between the middle and the major term which is independent of all conditions. It is an invariable and unconditional relation of concomitance (niyata anaupādhika saṁbandha) between the middle and the major term.

Vyāpti is an invariable and unconditional relation of concomitance between the middle and the major term.

The second question is : How is vyāpti known? How do we get a universal proposition like "all smoky objects are fiery", or "all men are mortal"? This is the problem of induction. For the Cārvākas, who are radical empiricists, there is no problem, because there is no inference as a source of true knowledge. All the other systems of Indian philosophy which admit the validity of inference try to slove this problem in some way or other. The Buddhists base the knowledge of universal propossitions on the pricipales of causality and essential endentity, which they regard as *a priori* and necessary principles of human thought and action. If two things are related as cause and effect, we know that they are universally related, for there cannot be any effect without its cause. To determine the casual relation between

Different methods of ascertaining vyāpti.

The Buddhist method.

them, the Buddhists adopt the method of pañcakāranī which is as fllows : (*a*) neither the cause nor the effect is perceived (*b*) the cause is perceived, (*c*) immediately, the effect is perceived, (*d*) the cause disappears, (*e*) immediately, the effect disappears. Similarly, if two things are essentially identical, (*i.e.*, possess a common essence) they must be universally related. All men are animals, because animality belongs to the essence of both, and men without animality will not be men.

The Vedāntin's method.

The Vedāntins hold that vyāpti or the universal proposition is the result of an induction by simple enumeration. It is derived from the uncontradicted experience of agreement in presence between two things. When we find that two things go together or co-exist, and that there is no exception to their relation (vyabhicārādarśane sati sahacāradarśanam) we may take them as univarsally related.

The Nyāya method which includes —

The Naiyāyikas agree with the Vedāntins in holding that vyāpti is established by the uncontradicted experience of the relation between two things, and not on any *a priori* principle like causality or essential identity. They, however, go further than the Vedāntins and supplement uncontradicted experience of the relation between two facts by tarka or indirect proof and by sāmānyalakṣaṇa perception, the Nyāya method of induction or generalisation may be analysed into the following steps : First we observe that there is a relation of agreement in presence (anvaya) between two things, or that in all cases in which one is present, the other also is present, *e.g.*, wherever there is smoke, there is fire.

(*a*) anvaya,

Secondly, we see that there is uniform agreement in absence (vyatireka) between them, *e.g.*, wherever there is no fire, there is no smoke. These two steps taken together correspond very well to Mill's Joint Method of Agreement in presence and in absence.

(*b*) vyatireka,

Thirdly, we do *not* observe any contrary instance in which one of them is present without the other (vyabhicārāgraha). From this

(*c*) vyabhicārāgraha,

we may conclude that there must be a natural relation of invariable concomitance between the two things.

Still we cannot be sure if the relation in question is unconditional or free from upādhis, which a real vyāpti must be. Hence the fourth step of the inductive method is elimination of upādhis or conditions on which the relation may possibly be dependent (upādhinirāsa). I put on the switch and there is light ; if I do not, there is no light. From this if anybody concludes that there is a vyāpti or invariable relation between switching on and lighting the room, then he would commit the mistake of ignoring the upādhi or condition, *viz.*, the electric current, in the presence of which alone there can be light. This upādhi, *viz.*, electric current, must be present when there is light, but it may not be present wherever there is switching on. So an upādhi is defined as a term which is co-extensive with the major (sādhyasamavyāpta) but not with the middle term of an inference (avyāptasādhana). Taking the stock example, when one infers the existence of smoke from fire, one relies on the conditional relation of fire to smoke, since fire is attended with smoke on the condition of its being fire from "wet fuel".[1] It will be seen here that the condition "wet fuel" is always related to the major term "smoky", but not so related to the middle term "fire", as there are cases of fire without "wet fuel". Hence to eliminate the suspected conditions of an invariable relation between two things we must make repeated observation (bhūyodarśana) of their agreement in presence and in absence under varying circumstances. If in the course of this process we see that there is no material circumstance which is present or absent just when the major term is present or absent, we are to understand that its concomitance with the middle term is unconditional. In this way we can exclude all the suspected conditions of a relation of invariable concomitance between

(*d*) upādhinirāsa,

1. The inference is like this : "Whatever is fiery is smoky ; X is fiery ; therefore X is smoky." Here the conclusion is contradicted by the red-hot iron ball, lighting, etc. The reason is that the relation of the middle "fiery" to the major "smoky" is conditional on its being fiery from "wet fuel."

the middle and the major term and say that it is a relation of vyāpti or invariable and unconditional concomitance.

But there is still room for a sceptical doubt about the vyāpti or universal proposition thus arrived at. It may be urged by a sceptic like Hume or the Cārvāka that so far as our past and present experience is concerned, there is no exception to the uniform relation of concomitance between smoke and fire. But there is no knowing whether this relation hold good in distant regions, like the planets, or will hold good in the remote future. To end this sceptical doubt, the Naiyāyikas try next to fortify the induction by tarka. The proposition "all smoky objects are firery" may be indirectly proved by a tarka like this : If this proposition is false, then its contradictory, "some smoky objects are not fiery", must be true. This means that there may be smoke without fire. But this supposition is contradicted by the law of universal causation, for to say that there may be smoke without fire is just to say that there may be an effect without a cause (since fire is the only known cause of smoke). If any one has the obstinacy to say that sometimes there may be effect without causes, he must be silenced by reference to the practical contradictions (vyāghāta) involved in his position. If there can be an effect without a cause, why seek for fire to smoke your cigar or to cook our food ? This process of indirect proof in the Nyāya may be said to correspond roughly to the method of *reductio ad absurdum* in Western logic.

(e) tarka

Although the Naiyāyikas take great pains to establish vyāpti or universal proposition on the ground of the observation of particular facts, still they feel that a generalisation from particulars as mere particulars cannot give us that certainty which we claim when we lay down a general proposition like "*all* men are mortal". We find it less difficult to think of a crow which is not black, than to think of a man who is not mortal. Just as a cuckoo may be black or grey and spotted, so crows may be black or dark, grey or brown. We cannot, however, seriously and honestly think of ourselves as immortal, and

(f) sāmānyalakṣaṇa perception.

regulate our prractical activities accordingly. Why this difference in the sense of security or certainty? The answer that naturally suggests itself and that not unreasonably is that while there is nothing in the *nature* of a crow to prevent it from being grey or brown, there seems to be something in the *nature* of a man that makes him mortal. We say that all crows are black, not because they cannot be otherwise, but because they *happen* to be so, as far as we have seen. On the other hand, we say that all men are mortal because they are men, *i.e.*, because they possess some essential nature, manhood, which is related to mortality. This becomes clear when we say that "A,B,C are mortal, not because they are A, B, C but because they are men". It follows from this that an inductive generalisation must be ultimately based on the knowledge of the essential nature of things, *i.e.*, the class-essence or the universal in them. Hence it is that the Naiyāyikas finally establish an induction by sāmānyalakṣaṇa perception.[1] They hold that a universal proposition like "all men are mortal", or "all smoky objects are fiery", must be due to the perception of the universal "manhood" as related to "mortality", or that of "smokeness" as related to "fireness". It is only when we perceive "manhood" as related to mortality that we can say that *all* men are mortal, for to perceive "manhood" is to perceive all men so far as they are *man-as-such*, and not this or that man. So we may say that the essence of induction is not an *inference* of the form "some men are mortal ; therefore, all men are mortal". This is not a logically valid inference, because there is an obvious illicit distribution of the subject term *men*. On the other hand, induction is a process of generalisation from the particulars of experience through the knowledge of the classessences or universals underlying such particulars.[2]

1. Vide *Muktāvali*, p. 280, *Tattvacintāmaṅi,* ii. pp. 153-54.

2. For a somewhat similar theory of induction the reader may be referred to R. M. Eaton, *General Logic,* Part IV; A. N. Whitehead, *Process and Reality,* Part II, Ch. IX, Sections VI-Viii. Vide *The Nyāya Theory of Knowledge,* Chaps. X, XII, for a fuller account.

(*iv*) The Classification of Inference

As we have seen before, inference is, in Indian logic, a combined deductive-inductive reasoning consisting of at least three categorical propositions. All inferences are thus pure syllogisms of the categorical type which are at once formally valid and materially true. Hence we have not here a classification of inferences into deductive and inductive immediate and mediate, syllogistic and non-syllogistic, pure and mixed types. The Naiyāyikas give us three different classifications of inferences which we shall now consider. According to the first classification, inference is of two kinds, namely, svārtha and parārtha. This is a psychological classification which has in view the use or purpose which an inference serves. An inference may be intended either for the acquisition of some knowledge on our part or for the demonstration of a known truth to other persons. In the first case we have svārthānumāna or inference for oneself. In the second, we have parārthānumāna or inference meant for others. The first is illustrated by a man who first perceives a mass of smoke in the hill, then remembers that there is a universal relation between smoke and fire, and finally infers that there is fire in the hill. On the other hand, an inference is parārtha when in making it a man aims at proving or demonstrating the truth of the conclusion to other men. This is illustrated when a man, having inferred or known the existence of fire in a hill, tries to convince another man who doubts or questions the truth of his knowledge, and argues like this: "The hill must be fiery ; because it smokes ; and whatever is smoky is fiery *e.g.* the kitchen : so also the hill is smoky ; therefore, it is fiery."[1]

Inference is svārtha or parārtha according as it is meant for oneself or for others.

According to another classification, we have three kinds of inference, namely, pūrvavat, śesavat and sāmānyatodrṣṭa.[2] This classification has reference to the nature of the vyāpti or universal relation between the middle and the major term. While

It is pūrvavat or śesavat, according as it passes from cause to effect, or from effect to cause.

1. Vide *Tarkasaṅgrāha,* pp. 46-49.
2. Vide *Nyāya -sūtra* and *Bhāṣya,* 1-1.5.

pūrvavat and śeṣavat inferences are based on causal uniformity, the last is based on non-causal uniformity. A cause is defined as the invariable and unconditional antecedent of an effect. Conversely, an effect is the invariable and unconditional consequent of a cause.[1] Accordingly, a pūrvavat inference is that in which we infer the unperceived effect from a perceived cause, *e.g.* the inference of future rain from the appearance of dark heavy clouds in the sky. A śeṣavat inference is that in which we infer the unperceived cause from a perceived effect *e.g.* the inference of past rain from the swift muddy current of the river. In these two kinds of inference, the vyāpti or universal relation between the middle and the major term is a uniform relation of causality between them. They are thus dependent on what is known as "scientific induction." In

It is sāmānyatodṛṣṭa when based on certain observed points of general similarity between objects of experience.

sāmānyatodṛṣṭa inference, however the vyāpti or universal relation between the middle and the major term does not depend on a causal uniformity. The middle term is related to the major neither as a cause nor as an effect. We infer the one from the other not because we know them to be casually connected, but because they are uniformly related in our experience. This is illustrated when, on seeing the different positions of the moon at long intervals, we infer that it moves, although the motion might not have been perceived by us. In the case of other things, whenever we perceive change of position, we perceive motion also. From this we infer motion in the moon, although the movement of the planet is not perceived. Similarly, we may infer the cloven hoof of an unknown animal simply by seeing its horns. These inferences depend not on a causal connection, but on certain observed points of general similarity between different objects of experience. Sāmānyatodṛṣṭa

---

1. Vide *Tarkabhāṣā*, p. 2 ; *Tarkasaṅgraha* and *Tarka-dīpikā*, pp. 35-36.

inference is thus similar to analogical argument.[1]

A third classification gives us the three kinds of kevalānvayi kevalovyatireki and anvayavyatireki inferences.[2] This classification is more logical in as much as it is based on the nature of the induction by which we get the knowledge of vyāpti,on which inferences depend. An inference is called kevalānvayi when it is based on a middle term which is *only positively* related to the major term. Hence the knowledge of vyāpti between the middle and the major term is arrived at only through the method of agreement in presence (anvaya), since there is no negative instance of their agreement in absence. This is illustrated by the following inference :

Inference is called kevalānvayi when based on a middle term which is only positively related to the major term.

All knowable objects are nameable :
The pot is a knowable object ;
Therefore the pot is nameable.

In this inference the major premise is a universal affirmative proposition in which the predicate "nameable" is affirmed of all knowable objects. It is not really possible for us to deny the predicate with regard to the subject and say that here is a knowable object which is not nameable, because we have at least to speak of it as an object. The minor premise and the conclusion of this inference are also universal affirmative propositions and cannot be otherwise. Hence, in its logical form, this inference is a syllogism of the first mood of the first figure, technically called Barbara.

---

1. According to another interpretation, pūrvavat inference is that which is based on previous experience of the concomitance between two things and śeṣavat is pariśesa or inference by elimination, *e.g.*sound is a quality, because it cannot be a substance or an activity or anything else.

2. Vide *Tarkasaṅgraha,* pp. 51-52, *Bhāṣāpariccheda* and *Muktāvali* pp. 142-43.

It is kevalavyatireki when the middle term is only negatively related to the major.

A kevalavyatireki inference is that in which the middle term is *only negatively* related to the major term. It depends on a vyāpti between the absence of the major term and that of the middle term. Accordingly, the knowledge of vyāpti is here arrived at only through the method of agreement in absence (vyatireka), since there is no positive instance of agreement in presence between the middle and the major term excepting the minor term. This is illustrated thus by the Naiyāyikas :

What is not different-from-other-elements has no smell ;
The earth has smell ;
Therefore the earth is different-from-other-elements.[1]

In this inference the major premise is a universal negative proposition in which the predicate of the middle term "smell" is denied of the subject or the negative of the major term "different-from-other-elements". It is not possible for us to affirm the predicate "smell" of any other subject excepting the earth which is the minor term of the inference. Hence the only way in which we can relate the middle to the major is the negative way of saying that "what is not different from the other elements has no smell." Hence the major premise is a universal negative proposition arrived at only through the method of agreement in absence between the major and the middle term. The minor premise is an affirmative proposition. But although one of the premises is negative, the conclusion is affirmative, which is against the general canons of the syllogism in Formal Logic. Hence we are to say that this inference is not any of the valid moods of syllogism recognized by Formal Logic, nor should we forcibly convert the conclusion into a negative proposition. But the validity of such an inference has been admitted by Bradley as a special case of negative reasoning.[2]

1. Another example of such inference would be : The sun is different from other planets, since it is stationary, and what is not different from other planets is not stationary.

2. *Cf. Bradley, Principles of Logic,* Vol. I, pp. 274-83.

An inference is called anvayavyatireki when its middle term is both positively and negatively related to the major term. In it there is a vyāpti or universal relation between the middle and the major term in respect of both their presence and absence. So the knowledge of the vyāpti or the universal proposition is based on the Joint Method of agreement in presence (anvaya) and in absence (vyatireka). The universal proposition is affirmative when it is the result of the observation of positive instances of agreement in presence, and negative when based on the observation of negative instances of agreement in absence, between the middle and the major term. The difference between the universal affirmative and negative propositions (anvaya and vyatirekavyāpti) is that the subject of the affirmative proposition becomes predicate and the condradictory of the predicate becomes subject in the corresponding negative proposition. Hence anvayavyatireki inference may be based on both universal affirmative and universal negative propositions. It is illustrated in the following pair of inferences :

It is anvayavyatireki when the middle term is both positively and negatively related to the major term.

(1) All smoky objects are fiery ;
The hill is smoky ;
Therefore the hill is fiery.

(2) No non-fiery object is smoky ;
The hill is smoky ;
Therefore the hill is fiery.

(v) The Fallacies of Inference[1]

Fallacies in Indian logic are all material fallacies.

The fallacies of inference (hetvābhāsa) in Indian logic are all material fallacies. So far as the logical form of inference is concerned, it is the same for all inferences. There is, strictly speaking, no fallacious form of inference in logic since all inferences must be put in one or other of the valid forms. Hence if there is any fallacy of inference, that must be due to the material conditions on which the truth of the constituent premises depends. It may be observed here that in the Aristotelian classification of fallacies into those *in dictione* and those *extra dictionem* there is no mention of the formal fallacies of inference like the undistributed middle, the illicit process of the major or minor term, and so forth. The reason for this, as Faton[2] rightly points out, is that "to one trained in the arts of syllogistic reasoning, they are not sufficiently persuasive to find a place even among sham arguments." As for Aristotle's fallacies *in dictione, i.e.,* those that occur through the ambiguous use of words, they are all included by the Naiyāyika among the fallacies of *chala, jāti* and *nigrahasthāna* with their numerous subdivisions.

There are five kinds of material fallacies.

In Indian Logic, a material fallacy is technically called *hetvābhāsa,* a word which literally means a hetu or reason which *appears as*, but really is not, a valid reason. The material fallacies being ultimately due to such fallacious reasons, the Naiyāyikas consider all these as being cases of hetvābhāsa. Accoring to the Naiyāyikas, there are five kinds of material fallacies. These are (1) Savyabhicāra (2)

1. Vide *Tarkasaṅgraha,* pp. 54-60
2. *General Logic,* p. 334.

Viruddha, (3) Satpratipakṣa, (4) Asiddha, (5) Bādhita.[1]

The first kind of fallacy is called savyabhicāra or irregular middle. To illustrate :

The first is called savyabhicāra or the irregular middle.

All bipeds are rational ;
Swans are bipeds ;
Therefore swans are rational.

The conclusion of this inference is false. But why ? Because the middle term 'biped' is not uniformly related to the major 'rational.' It is related to both rational and non-rational creatures. Such a middle term is called savyabhicāra or the irregular middle.

The savyabhicāra hetu or the irregular middle is found to lead to no one single conclusion, but to different opposite conclusions. This fallacy occurs when the ostensible middle term violates the general rule of inference, namely, that it must be universally related to the major term, or that the major term must be present in all cases in which the middle is present. The savyabhicāra middle, however, is not uniformly concomitant with the major term. It is related to both the existence and the non-existence of the major term, and is, therefore, also called *anaikāntika* or an inconstant concomitant of the major term. Hence from such a middle term we can infer both the existence and the non-existence of the major term. To take another illustration :

All knowable objects are fiery;
The hill is knowable ;
Therefore the hill is fiery ;

Here the middle 'knowable' is indifferently related to both fiery objects like the kitchen, and fireless objects like the lake. All knowables being thus not fiery, we cannot argue that a hill is fiery because it is knowable. Rather, it is as much true to say that, for the same reason, the hill is fireless.

1. *Vide The Nyāya Theory of Knowledge,* Ch, XIV, for a detailed account of the fallacies.

The second kind of fallacy is called viruddha or the contradictory middle. Take this inference : "Air is heavy, because it is empty." In this inference the middle term 'empty' is contradictory because it disproves the heaviness of air. Thus the viruddha or the contradictory middle is one which disproves the very proposition which it is meant to prove. This happens when the ostensible middle term, instead of proving the existence of the major, in the minor, which is intended by it, proves its non-existence therein. Thus to take the Naiyāyikas illustration, if one argues, "Sound is eternal, because it is caused," we have a fallacy of the viruddha or contradictory middle. The middle term, 'caused' does not prove the eternality of sound, but its non-eternality, because whatever is caused is non-eternal. The distinction between the savybhicāra and the viruddha is that while the former only fails to prove the conclusion, the latter disproves it or proves the contradictory proposition.

The second is viruddha or the contradictory middle.

The third kind of fallacy is called satpratipakṣa or the inferentially contradicted middle. This fallacy arises when the ostensible middle term of an inference is validly contradicted by other middle term which proves the non-existence of the major term of the first inference.Thus the inference "sound is eternal, because it is audible" is validly contradicted by another inference like this : "sound is *non*-eternal, because it is produced like a pot." Here the non-existence of *eternality* (which is the major term of the first inference) is proved by the second inference with its middle term 'produced' as against the first inference with its middle 'audible.' The distinction between the viruddha and the satpratipaksa is that, while in the former the middle *itself* proves the contradictory of its conclusion, in the latter the contradictory of the conclusion is proved by another inference based on *another* middle term.

The third is satpratipakṣa or the inferentially contradicted middle

The fourth kind of fallacy is called asiddha or sādhyasama, *i.e.* the unproved middle. The sādhyasama middle is one which is not yet proved, but requires *to be proved*, like the sādhya or the major term. This means that the sādhyasama middle is not a proved or an established fact, but an *asiddha* or unproved assumption. The fallacy

The fourth is asiddha or the unproved middle.

of the asiddha occurs when the middle term is wrongly assumed in any of the premises, and so cannot be taken to prove the truth of the conclusion. Thus when one argues, "the sky-lotus is fragrant because it has *lotusness* in it like a natural lotus," the middle has no *locus standi,* since the sky-lotus is non-existent, and is, therefore, asiddha or a merely assumed but not proved fact.

The fifth is called bādhita or the non-inferentially contradicted middle.

The last kind of fallacy is called bādhita or the non-inferentially contradicted middle. It is the ostensible middle term of an inference, the non-existence of whose major is ascertained by means of some *other pramāṇa* or source of knowledge. This is illustrated by the argument : "Fire is *cold*, because it is a substance." Here 'coldness' is the sādhya or major term, and 'substance' is the middle term. Now the non-existence of coldness, may more, the existence of hotness is perceived in fire by our sense of touch. So we are to reject the middle 'substance' as a contradicted middle. The fallacy of satpratipakṣa, as explained before, is different from this fallacy of bādhita, because in the former one inference is contradicted by another inference, while in the latter an inference is contradicted by perception or some other *non-inferential* source of knowledge. Another example of bādhita would be : Sugar is sour, because it produces acidity.

4. Upamāna or Comparison

Upamāna is the process of naming objects through a given description.

Upamāna is the third source of valid knowledge accepted by the Nyāya. It is the source of our knowledge of the relation between a name and things so named or between a word and its denotation (sañjñāsañjñisaṁbandha). We have such knowledge when we are told by some authoritative person that a word denotes a class of objects of a certain description and then, on the basis of the given description, apply the word to some object or objects which fit in with that description, although we might not have seen them before. For example, a man, who does not know what a gavaya[1] or wild cow is, may be told by a forester that it is an animal like the cow. If

1. In some parts of India, the 'gavaya' is more commonly known as nilgai.

subsequently he happens to meet with such an animal in the forest and knows or recognizes it *as a gavaya,* then his knowledge will be due to upamāna or comparison.[1] A boy who does not know what a jackdaw is, may be told by you that it is like a crow, but of bigger size and glazy black colour. When next he sees a jackdaw and says, 'this must be a jackdaw,' we know that he has learnt the denotation of the word. To take another example from Dr. L. S. Stebbing,[2] suppose you do not know what "saxophone" means. You may be told by a musician : "A saxophone is a musical instrument something like U-shaped trumpet." If, on subsequently seeing a saxophone, you are able to give its name, it will be clear that you understand what "saxophone" means. Now, upamāna is just this way of knowing the denotation of words, or the relation between names and the objects denoted by them. The grounds of our knowledge in upamāna are a given description of the objects to be known and a perception of their similarity, etc. to the familiar objects mentioned in the description. A man recognizes a gavaya *as such* just when he perceives its similarity of the cow and remembers the description, "the gavaya is an animal resembling the cow."[3]

Other systems on the nature of upamāna.

That upamāna or comparison, as explained by the Naiyāyikas, is a distinct source of valid knowledge, has not been recognized in the other systems of Indian philosophy. The Cārvākas[4] contend that upamāna is not a pramāṇa at all, since it cannot give us any true knowledge about the denotation of words as maintained by the Naiyāyikas. The Buddhist logicians recognize upamāna as a form of valid knowledge, but they reduce it to perception and testimony, so that we do not require a separate source of knowledge

1. Vide *Tarkasaṅgraha,* pp. 62-63
2. *Modern Introduction to Logic,* p. 13
3. Vide *Nyāya-bhāṣya* 1.1.6 ; Nyāyamañjarī, pp. 141-42.
4. Vide *Nyāya -sūt.* and *Bhāṣya,* 2.1.42

like upamāna.[1] So also, the Vaiśeṣika[2] and the Sāṅkhya[3] system explain upamāna as a form of inference, and therefore, neither a distinct type or knowledge nor an independent way of knowing. The jainas[4] reduce upamāna to pratyabhijñā or racognition. While recognizing upamāna as a separate source of knowledge, the Mīmā ṁsakas[5] and the Vedāntins[6] explain it in a different way which will be considered under the Mīmāṁsā.[7]

5. *Śabda or Testimony*

(*i*) The Nature and Classification of Śabda

Śabda consists in understanding the meaning of the statement of a trust worthy person.

Śabda is the last pramāṇa accepted by the Nyāya. Literally śabda means verbal knowledge. It is the knowledge of objects derived from words or sentences. All verbal knowledge, however, is not valid. Hence śabda, as a pramāṇa, is defined in the Nyāya as valid verbal testimony. It consists in the assertion of a trustworthy person.[8] A verbal statement is valid when it comes from a person who knows the truth and speaks the truth about anything for the guidance of other person.[9] But it is a matter of common observation that a sentence or statement is not by itself sufficient to give us any knowledge of things. Nor again does the mere perception of the words of a sentence leads to any knowledge about objects. It is only when one perceives the words and *understands* their meanings that he acquires any knowledge from a verbal statement. Hence while the validity of verbal knowledge depends on its being based on the statement of a

1. Vide *Nyāyavārttika,*1.1.6.
2. Vide *Tarkasaṅgraha* and *Dīpikā*, p. 63.
3. *Tattvakaumudi,* p. 5.
4. *Prameyakamalamārtaṇḍa,* Ch. III.
5. *Sāstradīpikā*, pp. 74-76.
6. *Vedanta -Paribhāṣā,* Ch. III.
7. Vide *The Nyāya Theory of Knowledge,* Ch. XVI, for a critical discussion of upamāna as a distinct source of knowledge.
8. *Nyāya -sūt*, 1.1.7.
9. *Tārkikarakṣā*, pp. 94-95.

trustworthy person, its possibility depends on the understanding of the meaning of that statement. Hence śabda or testimony, as a source of valid knowledge, consists in understanding the meaning of the statement of a trustworthy person.[1]

There are two ways of classifying śabda, which give us (a) dṛṣṭārtha and adṛṣṭārtha;

There are two ways of classifying śabda or verbal knowledge. According to the one, there are two kinds of śabda namely, that relating to perceptible objects (dṛṣṭārtha), and that relating to imperceptible objects (adṛṣṭārtha).[2] Under the first head we are to include the trustworthy assertions of ordinary persons, the saints and the scriptures in so far as they bear on the perceptible objects of the world, *e.g.* the evidence given by witnesses in the law courts, the statements of a reliable farmer about plants, the scriptural injunctions to perform certain rites to bring about rain-fall, etc. The second will include all the trustworthy assertions of ordinary persons, saints, prophets and the scripture in so far as they bear on supersensible realities, *e.g.* the scientists' assertions about atoms, ether, electrons,vitamins, etc., the prophets, instructions about virtue and vice, the scriptural texts on God, freedom and immortality.

(b) laukika and vaidika śabda.

According to another classification, there are two kinds of testimony, the scriptural (vaidika) and the secular (laukika).[3] In vaidika testimony we have the words of God.Vaidika or scriptural testimony is thus perfect and infallible by its very nature. But laukika or secular testimony is not all valid. It is the testimony of human beings and may, therefore, be true or false. Of laukika testimony, only that which proceeds from trustworthy persons is valid, but not the rest. It will be observed here that the first classification of testimony (śabda) has reference to the nature of the objects of knowledge, the second to the nature of the source of knowledge. But the two classifications, given by different

1. *Tarkasaṅgraha,* p. 73 ; *Bhāṣya*pariccheda and *Muktāvali,* 81.
2. *Nyāya-sūtra and Bhāṣya* 1.18.
3. *Tarkasaṅgraha,* p. 73 ; *Tarkabhāṣā,* p. 14.

Naiyāyikas, agree in implying that testimony must always be personal, *i.e.* based on the words of some trustworthy person, human or divine. In respect of their truth, however, there is no difference among the trustworthy statements of an ordinary person, a saint, a prophet, and the scriptures as revealed by God.[1]

(*ii*) The Logical Structure of a Sentence

Śabda or testimony, we have seen, gives us knowledge about certain things through the understanding of the meaning of sentences, either spoken or written by some authoritative person. Hence the question is : What is a sentence and how does it become intelligible? A sentence,we are told, is a group of words (pada) arranged in a certain way. A word again, is a group of letters arranged in a fixed order.[2] The essential nature of a word lies in its meaning. A word is that which has a fixed relation to some object, so as to recall it whenever it is heard or read, *i.e., it means* an object. So we may say that words are significant symbols. This capacity of words to mean their respective objects is called their śakti or potency, and it is said to be due to the will of God.[3] That a word has a fixed and an unalterable relation to certain things only, or that this word always means this object and not others, is ultimately due to the Supreme Being who is the ground and reason of all the order and uniformity that we find in the world.

A sentence is a group of words arranged in a certain way.

A sentence (vākya) is a combination of words having a certain meaning. Any combination of words, however, does not make a significant sentence. The construction of an intelligible sentence must conform to four conditions. These are ākāṅkṣā, yogyatā, sannidhi and tātparya.[4]

The four conditions of an intelligible sentence :

1. For a critical discussion of Śabda as an independent source of knowledge. vide *The Nyāya Theory of Knowledge,* pp. 381-89.
2. Tarkasaṅgraha, pp. 63-64.
3. Ibid., 64:
4. *Tarkasaṅgraha,* p. 72 ; *Bhāṣā*pariccheda p. 82.

(a) Ākāṅkṣā or the mutual need of the words of a sentence for expressing a complete sense.

By ākāṅkṣā or *expectancy* is meant that quality of the words of a sentence by which they expect or imply one another. Generally speaking, a word cannot by itself convey a complete meaning. It must be brought into relation with other words in order to express a full judgment. When one hears the word 'bring,' he at once asks : 'what?' The verb 'bring' has a need for some other words denoting some object or objects, e.g. 'the jar.' Ākāṅkṣā is this mutual need that the words of a sentence have for one another in order to express a complete sense.

(b) Yogyatā or the mutual fitness of the words.

The second condition of the combination of words in a sentence is their yogyatā or *mutual fitness*. It consists in the absence of contradiction in the relation of objects denoted by a sentence. When the meaning of a sentence is not contradicted, there is yogyatā or fitness between its constituent words. The sentence 'moisten with fire' is devoid of meaning, because there is a contradiction between 'fire' and 'moistening.'

(c) Sannidhi or the proximity between the words of a sentence.

Sannidhi or āsatti is the third condition of verval knowledge. It consists in the juxtaposition or *proximity* between the different words of a sentence. If there is to be an intelligible sentence then its constituent words must be continuous with one another in time or space. Spoken words cannot make a sentence when separated by long intervals of time. Similarly, written words cannot construct a sentence when they are separated by long intervals of space. Thus the words 'bring–a–cow' will not make a sentence when uttered on three days or written on three pages, even though they possess the first two marks of ākāṅkṣā or expectancy and yogyatā or fitness.

(d) Tātparya or the meaning intended to be conveyed by a sentence.

Tātparya as a condition of verbal knowledge stands for the meaning *intended* to be conveyed by a sentence. A word may mean different things in different cases. Whether it means this or that thing in a particular case depends on the intention of the person who uses the word. To understand the meaning of a sentence, therefore, we must consider the intention of the writer or the speaker who uses it. Thus when a man is asked to bring a 'bat' he is at a loss to understand whether he is told to bring a particular kind of animal or a playing implement, for the word means both. This can be ascertained only if we know the intention of the speaker. Hence the undrestanding of sentence depends on the understanding of its tātparya or intended meaning. In the case of ordinary sentences used by human beings, we can ascertain their tātparya from the context (prakaraṇa) in which they are used. For the understanding of the Vedic texts we are to take the help of the various rules of interpretation systematized by the Mīmāṁsā.

III. The Nyāya Theory of the Physical World[1]

Prameya is the world of objects of knowledge.

So far we have considered the Nyāya doctrine of pramāṇa or the methods of knowledge. Now we come to the second topic of *prameya* or the objects of knowledge. According to Gautama, 'as already seen[2], these are : the self, the body, the senses and their objects, knowledge, mind (manas), pravṛtti or activity, doṣa or the mental imperfections, pretyabhāva or rebirth, phala or the feelings of pleasure and pain, duḥkha or suffering, apavarga or absolute freedom from all sufferings. There are also such objects as dravya or substance, guṇa or quality, karma or motion, sāmānya or the universal, viśesa or particularity, samavāya or the relation of inherence, and abhāva or non-existence.

Of these, the physical elements, time, space and ākāśa constitute the physical world.

All of these prameyas or knowables are not to be found in the physical world, because it includes only those objects that are either physical (būhta) or somehow belong to the world of physical nature. Thus the self, its attribute of knowledge and manas are not at all physical. Time and space are two substances which

1. Vide *Nyāya-sūt. and Bhāṣya* 1.1.9-22.
2. See p. 165.

although different from the physical substances, yet somehow belong to the physical world. Āāśka is a physical substance which is not a productive cause of anything. The physical world is constituted by the four physical substances of earth, water, fire and air. The ultimate constituents of these four substances are the eternal and unchanging atoms of earth, water, fire and air. Ākāśa or ether, kāla or time, and dik or space are eternal and infinite substances, each being one single whole. Thus the physical world is the product of the four kinds of atoms of earth, water, fire and air. It contains all the composite products of these atoms, and their qualities and relations, including organic bodies, the senses, and the sensible qualities of things. To it belongs also the physical substance of ākāśa or ether. The non-physical, infinite substances of kāla or time and dik or space contain and interrelate all physical things and events in various ways. The Nyāya theory of the physical world, in respect of these and other connected subjects, is the same as that of the Vaiśeṣika. The Vaiśeṣika theory, which is a more detailed account of the subject, is accepted by the Nyāya as *samānatantra* or an allied theory common to the Nyāya and the Vaiśeṣika system. So we propose to take up this subject when we come to the Vaiśeṣika philosophy.

IV. The Individual Self and its Liberation

Different conceptions of the self: materialistic, empricist and idealistic.

The Nyāya is a philosophy of life and seeks to guide individual selves in their search for truth and freedom. With regard to the individual self (jīvātmā) we have to consider first its nature and attributes. There are four main views of the self in Indian philosophy. According to the Cārvākas, the self is the living body with the attribute of consciousness. This is the materialistic conception of the self. The Bauddhas reduce the self to a stream of thought or a series of congnitions. Like some empiricists and sensationalists, they admit only the empirical self. The Advaita Vedānta takes the self as one, unchanging and self-shining consciousness (svaprakāśa caitanya) which is neither a subject nor an object, neither the 'I' nor the 'me'. The Viśiṣṭādvaita Vedānta, however holds that the self is not pure consciousness as such but a conscious subject called the ego or the 'I' (jñātā ahamartha evātmā). Both these views of the self may be called idealistic in a broad sense.

The realistic view of the self in the Nyāya-Vaiśeṣika system.

The Nyāya-Vaiśeṣikas adopt the realistic view of the self. According to them, the self is a unique substance, to which all cognitions, feelings and conations belong as its attributes. Desire, aversion and volition, pleasure, pain and cognition are all qualities of the soul. These cannot belong to the physical substances, since they are not physical qualities perceived by the external senses. Hence we must admit that they are the peculiar properties of some substance other than different from all physical substances. There are different selves in different bodies, because their experiences do not overlap but are kept dissinct. The self is indestructible and eternal. It is infinite or ubiquitous (vibhu), since it is not limited by time and space.[1]

The self is distinct from the body, senses, manas and the stream of consciousness.

The body or the senses cannot be the self because consciousness cannot be the attribute of the material body or the senses. The body is, by itself, unconscious and unintelligent. The senses cannot explain functions like imagination, memory, ideation, etc., which are independent of the external senses. The manas too cannot take the place of the self. If the manas be, as the Nyāya Vaiśeṣikas hold, and atomic and therefore, imperceptible substance, the qualities of pleasure, pain, etc., which should belong to the manas, must be equally impreceptible. But pleasure and pain are experienced or perceived by us. Nor can the self be identified with the series of cognitions as in Baudha philosophy, for then memory becomes inexplicable. No member of a mere series of cognitions can, like a bead of the rosary, know

1. *Nyāya-bhāṣyā*, 1.1.10; *Padārthadharmasaṅgraha*, pp. 30f. ; *Tarkabhaṣya*, pp. 18-19.

what has preceded it or what will succeed it. The Advaita Vedāntin's idea of the self as eternal, self-shining consciousness is no more aceeptable to the Naiyāyika than that of the Buddhists. There is no such thing as pure consciousness unrelated to some subject and object. Consciousness cannot subsist without a certain locus. Hence the self is not consciousness as such, but a substance having consciousness as its attribute. The self is not mere consciousness or knowledge, but a knower, an ego or the 'I' (ahaṅkārāśraya), and also an enjoyer (bhoktā).[1]

Consciousness is not an essential attribute of the soul substance.

Although knowledge or consciousness belongs to the self as an attribute, yet it is not an essential and inseparable attribute of it. All cognitions or cnscious states arise in the self when it is related to the manas, and the manas is related to the senses and senses come in contact with the external objects. Otherwise, there will be no consciousness in the self. In its disembodied condition, therefore, the self will have no knowledge or consciousness. Thus the attributes of cognition, feeling and conation – in a word consciousness is an accidental attribute of the self, the accident being its relation to the body.[2]

Proofs for the existence of the self.

How do we know that there is any self of the individual, which is distinct from his body, his senses and mind? Some old Naiyāyikas[3] seem to think that there cannot be a perception or known either from the testimony of spiritual authorities or by feelings of pleasure and pain, and the phenomenon of knowledge in us. That we have desire, aversion, etc., nobody can doubt. But these cannot be explained unless we admit a permanent self. To desire an object is to strive to obtain it as something pleasurable. But before we obtain it we cannot get any pleasure out of it. so in desiring the object we only judge it to be similar to such objects as were found to be

1. *Bhāṣāpariccheda* and *Muktāvali* 4850 ; *Nyāya-sūt* and *Bhāṣya* 3. 1. 4 ff.
2. Vārttika, 2,1.22 ; *Nyāyamanjari*, p. 432.
3. Vide *Nyāya bhāṣya*, 1.1.9-10.

pleasurable in the past. This means that desire supposes some permanent self which had experienced pleasure in relation to certain objects in the past and which considers a present object to be similar to any of those past objects, and so strives to get possession of it. Similarly, aversion and volition cannot be explained without a permanent self. The feelings of pleasure or pain also arise in an individual when he gets something considered to be the means of attaining a remembered pleasure, or gets into something which had previously led to a painful experience. So too knowledge as a process of reflective thinking requires a parmanent self which first desires to know something, then reflects on it and finally attains certain knowledge about it. All these phenomena of desire, etc., cannot be explained either by the body or the senses or the mind as a series of cognitions or a stream of consciousness. Just as the experience of one man cannot be remembered by another man, so the present states of the body or the senses or the mind cannot remember their past states ; but without such memory we cannot explain the phenomena of desire, aversion and volition, pleasure, pain and cognition.[1]

Direct experience of the self in internal perception.

The later Naiāyikas go a step further and maintain that the self is directly known through internal or mental perception (mānasapratyaksa). Of course, when its existence is denied or doubted by anyone, the self must be inferred and proved in the way explained above. The mental perception of the self may take either of two forms. It may be a perception in the form of pure self-consciousness, which is due to a contact between the mind and the pure self, and is expressed in the judgment 'I am.' According to some Naiyāyikas, however, the pure self cannot be an object of perception. The self is perceived only as having a perceived quality like cognition, feeling or willing, and so the pereceptual judgment is in the form. 'I am knowing,' 'I am happy,' and so forth. We do not perceive the self as such, but as knowing or feeling or doing something. Hence self-consciousness is a mental perception of the self as present in some mode of consciousness. While one's own self can be perceived, other selves in other bodies can only be inferred from their intelligent bodily actions, since these cnanot be explained by the unintelligent body and require a conscious self for their performance.[2]

---

1. Vide *Bhāṣya* 1.1.10.
2. Vide *Tarkabhāṣā*, p. 6 ; *Tarkakaumudi*, p. 8 ; *Bhāṣāpariccheda* and *Muktāvali.* 47.50 and *Dinaharii* thereon.

Liberation is freedom from all pain and suffering.

The end of almost all the systems of Indian philosophy is the attainment of mukti or liberation for the individual self. This is especially true of the Nyāya system which purposes, at the very outset, to give us a knowledge of reality or relaties for the realization of the highest good or the *summun bonum* of our life. The different systems, however, give us different descriptions of this consummate state of the soul's existence. For the Naiyāyikas it is a state of negation, complete and absolute, of all paim and suffernig. Apavarga or liberation is absoulute freedom from pain. This implies that it is a state in which the soul is released from all the bounds of its connection with the body and the senses. So long as the soul is conjoined with a body, it is impossible for it to attain the state of utter freedom from pain. The body with the sense organs being there we cannot possibly prevent their contact with undesirable and unpleasant objects, and so must submit to the inevitable experience of painful feelings. Hence in liberation, the soul must be free from the shackles of the body, and the senses. But when thus severed from the body, the soul ceases to have not only painful but also pleasurable experiences, nay more, it ceases to have any experience or consciousness. So in liberation the self exists as a pure substance free from all connection with the body, neither suffering pain, nor enjoying pleasure, nor having consciousness even. Liberation is the negation of pain, not in the sense of a suspension of it for a longer or shorter period of time, as in a good sleep or a state of recovery from some disease or that of relief from some bodily or mental affliction. It is absolute freedom from pain for all time to come. It is just that supreme condition of the soul which has been variously described in the scriptures as 'freedom from fear' (abhayam), 'freedom from decay and change' (ajaram), 'freedom from death' (amṛtyupadam) and

In it the self ceases to have any experience, painful or pleasurable, and exists as a pure substance devoid of consciousness.

so forth.[1] Some later Naiyāyikas, however, hold that liberation is the soul's final deliverance from pain and attainment of eternal bliss.[2]

The way to attainment of liberation.

To attain liberation one must acquire a true knowledge of the self and all other objects of experience (tattva-jñāna). He must know the self as distinct from the body, the mind, the senses, etc. For this he should first listen to the scriptural instructions about the self (śravaṇa). Then he should firmly establish the knowledge of the self by means of reasoning (manana). Finally, he must meditate on the self in conformity with the principles of yoga (nididhyāsana). These help him to realize the true nature of the self as distinct from the body and all other objects. With this realization, the wrong knowledge (mithyā-jñāna) that 'I am the body and the mind' is destroyed, and one ceases to be moved to action (pravṛttii) by passions and impulses (doṣa). When a man becomes thus free from desires and impulses, he ceases to be affected by the effects of his present actions, done with no desire for fruits. His past karmas or deeds being exhusted by producing their effects, the individual has to undergo no more birth in this world (janma). The cessation of birth means the end of his connection with the body and coneequently, of all pain and suffering (duḥkha) ; and that is liberation.[3]

V. The Nyāya Theology

In the *Nyāya-sūtra* of Gautama we find short but explicit references to God. Though in the *Vaiśeṣika-sūtra* there is no explicit mention of God by name, yet the commentators

1. Vide *Bhāṣya* 1.1.22 *Cf. Praśna Upaniṣad,* 5.7.
2. Vide Bhāsarvajña. *Nyāyasāra* pp. 39-41 (Asiatic Society, Calcutta).
3. *Cf. Rhāṣya,* 1.1.2 ;*Tarkasaṅgraha* and *Dipikā* pp. 106-07.

interpret some of the sūtras as referring the God.[1] But the later Nyāya-Vaiśeṣika school gives us an elaborate theory of God and connects it with the doctrine of liberation. According to these thinkers the individual self can attain true knowledge of realities and, through it, the state of liberation only by the grace of God. Without God's grace neither the true knowledge of the categories of philosophy nor the highest end of liberation is attainable by any individual being of the world. So the questions that arise are : What is God? How do we know that God exists ?

Reference to God in the *Nyāya* and *Vaiśesika sūtras.*

1. The Idea of God

God is the ultimate cause of the creation, maintenance and destruction of the world. He does not create the world out of nothing, but out of eternal atoms, space, time, ether, minds(manas) and souls. The creation of the world means the ordering of the eternal entities, which are co-existent God. into a moral world, in which individual selves enjoy and suffer according to the merit and demerit of their actions, and all physical objects serve as means to the moral and spiritual ends of our life. God is thus the creator of the world in the sense of being the first efficient cause of the world and not its meterial cause, *i.e.* a sort of demiurgus or a builder of the ordered universe. He is also the preserver of the world in so far as the world is kept in existence by the will of God. So also He is the destroyer who lets loose the forces of destruction when the exigencies of the moral world require it. Then, God is one, infinite and eternal, since the world of space and time, minds and souls does not limit Him, but is related to Him as a body to the self which resides in it. He is omnipotent, although He is guided in His activities by moral considerations of the merit and demerit of human

God is the eternal infinite self who creates, maintains and destroys the world.

1. Vide *Nyāya-sūt*, 4.1.19-21 ; *Vaiśeṣka-sūt.*, 2.1.17-19.

actions. He is omniscient in so far as He possesses right knowledge of all things and events. he has eternal consciousness as a power of direct and steadfast cognition of all objects. Eternal consciousness is only an inseparable *attribute* of God, *not* His very *essence*, as maintained in the Advita Vedānta. He possesses to the full all the six perfection (ṣaḍaiśvaryya) and is majestic, almighty, allglorious, infinitely beautiful, and possessed of infinite knowledge and perfect freedom from attachment.[1]

He is also the moral governor of all living beings including ourselves.

Just as God is the efficient cause of the world, so He is the directive cause of the actions of all living beings. No creature, not even man, is absolutely free in his actions. He is relatively free, *i.e.* his actions are done by him under the direction and guidance of the Divine Being. Just as a wise and benevolent father directs his son to do certain things, according to his gifts, capacities and previous attainments, so God directs all living beings to do such actions and feel such natural consequence thereof as are consistent with their past conduct and character. While man is the efficient instrumental cause of his actions, God is their efficient directive cause (prayojaka kartā). Thus God is the moral governor of the world of living beings including ourselves, the impartial dispenser of the fruits of our actions (karmaphaladātā) and the supreme arbiter of our joys and sorrows.[2]

2. Proofs for the Existence of God

Now the more important question which naturally arises here is this : What are the proofs for the existence of God ? The Nyāya Vaśieṣikas have to their credit an array of proofs which include almost all the arguments given in Western

1. Vide *Saddarśana,* Ch. I ; *Kusumāñjali,* 5.
2. Vide *Nyāya-bhāṣya,* 4. 1. 21.

philosophy for God's existence. There are as many as ten proofs, of which the more important may be considered here.

(*i*) The Causal Argument

All composite and limited objects of the world must have an intelligent maker who is omnipotent and omniscient, and that maker is God.

All composite objects of the world, formed by the combination of atoms (*e.g.* mountains, seas, etc.), must have a cause because they are of the nature of effects, like a pot. That all such objects of the world are effects follows first from their being made up of parts (sāvayava) and secondly, from their possessing an intermediate magnitude (avāntaramahattva). Space, time, ether and self are not effects, because these are infinite substance, not made up of parts. Atoms of earth, water, light and air, and the mind are not the effects of any cause, because they are simple, indivisible and infinitesimal substances. All other composite objects of the world, like mountains and seas, the sun and the moon, the stars and the planets must be the effects of some cause, since they are both made up of parts and possess limited dimensions. These objects are what they are because of the concurrence of a number of material causes. Therefore, there must be an intelligent cause (kartā), for all these effects. Without the guidance of an intelligent cause the material causes of these things cannot attain just that order, direction and co-ordination which enable them to produce these difinite effects. This intelligent cause must have a direct knowledge of the material causes (the atoms) as means, a desire to attain some end, and the power of will to accomplish or realize the end, (jñāna-cikīrsā-kṛti). He must also be omniscient (sarvajña), since only an omniscient being can have direct knowledge of such absolutely simple and infinitely small entities as atoms and the like. That is, He must be God and none but God.[1]

A comparison of the Nyāyika's causal argument with that of Western theologians.

The first argument of the Naiyāyikas, it will be observed, resembles the causal argument for God's existence as explained by some Western thinkers like Paul Janet,[2] Hermann Lotze[3] and James Martineau.[4] According to them, the world of finite objects requires an intelligent cause which gives order and co-ordination to their concurrent physical causes. Thus Janet lays it down as a principle that all co-ordination between divergent phenomena implies a final cause or an intelligent agent who effects the complex combination of such separate phenomena. So also, both Lotze and Martineau start from the fact of physical causation in the world and rise up to the conception of an intelligent principle as its ultimate ground and reason. Indeed, the Naiyāyika view of an efficient cause as an intelligent agent strikingly anticipates Martineau's idea of cause as will directed to the realization of ends. There is, however, some difference between these theists and the Naiyāyikas. Western theists generally believe that God is not only the cause of the *order* and unity of things in the world, but also the creative energy that gives *existence* to the things of Nature. For the Naiyāyikas, however, God is only the cause of the *order* of Nature, and not of the existence of the ultimate constituents of it. Still the Nyāya conception of God cannot be called deistic. According to deism, God creates the world at a certatin point of time and then leaves it to itself. He has usually no concern with the affairs of the world, although he may occasionally interfere with them in case of grave emergency,

---

1. Vide *Kusumāñjali* 5 ; *Sarvadarśana*, Ch. XI ; *Tarkasaṅgraha* and *Dipikā*, pp. 21-22.
2. Vide *Final Causes*, BK. 1, Ch. I.
3. Vide *Outlines of a Philosophy of Religion*, Chs. I and II.
4. Vide *A Study of Religion*, BK. II, Ch. I.

as a clock-maker does when the clock made by him gets our of order. On the Nyāya theory, however, God maintains a continuous relation with the world (being conceived as not only the creator, but also as its maintainer and destroyer). This is the essence of theism as distinguished from deism and, as such, the Nyāya conception of God is rather theistic than deistic.

(ii) The Argument from Adṛṣṭa

The second argument of the Naiyāyikas is this : We often wonder : How are we to account for the differences in our lot here on earth? Some people are happy and some miserable, some wise and some ignorant. What may be the cause of all these variations in our worldly life? We cannot say that they have no causes, because these are so many events in our life, and every event must have its cause. Now the causes which produce our joys and sorrows in this life are our own actions in this or some previous life. We enjoy or suffer in this life because of our good or bad actions. The law that governs the lives of individual souls is the moral law of karma which requires that every individual being must reap the fruits of its own actions, good or bad, right or wrong. There is nothing strange or improbable in this. It follows logically from the law of universal causation, which means that every cause must produce its effect and every effect must be produced by its cause. That our moral actions are as good causes as our physical actions must be admitted by every one who believes in the law of causation and extends it to the moral world. Just as bodily acts produce bodily changes and mental functions produce mental changes and dispositions, so morally good or bad actions lead to good or bad moral consequences, such as reward or punishment, happiness or misery. Hence it is established

The differences in our lot require an explanation which must be given in terms of our good or bad deeds.

that our joys and sorrows are due to our own actions.[1]

But the next question is : How do our moral actions produce their consequences which may be separated from them by long intervals of time ? Many of our joys and sorrows cannot be traced to any work done by us in this life. Even those that are due to acts done in this life, do not arise out of them immediately, but afer some time. A sinner in the heyday of youth may be a sufferer in the infirmity of old age. So it is maintained that our good actions produce a certain efficiency called merit (puṇya), and bad actions produce some deficiency called demerit (pāpa) in our souls and these persist long after our actions have ceased and disappeared. This stock of merit and demerit accruing from good and bad actions is called adṛṣṭa. There is nothing more mysterious in the concept of adṛṣṭa than in those of virtue and vice. Just as good actions have a purifying, so bad actions have a corrupting effect on our mind. And just as virtue conduces to a sense of security, serenity and peace (in a word, happiness), so vice plunges the mind into the ruffled waters of suspicion, distraction and uneasiness (in a word, unhappiness). In the same way, adṛṣṭa, as the sum-total of merit and demerit accruing from our past actions, produces our present joys and sorrows.

Adṛṣṭa is the stock of merit and demerit accruing from our good and bad actions. So our lot is determined by our own actions.

But how is it that adṛṣṭa manages to produce the proper consequences ? It is an unintelligent principle which cannot by itself lead to just that kind or degree of joy and sorrow which are due to our past actions . So it is argued that adṛṣṭa must be guided by some intelligent agent to produce its proper

But adṛṣṭa being an unintelligent principle requires to be guided by a supremely wise person, namely, God.

1. If the world be created by God, who is not only omnipotent but also *morally perfect*, it is not unreasonable to think that good actions must produce good effects and bad actions must produce bad effects in our lives. If God is both the creator and moral governor of the world, it logically follows that human beings are responsible to God for their actions. It follows also that our actions are judged by God as good or bad, right or wrong, according as they do or do not help us to realize the end of our life, or to perform our own duties to God and man. And from this it is but natural and rational to conclude that God rewards us for our good acts and punishes us for bad ones. In other words, in a world created by God, good actions must lead to good results and evil actions must not fail to lead to evil consequences.

consequences. Individual selves cannot be said to direct or control adṛṣṭa, and further, it is not infrequently that adṛṣṭa defies the control of their will. So the intelligent agent who guides adṛṣṭa through the proper channels to produce the proper effects, is the eternal, omnipotent and omniscient Divine Being. It is God who controls our adṛṣṭa and dispenses all the joys and sorrows of our life, in strict accordance with it. Or, as Kant would say, it is God who combines happiness with virtue and misery with vice. God gives us the fruits of our actions in the shape of enjoyments or afflictions in a way similar to that in which a wise and potent monarch rewards or punishes his subjects according to the merit or guilt attaching to their good or bad actions.[1]

(iii) The Argument from the Authoritativeness of the Scriptures

The scriptures (Vedas) are valid and authoritative texts. This is due to the supreme authority of their author who must be omniscient, and so none other than God.

Another argument for God's existence is based on the authoritative character of the Vedas. The authority of the scriptures is accepted as unquestionable and infallible in all religions. Now the question, we are to consider here, is this : What is the source of authority of the Vedas ? According to the Naiyāyikas the authority (prāmānya) of the Vedas has its source in the supreme authority of their author (āptaprāmānya). Just as the authoritativeness of the medical science, or for the matter of that, of all sciences, is derived from the scientists who founded them so the authoritativeness of the Vedas is derived from some person who imparted that character to them. The validity of the Vedas may be tested like that of any science, by following their injunctions about worldly objects and seeing how they produce the desired result. Of course, the truth of other Vedic texts bearing on supersensible objects cannot, like some scientific truths,

1. Vide *Kusumāñjali*, 1.

be tested in this way. Still, we may accept the whole of the Vedas as valid and authoritative, in the same way in which we accept the whole of a science as true when, as a matter of fact, we can verify only some parts of it. So we must explain the authority of the Vedas by referring them to some authoritative person. Now the individual self (Jīva) cannot be the author of the Vedas since the supramundane realities and the transcendent principles related in the Vedas cannot be objects of the knowledge of any ordinary individual. Hence the author of the Vedas must be the supreme person who has a direct knowledge of all objects, past, present and future, finite, infinite and infinitesimal, sensible and supersensible. That is, the Vedas, like other scriptures, are revealed by God.[1]

(*iv*) The Testimony of Śruti

The Sruti bears testimony to the existence of God.

Another proof of God's existence is this : God exists because the Vedic scripture (śruti) bears testimony to His existence. Here are some of the scriptural texts : "The highest eternal self is the Lord of all, the ruler of all, the protector of all......" "The great unborn spirit is the receiver of all offerings and the giver of all gifts."[2] "The one god lies hidden in all, is all-pervading is the inmost self of all and the controller and sustainer of all."[3] "He is the ruler of all selves and the creator of the world."[4] In the *Bhagavadgītā* also, the Lord says : "I am the Father and the Mother of this world, its Foster-parent, and its eternal and immutable God." "I am the highest end of all, the maintainer of all, the controller of all the witness of all, the abode of all, the shelter of all, the friend of all, the creator

1. *Nyāya-bhāṣya*, 2.1.68 ; *Kusumāñjali*. 5, p. 62.
2. *Bṛhadāraṇyaka Upaniṣad*, 4.4.22, 4.24.
3. Svetāṣvatara *Upaniṣad*, 6.11.
4. *Kauṣitaki Upaniṣad*, 4.18.

of all, the destroyer of all, the substratum of all, and the unchanging ground of the origin and destruction of all."[1]

But why should one accept the testimony of the scripture on this point?

It will appear from the above that the śruti or the scripture bears unmistakable testimony to the esistence of God. But the question that may agitate the mind of the reader is : Why should one believe in God simply on the authority of the scriptures? An ordinary man may be inclined to do so, if he has not the spirit of critical enquiry in him. But a critical philosopher may say that scriptural testimony has no importance for philosophy, which is satisfied with nothing short of logically valid arguments in the attainment of true knowledge about anything human or divine. So long as these are not forthcoming, the appeal to authority is of no avail. It may also be thought that such logical support for the belief in God is afforded by the traditional proofs of God's existence. But as Immanuel Kant[2] and, after him Hermann Lotze[3] have clearly shown, none of the so-called proofs can really prove the existence of God. To prove anything is to deduce it as a necessary conclusion from certain given premises. But God being the highest of all premises, *i.e.* the ultimate reality, there cannot be any anterior premise or premises from which we can deduce God as a conclusion. The ontological proof starts from the idea of the most perfect being and infers its existence on the ground that without existence it would not be most perfect. So, the cosmological argument starts from the sensible world as a finite and conditioned reality, and argues to the existence of an infinite, unconditioned and supersensible reality as the ground thereof. Similarly, the teleological proof lays stress on the adaptation of means to

An examination of the so-called proofs for God's existence shows that God cannot be proved in any way, for all proofs presuppose the reality of God as spirit.

1. *Bhagavadgītā*, 9. 17-18.
2. Vide E. Caird, *The Critical Philosophy of Kant.* Vol. II. Ch. XIII.
3. Vide *Outlines of a Philosophy of Religion,* Ch. 1.

ends which we find so often in nature and infers the existence of an infinitely intelligent creator of the world. But all these proofs are vitiated by the fallacy of deducing the existence of God from the mere idea of Him. The idea of the most perfect being may involve the idea of exitence but not actual exsistence, just as the thought of one hundred rupees in my pocket involves the image or the idea of their existence, but not their real physical existence. So, to think of the unconditioned or to explain the adaptation of thing we have to think of an intelligent cause. But to think of the existence of something is not to prove its existence, since the *thought of existence* is not actual existence.

Experience is the only source of our knowledge about fact or existence.

The conclusion to be drawn from all this is that the existence of God cannot be proved by any argument. In truth, mere reasoning or logical argument cannot prove the existence of anything. The existence of a thing is to be known, if at all, through experience, direct or indirect. A man of normal vision may indirectly know what orange colour is, if he has seen red and yellow, but no orange as yet. But a man who is born blind can never know what colour is, however much he may argue and reason logically. If by some surgical operation, the man is blessed with the power of vision, a single glance at some coloured objects shall reveal to him the world of colours. Lotze[1] told us the truth about our knowledge of God when he said : "Therefore, all proofs that God exists are please put forward in justification of our faith and of the particular way in which we feel that we must apprehend this highest principle." This point becomes more clear when in his criticism of Anselm's form of the ontological proof, he observes : "To him (Anselm) the assumption that it (God) does not exist seemed to conflict with that *immediate*

1. *Op. cit.*, pp. 9.12 (italics ours).

conviction of its reality, which all our theoretic, aesthetic, and moral activities constrain our soul to entertain." "Although", he goes on to say, "weak enough as a proof. Anselm's argument expresses an *immediate fact* about our minds, namely that *impulse which we experience towards the supersensuous* and that *faith* in its truth which is the starting - point of all religion." It becomes abundantly clear from all this that God must be known through any process of reasoning. If there is this direct experience, on proof is necessary, just as no reasoning is needed to convince you that you are now reading this book. If there is no direct experinnce of God, we may pile up proof after proof and yet remain as unconvinced as ever with regard to the existence of God.

God's existence must be known through direct experience and not by means of reasoning.

For the knowledge of God or of any supersensuous reality, those who have no direct experience must depend on the authority of those rare blessed souls who are pure in heart and have seen God, like the Upanisadic seers and the Christian saints. So, śruti or the scripture, being the embodiment of the knowledge imparted by the enlightened sages and seers of God, may be accepted as a source of right knowledge about God. Just as the great scientists and their sciences have been for all ages, the source of our knowledge of many scientific truths, so the Vedas and Upanisads (śruti) constitute a just ground of our belief in one universal

Those who have no direct experience of God, must depend for their knowledge about God, on others who have that direct experience. The śruti being the expression of such direct experience of God is a just source of our belief in God.

spiritual truth *i.e.* God.[1]

3. Anti-theistic Arguments

It may be objected here that the last two proofs given above involve us in the fallacy of reasoning in a circle. In the third proof, it is shown that God is the author of the Vedas, while in the fourth, the Vedas are exhibited as the ground of our knowledge of God. It appears, therefore, that we prove God's existence from the Vedas and the authoritativeness of the Vedas as being the revelation of God. But that there is really no circular reasoning here becomes clear when we distinguish between the order of *knowledge* and the order of *existence*. In the order of existence, God is prior of the Vedas, and He reveals them. In the order of knowledge, however, the Vedas are known first, and we rise from them to a knowledge of God. But for our knowledge of the Vedas, we need not be necessarily and absolutely dependent on God, since these may be learned from an eligible and efficient teacher. All reciprocal dependence is not reasoning in a circle. It is only when there is reciprocal dependence with reference to the same order or within the same universe of discourse, that there arises the fallacy of resoning in a circle. In the present case, however, the Vedas depend on God for their existence but not for their knowledge by us, while God depends on the Vedas for our knowledge of Him but not for His existence. So there is really no fallacy of reasoning in a circle.[2]

The charge of arguing in a circle against the last two proofs is answered.

Another objection to the Nyāya theory of God is this : If God be the creator of the world, He must have a body, since without body no action is possible. This objection, the Naiyāyikas reply, fails because it is caught between the two horns of a dilemma. If God's existence is proved by śruti, then the objection stands precluded, for there is no point in arguing against what is already proved. On the other hand, if the very *existence* of God is not proved, there is no basis for an argument against the possibility of his *action* without a body.[3]

Reply to the second objection.

---

1. Cf. *Kusumāñjali*, 5.
2. Vide *Sarvadarśana*, Ch. XI.
3. *Ibid.*

Still another anti-theistic argument is based on the problem of the end of creation. In creating the world God must have some end in view, for nobody acts without a desire to realize some end. But what may be the end of God's creative activity ? It cannot be any end of His own because there are no unfulfilled desires or unattained ends in the Divine Being who is perfect. Nor can it be the end or good of others. He who labours only for others must not be regarded as an intelligent person. It cannot be said that God was moved by compassion (karuṇā) in the act of creation. If it were really so, He should have made all his creatures perfectly happy and not so miserable as we actually find them. Compassion is just the desire to relieve the suffering of other creatures without any selfinterest. So it follows that the world is not created by God. The Naiyāyikas meet this objection thus : "God's action in creation is indeed caused by compassion. But we must not forget that the idea of creation which consists only of happiness is in consistent with the nature of things. Certain eventual differences in the form of happiness or misery are bound to arise out of the good or bad actions of the beings who are to be created. It cannot be said that this will limit God's independence in so far as His compassionate creative act depends on the actions of other beings. One's own body does not hinder one. Rather, it helps one to act and achieve one's end. In a like manner, the created world does not hinder and limit God, but serves as the means for the realization of God's moral ends and rational purposes"[1]

The third objection and the Naiyāyik's reply to it.

VI. Conclusion

The value of Nyāya system lies especially in its methodology or theory of knowledge on which it builds its philosophy. One of the charges against Indian philosophy is that it is based on religious authority and is, therefore,

1. *Ibid.*

dogmatic and not critical. The Nyāya philosophy is a standing repudation of this charge. The theory of knowledge, formulated by the Nyāya, is made the basis not only of the Nyāya-Vaiśeṣika, but also of other Indian systems, with slight modifications. The Nyāya applies the method of logical criticism to solve the problems of life and reality. It is by means of a sound logic that it tries to find out the truth and defend it against hostile criticism. But the Nyāya theory of pluralistic realism is not as satisfying as its logic. Here we have a common-sense view of the world as a system of many independent realities, like material atoms, minds, individual souls and God, which are externally related to one another in space, time and ākāśa. It does not give us a systematic philosophy of the world as a whole in the light of one universal absolute principle. The philosophical position of the Nyāya is said to be lower than that of the Sāṅkhya or the Vedānta. This becomes mainfest when we consider its theory of the individual self and God. According to it, the individual self is a substance which is not essentially conscious and intelligent, but is accidentally qualified by consciousness when associated with a body. But such a view of the self is contradicted by the evidence of our direct experience which reveals the self as an essentially conscious subject and not as a *thing* with the quality of consciousness. Further, on this view, the liberated self has no consciousness and is, therefore, indistinguishable from a material substance. The Nyāya conception of God as the architect of the world, its efficient but not material cause, has an obvious reference to human analogy and reduces God to the position of a human artificer who makes things out of given material. There is indeed the suggestion that the world of things and beings is related to God as one's body is to one's self. But this idea is not properly developed in the direction of a full-fledged theism. Still, as a philosophy of life, the Nyāya theism is no less edifying and assuring than other forms of it.

dogmatic and not critical. The Nyaya philosophy is a standing repudiation of this charge. The theory of knowledge, formulated by the Nyaya, is made the basis not only of the Nyaya-Vaiśeṣika, but also of other Indian systems, with slight modifications. The Nyaya applies the method of logical criticism to solve the problems of life and reality. It is by means of a sound logical that it tries to find out the truth and defend it against hostile criticism. But the Nyaya theory of pluralistic realism is not as satisfying as its logic. Here we have a common-sense view of the world as a system of many independent realities, like material atoms, minds, individual souls and God, which are externally related to one another in space, time and ākāśa. It does not give us a systematic philosophy of the world as a whole in the light of one universal, absolute principle. The philosophical position of the Nyaya is said to be lower than that of the Sankhya or the Vedanta. This becomes manifest when we consider its theory of the individual self and God. According to it, the individual self is a substance which is not essentially conscious and intelligent, but is accidentally qualified by consciousness when associated with a body. But such a view of the self is contradicted by the evidence of our direct experience, which reveals the self as an essentially conscious subject and not as a thing with the quality of consciousness. Further, on this view, the liberated self has no consciousness and is, therefore, indistinguishable from a material substance. The Nyaya conception of God as the creator of the world, or efficient but not material cause, raises obvious references to human analogy and reduces God to the position of a human architect who makes things out of given materials. There is, indeed, the suggestion that the world of things and minds is related to God as one's body is to one's self. But the view is not properly developed into the theory of a qualified monism. Still as a theistic philosophy, the Nyaya theism is no less satisfying and sustaining than other forms of it.

THE VAIŚEṢIKA PHILOSOPHY

A SELECT BIBLIOGRAPHY

Nandalal Sinha ... *The Vaiśeṣika Sūtras of Kaṇāda* (with Eng. trans., Indian Press, Allahabad).

Praśastapāda ... *Padārtha-dharma-saṅgraha* with *Upaskāra* (Chowkhampa, Benares, 1923).

Śridhara ... *Nyāya-kandalī* with *Praśastapāda-bhāṣya* (Lazarus & Co., Benares, 1895).

Gangānāth Jhā ... *Padārtha-dharma-saṅgraha of Praśastapāda with Nyāya-kandalī of Śrīdhara* (Eng. trns., Lazarus 1916).

Jagadiśa Tarkālaṅkāra ... *Tarkāmṛta* (Calcutta, c. 1919).

Vallabhācārya ... *Nyāya-līlāvatī* (Nirnaya Sagar, 1915).

Laugāksi Bhāskara ... *Tarka-kaumudī* (Nirnaya Sagar, 1914).

A.B. Keith ... *Indian Logic atomism* (Oxford, 1921).

Mādhavācārya ... *Sarva-darśana-saṅgraha*, Ch. on Vaiśeṣika.

J.N. Sinha ... *Indian Realism* (Kegan Paul, London, 1938).

CHAPTER VI
THE VAIŚEṢIKA PHILOSOPHY

I. INTRODUCTION

The Vaiśeṣika system was founded by Kaṇāda.

The Vaiśeṣika system was founded by Kaṇāda. It is so named in view of the fact that 'viśesa' as a category of knowledge has been elaborately discussed in it. The founder of this philosophy, we are told, was surnamed 'Kaṇāda' because he led the life of an ascetic and used to live on grains of corn gleaned from the field. He was also named Ulūka. So the Vaiśesika philosophy is also known as the Kāṇāda or Aulūkya system.

Some important works of the system.

The first systematic work of this philosophy is the *Vaiśeṣika-sūtra* of Kaṇāda. It is divided into ten adhyāyas or books, each consisting of two āhnikas or sections. Praśastapāda's *Padārtha-dharma-saṅgraha,* usually known as the Bhāsya, reads like an inpepended exposition of the Vaiśeṣika philosophy. Further, we know from two commentaries[1] on Śaṇkara's *Śāriraka Bhāṣya* that Rāvaṇa, King of Ceylon, wrote a commentary on the *Vaiśeṣika-sūtra*. Vyomaśiva's *Vyomavatī*, Udayana's *Kiraṇavalī* and Śrīdhara's *Nyāya-Kandalī* are three well known and excellent commentaries on Praśastapāda's work. Jagadiśa Tarkālaṅkāra's Sūkti and Padmanābha Miśra's *Setu* are two less known commentaries on the same work. Vallabhācārya's *Nyāya-līlāvatī* and Udayana's *Lakṣaṇāvalī* are two valuable compendiums of Vaiśeṣika Philosophy. The later works on the Vaiśeṣika combine this system with the Nyāya. Of these Śivāditya's *Sapta-padārthi,* Laugākṣi Bhāskara's *Tarka-kaumudī* and *Visvanatha's Bhāṣā paricċheda* with its commentary *Siddhānta muktāvalī* are important.

1. Vide *Prabaṭārtha* and *Ratnaprabhā*, 2.2.11.

Its relation to the Nyāya system.

The Nyāya and the Vaiśeṣika are allied systems of philosophy (samānatantra). They have the same end in view, namely, liberation of the individual self. According to both, ignorance is the root cause of all pain and suffering; and liberation, which consists in their absolute cessation, is to be attained through a right knowledge of reality. There is, however, some difference between the two systems on two fundamental points. While the Nyāya accepts four independent sources of knowledge, namely, perception, inference, comparison and testimony, the Vaiśeṣika recognizes only two, *viz.* perception and inference, and reduces comparison and verbal testimony to perception and inference. Secondly, the Naiyāyikas give us a list of sixteen padārthas which, according to them, cover the whole of reality and include those accepted in the other system. The Vaiśeṣikas, on the other hand, recognize only seven padārthas and comprehend all reals under them. These seven categories of reality are (1) dravya or substance, (2) guṇa or quality, (3) karma or action, (4) sāmānya or generality, (5) viśesa or particularity, (6) samavāya or the relation of inherence, and (7) abhāva or non-existence. The Vaiśesika philosophy is an elaboration and a critical study of these seven categories.

The seven categories of the Vaisesika system.

Padārtha literally means the object denoted by a word.[1] So by padārtha we propose to mean all objects of knowledge or all reals. Now, according to the Vaiśeṣikas, all objects, denoted by words, may be broadly divided into two classes, namely, being and non-being (bhāva and abhāva). Being stands for all that is or for all positive realities, such as existent physical things, minds, souls, etc. Similarly, non-being stands for all negative facts like the non-existence of things. There are six kinds of being or positive realities, namely, substance, quality, action,

of which six are positive and one negative.

1. 'Abhidheyāḥ padārthāḥ'. *Tarkakamudi*, p. 1. see also *Tarkadipikā*, p. 4. ; *Padārtha-dharmasangraha*, p.5. P. 224

generality, particularity and inherence. To these the later Vaiśeṣikas added a seventh padārtha called abhāva which stands for all negative facts.[1]

II. The Categories

1. Substance or Dravya [2]

Substance is the substratum of qualities and actions and the material cause of composite things.

A dravya or substance is that in which a quality or an action can exist, but which is distinct from both. Without substance there can be no quality or action. A thing must *be* or exist, if it is to have any quality or action belonging to it. So a substance is the substratum of qualities and actions. It is also the constitutive or material cause (samavāyikāraṇa) of other composite things produced from it. Thus a cloth is a composite thing formed by the combination of a number of threads of a certain colour. Now the threads are the material or constitutive causes of the cloth, because it is made of threads and subsists in them. Similarly, wood and lead are the material causes of a wooden pencil because it is made of them.[3]

There are nine kinds of substances.

There are nine kinds of substances, namely, earth or prithivī, water or jala, light or tejas, air or vāyu, ether or ākāśa, time or kāla, space or dik, soul or ātmā, and mind or manas. Of these the first five are called physical elements (pañcabhūta), since each of them possesses a specific or peculiar quality (viśeṣa guṇa) which is sensed by an external sense. Smell is the peculiar property of earth. Other substances have smell only as they are mixed up with some quantity of earth. There is smell in muddy water, but no smell in water which is pure. Taste is the peculiar property of water, colour of light, touch of air, and sound of

1. Vide *Tarkāmṛta*, Ch.1 ; *Tarkabhāṣā*, p. 29; *Vaiśesika-sūt*., 1.1.14.
2. Vide *Tarkasaṅgraha*, Secs. on Uddeśa and Dravya; *Tarkabhāsā*, pp. 20- 23; *Vaiśeṣika-sūt*., 1.1.15.
3. As distinguished from samavāyikārana, the colour of the threads is the asamavāyikārana or non-constitutive cause of the colour of the cloth. It is the indirect cause of an effect. The colour of the threads determines the colour

ākāśa or ether. These five specific qualities are sensed by the five external senses. Each of the senses is constuted by the physical element whose specific quality is sensed by it. The sense of smell is constituted by the element of earth, the sense of taste by water, the sense of sight by light, that of touch by air, and that of hearing by ākāśa. We find that earthy substances, like odoriferous particles in smelling objects, manifest the quality of smell. From this we conclude that the sense of smell which manifests smell is constituted by earth. For similar reasons it is held that the senses of taste, sight, touch and hearing are respectively made of the elements of water, light, air and ether.

The atoms of earth, water, light and air are eternal while compounds made of earth.etc, are non-eternal.

The substances of earth, water, light and air are of two kinds, namely, eternal (nitya) and non-eternal (anitya). The atoms (paramāṇu) of earth, water, light and air are eternal, because an atom is partless and can be neither produced nor destroyed. All other kinds of earth, water, etc. are non-eternal, because they are produced by the combination of atoms and are, therefore, subject to disintegration and destruction. We cannot ordinarily perceive an atom. The existence of atoms is known by an inference like this : The ordinary composite objects of the world like jars, tables, and chairs, are made up of parts. Whatever is produced must be made up of parts, for to produce a thing is to combine certain parts in a certain way. Now if we go

The existence of atoms is proved by inference.

---

of the cloth through being related to the threads which are the constitutive causes. There is still another kind of cause, namely, the nimittakāraṇa or efficient cause. It stands for that cause of an effect which is neither constitutive, nor non-constitutive, but still necessary for the effect. Thus the shuttle is the efficient cause of the cloth, because it is the instrument by which the combination of threads is effected in order to manufacture a piece of cloth. The nimittakārana includes also the directive cause (prayojaka or nirvartaka) and final cause (bhoktā) of the effect. Vide *Tarkāmṛta* pp. 9-11; *Tarkabhāṣā*, pp. 2f.; *Tarkaumudī*, p.7; *Tarkasangraha*. pp. 37-38; *Bhāṣāpariccheda* and *Muktāvalī* 16-18. *Cf.* Aristotle's classification of causes into the formal material efficient and final.

on separating the parts of a composite thing, we shall pass from larger to smaller, from smaller to still smaller, and from these to the smallest parts which cannot be further divided in any way. These indivisible and minutest parts are called paramāṇus or atoms. An atom cannot be produced, because it has no parts, and to produce means to combine parts. Nor can it be destryoed, for to destroy a thing is to break it up into its parts, whereas the atom has no parts. Thus being neither produced nor destructible the atoms or the smallest parts of a thing are eternal. The atoms are different in kind. There are four kinds of atoms, namely, of earth, water, light and air, each having its peculiar quality. The Vaiśeṣika view is thus different from that of the Greek atomists like Democritus who believe that all atoms are of the same kind, and that they differ in quantity and not in quality.

Ākāśa is one, eternal and all-pervading physical substance which is imperceptible.

Ākāśa is the fifth physical substance which is the substratum of the quality of sound. While sound is perceived, ākāśa cannot be perceived. There are two conditions of the external perception of a substance, namely, that it must have a perceptible dimension (mahattva) and manifest colour (udbhūtarūpavattva). Ākāśa is not a limited and coloured substance. Ākāśa is an all-pervading bearer of the quality of sound and is inferred from the perception of that quality. Every quality must belong to some substance. Sound is not a quality of earth, water, light and air, because the qualities of these substances are not perceived by the ear, while sound is perceived by our ears. Further, there may be sound in regions relatively free from the influence of these substances. Nor can sound belong as a quality to space, time, soul and mind, for these exist even when there is no sound to qualify them. So there must be some other substance called ākāśa or ether of which sound is the quality. It is one and eternal because it is not made up of parts and does not depend on any other substance for its existence. It is all-pervading in the sense that it has an unlimited dimension and its quality, sound, is perceived everywhere.

Space and time also are imperceptible substances.

Space (dik) and time (kāla) are, like ākāśa, imperceptible substances each of which is one, eternal and all-pervading. Space is inferred as the ground of our cognitions of 'here' and 'there', 'near' and 'far'. Time is the cause of our cognitions of 'past', 'present' and 'future', 'older' and 'younger'. Although one and indivisible, ākāśa, space and time are distinguished into different parts and thus conventionally, spoken of as many by reason of certain limiting conditions (upādhi) which affect our knowledge of them. Thus the expressions 'the ether enclosed by a jar', 'that by a house', 'filled and empty space', 'the east and the west', 'a minute and hour and a day' are due to the apparent distinctions, made by certain conditions, in what is really one ether, one space and one time.

The soul is an eternal and all-pervading substance which is the substratum of consciousness.

The soul (ātmā) is an eternal and all-pervading substance which is the substratum of the phenomena of consciousness. There are two kinds of souls, namely, the individual soul (jīvātmā) and the supreme soul (paramātmā or Īśvara). The latter is one, and is inferred as the creator of the world. The former is internally or mentally perceived as possessing some quality when, for example, one says, 'I am happy', 'I am sorry,' and so forth. The individual self is not one but many being different in different bodies.

Manas is an atomic imperceptible substance. Proofs for the existence of manas or the mind.

Manas, which is a substance, is the internal sense (antarindriya) for the perception of the individual soul and its qualities, like pleasure and pain. It is atomic and cannot, therefore, be perceived. Its existence is inferred from the following grounds : (a) Just as in the perception of the external objects of the world, we require the external senses, so in the perception of internal objects, like the soul, cognition, feeling and willing, there must be an internal sense, to which we give the name of mind (manas). (b) Secondly, we find that although the five external senses may be in contact with their respective objects at the same time, we have not simultaneous perceptions of colour, touch, sound, taste and smell. But why must this be so? If when talking to a friend in your house, your eyes are in contact with his facial expressions, your ears are in contact with the rumbling sound of the tram car outside, and your skin is in contact with the clothes you wear, you should have simultaneous perceptious of the friend's face, of the tram car and of the clothes. But you do not get all these perceptions at the same time. This shows that over and above the contact between the external senses and their objects, there must be some other cause which limits the number of perceptions to one at a time, and the order of perceptions to one of sucession, *i.e.* one after the other and not all together. Of the different objects which may be in contact with our external senses at one and the same time, we perceive only that to which we are attentive. This means that we must *attend* to, or turn our mind (manas) and fix it on (manoyoga), the object of perception. So every perception requires the contact of the mind (manas) with the object through its contact with the sense organ in question.That is, we must admit the existence of manas as an internal sense. That the manas is partless or atomic also follows from the order of succession among our experiences. If the mind were not an infinitesimal or partless entity, there could have been simultaneous contract of its many parts with many senses, and so the appearance of many perceptions at one and the same time. But as this is not the case, we are to say that the manas is partless or atomic, and functions as an internal sense of perception. It is the organ through which the soul attends to objects.

2. *Quality or Guṇa*[1]

A quality exists in a substance and has no quality or activity in it.

A quality or guṇa is defined as that which exists in a substance and has no quality or activity in itself. A substance exists by itself and is the constituent (samavāyi) cause of things. But a quality

1. Vide *Vaiśeṣika-sut.*, 1.1.16; *Tarkasangraha*, Sec. on guṇa; *Tarkabhāṣā*, pp. 24-28.

depends for its existence on some substance and is never a constitutive cause of anything. It is a non-constitutive or non-material cause of things in so far as it determines only their nautre and character, but not their existence. All qualities must belong to substances and so there cannot be qualities of a quality. A red colour belongs to some thing and not to any other colour. A quality (guṇa) is an unmoving or motionless property of things. It inheres in the thing as something passive and inactive (niṣkriya). So it is different from both substance (dravya) and action (karma).

There are twenty-four kinds of qualities.

There are altogether twenty-four kinds of qualities. These are rūpa or colour, rasa or taste, gandha or smell, sparśa or touch, śabda or sound, sāṅkhyā or number, parimāṇa or magnitude, pṛthaktva or distinctness, saṁyoga or conjuction, vibhāga or disjunction, paratva or remoteness, aparatva or nearness, buddhi or cognition, sukha or pleasure, duḥkha or pain, iccha or desire, dveṣa or aversion, prayatna or effort, gurutva or heaviness, dravatva or fluidity, sneha or viscidity, saṁskāra or tendency, dharma or merit, and adharma or demerit. Many of these qualities have sub-divisions. Thus there are different kinds of colour like white and black, red and blue, yellow and green. There are different kinds of taste, such as sweet, sour, bitter, etc. Smell is of two kinds, namely, good and bad. The quality of touch is of three kinds, *viz.* hot, cold, and neither hot nor cold. Sound is of two kinds, *viz.* dhvani or an inarticulate sound (*e.g.* the sound of a bell) and varna or an articulate sound (*e.g.* a letter sound).

Number is a quality of things.

Number is that quality of things for which we use the words, one, two, three. There are many kinds of number from one upwards. Magnitude is that quality by which things are distinguised as large or small. It is of four kinds, *viz.* the atomic or extremely small, the extremely great, the small and the large. Pṛthaktva is that quality by which we know that one thing is different and distinct from another, *e.g.* a jar from a picture, a table from a chair.

Magnitude is a quality of which there are four kinds.

Conjunction is the union between two or more things which can exist separately, *e.g.* a book and a table. The relation between an effect and its cause is not one of conjuction, since the effect cannot exist without relation to the cause. Disjunction is the disconnection between things, which ends their previous conjuction. Conjunction is of three kinds, according as it is due to motion in one of the things conjoined (as when a flying kite sits on a hill-top), or to that of both the things (as when two balls moving from opposite directions meet and impinge). It may also be due to another conjunction. When the pen in my hand touches the table, there is conjunction between my hand and the table, brought about by the conjunction between my hand and the pen. Similarly, disjuction may be caused by the motion of one of the things disjoined, as when a bird flies away from a hill-top. Or, it may be due to the motion of both the things, as when the balls rebound after impact. It may also be caused by another disjunction as when I drop the pen from my hand and thereby disconnect my hand from the table.

Conjunction is union between two separable things, and disjunction is their separation after conjuction.

Remoteness and nearness are each of two kinds, namely, the temporal and the spatial. As temporal, they mean the qualities of being older and younger, and as spatial, those of being far and near.

There are two kinds of remoteness and nearness.

Buddhi, knowledge or cognition, and its different forms have been explained before.[1] Pleasure and pain, desire and aversion are well-known facts. Prayatna or effort is of three kinds, namely, pravṛtti or striving towards something, nivṛtti or striving away from something, and jīvanayoni or vital function. Gurutva or heaviness is the cause of the fall of bodies. Dravatva or fluidity is the cause of the flowing of certain substances like water, milk, air etc. Sneha or viscidity is the cause of the adhesion of different particles of matter into the shape of a ball or a lump. This quality belongs exclusively to water.

Prayatna is of three kinds.

---

1. *Vide* Ch. V. pp. 173-75.

Saṁskāra or tendency is of three kinds, *viz.* vega or velocity which keeps a thing in motion, bhāvanā or mental impressions which help us to remember and recognize things, and sthitisthāpakatva or elasticity, by which a thing tends towards equilibrium when disturbed, *e.g.* a rubber garter. Dharma and adharma respectively mean virtue and vice and are due to the performance of enjoined and forbidden acts. One leads to happiness and the other to misery.

So also Saṁskāra.

Thus we get a list of twenty-four qualities in the Vaiśeṣika system. Now one may ask : Why should we admit just this number? Can it not be more or less than that ? To this we reply that if one takes into consideration the numerous subdivisions of these qualities, then their number would be very great. But in a classification of objects we are to reduce them to such kinds as are ultimate from a certain standpoint, *i.e.*, do not admit of further reduction. So we come to the simplest forms or kinds of qualities. Thus while one compound colour like orange may be reduced to red and yellow, or a complex sound may be shown to arise out of the combination of other sounds, it is not possible for us to reduce colour to sound or any other quality. It is for this reason that we have to recognize colour, sound, touch, taste and smell as distinct and differnt kinds of qualities. The Vaiśeṣika classification of qualities into twenty four kinds is guided by these considerations of their simplicity or complexity, and reducibility or irreducibility. The guṇas are what the Vaiśeṣikas thought to be the *simplest, passive* qualities of substances.

Why just this number of twenty-four qualities ?

3. Action or Karma[1]

Karma or action is physical movement. Like a quality, it belongs only to substance, but is different from both. A substance is the support of both quality and action : a

Karma or action means physical movement.

1. *Tarkasangraha*, p. 87; *Tarkabhāṣā*, p.28; *Vaiśeṣika-sut.*, 1.1.17; *Tarkāmṛta*, p.30.

quality is a static character of things, but an action is dynamic. While a quality is a passive property that does not take us beyond the thing it belongs to, action is a transitive process by which one thing reaches another. So it is regarded as the independent cause of the conjunction and disjunction of things. An action has no quality, because the latter belongs only to substance. All actions or movements must subsist in limited corporeal substances (mūrtadravya), such as earth, water, light, air and the mind. So there can be no action or motion in the all-pervading substances like ākāśa, space, time and the soul. There can be no movement of an all-pervading thing because it cannot change its position.

There are five kinds of action.

There are five kinds of action or movement, namely, utkṣepaṇa or throwing upward, avakṣepaṇa or throwing downward, ākuñcana or contraction, prasāraṇa or expansion and gamana or locomotion. Of these, utkṣepaṇa is the cause of the contact of a body with some higher region, *e.g.* throwing a ball upward. Avakṣepaṇa is the cause of the contact of a body with some lower region, *e.g.* throwing down a ball from a house-top. Ākuficaña is the cause of such closer contact of the parts of a body as did not previously exist, *e.g.* clenching the fingers or rolling up a cloth. Prasāraṇa is the cause of the destruction of previous closer contact among the parts of a body, *e.g.* opening one's clenched hand. All other kinds of actions are denoted by gamana. Such actions as the walking of a living animal, going up of flames, etc. are not separately classed in so far as they may all be included within gamana. All kinds of actions cannot be perceived. The action of the mind (manas) which is an imperceptible substance does not admit of ordinary perception. The actions or movements of perceptible substances like earth, water and light can be perceived by the senses of sight and touch.

4. Generality or Sāmānya

Sāmānya is the class-essence or the universal.

Things of a certain class bear a common name because they possess a common nature. Men, cows and swans have, severally, something in common on account of which they bear these general names. The thought of what they have in common, is called a general idea or class-concept. Now the question is : What is it that they have in common? Or, what is the something that is common in them, and is the ground of their being brought under one class and called by the same name? The first answer, which is only provisional, is that it is the class-essence corresponding to the class-concept. The Nyāya-Vaiśeṣikas would say that it is their sāmānya or generality. Or, in the words of modern Western philosophers,[1] it is the "universal" in them. Hence the previous question leads to a second, *viz.* what is sāmānya or the universal?

There are three views of the universal: The Bauddha view.

There are three main views of the universal or the class-essence in Indian philosophy. In the Buddhist philosophy we have the nominalistic view. According to it, the individual (svalakṣaṇa) alone is real and there is no class or universal other than the particular objects of experience. The idea of sameness that we may have with regard to a number of individuals of a certain character is due to their being called by the same name. It is only the name that is general, and the name does not stand for any positive essence that is present in all the individuals. It means only that the individuals called by one name are different from those to which a different name is given. Thus certain animals are called cow, not because they possess any common essence but because they are different from all animals that are not cows. So there is no

1. *Vide* S.C. Chatterjee, *The Problems of Philosophy*, Ch. XI, for a full account of their views on the nature of universals.

universal but the name with a negative connotation.[1]

The Jainas[2] and the Advaita Vedāntins[3] adopt the conceptualistic view of the universal. According to them, the universal does not stand for any independent entity over and above the individuals. On the other hand, it is constituted by the essential common attributes of all the individuals. So the universal is not separate from the individuals but is indentical with them in point of existence. The universal and the individual are related by way of identity. The universal has existence, not in our mind only, but also in the particular objects of experience. It does not, however, come to them from ourside and is not anything like a separate 'essence', but is only their common nature.

The Jaina and the Vedānta view.

The Nyāya-Vaiśeṣikas[4] enunciate the realistic theory of the universal. According to them, universals are eternal (nityạ) entities which are distinct from, but inhere in, many individuals (anekānugata). There is the same (eka) universal in all the individuals of a class. The universal is the basis of the notion of sameness that we have with regard to all the individuals of a certain class. It is because there is one common essence present in different individuals that they are brought under a class and thought of as essentially the same. Thus sāmānya or the universal is a real entity which corresponds to a general idea or class-concept in our mind. Some of the modern realists[5] also hold that a 'universal is an eternal timeless entity which may be shared by many particulars'. They agree further with the Naiyāyikas in maintaining that universals do not come under *existence* (sattā). These do

The Nyāya-Vaiśeṣika view.

1. Vide *Tarkabhāṣā*, p. 28; *Six Buddhist Nyāya Tracts*. Ch. V.
2. Vide *Outlines of Jainism*. p. 115 : *Prameya-kamala-mārtaṇḍa* Ch.IV.
3. Vide *Paribhāṣā*. Ch.I.
4. Vide *Tarkasangraha*, p. 87; *Bhāṣāparicheda* and *Muktārvali*, 8.14.15 : *Tarkabhāṣā*, p. 28; *Tarkāmṛta*, Ch. I : *Padārthadharma*., p.164.
5. *Cf.* Russell, *The Problems of Philosophy*, Ch. IX.

not exist in time and space, but have being and *subsist* in substance, attribute and action (dravya-guṇa-karmavṛtti). There is no universal subsisting in another universal, because there is but one single universal for one class of objects. If there are two or more universals in the same class of things, then they would exhibit contrary and even contradictory natures and we could not classify them one way or the other. The same individuals could have been men and cows at the same time.

Universal may be distinguished into three kinds—para, apara and parāpara.

In respect of their scope or extent, universals may be distinguished into para or the highest and all-pervading, apara or the lowest, and the parāpara or the intermediate[1] 'Being-hood' (sattā) is the highest universal, since all other universals come under it. Jarness (ghaṭatva) as the universal present in all jars is apara or the lowest, since it has the most limited or the narrowest extent. Substantiality or thinghood (dravyatva) as another universal is parāpara or intermediate between the highest and the lowest. It is para or wider in relation to substances like earth, water, etc. and apara or narrower in relation to the universal 'being-hood' which belongs to substance, quality and action.

5. *Particularity or Viśeṣa*[2]

Particularity is the unique individuality of the eternal substances.

Particularly (viśesa) is the extreme opposite of the universal (sāmānya). By particularity we are to understand the unique individuality of substances which have no parts and are, therefore eternal, suca as space, time, ākāśa, minds, souls and the atoms of earth, water, light and air, How are we to distinguish one mind or soul from another? How again is one atom of water

1. Vide *Bhāṣāpariccheda* and *Muktāvali*, 8,9; *Nyāyalilāvati*, pp. 80-81 Cf. *Tarkāmṛta*, Ch. I.

2. Vide *Tarkasangraha*, pp. 11, 88; *Bhāṣāpariccheda* and *Muktāvali*, 10; *Tarkabhāṣā*, p. 28; *Tarkāmṛta*, Ch. I; *Padārthadharma*., p. 168.

distinguished from another atom of water? That they are different from one another must be admitted by us. Yet we cannot explain it by the difference of their parts because they have no parts at all. On the other hand, they are similar in other respects. So we have to admit some peculiarity or unique character whereby they are distinguished from one another. The category of viśeṣa stands for this peculiar character of the otherwise indistinguishable substances.

Particularities are eternal and distinguished by themselves.

As subsisting in the eternal substances, viśeṣas are themselves eternal (nitya). We should not suppose that viśeṣa pertains to the ordinary things of the world like pots, chairs and tables. It does not belong to anything made up of parts. Things which are made up of parts, *i.e.* composite wholes, are easily distinguishable by the differences of their parts. So we do not require any category like viśeṣa to explain their distinction. It is only when we come to the ultimate differences of the partless eternal substances that we have to admit certain original or underived peculiarities called viśeṣas. There are innumerable particularities, since the individuals in which they subsist are innumerable. While the individuals are distinguished by their particulars, the latter are distinguished by themselves (svataḥ). Hence particularities are so many ultimates in the analysis and explanation of the differences of things. There cannot be any perception of them; like atoms, they are supersensible entities.

6. Inherence or Samavāya[1]

Samavāya and saṁyoga are the two main relations in the Nyāya-Vaiśeṣika system.

There are two main relations recognized in the Nyāya Vaiśeṣika philosophy. These are saṁyoga or conjuction is a temporary inherence. Conjunction is a temporary or non-eternal relation between two things which can, and usually do, exist in separation from

1. *Tarkasangraha*, p.88; *Tarkabhāsā*, p.2; *Padārthadharma*, pp.171-75 : *Bhāṣāpariccheda* and *Muktāvali*, 11.60.

each other. Two balls moving from opposite directions meet at a certain place. The relation which holds between them when they meet is one of conjuction. It is a temporary contact between two *substances* which may again be separated and yet exist (yutasiddha). So long as the relation of conjunction *is,* it exists as a quality of the terms related by it. But it does not affect the existence of those terms. It makes no difference to the existence of the balls whether they are conjoined to each other or not. Thus conjuction is an external relation which exists as an *accidental quality of two substances* related by it.

How the two are distinguished from each other.

As distinguished from conjunction, samavāya is a permanent or eternal relation between two entities, of which *one* inheres *in* the other. The whole is *in* its parts, a quality or an action is *in* a substance, or the universal is *in* the individuals, and particularly is *in* some simple eternal substance. Thus we say that the cloth as a whole is in the threads, the colour *red* as a quality is in the rose, motion as an action belongs to the moving ball, manhood as a universal is in individual men, and the peculiarity or the distinctive character of one mind or soul is in that mind or soul. Samavāya is perceptible, according to Nyāya, but not so, according to Vaiśeṣika.[1]

Conjuction is a temporary relation between two things which can exists separately, and it is produced by the action of either or both of the things related, *e.g.* the relation between a man and the chair on which he may be seated for the time being. On the other hand, the whole is *always* related to its parts, a quantity or an action is *always* related to some substance, and so forth. So long as any whole, say a jar, is not broken up, it must exist in the parts. So also, any quality or action must be related to some substance as long as it exists. Thus we see that the relation of a whole to its parts, of any quality or action to its substance, of the

1. Vide *Tarkakaumudī*, p.8; *Bhāṣāpariccheda* and *Muktāvalī*, p. 260.

universal to the individual, and of particularity to the eternal substances is not produced by the conjuction of two separate things. Hence it is that they are said to be related without conjuction (ayutasiddha). Samavāya is thus an *eternal* relation between any two entities, one of which cannot exist without the other. Terms related by samavāya cannot be reversed like those related by saṁyoga. If there is a contact of the hand with a pen, the pen also must be in contact with the hand; but though a quality is in a substance, the substance is not in the quality.

7. *Non-existence or Abhāva*

We have dealt with the six positive categories above. Now we come to the negative category of abhāva or non-existence, which does not come under any of the six categories. The reality of non-existence cannot be denied. Looking at the sky at night you feel as much sure of the non-existence of the sun there, as of the existence of the moon and the stars. The Vaiśeṣika recognizes, therefore, non-existence as the seventh category of reality. It is true that Kaṇāda did not mention abhāva as a separate category in the enumeration of the ultimate objects of knowledge (padārtha). Hence some people think that he was in favour of accepting only six categories. But in view of the facts that non-existence as a possible object of knowledge has been discussed in other parts of the *Vaiśeṣika-Sūtra* and that later commentators have treated it as the seventh category, we propose to consider it as such.[1]

Abhāva is the seventh category.

Abhāva or non-existence is of two kinds, namely, saṁsargābhāva and anyonyābhāva. Saṁsargābhāva means the absence of something in something else. Anyonyābhāva means the fact that one thing is not another thing. Saṁsargābhāva is of three kinds,

Abhāva is of two kinds, *viz.*, saṁsargābhāva and anyonyābhāva.

1. Vide *Vaiśeṣika., sit* 1.4., 9.1.1-10. *Kiraṇavalī*, p.6; *Nyāya-kandali*, p.7.

namely, prāgabhāva, dhvaṁsābhāva and atyantābhāva.[1] All kinds of saṁsargābhāva can be expressed by a judgment of the general form 'S is not *in* P', whereas anyonyābhāva can be expressed by a judgment like 'S is not P'.

Prāgabhāva is non-existence before production.

Prāgabhāva or antecedent non-existence is the non-existence of a thing before its production. When one says, 'a house will be built with bricks three is non-existence of the house *in* the bricks. This non-existence of a house in the bricks before its construction is prāgabhāva. It means the absence of a connection between the bricks and the house which has not yet been built with them. The house *never* existed before being built, so that its non-existence before construction has no beginning (anādi). When, however, the house is built, its previous non-existence comes to an end (anta). Hence it is that prāgabhāva is said to be without a beginning, but having an end (anādi and sānta).

Dhvaṁsābhāva is non-existence after destruction.

Dhvaṁsābhāva is the non-existence of a thing on account of its destruction after production. A jar which has been produced by a potter may be subsequently broken into pieces. When the jar is broken into pieces, there is its non-existence *in* those pieces. This non-existence of a previously existing thing, due to its destruction is called dhvaṁsābhā va. It is said to have a beginning (sādi), but no end (ananta). The non-existence of the jar begins with its destruction, but it cannot be ended in any way, for the very same jar cannot be brought back into existence. It will be seen here that although in the case of positive entities (bhāva padārtha), the general rule is that, whatever is produced must be destroyed, in the case of negative entities (abhāva padārtha), something which is produced cannot be destroyed, in the case of negative entities (abhāva padā rtha), something which is produced cannot be destroyed. The non-existence of the jar is produced by its destruction, but that non-existence cannot itself be destroyed. To destroy or end the jar's non-existence, we are to restore the same jar to existence, which is impossible.

1. *Bhāṣāpariccheda* and *Muktāvali*, p. 12; *Tarkabhāṣā*, p.29; *Tarkasangraha*, p. 89; *Tarkāmṛta*, Ch.I.

Atyantābhāva is absolute non-existence in the past, present and future.

Atyantābhāva or absolute non-existence is the absence of a connection between two things for all time—past, present and future, *e.g.* the non-existence of colour *in* air. It is thus different from prāgabhāva and dhvaṁsābhāva. Prāgabhāva is the non-existence of a thing before its production. Dhvaṁsābhāva is the non-existence of a thing after its destruction. But atyantābhāva is the non-existence of a thing, not in any particular time, but for all time. So it is subject neither to origin nor to cessation, *i.e.* it is both beginningless and endless (anādi and ananta).

Anyonyābhāva implies the difference of one thing from another.

While saṁsargābhāva is the absence of a connection between two things, anyonyābhāva underlies the difference (bheda) of one thing from another thing. When one thing is different from another thing, they mutually exclude each other and there is the non-existence of either as the other. A table is different from a chair. This means that a table does not exist as a chair, or, more simply, a table is not a chair. Anyonyābhāva is this non-existence of one thing as another, from which it is different. Thus saṁsargābhāva is the absence of a connection (saṁsarga) between two entities, and its opposite is just their connection. On the other hand, anyonābhāva is the absence of one thing as another, and its opposite is just their sameness or identity. Take the following illustrations: 'A hare has no horn,' 'there is no colour in air' are propositions which express the absence of a connection between a hare and a horn, between colour and air. The opposite of these will be the propositions 'a hare has horns,' 'there is colour in air.' 'A cow is not a horse,' 'a jar is not a cloth' are propositions which express the difference between a cow and a horse, a jar and a cloth. The opposite of these will be the propositions 'a cow is a horse', 'a jar is a cloth.' Thus we may say that saṁsargābhāva is relative non-existence in the sense of a negation of the presence (saṁsarga) of some thing in some other thing, while anyonyābhāva is mutual non-existence or difference in the sense of a negation of the identity (tādātmya) between two objects. Like atyantābhāva or absolute non-existence anyonyābhāva or mutual non-existence is without a beginning and an end *i.e.* is eternal.

III. The Creation and Destruction of the World[1]

The Vaiśesika theory of the world is guided by the general spiritual outlook of Indian philosophy.

From the standpoint of Indian philosophy the world including physical nature is a moral stage for the education and emancipation of individual souls. The Vaiśeṣika theory of the world is guided by this general spiritual outlook of Indian philosophy. In its attempt to explain the origin and destruction of the world it does indeed reduce all composite objects to the four kinds of atoms of earth, water, fire and air. So it is sometimes characterized as the atomic theory of the world. But it does not ignore the moral and spiritual principles governing the processes of composition and decomposition of atoms. Further, five of the nine kinds of substances, to which all things may be reduced, are not and cannot be reduced to material atoms. So the atomic theory of the Vaiśeṣika has a background different from that of the atomism of Western science and philosophy. The later is in principle a materialistic philosophy of the world. It explains the order and history of the world as the mechanical resultant of the fortuitous motions of innumerable atoms in infinite space and time, and in different directions. There is no mind or intelligent power governing and guiding the operations of the material atoms; these act according to blind mechanical laws. The atomism of the Vaiśeṣika, however, is a phase of their spiritual philosophy. According to it, the ultimate source of the actions of atoms is to be found in the creative or the destructive will of the Supreme Being who directs the

It is different from the atomism of Western philosophy.

1. Vide *Padārthadharma.*, pp. 19-23; *Nyāyakandalī*, pp. 50-54; *Kusumāñjali*, 2; *Tattvacintāmaṇi*, ii.

operations of atoms according to the unseen deserts (adṛṣṭa) of individual souls and with reference to the end of moral dispensation. On this view, the order of the world is like that of a monarchical state, which ultimately expresses the will of a wise monarch and in which all things are so ordered and adjusted that the citizens get ample opportunities for self-expansion and self-development as free and responsible beings.

The atomic theory of the Vaiśeṣika explains the order of creation and destruction of non-eternal objects.

The atomic theory of the Vaiśeṣika explains that part of the world which is non-eternal, *i.e.* subject to origin and destruction in time. The eternal constituents of the universe, namely, the four kinds of atoms, and the five substances of ākāsa, space, time, mind, and soul, do not come within the purview of their atomic theory, because these can neither be created nor destroyed. On the other hand, all composite objects, beginning with a dyad or the first compound of only two atoms (dvyaṇuka), are non-eternal. So the atomic theory explains the order of creation and destruction of these non-eternal objects. All composite objects are constituted by the combination of atoms and destroyed through their separation. The first combination of two atoms is called a dvyaṇuka or dyad, and a combination of three dyads (dvyaṇukas) is called a tryaṇuka or triad. The tryaṇuka is also called the trasareṇu and it is the minimum perceptible object according to the Vaiśeṣika philosophy. The paramāṇu or atom and the dvyaṇuka or dyad, being smaller than the tryaṇuka or triad, cannot be perceived, but are known through inference.

The world is composed of the four kinds of atoms.

All the finite objects of the physical world and the physical world itself are composed of the four kinds of atoms in the form of dyads, triads and other larger compounds arising out of these. How can we account for the action or motion of atoms, which is necessary for their combination? How, again, are we to explain this particular order and arrangement of things in the world? In the

Vaiśeṣika philosophy the order of the world is, in its broad outlines, conceived like this :

The world, or better, the universe is a system of physical things and living beings having bodies with senses and possessing mind, intellect and egoism. All these exist and interact with one another, in time, space and ākāśa. Living beings are souls who enjoy or suffer in this world according as they are wise or ignorant, good or bad, virtuous or vicious. The order of the world is, on the whole, a moral order in which the life and destiny of all individual selves, are governed, not only by the physical laws of time and space, but also by the universal moral law of karma. In the simplest form this law means 'as you sow, so you reap,' just as the physical law of causation, in its most abstract form, means that there can be no effect without a cause.

It is a system, of physical things and living beings which interact with one another.

The moral order of the world.

Keeping in view this moral order of the universe, the Vaiśeṣikas explain the process of creation and destruction of the world as follows : The starting-point of the process of creation of destruction is the will of the Supreme Lord (Maheśvara) who is the ruler of the whole universe. The Lord conceives the will to create a universe in which individual beings may get their proper share of the experience of pleasure and pain according to their deserts. The process of creation and destruction of the world being beginningless (anādi), we cannot speak of a first creation of the world. In truth every creation is preceded by a state of destruction, and every destruction is preceded by some order of creation. To create is to destroy an existing order of things and usher in a new order. Hence it is that God's creative will has reference to the stock of merit and demerit (adṛṣṭa) acquired by individual souls in a previous life lived in some other world. When God thus wills to create a world, the

The creation of the world has its starting-point in the creative will of the Supreme Lord.

The adrsta of individual souls guides the process of creation.

unseen forces of moral deserts in the eternal individual souls beign to function in the direction of creation and the active life of experiences (bhoga). And it is the contact with souls, endowed with the creative function of adṛṣṭa, that first sets in motion the atoms of air. Out of the combination of air-atoms, in the form of dyads and triads, arises the gross physical element (mahābhūta) of *air*, and it exists as an incessantly vibrating medium in the eternal ākāśa. Then, in a similar way, there is motion in the atoms of water and the creation of the gorss element of *water* which exists in the air and is moved by it. Next, the atoms of earth are set in motion in a similar way and compose the gross element of *earth* which exists in the vast expanse of the gross elemental water. Then from the atoms of light arises in a similar way, the gross element of *light* and exists with its luminosity in the gross water. After this and by the mere thought (abhidhyāna) of God, there appears the embryo of a world (brahmāṇda) out of the atoms of light and earth. God animates that great embryo with Brahmā, the world-soul, who is endowed with supreme wisdom, detachment and excellence (jñāna, vairāgya and aiśvaryya). To Brahmā God entrusts the work of creation in its concrete details and with proper adjustment between merit and demerit on the one hand, and happiness and misery on the other.

Brahmā is the architect of the world.

The created world runs its course for many years. But it cannot continue to exist and endure for all time to come. Just as after the stress and strain of the day's work God allows us rest at night, so after the trials and tribulations of many lives in one created world, God provides a way of escape from suffering for all living beings for sometime. This is done by Him through the destruction of the world. So the period of creation is followed by a state of destruction. The periods of creation and destruction make one complete cycle called Kalpa which has been repeating itself eternally. The theory of cycles (kalpas) or recurring periods of creation and destruction is accepted by most of the orthodox systems of Indian philosophy. The belief that the world in which we live is not eternal, and

Creations is followed by destruction.

The theory of cycles of creation and destruction.

that at some distant time there shall be its dissolution, is supported by an analogical argument. Just as earthen substances like jars are destroyed, so mountains which are earthy shall be destroyed. Ponds and tanks are dried up. Seas and oceans being only very big reservoirs of water shall dry up. The light of a lamp is blown out. The sun being but a glorious orb of light must be extinguished at some distant time.

The process of the world's dissolution is as follows : When in the course of time Brahmā, the worldsoul, gives up his body like other souls, there appears in Maheśvara or the Supreme Lord a desire to destroy the world. With this, the creative adṛṣta or unseen moral agency in living beings is counteracted by the corresponding *destructive* adṛṣta and ceases to function for the active life of experience. It is in contact with such souls, in which the destructive adṛṣta begins to operate, that there is motion in the constituent atoms of their body and senses. On account of this motion there is disjunction of the atoms and consequent disintegration of the body and the senses. The body with the senses being thus destroyed, what remain are only the atoms in their isolation. So also, there is motion in the constituent atoms of the elemental earth, and its consequent destruction through the cessation of their conjuction. In this way there is the destruction of the physical elements of *earth, water, light* and *air*, one after the other. Thus these four physical elements and all bodies and sense organs are disintegrated and destroyed. What remain are the four kinds of atoms of earth, water, light and air in their isolation, and the eternal substances of ākāśa, time, space, minds and souls with their stock of merit, demerit and past impressions (bhāvanā). It will be observed here that while in the order of destruction, earth compounds come first, and then those of water, light and air in succession, in the order of creation, air compounds come first, water compounds next, and then those of the great earth and light appear in succession.[1]

The process of the world's destruction is started by the destructive will of God.

1. The details of this account of creation and destruction are found in Praśastapādas's *Padārthadharmasangraha* which seems to draw on the Paurāṇika accounts.

IV. Conclusion

Like the Nyāya system, the Vaiśeṣika is a realistic philosophy which combines pluralism with theism. It traces the variety of the objects of the world to the combination of material atoms of different kinds and qualities. But the creation of the world out of the combination of eternal atoms, in eternal time and space, has reference to the moral life of individual selves. The world is created and destroyed by God according to the moral deserts of individual souls and for the proper realization of their moral destiny. But the realistic idea of the soul and the apparently deistic conception of God in the Vaiśeṣika labour under the difficulties of the Nyāya theory and are as unsatisfactory as the latter. For it, the soul is an independent substance, of which consciousness is an accidental property. It may be admitted by us that the mind or the empirical consciouness is not the real self and that the latter is different from the former. Still it is not possible for us to explain mental phenomena or the empirical consciousness unless we admit that the real or the nonmenal self is an essentially conscious and intelligent reality. So also the Vaiśeṣika idea of God as wholly transcendent to and separate from man and the world, is not favourable for a deeply religious view of life and the genuine religious consciousness of communion with God.

The special contributions of the Vaiśeṣika philosophy are its comprehensive conception of padārtha or object as that which is denoted by a word, its classification of objects and its atomic cosmology. In the classification of objects it recognizes the distinction between positive and negative objects, or between those that have being and those which have no being, but are as real and as much denoted by words as the former. Again, it is here pointed out that while most objects can be classified and brought under certain genera (jāti), there are some like ākāśa or ether, sāmānya, viśeṣa, samavāya and abhāva which do not come under any corresponding genera like ākāśatva, sāmānyatva, etc., because none of them is a genus or jāti at all. The Vaiśeṣika division of objects into seven classes and of these into many other sub-classes is a logical classification of them based on their distinctive characters and ultimate differences. The atomic theory of the Vaiśeṣika is an improvement on the ordinary view of the world as constituted by the physical elements of earth, water, air and fire. It is also an advance on the materialistic theory that all things including life, mind and consciousness are transformations and mechanical products of material atoms. The Vaiśeṣikas harmonize the atomic theory with the moral and spiritual outlook of life and the theistic faith in God as the creator and moral governor of the world. But they do not carry their theism far enough and make God the author not only of the order of nature but also of its ultimate constituents, *viz.* the atoms, minds and souls, and see God at the heart of all reality.

THE SĀṄKHYA PHILOSOPHY

A SELECT BIBLIOGRAPHY

Kṛṣṇanātha Nyāyapañcānana *Tattvakaumudī* (Calcutta C. 1904).

Kālīvara Vedāntavāgīśa ... *Sāṅkhya-sūtra* (with Aniruddha's *Vṛtti*, Calcutta)

S. S. Sūryanārayaṇa Śāstrī ... *The Sāṁkhya Kārikā of Iśvara Kṛṣṇa* (with Eng. trans., Madras University, 1933)

R.G. Bhatta ... *Sāṅkhya-pravacana-bhāṣya* (Chowkhamba, Benares)

Mādhavācārya ... *Sarva-darśana-saṅgraha*, Ch. on Sāṅkhya

Nandalal Sinha ... *The Sāṁkhya Philosophy* (Panini Office, Allahabad, 1915).

S. Radhakrishnan ... *Indian Philosophy*, Vol. II, Ch. IV.

S. N. Dasgupta ... *History of Indian Philosophy*, Vol. I, Ch. VII.

A. B. Keith ... *The Sāṁkhya System* (Oxford, 1918).

A. K. Majumdar ... *The Sāṅkhya Conception of Personality* (Calcutta University, 1930).

B. N. Seal ... *The Positive Science of the Ancient Hindus*. Ch. I.

M. C. Pandya ... *Origin of the Sāṅkhya* (Bombay, 1953).

CHAPTER VII

THE SĀṄKHYA PHILOSOPHY

I. Introduction

The Sāṅkhya system is the work of a great sage of the name of Kapila. The Sāṅkhya must be a very old system of thought. Its antiquity appears from the fact that the Sāṅkhya tendency of thought pervades all the literature of ancient India including the śrutis, smṛtis and purāṇas. According to tradition, the first work of the Sāṅkhya school is the *Sāṅkhya-sūtra* of Kapila. This being very brief and terse, Kapila, we are told, wrote an elaborate work entitled the *Sāṅkhya-pravacana-sūtra.* Hence the Sāṅkhya philosophy is also known as Sāṅkhyaprayacana. This system is sometimes described as the 'atheistic Sāṅkhya' (nirīśvara-sāṅkhya), as distinguished from the Yoga which is called the 'theistic Sāṅkhya' (seśvara-Sāṅkhya). The reason for this is that Kapila did not admit the existence of God and also thought that God's existence could not be proved. But this is a controversial point.

The Sāṅkhya system is the work of the great sage Kapila.

Next to Kapila, his disciple Āsuri's, and Āsuri's disciple Pañcaśikha wrote some books which aimed at a clear and elaborate exposition of the Sāṅkhya system. But these works were lost in course of time and we have no information about their contents. Iśvarakṛṣṇa's *Sāṅkhya-Kārikā* is the earliest available and authoritative text-book of the Sāṅkhya. Gauḍapāda's *Sāṅkhya-Kārikā-bhāṣya*, Vācaspati's *Tattvakaumudi,* Vijñānabhikṣu's *Sāṅkhya-pravacana-bhāṣya* and *Sāṅkhya-sāra,* and Aniruddha's *Sāṅkhya-pravacana-sūtra-vṛtti* are some other important works of the Sāṅkhya system.

Some important works of the Sāṅkhya.

The name 'sāṅkhya' is explained in different ways.

The origin of the name 'sāṅkhya' is shrouded in mystery. According to some thinkers,[1] the name 'sāṅkhya' is an adaptation from 'sāṅkhya' meaning number and has been applied to this philosophy because it aims at a right knowledge of reality by the enumeration of the ultimate objects of knowledge. According to others however the word 'sāṅkhya' means perfect knowledge (samyag-jñāna), and a philosophy in which we have such knowledge is justly named sāṅkhya. Like the Nyāya-Vaiśeṣika system, the Sāṅkhya aims at the knowledge of reality for the practical purpose of putting an end to all pain and suffering. It given us a knowledge of the self which is clearly higher than that given by the other systems, excepting perhaps the Vedānta. So it may very well be characterized as the 'sāṅkhya' in the sense of a pure metaphysical knowledge of the self. It is a metaphysic of dualistic realism. While the Nyāya and the Vaiśeṣika admit the ultimate reality of many entities—atoms, minds and souls—the Sāṅkhya recognizes only two kinds of ultimate realities, namely, spirit and matter (puruṣa and prakṛti). The nature of these two ultimate and other derivative realities will be considered in the Sāṅkhya metaphysics.

II. The Sāṅkhya Metaphysics

1. *Theory of Causation*[2]

The Sāṅkhya Metaphysics, especially its doctrine of prakṛti, rests mainly on its theory of causation which is known as satkārya-vāda. It is a theory as to the relation of an effect (kārya) to its material cause. The specific question discussed here is this : Does an effect originally exist in the material cause prior to its production, *i.e.* appearance as an effect ? The Bauddhas and the Nyāya-Vaiśeṣikas

The Bauddha and the Nyāya-Vaiśesika theory of causation.

1. Vide *Bhāgavata*, 3. 25, *et passim* and Srīdhara svāmin thereon.

2. Vide *Sāṅkhya - kārikā* and *Tattvakaumudī*, 8. 9; *Sāṅkhya-pravacanabhāṣya*, 1. 113-21 : Aniruddha's *Vṛtti*, 1. 113-21.

answer this question in the negative. According to them, the effect cannot be said to exist before it is produced by some cause. If the effect already existed in the material cause prior to its production, there is no sense in our speaking of it as being caused or produced in any way. Further, we cannot explain why the activity of any efficient cause is necessary for the production of the effect. If the pot already existed in the clay, why should the potter exert himself and use his implements to produce it ? Moreover, if the effect were already in its material cause, it would logically follow that the effect is indistinguishable from the cause, and that we should use the same name for both the pot and that we should use the same name for both the pot and the clay, and also that the same purpose would be served by a pot and a lump of clay. It cannot be said that there is a distinction of form between the effect and its material cause, for then we have to admit that there is something in the effect which is not to be found in its cause and, therefore, the effect does not really exist in the cause. This theory that the effect does not exist in the material cause prior to its production is known as asatkārya-vāda (*i.e.* the view that the kārya or the effect is asat or non-existent before its production). It is also called ārambhavāda *i.e.* the theory of the beginning of the effect anew.

The Sāṅkya theory of satkārya-vāda and its grounds.

The Sāṅkhya repudiate this theory of causation and establish their view of satkārya-vāda, namely, that the effect exists in the material cause even before it is produced. This view is based on the following grounds : *(a)* If the effect were really non-existent in the material cause, then no amount of effort on the part of any agent could bring it into existence. Can any man turn bule into red, or sugar into salt ? Hence, when an effect is produced from some material cause, we are to say that it pre-exists in the cause and is only manifested by certain favourable conditions, as when oil is produced by pressing seeds. The activity of efficient causes, like the potter and his tools, is necessary to *manifest* the effect, pot, which exists *implicitly* in the clay. *(b)* There is an invariable relation between a material cause and its effect. A material cause can produce only that effect with which it is causally related. It cannot produce an effect which is in no way related to it. But it cannot be related to what does not exist. Hence the effect must exist in the material cause before it is actually produced. *(c)* We see that only certain effects can be produced from certain causes. Curd can be got only out of milk and a cloth only out of threads. This shows that the effect somehow exists in the cause. Had it not been so, any effect could be produced from any cause ; the potter would not have taken clay to produce pots, instead of taking milk or threads or any other thing. *(d)* The fact that only a *potent* cause can produce a desired effect goes to show that the effect must be *potentially* contained in the cause. The potent cause of an effect is that which possesses some power that is definitely related to the effect. But the power cannot be related to the effect, if the latter does not exist in some form. This means that the effect exists in the cause in an *unmanifested* form before its production or manifestation. *(e)* If the effect be really non-existent in the cause, then we have to say that, when it is produced, the non-existent comes into existence, *i.e.* something comes out of nothing, which is absurd. *(f)* Lastly, we see that the effect is not different from, but essentially identical with, the material cause. If, therefore, the cause exists, the effect also must exist. In fact, the effect and the cause are explicit and implicit states of the same substance. A cloth is not really different from the threads, of which it is mades ; a statue is the same as its material cause, stone, with a new shape and form ; the weight of a table is the same as that of the pieces of wood used in it. The conclusion drawn by the Sāṅkhya from all this is that the effect exists in the material cause even before its production or appearance. This is the theory of satkārya-vāda (*i.e.* the view that the effect is existent before its appearance).

Two different forms of satkārya-vāda.

The theory of satkārya-vāda has got two different forms, namely, pariṇāma-vāda and vivarta-vāda. According to the former, when effect is produced, there is a *real* transformation (pariṇāma) of the cause into the effect, *e.g.* the production of a pot from clay, or of curd from milk. The Sāṅkhya is in favour of this view as a further specification of the theory of satkārya-vāda. The second, which is accepted by the Advaita Vedāntins, holds that the change of the cause into the effect is merely *apparent*. When we see a snake in a rope, it is not the case that the rope is really transformed into a snake ; what happens is that the rope only appears as, but is not really, a snake. So also, God or Brahman does not become really transformed into while we may wrongly think that He undergoes change and becomes the world.

2. *Prakṛti and the Guṇas*[1]

Prakṛti is the ultimate cause of the world of objects.

The Sāṅkhya theory that causation means a real transformation of the material cause into the effect logically leads to the concept of prakṛti as the ultimate cause of the world of objects. All objects of the world, including our body and mind, the senses and the intellect, are limited and dependent things produced by the combination of certain elements. So we see that the world is a series of effects and that it must have a cause. What, then, is the cause of the world ? it cannot be the puruṣa or the self, since the self is neither a cause nor an effect of any thing. So the cause of the world must be the not-self, *i.e.* some principle which is other than and different from spirit, self or consciousness. Can this not-self be the physical elements or the material atoms? According to the Cārvākas or the materialists, the Bauddhas, the Jainas and the Nyāya-Vaiśeṣikas, the atoms of earth, water, light and air are the

1. Vide *Kārikā* and *Kaumudī*, 3, 10-16; *Pravacana-bhāṣya* and *vṛtti* 1.110, 1.122-37

material causes of the objects of the world. The Sāṅkhya objects to this on the ground that material atoms cannot explain the origin of the subtle products of nature, such as the mind, the intellect and the ego. So we must seek for something which can explain the gross objects of nature like earth and water, trees and seas, as well as its subtle products. Now it is found that in the evolution of things the cause is subtler than the effect and that it pervades the effect, as when a seed develops into a tree or a wish into a dream-object. Hence the ultimate cause of the world must be some unintelligent or unconscious principle which is uncaused, eternal and all-pervading, very fine and always ready to produce the world of objects. This is the prakṛti of the Sāṅkhya system. It is the first cause of all things and, therefore, has itself no cause. As the uncaused root-cause of all objects it is eternal and ubiquitous, because nothing that is limited and non-eternal can be the first cause of the world. Being the ground of such subtle products of nature as mind and the intellect, prakṛit is a very subtle, mysterious and tremendous power which evolves and dissolves the world in a cyclic order.

Proofs for the existence of Prakṛti.

The existence or prakṛti as the ultimate subtle cause of the world is known by inference from the following grounds : *(a)* All particular objects of the world, from the intellect to the earth are limited and dependent on one another. So there must be an unlimited and independent cause for their existence. *(b)* Things of the world possess certain common characters, owing to which everyone of them is capable of producing pleasure, pain and indifference. Therefore, they must have a common cause having these three characters. *(c)* All effects proceed from the activity of some cause which contains their potentiality within it. The world of objects which are effects must, therefore, be implicitly contained in some world-cause. *(d)* An effect arises from its cause and is again resolved into it at the moment of its destruction. That is, an existent effect is manifested by a cause, and eventually it is re-absorbed into the latter. So the particular objects of experience must arise from their particular causes, and these again from other general causes, and so on, till we come to the first cause of the world. Contrariwise, at the time of destruction, the physical elements must be resolved into atoms, the atoms into energies and so on, till all products are resolved into the unmanifested, eternal prakṛti. Thus we get one unlimited and unconditioned, all-pervading and ultimate cause of the whole world including everything but the self. This is the eternal and undifferentiated casual matrix of the world of not-self, to which the Sāṅkhya gives the different names of prakṛti, pradhāna, avyakta, etc. We whould not imagine a cause of this ultimate cause, for that will land us in the fallacy of infinite regress. If there be a cause of prakṛti, then there must be a cause of that cause, and so on, *ad infinitum*. Or, if we stop anywhere and say that here is the first cause, then that first cause will be the prakṛti which is specifically described as the supreme root cause of the world (parā or mūlā prakṛti).[1]

Prakṛti is constituted by three guṇas called sattva, rajas and tamas.

Prakṛti is constituted by the three guṇas of sattva, rajas and tamas. It is said to be the unity of guṇas held in a state of equilibrium (sāmyāvasthā). Now the question is : What are these guṇas ? Guṇa here means a constituent element or component and *not* an attribute or quality. Hence by the guṇas of sattva, rajas and tamas we are to understand the elements of the ultimate substance called prakṛti. The reason why they are

1. Vide *Pravacana-bhāṣya*, 1. 67-68, 1. 76-77, 6.35.

called guṇas is either their being *subservient* to the ends of the puruṣa which is other than themselves, or their being intertwined *like* the three *strands* of a rope which binds the soul to the world.[1]

Proofs for the existence of guṇas.

The guṇas are not perceived by us. They are inferred from the objects of the world which are their effects. Since there is an essential indentity (tādātmya) between the effect and its cause, we know the nature of the guṇas from the nature of their products. All objects of the world, from the intellect down to the ordinary objects of perception (*e.g.* tables, pots, etc.), are found to possess three characters capable of producing pleasure, pain and indifference, respectively. The same things are pleasureable to some person, painful to another, and neutral to a third. The cuckoo's cry is a pleasure to the artist, a pain to his sick friend and neither to the plain rustic. A rose delights the youth, dejects the dying man and leaves the gardener cold and indifferent. Victory in war elates the victor, depresses the vanquished and leaves the third party rather apathetic. Now, as the cause must contain what is in the effect, we can infer that the ultimate cause of things must have been constituted also by the three elements of pleasure, pain and indifference. The Sāṅkhya calls these three sattva, rajas and tamas respectively. These are constitutive of both prakṛti, the ultimate substance, and the ordinary objects of the world.

Sattva is of the nature of pleasure and is light and illuminating.

Sattva is that element of prakṛti which is of the nature of pleasure, and is buoyant or light (laghu), and bright or illuminating (prakāśaka). The manifestation of objects in consciousness (jñana), the tendency towards conscious manifestation in the senses, the mind and the intellect, the luminosity of light, and the power of reflection in a mirror or the crystal are all due to

1. *Op. cit.,* 1. 65. The word *guṇa* has many senses, such as 'quality,' 'strands,' 'subservient.'

the operation of the element of sattva in the constitution of things. Similarly, all sorts of lightness in the sense of upward motion, like the blazing up of fire, the upward courses of vapour and the winding motion of air, are induced in things by the element of sattva. So also pleasure in its various forms, such as satisfaction, joy, happiness, bliss, contentment, etc. is produced by things in our minds through the operation of the power of sattva inhering in them both.

Rajas is of the nature of pain, and is mobile and stimulating.

Rajas is the principle of activity in things. It always moves and makes other things move. That is, it is both mobile (cala) and stimulating (upaṣṭambhaka). It is on account of rajas that fire spreads, the wind blows, the senses follow their objects and the mind becomes restless. On the affective side of our life, rajas is the cause of all painful experiences and is itself of the nature of pain (duḥkha). It helps the elements of sattva and tamas, which are inactive and motionless in themselves, to perform their functions.

Tamas is of the nature of indifference and is heavy and enveloping.

Tamas is the principle of passivity and negativity in things. It is opposed to sattva in being heavy (guru) and in obstructing the manifestation of objects (varaṇaka). It also resists the principle of rajas or activity in so far as it restains (niyam) the motion of things. It counteracts the power of manifestation in the mind, the intellect and other things, and thereby produces ignorance and darkness, and leads to confusion and bewilderment (moha). By obstructing the principle of activity in us it induces sleep, drowsiness and laziness. It also produces the state of apathy or indifference (viṣāda). Hence it is that sattva, rajas and tamas have been compared respectively to whiteness, redness, and darkness.

The guṇas are in the state of both conflict and co-operation with one another.

With regard to the relation among the three guṇas constituting the world, we observe that it is one of constant conflict as well as co-operation. They always go together and can never be separated from one another. Nor can any one of them produce anything without the help and support of the other two. Just as the oil, the wick and the flame, which are relatively, opposed to one another, co-operate to produce the light of a lamp, so the guṇas co-operate to produce the objects of the world, although they possess different and opposed qualities. So all the three guṇas are present in everything of the world, great or small, fine or gross. But each of them tries to suppress and dominate the others. The nature of things is determined by the predominant guṇa, while the others are there in a subordinate position. We cannot point to anything of the world which does not contain within it all the three elements, of course, in different proportions. The classification of objects into good, bad and indifferent, or into pure, impure and neutral, or into intelligent, active and indolent, has reference to the preponderance of sattva, rajas and tamas respectively.

They are subject to constant change and transformation.

Another characteristic of the guṇas is that they are constantly changing. "Change or transformation belongs to the very essence of the guṇas, and they cannot help changing even for a moment." There are two kinds of transformation which the guṇas undergo. During pralaya or dissolution of the world, the guṇas change, each within itself, without disturbing the others. That is, sattva changes into sattva, rajas into rajas and tamas into tamas. Such transformation of the guṇas is called svarūpapariṇāma or change into the homogeneous. At this stage, the guṇas cannot create or produce anything, because they do not oppose and co-operate with one another. No object of the world can arise unless the guṇas combine, and one of them predominates over the others. So before creation, the guṇas exist as a homogeneous mass in which there is no motion (although there is transformation), no thing, and none of the qualities of sound, touch, colour, taste and smell. This is the state of equilibrium (sāmyāvasthā) for the guṇas to which the Sāṅkhya gives the name of prakṛti. The other kind of transformation takes place when one of the guṇas dominates over the others

Two kinds of transformation of the guṇas.

which become subordinate to it. When this happens, we have the production of particular objects. Such transformation is called virūpa-pariṇāma or change into the heterogeneous, and it is the starting-point of the world's evolution.

3. Puruṣa or the Self[1]

The self is an indubitable reality.

The second type of ultimate reality admitted by the Sāṅkhya is the self. The existence of the self must be admitted by all. Everybody feels and assests that he or she exists, and has this or that thing belonging to him or her. The feeling of one's own existence is the most natural and indubitable experience that we all have. In fact, no one can consistently deny the existence of his self, for the act of denial presupposes the reality of the denying self. So it has been said by the Sāṅkhyas that the self exists, because it is self-manifest and its non-existence cannot be proved in any way.

Different conceptions of the self.

But while there is general agreement with regard to the existence of the self, there is a wide divergence of opinion about its nature. Some Cārvākas or materialists identify the self with the gross body, some with the senses, some with life, and some others with the mind. The Buddhists and some empiricists regard the self as identical with the stream of consciousness. The Nyāya-vaiśeṣika and the Prābhākara Mīmāṁsakas maintain that the self is an unconscious substance which may acquire the attribute of consciousness under certain conditions. The Bhāṭṭa Mīmāṁsakas, on the other hand, think that the self is a conscious entity which is partially hidden by ignorance, as appears from the imperfect and partial knowledge that men have of their own selves. The Advaita Vedānta holds that the self is pure eternal

1. Vide *Vedāntasāra*, 51-59 ; *Kārikā* and *Kaumudi*., 17-20; *Pravacana-bhāṣya* and *Vṛtti*, 1. 66., 1. 138-64., 5. 61-68.

consciousness which is also a blissful existence (saccidānanda svarūpa). It is one in all bodies, and is eternally free and self-shining intelligence.

The self is pure, eternal and all-pervading consciousness.

According to the Sāṅkhya, the self is different from the body and the senses, the manas and the intellect (buddhi). It is not anything of the world of objects. The self is not the brain, nor the nervous system, nor the aggregate of conscious states. The self is a conscious spirit which is always the subject of knowledge and can never become the object of any knowledge. It is not a substance with the *attribute* of consciousness, but it is pure consciousness *as such.* Consciousness is its very *essence* and not a mere *quality* of it. Nor should we say that it is a blissful consciousness (ānandasvarūpa), as the Advaita Vedāntin thinks; bliss and consciousness being different things cannot be the essence of the same reality. The self is the transcendent subject whose essence is pure consciousness. The light of the self's consciousness ever remains the same, although the objects of knowledge may change and succeed one another. It is a steady constant consciousness in which there is neither change nor activity. The self is above all change and activity. It is an uncaused, eternal and all-pervading reality which is free from all attachement and unaffected by all objects. All change and activity, all pleasures and pains belong really to matter and its products like the body, mind and intellect. It is sheer ignorance to think that the self is the body or the senses or the mind or the intellect. But when, through such ignorance, the self confuses itself with any of these things, it *seems* to be caught up in the flow of changes and activities, and merged in the mire of sorrows and miseries.

Proofs for the existence of the self.

The existence of the self as the transcendent subject of experience is proved by the Sāṅkhya by several arguments : *(a)* Objects of the world like tables, chairs, etc. which are composed of parts are means to the ends of other beings. These beings whose purpose is served by the things of the world must be quite different and distinct from them all. That is, they cannot be said to be unconscious things, made up of parts like physical objects, for that would make them means to the ends of others and not ends in themselves. They must be conscious selves, to whose ends all physical objects are the means. *(b)* All material objects including the mind and intellect must be controlled and directed by some intelligent principle in order that they can achieve anything or realize any end. A machine or a car does its work when put under the guidance of some person. So there must be some selves who guide the operations of prakṛti and all her products. *(c)* All objects of the world of the nature of pleasure, pain and indifference. But pleasure and pain have meaning only as they are experienced by some conscious experiencer. Hence there must be some conscious subjects or selves who enjoy and suffer pleasure and pain respectively. *(d)* Some persons at least of this world make a sincere endeavour to attain final release from all suffering. This is not possible for anything of the physical world, for by its very nature, the physical world cause suffering rather than relieve it. So there must be some immaterial substances or *selves* transcending the physical order. Otherwise, the concept of liberation or salvation and the will to liberate or to be liberated as found in saints and the saviours of mankind would be meaningless.

Proofs for the reality of many selves.

There is not, as the Advaita Vedāntin says, one universal self pervading all bodies alike. On the other hand, we must admit a plurality of selves, of which one is connected with each body. That there are many selves in the world follows from the following considerations : *(a)* There is an obvious difference in the *birth* and *death*, and the *sensory* and *motor endowments* of different individuals. The birth or death of one individual does not mean the same for all other individuals. Blindness or deafness in one man does not imply the same for all men. But if all person had one and the same self, then the birth and death of one would cause the birth and death of all, and the blindness or deafness of one would make all others blind or deaf. Since, however, that is not the case, we are to say that there is not one but many selves. *(b)* If there were but one self for all living beings, then the *activity* of any one would make all others active. But as a matter of fact, when we sleep, others make restless efforts, and *vice versa*. *(c)* Men and women are different from the gods, on the one hand, and birds and beasts, on the other. But there could not have been these distinctions, if gods and human beings, birds and beasts possessed the *same* self. Thus we see that there must be a *plurality* of selves, which are eternal and intelligent subjects of knowledge, as distinguished from prakṛti which is the one, eternal and non-intelligent ground of the objects of knowledge, including manas, intellect and the ego.

4. Evolution of the World[1]

The evolution of the world has its starting point in contact between puruṣa and prakṛti.

Prakṛti evolves the world of objects when it comes into relation with the puruṣa. The evolution of the world has its starting-point in the contact (saṁyoga) between puruṣa or the self and prakṛti or primal matter. The contact (saṁyoga) between puruṣa and prakrti does not, however, mean any kind of ordinary conjunction like that between two finite material substances. It is a sort of effective relation through which prakṛti is influenced by the presence of puruṣa in the same way in which our body is sometimes moved by the presence of a thought. There can be no evolution unless the two become somehow related to each other. The evolution of the world cannot be due to the self alone, for it is inactive; nor can it be due to matter (prakṛti) alone, for it is non-intelligent. The activity of prakṛti must be guided by the intelligence of puruṣa, if there is to be any evolution of the world. It is only when

1. Vide *Kārikā* and *Kaumudī*, 21-41; *Pravacana-bhāṣya* and *Vṛtti*, 1. 64-74, 2. 10-32.

puruṣa and prakṛti co-operate that there is the creation of a world of objects. But the question is : How can two such different and opposed principles like puruṣa and prakṛti co-operate ? What brings the one in contact with other ? The answer given by the Sāṅkhya is this : Just as a blind man and a lame man can co-operate in order to get out of a forest, so the non-intelligent prakṛti and the inactive puruṣa combine and co-operate to serve their respective interests. Prakṛti requires the presence of puruṣa in order to be known or appreciated by someone (darśanārtham), and puruṣa requires the help of prakṛti in order to discriminate itself from the latter and thereby attain liberation (kaivalyārtham).

This contact disturbs the original equilibrium of prakṛti.

With the contact between puruṣa and prakṛti, there is a disturbance of the equilibrium in which the guṇas were held before creation. One of the guṇas, namely, rajas, which is naturally active, is disturbed first, and then, through rajas, the other guṇas begin to vibrate. This produces a tremendous commotion in the infinite bosom of prakṛti and each of the guṇas tries to preponderate over the rest. There is a gradual differentiation and integration of the three guṇas, and as a result of their combination in different proportions, the various objects of the world originate. The course of evolution is as follows :

The first product of evolution is mahat or buddhi.

The first product of the evolution of prakṛti is mahat or buddhi.[1] Considered in its cosmic aspect, it is the great germ of this vast world of objects and is accordingly called mahat or the great one. In its psychological aspect, *i.e.* as present in individual beings, it is called buddhi or the intellect. The special functions of buddhi are ascertainment and decision. It is by means of the intellect that the distinction between the subject and other objects is understood, and one makes decisions about things. Buddhi arises out of the preponderance of the element of sattva in prakṛti.

1. Vide *Sāṅkhya-sūt.,* 1.71.

It is the natural function of buddhi to manifest itself and other things. In its pure (sāttvika) condition, therefore, it has such attributes as virtue (dharma), knowledge (jñāna), detachment (vairāgya) and excellence (aiśvaryya). But when vitiated by tamas, it has such contrary attributes as vice (adharma), ignorance (ajñāna), attachment (āsakti or avairāgya) and imperfection (aśakti or anaiśvaryya). Buddhi is different from puruṣa or the self which transcends all physical things and qualities. But it is the ground of all intellectual processes in all individual beings. It stands nearest to the self and reflects the consciousness of the self in such a way as to become apparently conscious and intelligent. While the sense and the mind function for buddhi or the intellect, the latter functions directly for the self and enables it to discriminate between itself and prakṛti.[1]

The second is ahaṅkāra or the ego.

Ahaṅkāra or the ego is the second product of prakṛti, which arises directly out of mahat, the first manifestation. The function of ahaṅkāra that the self considers itself (wrongly indeed) to be an agent or a cause of action, a desirer of and striver for ends, and an owner of properties. We first perceive objects through the senses. Then the mind reflects on them and determines them specifically as of this or that kind. Next there is an appropriation of those objects as belonging to and intended for me, and also a feeling of myself as somehow concerned in them. Ahaṅkāra is just this sense of the self as 'I' (aham), and of objects as 'mine' (mama). When ahaṅkāra thus determines our attitude towards the objects of the world, we proceed to act in different ways in relation to them. The potter constructs a pot when he accepts it as one of his ends and resolves to attain it by saying within himself : 'Let *me* construct a pot'.

There are three kinds of ahaṅkāra.

Ahaṅkāra is said to be of three kinds, according to the predominance of one or other of the three guṇas. It is called vaikārika or sāttvika when the element of sattva predominates in it, taijasa or

1. Vide *Kārikā,* 36-37 : *Sāṅkhya-sūt.,* 2. 40-43.

rājasa when that of rajas predominates, and bhūtādi or tāmasa when tamas predominates. From the first arise the eleven organs, namely, the five organs of perception (jñānendriya), the five organs of action (karmendriya), and the mind (manas). From the third (*i.e.* tāmas ahaṅkāra) are derived the five subtle elements (tanmātras). The second (*viz.*rājasa) is concerned in both the first and the third, and supplies the energy needed for the change of sattva and tamas into their products.

The above order of development from ahaṅkāra is laid down in the *Sāṅkhya-kārikā* and accepted by Vācaspati Miśra.[1] Vijñānabhikṣu,[2] however, gives a different order. According to him, manas or the mind is the only sense which is pre-eminently sāttvika or manifesting, and is, therefore, derived from sāttvika ahaṅkāra. The other ten organs are developed from rājasa ahaṅkāra and the five subtle elements from the tāmasa.

Five organs of knowledge.

The five organs of perception (buddhindriya) are the senses of sight, hearing, smell, taste and touch. These perceive respectively the physical qualities of colour, sound, smell, taste and touch, and are developed from ahaṅkāra for the enjoyment of the self. It is the self's desire to enjoy objects that creates both the objects of and the organs for, enjoyment. The organs of action (karmendriya) are located in the mouth, hands, feet, anus and the sex organ. These perform respectively the functions of speech prehension, movement, excretion and reproduction. The *real* organs are not the perceptible external organs, like the eye-balls, ear-holes, skin, hands, feet, etc. There are certain *imperceptible* powers (śakti) in these perceptible end-organs which apprehend physical objects and act on them, and are, therefore, to be regarded as the organs (indriyas) proper. As such, an indriya cannot be sensed or perceived, but must be known by inference.[3] The mind (manas) is the central organ which partakes of the nature of the organs of both knowledge and action. Without the guidance of the manas neighter of them can function in relation to their objects. The manas is a very subtle, sense indeed, but it is

Five organs of action.

Manas or mind is the central organ.

1. Cf. *Kārikā* and *Kaumudī*, 25
2. Cf. *Pravacana-bhāṣya*, 2. 18.
3. Cf. *Sāṅkhya-sūt.*, 2. 23; *Kārikā* and *Kaumudī*, 26 and 28.

made up of parts, and so can come into contact with several senses at the same time. The mind, the ego and the intellect (manas, ahaṅkāra and buddhi) are the three internal organs (antaḥkaraṇa), while the senses of sight, hearing, etc. and the organs of action are called the external organs (bāhyakarana). The vital breaths or processes are the functions of the internal organs. The ten external organs condition the function of the internal ones. The mind (manas) interprets the indeterminate sense-data supplied by the external organs into determinate perceptions ; the ego owns the perceived objects as desirable ends of the self or dislikes them ; and the intellect decides to act to attain or avoid those objects. The three internal and the ten external organs are collectively called the thirteen karanas or organs in the Sāṅkhya philosophy. While the external organs are limited to present objects, the internal ones deal with the past, present and future.[1]

The Antaḥkaraṇas and bāhyakaraṇas.

The Sāṅkhya view of the manas and other organs has certain obvious differences from those of the other systems. According to the Nyāya-Vaiśeṣika, manas is an eternal atomic substance which has neither parts nor any simultaneous contact with many senses. So we cannot have many experiences—many perceptions, desires and volitions—at the same time. For the Sāṅkhyas, the manas is neither atomic not eternal, but a composite product of prakṛti, and so subject to origin and destruction in time. It is also held by them that we may have many experiences—sensation, perception, feeling and volition—at the same time, although ordinarily our experiences come one after the other. The Nyāya-Vaiśeṣikas admit only the manas and the five external senses as indriyas and hold that the external senses are derived from the physical elements (mahābhūta). The Sāṅkhyas enumerate eleven indriyas, *e.g.* the manas, the five sensory organs and the five motor organs and derive them all from the ego (ahaṅkāra), which is not recognized as a separate principle by the other systems. The Vedāntins treat the five vital breaths (pañca-prāṇa) as independent principles, while the Sāṅkhyas reduce them to the general functions of antaḥkaraṇa.[2]

The Sāṅkhya view of manas and other organs is different from those of the other systems.

1. Cf. *Sāṅkhya-sūt.*, 2. 26-32, 2. 1. 38, 5. 71; *Kārikā* and *Kaumudī*, 27. 29-30, 32-33.
2. Cf. *Sāṅkhya-sūt.*, 2. 20-22, 2. 31-32, 5. 84; *Kārikā*, 24 and 29-30.

Five tanmātras

The five tanmātras are the potential elements or generic essence of sound, touch, colour, taste and smell. These are very subtle and cannot be ordinarily perceived. We know them by inference, although the yogins may have a perception of them. The gross physical elements arise from the tanmātras as follows : *(i)* From the essence of sound (śabdatanmātra) is produced *ākāśa* with the quality of sound which is perceived by the ear. *(ii)* From the essence of touch (sparśatanmātra) combined with that of sound, arises *air* with the attributes of sound and touch. *(iii)* Out of the essence of colour (rūpatanmātra) as mixed with those of sound and touch, there arises *light* or *fire* with the properties of sound, touch and colour. *(iv)* From the essence of taste (rasatanmātra) combined with those of sound, touch and colour is produced the element of *water* with the qualities of sound, touch, colour and taste. *(v)* The essence of smell (gandhatanmātra) combined with the other four gives rise to *earth* which has all the five qualities of sound, touch, colour taste and smell. The five physical elements of ākaśa, air, light, water and earth have respectively the specific properties of sound, touch, colour, taste and smell. In the order in which they occur here, the succeeding element has the special qualities of the preceding ones added to its own, since their essences go on combining progressively.[1]

Five gross physical elements.

Two stages of evolution, *viz*, the psychical and the physical.

The whole course of evolution from prakṛti to the gross physical elements is distinguished into two stages, namely, the psychical (pratyayasarga or buddhisarga) and the physical (tanmātrasarga of bhautikasarga). The first includes the developments of prakṛti as buddhi, ahaṅkāra and the eleven sense-motor organs. The second is constituted by the evolution of the five subtle physical essences (tanmātra), the gross elements (mahābhūta) and the products. The tanmātras, being supersensible and unenjoyable to ordinary beings, are called *aviśeṣa*, *i.e.*,

1. Cf. *Kārikā* and *Kaumudī*, 22.

devoid of specific perceptible characters. The physical elements and their products, being possessed of specific characters, pleasurable or painful or stupefying, are designated as *viśeṣas* or the specific. The viśeṣa or specific objects are divided into three kinds, namely, the gross elements, the gross body born of parents (sthūlaśarīra) and the subtle body (sūkṣma or liṅga śarīra) and the subtle body (sūkṣma or liṅga śarīra). The gross body is composed of the five gross elements, although some think that it is made of four elements or of only one element. The subtle body is the combination of buddhi, ahaṅkāra, the eleven sense-motor organs and the five subtle elements (tanmātra). The gross body is the support of the subtle body, in so far as the intellect (buddhi), the ego (ahaṅkāra) and the senses cannot function without some physical basis. According to Vācaspati there are only these two kinds of bodies as mentioned before. Vijñānabhikṣu, however, thinks that there is a third kind of body called the adhiṣṭhāna body which supports the subtle one when it passes from one gross body into another.[1]

The history of the evolved universe is a play of twenty-four principles, of which prakṛti is the first, the five gross elements are the last, and the thirteeen organs (karaṇas) and five tanmātras are the intermediate ones. But it is not complete in itself, since it has a necessary reference to the world of selves as the witnesses and enjoyers thereof. It is not the dance of blind atoms, nor the push and pull of mechanical forces which produce a world to no purpose. On the other hand, it serves the most fundamental ends of the moral, or better, the spiritual, life. If the spirit be a reality, there must be proper adjustment between moral deserts and the joys and sorrows of life. Again, the history of the world must be, in spite of all appearances to the contrary, the progressive realization of the life of spirit. In the Sāṅkhya, the evolution of prakṛti into a world of objects makes it possible for spirits to enjoy or suffer according to their merits or demerits. But the ultimate end of the

1. Cf. *Kārikā* and *Kaumudī*, 38-41; *Sāṅkhya-sūt.*, 3. 1-17; *Pravacana-bhāṣya*, 8. 11.

evolution of prakṛti is the freedom (mukti) of self. It is through a life of moral training in the evolved universe that the self realizes its true nature. What that nature is and how it can be realized, we shall consider presently. Now the evolution of prakṛti in relation to the puruṣa may be represented by the following table :

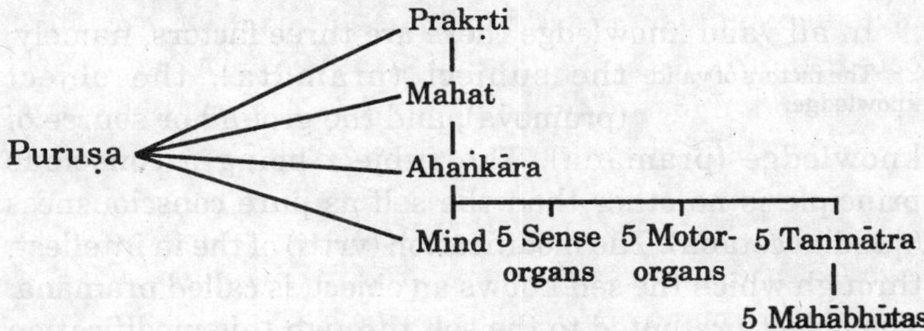

III. The Sāṅkhya Theory of Knowledge[1]

The Sāṅkhya theory of knowledge follows in the main its dualistic metaphysics. It accepts only three independent sources of valid knowledge (pramāṇa). These are perception, inference and scriptural testimony (śabda). The other sources of knowledge, like comparison, postulation (arthāpatti) and non-cognition (anupalabdhi), are included under these three, and not recognized as separate sources of knowledge.

The Sāṅkhya accepts only three independent sources of valid knowledge.

Valid knowledge (pramā) is a definite and an unerring cognition of some object (arthaparicchitti) through the modification of buddhi or the intellect which reflects the consiousness of the self in it. What we call the mind or the intellect is an unconscious material entity in the Sāṅkhya philosophy. Consciousness or intelligence (caitanya) really belongs to the self. But the self cannot immediately apprehend the objects of the world. If it could, we should always know all objects, since the self

Nature and condition of valid knowledge.

1. Vide *Kārikā* and *Kaumudī'* 4-6; *Pravacana-bhāṣya*, 1. 87.89.99-103; 5, 27, 37, 42-51. Cf. *Nyāya Theory of Knowledge* (Ch. V. *ante*) for a fuller account of this subject.

in us is not finite and limited, but all-pervading. The self knows objects through the intellect, the manas, and the senses. We have a true knowledge of objects when, through the activity of the senses and the manas, their forms are impressed on the intellect which in its turn, reflects the light or consciousness of the self.

The factors of valid knowledge.

In all valid knowledge there are three factors, namely, the subject (pramātā), the object (prameya), and the ground or source of knowledge (pramāṇa). The subject being a conscious principle is no other than the self as pure consciousness (śuddha cetana). The modification (vṛtti) of the in intellect, through which the self knows an object, is called pramāṇa. The object presented to the self through this modification is the prameya. Pramā or valid knowledge is the reflection of the self in the intellect as modified into the form of the object, because without the self's consciousness the unconscious intellect cannot cognise anything.

The nature of perception.

Perception is the direct cognition of an object through its contact with some sense. When an object like the table comes within the range of your vision, there is contact between the table and your eyes. The table produces certain inpressions or modifications in the sense organ, which are analysed and synthesised by manas or the mind. Through the activity of the senses and the mind, budhi or the intellect becomes modified and transformed into the shape of the table. The intellect, however, being an unconsious material principle, cannot by itself know the object, although the form of the object is present in it. But as the intellect has an excess of sattva, it reflects, like transparent mirror, the consciouseness of the self (puruṣa). With the reflection of the self's consciousness in it, the unconscious modification of the intellect into the form of the table becomes illumined into a conscious state of perception. Just as a mirror reflects the light of a lamp and thereby manifests other things, so the material principle of buddhi, being transparent and bright (sāttvika), reflects the consciousness of the self and illuminates or cognises the objects of knowledge.

It is to be observed here that the reflection theory of knowledge has been explained in two different ways by Vācaspati Miśra and Vijñānabhikṣu. We have followed the former in the account of the knowledge process given above, Vācaspati thinks that the knowledge of an object takes place when there is reflection of the self in the intellect which has been modified into the form of the object. According to Vijñānabhikṣu, the process of perceptual knowledge is like this : When any object comes in contact with its special sense organ, the intellect becomes modified into the form of the object. Then, because of the predominance of sattva in it, the intellect reflects the conscious self and seems to be conscious, in the same way in which a mirror reflects the light of a lamp and becomes itself luminous and capable of manifesting other objects. But next, the intellect, which is thus modified into the form of the object, is reflected back in the self. That is the object is presented to the self through a mental modification corresponding to the form of the object. Thus on Vācaspati's view, there is a reflection of the self in the intellect, but no reflection of the intellect back into the self. Vijñānabhikṣu, on the other hand, thinks that there is a reciprocal reflection of the self in the intellect and of the intellect in the self. This view is accepted also in Vedavyāsa's commentary on the *Yoga-Sūtra*.[1] What induces Vijñānabhikṣu to suppose that the modified intellect is reflected in the self is perhaps the necessity of explaining the self's experience of pleasure and pain. The self, being pure consciousness, free from all pleasure and pain, cannot be subjected to these experiences. It is the intellect which really enjoys pleasure and suffers pain. So, the apparent experiences of pleasure and pain in the self should be explained by some sort of reflection of the intellect in the self.

1. Vide *Pravacana-bhāṣya*, 1. 99; *Vyāsa-bhāṣya*, 4, 22.

Nirvikalpaka and savikalpaka perceptions.

There are two kinds of perception, namely, nirvikalpaka or the indeterminate and savikalpaka or the determinate. The first arises at the first moment of contact between a sense and its object, and is antecendent to all mental analysis and sythesis of the sense-data. It is accordingly called ālocana or a mere sensing of the object. In it there is a cognition of the object as a mere something without any recognition of it as this or that kind of thing. It is an unverbalised experience like those of the infant and the dumb. Just as babies and dumb persons cannot express their experience it words, so we cannot communicate this indeterminate perception of objects to other people by means of words and sentences. The second kind of perception is the result of the analysis, synthesis and interpretation of sense-data by manas or the mind. So it is called vivecana or a judgement of the object. It is the determinate cognition of an object as a particular kind of thing having certain qualities and standing in certain relations to other things. The determinate perception of an object is expressed in the form of a subject-predicate proposition, *e.g.* 'this is a cow,' 'that rose is red.'[1]

The nature and conditions of inference.

Inference is the knowledge of one term of a relation, which is not perceived, through the other which is perceived and known to be invariably related to the first. In it what is perceived leads us on to the knowledge of what is unperceived through the knowledge of a universal relation (vyāpti) between the two. We get the knowledge of vyāpti between two things from the repeated observation of their concomitance. One single instance of their relation is not, as some logicians wrongly think, sufficient to establish the knowledge of universal relation between them.

---

1. For a fuller account of nirvikalpaka and savikalpaka perceptions, *vide* S. C. Chatterjee, *The Nyāya Theory of Knowledge,* Ch. IX.

With regard to the classification of inference, the Sāṅkhya adopts the Nyāya view, although in a slightly different form.

The classification of inference.

Inference is first divided into two kinds, namely, vīta and avīta. It is called vīta or affirmative when it is based on a universal affirmative proposition, and avīta or negative when based on a universal negative proposition. The *vīta* is subdivided into the pūrvavat and the sāmānyatodṛṣṭa. A pūrvavat inference is that which is based on the *observed* uniformity of concomitance between two things. This is illustrated when one infers the existence of fire from smoke because one has observed that smoke is always accompanied by fire. Sāmānyatodṛṣṭa inference, on the other hand, is not based on any observation of the concomitance between the middle and the major term, but on the similarity of the middle with such facts as are uniformly related to the major. How do we know that we have the visual and other senses ? It cannot be by means of perception. The senses are supersensible. We have no sense to perceive our senses with. Therefore, we are to know the existence of the senses by an inference like this : "All actions require some means or instruments, *e.g.* the act of cutting; the perceptions of colour, etc. are so many acts; therefore, there must be some means or organs or perception." It should be noted here that we infer the existence of organs from acts of perception, not because we have *observed* the organs to be invariably related to perceptive acts, but because we know that perception is an action and that an action requires a means of action. The other kind of inference, namely, *avīta* is what some Naiyāyikas call śeṣavat or pariśeṣa inference. It consists in proving something to be true by the elimination of all other alternatives to it. This is illustrated when one argues that sound must be a quality because it cannot be a substance or an activity or a relation or anything else. As regards the logical form of inference, the Sāṅkhyas admit, like the Naiyā yikas, that the five-membered syllogism is the most convincing form of inferential proof.[1]

1. Vide, p. 183 *ante*. For an elaborate account of the theory of inference, *vide* S.C. Chatterjee, *The Nyāya Theory of Knowledge,* B.K. III.

The nature and forms of sabda or testimony.

The third pramāṇa is śabda or testimony. It is constituted by authoritative statement (āptavacana), and gives the knowledge of objects which cannot be known by perception and inference. A statement is a sentence made up of words arranged in a certain way. A word is a sign which denotes something (vācaka), and its meaning (artha) is the thing denoted by it (vācya). That is, a word is a symbol which stands for some object. The understanding of a sentence requires the understanding of the meanings of its constituent words. Śabda is generally said to be of two kinds, namely, laukika and vaidika. The first is the testimony of ordinary trustworthy persons. This, however, is not recognised in the Sāṅkhya as a separate pramāṇa, since it depends on perception and inference. It is the testimony of Śruti or the Vedas that is to be admitted as the third independent pramāṇa. The Vedas give us true knowledge about supersensuous realities which cannot be known through perception and inference. As not made by any person, the Vedas are free from all defects and imperfections that must cling to the works of personal agencies. They are, therefore, infallible, and possess self-evident validity. The Vedas embody the intuitions of enlightened seers (ṛṣis). These intuitions being universal and eternal experiences are not dependent on the will or consciousness of individual persons. As such the Vedas are impersonal (apaurṣeya). Yet they are not eternal since they arise out of the spiritual experiences of seers and saints, and are conserved by a continuous line of instruction from generation to generation.

IV. The Doctrine of Liberation[1]

Our life on earth is a mixture of joys and sorrows. There are indeed many pleasures of life, and also many creatures who have a good share of them. But many more are the

1. Vide *Kārikā* and *Kaumudī*, 44-68; *Sāṅkhya-sūt.*, *Pravacana-bhāṣya* and *vṛtti*, 3. 65-84.

pains and sufferings of life and *all* living beings are more or less subject to them. Even if it be possible for any individual being to shun all other pains and miseries, it is impossible for him to evade the clutches of decay and death. Ordinarily, however, we are the victims of three kinds of pains, *viz.*, the ādhyātmika, ādhibhautika and ādhidaivika. The first is due to intraorganic causes like bodily disorders and mental affections. It includes both bodily and mental sufferings, such as fever and headache, the pangs of fear, anger, greed, etc. The second is produced by extra-organic natural causes like men, beasts, thorns, etc. Instances of this kind are found in cases of murder, snake-bite, prick of thorns and so forth. The third kind of suffering is caused by extra-organic supernatural causes, *e.g.* the pains inflicted by ghosts, demons, etc.

The three kinds of pains, ādhyātmika, ādhibhautika and ādhidaivika.

Now all men earnestly desire to avoid every kind of pain. Nay more, they want, once for all, to put an end to all their sufferings, and have enjoyment at all times. But that is not to be. We cannot have pleasure only and exclude pain altogether. So long as we are in this frail body with its imperfect organs, all pleasures are bound to be mixed up with pain or, at least, be temporary. Hence we should give up the hedonistic ideal or pleasure and rest content with the less attractive but more rational end of freedom from pain. In the Sāṅkhya system, liberation (mukti) is just the absolute and complete cessation of all pain without a possibility of return. It is the ultimate and or the *summum bonum* of our life (apavarga or puruṣārtha).

All men want to get rid of pain.

Sāṅkhya mukti or liberation is the absolute cessation of all pain.

How are we to attain liberation or absolute freedom from all pain and suffering ? All the arts and crafts of the modern man and all the blessings of modern science give us but temporary relief from pain or short-lived pleasures. These do not ensure a total

Ignorance is the cause of suffering. So freedom from suffering is to be attained through right knowledge of reality.

and final release from all the ills to which our mind and body are subject. So the Indian philosopher wants some other more effective method of accomplishing the task, and this he finds in the right knowledge of reality (tattvajñana). It is a general rule that our sufferings are due to our ignorance. In the different walks of life we find that the ignorant and uneducated man comes to grief on many occasions because he does not know the laws of life and nature. The more knowledge we have about ourselves and the world we live in, the better fitted are we for these struggle for existence and the enjoyments of life. But the fact remains that we are not perfectly happy, nor even completely free from pain and misery. The reason for this is that we have not the perfect knowledge about reality.

The nature and constitution of reality.

When we have that knowledge, we shall attain freedom from all suffering. Reality is, according to the Sāṅkhya, a plurality of selves and the world of objects presented to them. The self is an intelligent principle which does not possess any quality or activity but is a pure consciousness free from the limitations of space, time and causality. It is the pure subject which transcends the whole world of objects including physical things and organic bodies, the mind and the senses, the ego and the intellect. All changes and activities, all thoughts and feelings, all pleasures and pains, all joys and sorrows belong to what we call the mind-body system. The self is quite distinct from the mind-body complex and is, therefore, beyond all the affections and afflictions of the psychical life. Pleasure and pain are mental facts which do not really colour the pure self. It is the mind, and not self, that feels pleasure or pain, and is happy or unhappy. So also, virtue and vice, merit and demerit, in short, all moral properties belong to the ego (ahaṅkāra) who is the striver and doer of all acts.[1] The self is different from the ego or the moral agent who strives for good or bad ends, attains them and enjoys or suffers accordingly. Thus we see that the self is the transcendent subject whose very essence is pure consciousness, freedom, eternity and immortality. It is pure consciousness (jñānasvarūpa) in the sense that the changing states and processes of the mind, which we call empirical consciousness, do not belong to the self. The self is the subject or witness of mental changes as of bodily and physical changes, but is as much distinct from the former as from the latter. It is freedom itself in so far as it is above the space-time and the cause-effect order of existence. It is eternal and immortal, because it is not produced by any cause and cannot be destroyed in any way.[2]

Ignorance or aviveka is non-discrimination between self and not-self.

Pleasure and pain, joy and sorrow really belong to buddhi or the intellect and the mind. The puruṣa or self is by its nature free from them all. But on account of ignorance it fails to distinguish itself from the mind and the intellect, and owns them as parts of itself so much so that it identifies itself with the body, the senses, the mind and the intellect. It becomes, so to say, *somebody* with a certain name, and a particular 'combination of talent, temperament and character.' As such, we speak of it as the 'material self,' the 'social self,' the 'sensitive and appetitive self,' the 'imagining and desiring self,' or the 'willing and thinking self.'[3] According to the Sāṅkhya, all these are not-self which reflects the pure self and apparently imparts its affections and emotions to the latter. The self considers itself to be happy or unhappy when the mind and the intellect, with which it identifies itself, become so, in the same way in

1. Cf. *Sāṅkhya-sūt are Vṛtti*, 5. 25-26.

2. Cf. *Pravacana-bhāṣya*, 1. 146-48.

3. For an account of the different kinds of selves *vide* James, *principles of Psychology, Vol. I.* Chap. X, and Ward, *Psychological Principles*, Chap. XV.

which a father considers *himself* fortunate or unfortunate in view of his beloved *son's* good or bad luck, or a master feels insulted by an insult to his own servant. It is this want of discrimination of feeling of identity (aviveka) between the self and the mind-body that is the cause of all our troubles. We suffer pain and enjoy pleasure because the experiencing subject in us (draṣṭā) wrongly identifies itself with the experienced objects (dṛśya) including pleasure and pain.[1]

Vivekajñāna or discrimination between the two leads to freedom from suffering.

The cause of suffering being ignorance (ajñāna) in the sense of non-discrimination (aviveka) between the self and the not-self, freedom from suffering must come from knowledge of the distinction between the two (vivekajñāna).[2] But this saving knowledge is not merely an intelletual understanding of the truth. It must be a direct knowledge or clear realization of the fact that the self is not the body and the senses, the mind and the intellect. Once we realize or *see* that our self is the unborn and undying spirit in us, the eternal and immortal subject of experience, we become free from all misery and suffering. A direct knowledge of the truth is necessary to remove the illusion of the body or the mind as my self. Now I have a direct and an undoubted perception that I am a particular psychophysical organism. The knowledge that the self is distinct from all this must be an equally direct perception, if it is to contradict and cancel the previous one. The illusory perception of snake in a rope is not to be sublated by any argument or instruction, but by another perception of the rope as such. To realize the self we require a long course of spiritual training with devotion to and constant comtemplation of, the truth that the spirit is not the body,

---

1. Cf. *Kārikā* and *Kaumudī*, 62; *Pravacana-bhāṣya* and *Vṛtti*, 3. 72.
2. *Kārikā* and *Kaumudī*, 44, 63; *Sāṅkhya-sūt. and Vṛtti*, 3, 23-24.

the senses, the mind or the intellect.[1] We shall consider the nature and methods of this training when we come to the Yoga philosophy.

When the self attains liberation, no change takes place in it and no new property or quality accrues to it. Liberation or freedom of the self does not mean the development from a less perfect to a more perfect condition. So also immortality and eternal life are not to be regarded as future possibilities or events in time. If these were events and temporal acquisitions, they would be governed by the laws of time, space and casuality, and, as such, the very opposite of freedom and immortality. The attainment of liberation means just the clear recognition of the self as a reality which is beyond time and space, and above the mind and the body, and, therefore, essentially free, eternal and immortal.[2] When there is such realization, the self ceases to be affected by the vicissitudes of the body and the mind and rests in itself as the disinterested witness of physical and psychical changes. "Just as the dancing girl ceases to dance after having entertained the spectators, so prakṛti ceases to act and evolve the world after manifesting her nature to the self."[3] It is possible for every self to realize itself in this way and thereby attain liberation in life in this world. This kind of liberation is known as jīvanmukti or emancipation of the soul while living in this body. After the death of its body, the liberated self attains what is called videhamukti or emancipation of the spirit from all bodies, gross and subtle. This ensures absolute and complete

The nature of liberation.

Two kinds of mukti, *viz.*, jīvanmukti and videhamukti.

---

1. Cf. *Sāṅkhya-sūt.* and *Vṛtti*, 3. 66 and 75; *Kārikā* and *Kaumudi*, 64;
2. Cf. *Sāṅkhya-sūt.* and *Vṛtti*, 5. 74-83; *Sāṅkhya-sūt.*, 1, 56, 6, 20.
3. Cf. *Kārikā* and *Kaumudi*, 59. 65-66.

freedom.[1] Vijñānabhikṣu, however, thinks that the latter is the real kind of liberation, since the self cannot be completely free from the influence of bodily and mental changes so long as it is embodied.[2] But all Sāṅkhyas agree that liberation is only the complete destruction of the threefold misery (duḥkhatrayā-bhighāta). It is not a state of joy as conceived in the Vedānta. Where there is no pain, there can neither be any pleasure ; because the two are relative and inseparable.

V. The Problem of God[3]

Controversy among Sāṅkhyas with regard to God's existence.

The attitude of the Sāṅkhya towards theism has been the subject of controversy among its commentators and interpreters. While some of them clearly repudiate the belief in God, others take great pains to make out that the Sāṅkhya is no less theistic than the Nayāya. The classical Sāṅkha argues against the existence of God on the following grounds : *(a)* That the world as a system of effects must have a cause is no doubt true. But God or Brahman cannot be the cause of the world. God is said to be the eternal and immutable self : and what is unchanging cannot be the active cause of anything. So it follows that the ultimate cause of the world is the eternal but ever-changing (pariṇāmī) prakṛti or matter. *(b)* It may be said that prakṛti being non-intelligent must be controlled and directed by some intelligent agent to produce the world. The individual

Anti-theistic proofs of the classical Sāṅkhya.

1. Cf. *Kārikā* and *Kaumudī*, 67-68 : *Sāṅkhya-sūt.* and *Vṛtti*, 3. 78-84.

2. Cf. *Pravacana-bhāṣya*, 3. 76-84, 5. 116.

3. Cf. *Kārikā* and *Kaumudī*, 56-57 ; *Sāṅkhya-sūt.*, *Vṛtti.* and *Pravacana*, 1. 92-95, 3. 56-57, 5. 2-12. *Vide* also Gaudapāda, *Sāṅkhya-Kārikā bhāṣya* and A. K. Majumder, *The Sāṅkhya Conception of Personality*, Chapters I and II.

selves are limited in knowledge and, therefore, cannot control the subtle material cause of the world. So there must be an infinitely wise being, *i.e.* God, who directs and guide prakṛti. But this is untenable. God, as conceived by the theists, does not act or exert Himself in any way ; but to control and guide prakṛti is to act or do something. Supposing God is the controller of prakṛti, we may ask : What induced God to control prakṛti and thereby create the world ? It cannot be any end of His own, for a perfect being cannot have any unfulfilled desires and unattained ends. Nor can it be the good of His creatures. No prudent man bothers himself about the welfare of other beings without his own gain. As a matter of fact the world is so full of sin and suffering that it can hardly be said to be the work of God who had the good of His creatures in view when He created. *(c)* The belief in God is inconsistent with the distinctive reality and immortality or individual selves (jīva). If the latter be included within God as His parts, they ought to have some of the divine powers which, however, is not the case. On the other hand, if they are created by God, they must be subject to destruction. The conclusion drawn from all this is that God does not exist and that prakṛti is the sufficient reason for there being a world of objects. Prakṛti creates the world unconsciously for the good of the individual selves (puruṣa) in the same way in which the milk of the cow flows unconsciously through her udder for the nourishment of the calf.

Theistic interpretation of the Sāṅkhya.

According to another interpretation of the Sāṅkhya, which is not generally accepted, this system is not atheistic. This is the view of Vijñānabhikṣu and some modern writers.[1] They hold that the existence of God as possessed of creative activity cannot be admitted. Yet we must believe in God as the eternally perfect spirit who is the witness of the world and whose mere presence (sannidhimātra) moves

1. Vide *Pravacana-bhāṣya, ibid* ; A. K. Majumdar. *The Sāṅkhya Conception of Personality, ibid.*

prakṛti to act and create, in the same way in which the magnet moves a piece of iron. Vijñānabhiksu thinks that the existence of such a God is supported by reason as well as by the scriptures.

VI. Conclusion

The Sāṅkhya may be called a philosophy of dualistic realism. It traces the whole course of the world to the interplay of two ultimate principles, *viz.* spirit and primal matter (puruṣa and prakṛti). On the one hand, we have prakṛti which is regarded as the ultimate cause of the world of objects including physical things, organic bodies and psychical products like the mind (manas), the intellect and the ego. Prakṛti is both the material and the efficient cause of the world. It is active and ever-changing, but blind and unintelligent. How can such a blind principle evolve an orderly world and direct it towards any rational end ? How again are we to explain the first disturbance or vibration in prakṛti which is said to be originally in a state of equilibrium ? So, on the other hand, the Sāṅkhya admits another ultimate principle, *viz.* puruṣa or the self. The category of puruṣa includes a plurality of selves who are eternal and immutable principles of pure consciousness. These selves are intelligent but inactive and unchanging. It is in contact with such conscious and intelligent selves that the unconscious and unintelligent prakṛti evolves the world of experience. But how can the inactive and unchanging self at all come in contact with and influence prakṛti or matter ? The Sāṅkhya holds that the mere presence (sannidhi) of puruṣa or the self is sufficient to move prakṛti to act, although it itself remains unmoved. Similarly, it is the reflection of the conscious self on the unconscious intellect that explains the cognitive and other psychical functions performed by the latter. But how the mere presence of the self can be the cause of changes in prakṛti, but not in the self itself, is not clearly explained. Nor, again, is it quite clear how an unintelligent material principle like the intellect can reflect pure consciousness (which is immaterial) and thereby become conscious and intelligent. The physical analogies given in the Sāṅkhya are not sufficiently illuminating. Further, the existence of many selves is proved by the Sāṅkhya from the difference in the nature, activity, birth and death, and sensory and motor endowments of different living beings. But all these differences pertain, not to the self as pure consciousness but to the bodies associated with it. So far as their intrinsic nature (*i.e.,* pure consciousness) is concerned, there is nothing to distinguish between one self and another. So there seems to be no good ground for the Sāṅkhya theory of many ultimate selves. It may be that the many selves of which we speak, are the empirical individuals or egos dealt with in ordinary life and experience. From the speculative standpoint there seem to be certain gaps in the Sāṅkhya philosophy. Still we should not underrate its value as a system of self-culture for the attainment of liberation. So far as the practical end of attaining freedom from suffering is concerned, this system is as good as any other and enables the religious aspirant to realize the highest good of his life, *viz.* liberation.

THE YOGA PHILOSOPHY

A SELECT BIBLIOGRAPHY

Pūrṇacandra Vedāntacuñcu ... *Yoga-sūtra* with *Bhāṣya* Sanskrit Book Depository, Calcutta, 1907).

Kālīvara Vedāntavāgīśa ... *Pātañjala-sūtra* with *Bhoja-Vṛtti* (Calcutta, C. 1930).

Mādhavācārya ... *Sarva-darśana-saṅgraha*, Ch. on Pātañjala.

S. Radhakrishnan ... *Indian Philosophy* Vol. II, Ch. V.

S. N. Dasgupta ... *The Study of Patañjali* (Cal. Univ., 1920). *Yoga as Philosophy and Religion* (Kegan Paul, London, 1924).

G. Coster ... *Yoga and Western Psychology* (Oxford University Press, London, 1935).

N. K. Brahma ... *The Philosophy of Hindu Sādhanā* (Kegan Paul, 1932).

Hariharānanda Āraṇya ... *Pātañjala Yoga-darśana* (Kapilāśrama, Hugli, 1925).

Swami Akhilānanda ... *Mental Health and Hindu Psychology* (G. Allen and Unwin, 1950).

Swami Prabhavānanda and Christopher Isherwood ... *How to know God : The Yoga Aphorism of Patañjali* (Harper & Brothers, New York, 1953).

CHAPTER VIII

THE YOGA PHILOSOPHY

I. Introduction

The Yoga philosophy is an invaluable gift of the great Indian sage Patañjali to all bent upon spiritual realization. It is a great aid to those who wish to realize the existence of the spirit as an independent principle, free from all limitations of the body, the senses and the mind.[1] It is known also as the Pātañjala system after the name of its founder. The *Yoga-sūtra* or the *Pātañjala-sūtra* is the first work of this school of philosophy. Vyāsa wrote a brief but valuable commentary on the *Yoga-sūtra* called *Yoga-bhāṣya* or *Vyāsa-bhāṣya.* Vācaspati's *Tattva-vaiśāradī* is a reliable sub-commentary on Vyāsa's Commentary. Bhojarāja's *Vṛtti* and *Yoga maṇiprabhā* are very simple and popular works on the Yoga system. Vijñānabhikṣu's *Yoga-vārtika* and *Yoga-sāra saṅgraha* are other useful manuals of the Yoga Philosophy.

Patañjali was the founder of the Yoga system.

Some important works of this system.

The *Pātañjala-sūtra* is divided into four pādas or parts. The first is called the samādhipāda and treats of the nature, aim and forms of yoga, the modifications of citta or the internal organ, and the different methods of attaining yoga. The second, *viz.*, the sādhanapād, deals with kriyāyoga as a means of attaining

There are four pādas or parts of Yoga-sūtra.

1. Miss G. Coster has the Yoga system in view when she says : "We need a new kind of society for Psychical Research....to demonstrate to the ordinary public the possibility (or impossibility) of genuine super physical experience on this side" (vide *Yoga and Western Psychology* p. 246).

samādhi, the kleśas[1] or mental states causing afflictions, the fruits of action (karmaphala) and their painful nature, and the fourfold theme of suffering, its cause, its cessation and the means thereof. The third or vibhūtipāda gives an account of the inward aspects of yoga and the supernormal powers acquired by the practice of yoga and so forth. The fourth part is called the kaivalyapāda and describes the nature and forms of liberation, the reality of the transcendent self and the other world and so on.

Its relation to the Sāṅkhya system.

The Yoga is closely allied to the Sāṅkhya system. It is the application of the theory of the Sāṅkhya in practical life. The Yoga mostly accepts the Sāṅkhya epistemology and admits the three pramāṇas of perception, inference and scriptural testimony. It mostly accepts also the metaphysics of the Sāṅkhya with its twenty-five principles, but believes in God as the supreme self distinct from other selves. The special interest of this system is in the practice of yoga as the sure means of attaining vivekajñāna or discriminative knowledge which is held in the Sāṅkhya as the essential condition of liberation.

The value of yoga for life and philosophy.

The value of yoga as an important method of realizing the spiritual truths of Indian philosophy has been recognized by almost all the Indian systems. We have clear evidence of the recognition of yoga practices even in the Upaniṣads, the Smṛtis and the Purāṇas.[2] So long as the mind or the intellect of a man is impure and unsettled, he cannot

1. The verb, 'kliś' is ordinarily intransitive ('kliśyati), meaning 'to be afflicted.' Kleśa', then means affliction or suffering. But 'kliś' is sometimes also transitive (kliśnāti) meaning 'cause affliction,' 'torment.' The present word is more conveniently derived from this transitive sense. Vide *Vyāśa-bhāṣya*, 1. 5, where *kliṣṭa=kleśa-hetuka.*

2. Cf. *Kaṭha Upaniṣad*, 6. 11. 6. 18 : *Śvetāśvatara*, 2. 8. 3. 11.

properly understand anything profound and spiritual. We must have a pure heart and a tranquil mind if we are to know and realize the truths of philosophy and religion. Now the practice of yoga is the best way of self-purification, *i.e.* purification of the body and the intellect. Hence it is that almost all the systems of Indian philosophy insist on the practice of yoga as the necessary practical side of a philosophy of life.

The Yoga lays down a practical path for attaining liberation.

The Pātañjala system makes a special study of the nature and forms of yoga, the different steps in yoga practice, and other important things connected with these. It holds, like the Sāṅkhya and some other Indian systems, that liberation is to be attained through the direct knowledge of the self's distinction from the physical world including our body, mind and the ego (vivekajñāna). But this can be realized only if we can manage to suppress and terminate the functions of the body and the senses, the manas and the intellect, and finally, the ego (*i.e.* the empirical self) and yet have self-consciousness or experience of the transcendent spirit (puruṣa). This would convince us that the self is above the mind-body complex, the senses and the intellect and also the suffering or enjoying individual ego. It will be seen to be above all physical reality with its spatio-temporal and cause-effect order. This is the realization of the self as the free, immortal spirit which is above sin and suffering, death and destruction. In other words, it is the attainment of freedom from all pain and misery, *i.e.* liberation. The Yoga system lays down a practical path of self-realization for the religious aspirant and the sincere seeker after the spirit. The Sāṅkhya lays greater stress on discriminative knowledge as the means of attaining liberation, although it recommends such practical methods as study, reasoning and constant meditation on the truth.[1] The Yoga, on the other hand, emphasizes the importance of the practical methods of purification and concentration for realizing the self's distinction from the body and the mind, and thereby attaining liberation. These will be explained in the Yoga ethics. Before we come to that we have to study the Yoga psychology which deals with the nature of the self, the mind and its functions, and the relation between mind, body and the self.

II. Yoga Psychology

The self knows the objects of the world through the modifications of citta or the mind.

In the Sāṅkhya-Yoga system, the individual self (jīva) is regarded as the free spirit associated with the gross body and more closely related to a subtle body constituted by the senses, the manas, the ego and the intellect. The self is, in its own nature, pure consciousness, free from the limitations of the body and the fluctuations of the mind (citta). But in its ignorance it confuses itself with citta. The citta is the first product of prakṛti, in which the elements of sattva or the power of manifestation naturally predominates over those of rajas and tamas. It is essentially unconscious ; but being in the closest proximity to the self it reflects, through its manifesting power, the self's consciousness so as to become apparently conscious and intelligent. It is different from manas which is the internal sense. When the citta is related to any object through manas, it assumes the form of that object. The self knows the objects of the world through the modifications of citta which correspond to the forms of the objects known. Although the self really undergoes no change or modification, yet because of its reflection in the changing states and processes of citta, the self appears to be subject to changes and to pass through different states

1. Vide *Kārikā* and *Kaumudī*, 51.

of the mind or citta, in the same way in which the moon appears to be moving when we see it reflected in the moving waves.[1]

There are five kinds of mental modifications or citta-vṛtti.

The modifications of citta, *i.e.* cognitive mental states are many and varied. These may be classified under five heads, namely, pramāṇa or true cognition, viparyaya or false cognition, vikalpa or merely verbal cognition, nidrā of sleep, and smṛti or memory. There are three kinds of true cognition, *viz.* perception, inference and verbal testimony. These have been explained in almost the same way as in the Sāṅkhya. Viparyaya is the wrong knowledge of objects as what they really are not and it includes doubt or uncertain cognitions. Vikalpa is a mere verbal idea caused by words, to which no real facts correspond. When you hear the words "Rāhu's head," you have the idea of a distinction between Rāhu and its head, although really there is no distinction between the two, Rāhu being only a head. Similarly, the phrase "consciousness *of* the soul" arouses the ideas of two different entities (soul and consciousness) related together, whereas in reality there is no distinction between them (soul and consciousness being identical).[2] Sleep (nidrā) is another kind of mental modification (citta-vṛtti). It is due to the preponderance of tamas in citta and the consequent cessation of waking consciousness and dream experience. It thus stands for deep dreamless sleep (suṣupti). Some philosophers think that in sound sleep there is no mental function or conscious state at all. But this is wrong. On waking from sound sleep we say, "I slept well," "I knew nothing," etc. Such memory of what took place during sleep suppose direct experience of the state of sleep. So there

1. Vide *Yoga-sūt.*, and *Vṛtti*, 1. 4. *Cf.* Sāṅkhya theory of "Evolution of the World," *ante*.

2. *Yoga-bhāṣya*. 1. 9.

must be in sleep some cognitive mental state or process which is concerned in the experience of the absence of knowledge (abhāvapratyayālambanā vṛtti). Smrti or memory is the reproduction of past experiences without any alteration or innovation. All cognitive mental states and processes (citta-vṛtti) may be included in these five kinds of modifications. We need not admit any other kinds of cognitive functions of the mind (citta-vṛtti).[1]

Relation of the self to the mind or citta and the body.

When citta is modified into any kind of vṛtti or cognitive mental state, the self is reflected in it and is apt to appropriate it as a state of itself. Hence it is that it appears to pass through different states of the mind (citta) and stages of life. It considers itself to be subject to birth and growth, decay and death at different periods of time. It is led to believe that it sleeps and wakes up, imagines and remembers, makes mistakes and corrects errors and so on. In truth, however, the self (puruṣa) is above all the happenings of the body and the mind (citta), all physical and psychical changes, like sleeping and waking, birth and death, etc. It is citta or the mind that really performs these functions of sleeping and waking, knowing and doubting, imagining and remembering. The self appears to be concerned in these functions because it is reflected in citta or the mind which is held up before it as a mirror before a person. It also appears to be subject to the five kleśas or sources of afflictions, namely, *(i)* avidyā or wrong knowledge of the non-eternal as eternal of the not-self as the self, of the unpleasant as the pleasant, and of the impure as pure, *(ii)* asmitā, *i.e.* the false notion or perception of the self as indentical with buddhi or the mind, *(iii)* rāga or desire for pleasure and the means of its attainment, *(iv)* dveṣa or aversion to pain and the causes

---

1. Vide *Yoga-sūt., Bhāṣya and Vṛtti*, 1. 5. 11.

thereof *(v)* abhiniveśa or the instinctive fear of death in all creatures.[1]

The self's bondage is due to its identification with mental modifications. So liberation requires their cessation.

So long as there are changes and modifications in citta, the self is reflected therein and, in the absence of discriminative knowledge, identifies itself with them. As a consequence, the self feels pleasure or pain out of the objects of the world, and loves or hates them accordingly. This means bondage for the self. If, therefore, we are to attain liberation, we must somehow restrain the activities of the body, the senses and the mind (manas) and finally suppress all the modifications of citta. When the waves of the empirical consciousness (kārya-citta) die down and leave the citta in a state of perfect placidity (kāraṇa-citta), the self realizes itself as distinct from the mind-body complex and as free, immortal and self-shining intelligence. It is the aim of yoga to bring about this result through the cessation of the functions of citta.

III. Yoga Ethics

1. The Nature and Forms of Yoga[2]

Yoga is just the cessation of mental modifications.

Yoga here means the cessation of mental functions or modifications (cittavṛttinirodha). It does not mean any kind of contact between the individual self and some other reality like God or the Absolute. The aim of yoga, as we have already said, is to prevent the self from identifying itself with mental modifications. But this is not possible so long as the modifications are there and the self has not realized its distinction from citta or the mind. So

1. *Op. cit.*, 2. 3-9.
2. *Yoga-sūt.*, and *Bhāṣya*, 1. 1-4, 1. 12-18, 1. 23. 2. 1-2, 4. 29-34.

what yoga, really stands for is the arrest and negation of all mental modifications.

There are five levels of mental life. The first three are not conducive to yoga.

There are five conditions or levels of the mental life (cittabhūmi). The citta is constituted by the elements of sattva, rajas and tamas. Its different conditions are determined by the different degrees in which these elements are present and operative in it. These conditions are called kṣipta or restless, mūḍha or torpid, vikṣipta or distracted, ekāgra or concentrated, and niruddha or restrained. In each of these there is some kind of repression of mental modifications. One state of the mind excludes other different states. Love and hate, for example, naturally oppose and cancel each other. But still yoga cannot be attained in all the levels of citta. In the first, called kṣipta, the mind or citta is under the sway of rajas and tamas, and is attracted by objects of sense and the means of attaining power. It flits from one thing to another without resting in any. This condition is not at all conducive to yoga, because it does not help us to control the mind and the senses. The second, *viz.* mūḍha, is due to an excess of tamas in citta or the mind which, therefore, has a tendency towards vice, ignorance, sleep and the like. In the third level, called vikṣipta or distracted, the mind or citta is free from the sway of tamas and has only a touch of rajas in it. It has the capacity of manifesting all objects and makes for virtue, knowledge, etc. This is a stage of temporary concentration of citta or the mind on some object, which is followed by distraction. It cannot be called yoga, because it does not permanently stop the mental modifications nor end our troubles and destroys the mental afflictions of avidyā and the rest.

The last two levels are conducive to yoga : Saṁprajñāta and asaṁprajñāta samādhi.

The fourth level of citta is called ekāgra or concerntrated. Here citta is purged of the impurity of rajas and there is the perfect manifestation of sattva. It marks the beginning of prolonged concentration of the mind or citta on any object so as to reveal its true nature, and it prepares the way for the cessation of all mental modifications. In this state, however, the mind or citta continues to think. or meditate on some object, and so, even here the mental processes are not altogether arrested. At the last level, called niruddha, there is the cessation of all mental functions including even that of concentration which marks the previous stage. Here the succession of mental states and processes is completely checked, and the mind (citta) is left in its original, unmodified state of calmness and tranquility. These last two levels are conducive to yoga in so far as both manifest the sattva element of the mind to the highest degree and are helpful for the attainment of the ultimate goal, *viz.* liberation. In fact, ekāgra or the state of concentration, when permanently established, is called saṁprajñāta yoga or the trance of meditation, in which there is a clear and distinct *consciousness of the object* of comteplation. It is known also as samāpatti or saṁprajñāta samādhi inasmuch as citta or the mind is, in this state, entirely put into the object and assumes the form of the object itself. So also the state of niruddha is called as asaṁprajñāta yoga or asaṁprajñāta samādhi, because all mental modifications being stopped in this state, *nothing is known* or thought of by the mind. This is the trance of absorption in which all psychoses and appearances of objects are stopped and there are no ripples in the placid surface of citta or the mind. Both these kinds of samādhi are known by the common name of samādhi-yoga or the cessation of mental modifications, since both conduce to self-realization.

There are four kinds of Saṁprajñāta samādhi.

There are, then, two main kinds of yoga or samādhi, *viz.* the saṁprajñāta and the asaṁprajñāta. Four kinds of saṁprajñāta samādhi are distinguished according to the different objects of contemplation. It is called savitarka when the mind (citta) is concentrated on any *gross* physical object of the external world, *e.g.* the image of a god or goddess. Having realized the nature of this object, one should concentrate on *subtle* objects like the tanmātras or subtle essences of the physical elements. The mind's concentration on these subtle objects is called savicāra samādhi. The next step is to take some *subtler* objects like the senses and concentrate the mind (citta) on them, till their real nature becomes manifest to it, in what is called sānanda samadhī. The last kind of saṁprajñāta samādhi is called sāsmita inasmuch as the object of concentration herein is asmitā or the ego-substance with which the self is ordinarily identified. The fruition of this stage of concentration is the realization of the true nature of the ego. But it also gives us a glimpse of the knowing self as something almost indistinguishable from the ego.[1]

Asaṁprajñāta samādhi is yoga *par excellence.*

Thus the mind (citta) realizes the nature of different objects within or without the body and leaves them behind, one after the other, till it becomes completely free from the thoughts of all objects and attains what is called asaṁprajñāta samādhi or yoga *par excellence*. It puts a stop to all mental modifications and does not rest on any object at all. This is the final stage of samādhi because when it is attained the whole world of objects ceases to affect, and to exist for, the yogin. In this state the self abides in its own essence as pure consciousness, enjoying the still vision of isolated self-shining existence. When one attains this state, one reaches the final goal of life, namely, liberation or freedom from all pain and suffering. All life is a quest of peace and a search for the means thereof. Yoga is one of the spiritual paths that leads to the desired goal of a total extinctions of all pain and misery through the realization of the self's distinction from the body, the mind and the individual ego. But this final goal cannot be attained all at once. Even if it be possible for a self to attain once the state of samādhi and thereby release from pain, there is the

1. The final stage of saṁprajñāta is called dharmamegha samādhi because it showers on the Yogin the blessing of self-realization. Vide *Yoga-sūt.*, and *Bhāṣya,* 4. 29.

possibility of a relapse and consequent recurrence of pain, so long as all the impressions and tendencies of the mind (citta) due to its past and present deeds are not wiped out. It requires a long and arduous endeavour to maintain oneself steadily in the state of samādhi and destroy the effects of the different kinds of karma, past and present. For this it is necessary to practise yoga with care and devotion for a sufficiently long time. The auxiliary means to the practice of yoga will be explained in the next section.

2. *The Eightfold Means of Yoga*[1]

There are eight means of yoga called yogāṅgas.

As we have already said, a man cannot realize spiritual truths so long as his mind is tainted with impurities and his intellect vitiated by evil thoughts. It is in the pure heart and the clear understanding that the truth of the spirit is revealed and directly experienced. The Sāṅkhya Yoga system holds that liberation is to be attained by means of spiritual insight (prajñā) into the reality of the self as the pure immortal spirit which is quite distinct from the body and the mind. But spiritual insight can be had only when the mind is purged of all impurities and rendered perfectly calm and serene. For the *purification and enlightenment of citta* or the mind, the Yoga gives us the eightfold means which consists of the disciplines of (1) yama or restraint, (2) niyama or culture, (3) āsana or posture, (4) prāṇāyāma or breath control, (5) pratyāhāra or withdrawal of the senses, (6) dhāraṇā or attention, (7) dhyāna or meditation, and (8) samādhi or concentration. These are known as aids to yoga (yogāṅga). When practised regularly with devotion and dispassion, they lead to the attainment of yoga, both saṁprajñāta and asaṁprajñāta.

1. Cf. *Yoga-sūt.*, and *Bhāṣya*, 2. 28-55, 3. 1-4.

(1) Yama consists in abstention from injury to life, from falsehood, theft, incontinence and avarice.

The first discipline of yama or restraint consists in *(a)* ahiṁsā or abstention from all kinds of injury to any life *(b)* satya or truthfulness in thought and speech, *(c)* asteya or non-stealing, *(d)* brahmacarya or control of the carnal desires and passions, and *(e)* aparigraha or non-acceptance of unnecessary gifts from other people. Although these practices seem to be too well known to require any elaboration, yet the Yoga explains all their details and insists that a yogin must scrupulously follow them. The reason for this is obvious. It is a psychological law that a sound mind resides in a sound body, and that neither can be sound in the case of a man who does not control his passions and sexual impulses. So also, a man cannot concentrate his attention on any object when his mind is distracted and dissipated by sin and crime and other evil propensities. This explains the necessity or complete abstention from all the evil courses and tendencies of life on the part of yogin who is eager to realize the self in samādhi or concentration.

(2) Niyama consists in the cultivation of good habits.

The second discipline is niyama or culture. It consists in the cultivation of the following good habits : *(a)* śauca or purification of the body by washing and taking pure food (which is bāhya or external purification), and purification of the mind by cultivating good emotions and sentiments, such as friendliness, kindness, cheerfulness for the virtues and indifference to the vices of others (which is called ābhyantara or internal purification), *(b)* santoṣa or the habit of being content with what comes of itself without undue exertion, *(c)* tapas or penance which consists in the habit of enduring cold and heat, etc., and observing austere vows, *(d)* svādhyāya or the regular habit of study of religious books, and *(e)* Īśvarapranidhāna or meditation of and resignation to God.

Āsana is a discipline of the body and consists in the adoption of steady and comfortable postures. There are various kinds of āsana, such as padmāsana, vīrāsana, bhadrāsana, etc. These can be properly learnt only under the guidance of experts. The discipline of the body is as much necessary for the attainment of concentration as that of the mind. If the body is not completely free from disease and other disturbing influences, it is very difficult to attain concentration. Hence the Yoga lays down elaborate rules for maintaining the health of the body and making it a fit vehicle for concentrated thought. It prescribes many rules for preserving the vital energy, and strengthening and purifying the body and the mind. The āsanas or postures recommended in it are effective ways by which the body can be kept partially free from diseases, and all the limbs, especially the nervous system, can be brought under control and prevented from producing disturbances in the mind.

(3) Āsana is the adoption of steady and comfortable postures.

Prāṇāyāma is the regulation of breath. It consists in suspension of the breathing process either after exhalation (recaka), or inhalation (pūraka), or simply by retention of the vital breath (kumbhaka). The details of the process should be learnt from experts. That respiratory exercises are useful for strengthening the heart and improving its function is recognized by medical men when they recommend walking, climbing, etc., in a graduated scale, for patients with weak hearts. The yoga goes further and prescribes breath control for concentration of the mind, because it conduces to steadiness of the body and the mind. So long as the function of breathing continues, the mind also goes on fluctuating and noticing the current of air in and out. If, and when, it is suspended, the mind is in a state of undisturbed concentration. Hence by practising the control of breath, the yogin can suspend breathing for a long time and thereby prolong the state of concentration.

(4) Prāṇāyāma is regulated suspension of the breathing processes.

(5) Pratyāhāra consits in withdrawing the senses from their objects.

Pratyāhāra consists in withdrawing the senses from their respective external objects and keeping them under the control of the mind. When, the senses are effectively controlled by the mind, they follow, not their natural objects, but the mind itself. So in this state the mind is not disturbed by sights, sounds, etc., coming through the eye, the ear, and other senses, but keeps all of them under perfect control. This state is very difficult, although not impossible, of attainment. It requires a resolute will and long practice to gain mastery over one's senses. The five disciplines of restraint and culture (yama and niyama), bodily posture (āsana), breath-control (prāṇāyāma) and control over the senses (pratyāhāra) are regarded as the external aids to yoga (bahiraṅga-sādhana). As compared with these, the last three disciplines are said to be internal to yoga (antaraṅga-sādhana), because they are directly related to some kind of samādhi or yoga. These are dhāraṇā, dhyāna and samādhi.

(6) Dhāraṇa consists in fixing the mind on the desired object.

Dhāraṇa or attention is a mental discipline which consists in holding (dhāraṇa) or fixing the mind (citta) on the desired object. The object thus attended to may be a part of one's body, like one's navel, the midpoint of the eyebrows, etc. or it may be external to the body, like the moon, the images of gods, etc. The ability to keep one's attention steadily fixed on some object is the test of fitness for entering on the next higher stage of yoga.

(7) Dhyāna is the steady contemplation of the object without any break.

Dhyāna or meditation is the next step. It means the even flow of thought about, or rather, round about, the object of attention. It is the steadfast contemplation of the object without any break or disturbance. This has the effect of giving us a clear and distinct representation of the object first by parts and aspects. But by long-continued meditation the mind can develop the partial representation of the object into a full and live presentation of it. Thus dhyāna reveals the reality of the contemplated object to the yogin's mind.

(8) Samādhi is the mind's absorption in the object of contemplation.

Samādhi or concentration is the final step in the practice of yoga. In it the mind is so deeply absorbed in the object of contemplation that it loses itself in the object and has no awareness of itself. In the state of dhyāna, the act and the object of thought remain distinct and separate states of consciousness. But in samādhi the act of meditation is not separately cognised : it takes on the form of the object and loses itself, as it were. So here only the object of thought remains shining in the mind, and we do not even know that there is a process of thought in the mind. It should be observed here that *this samādhi as a discipline is different from the samādhi or the yoga previously defined as "the restraint of the mind"* (cittavṛttinirodha). The former is but the *means* for the attainment of the latter which is its *end*. A long-continued practice of the one leads to the other. These last three steps in the practice of yoga are called internal means (antaraṅga-sādhana). They should have the same object, *i.e.* the same object should be first attended to, then mediated and lastly concentrated upon. When thus combined they are said to constitute saṁyama which is very necessary for the attainment of samādhi-yoga.

The supernormal powers accruing from yoga.

A yogin is believed to acquire certain extraordinary powers by the practice of yoga in its different stages. Thus we are told that the yogins can tame all creatures including even ferocious animals, get any object by the mere wish of it, know directly the past, present and future, produce supernatural sights, sounds and smells and see subtle entities, angels and gods. They can also see through closed doors, pass through stone walls, disappear from sight, appear at different places at the same time, and so forth. While these may be possible, the Yoga system warns all religious aspirants not to practise yoga with these ends in view. Yoga is for the attainment of liberation. The yogin must not get entangled in the quagmire of supernormal powers. He must overcome the lure of yaugic powers and move onward till he comes to the end of journey, *viz.* liberation.[1]

---

1. Vide *Yoga-sūt.*, and *Bhāṣya*, 3. 37, 3. 51. 4. 1.

IV. The Place of God in The Yoga[1]

As distinguished from the Sāṅkhya, the Yoga is theistic. It admits the existence of God on both practical and theoretical grounds. Patañjali himself, however, has not felt the necessity of God for solving any theoretical problem of philosophy. For him God has more a practical value than a theoretical one. Devotion to God is considered to be of great practical value, inasmuch as it forms a part of the practice of yoga and is *one* of the means for the final attainment of samādhi-yoga or "the restraint of the mind." The subsequent commentators and interpreters of the Yoga evince also a theoretical interest in God and discuss more fully the speculative problems as to the nature of God and the proofs for the existence of God. Thus the Yoga system has come to have both a theoretical and a practical interest in the Divine Being.

The Yoga has both a theoretical and a practical interest in God.

According to the Yoga, God is the Supreme Person who is above all individual selves and is free from all defects. He is the Perfect Being who is eternal and all-pervading, omnipotent and omniscient. All individual selves are more or less subject to the afflictions (kleśa) of ignorance, egoism, desire, aversion and dread of death. They have to do various kinds of works (karma)—good, bad and indifferent—and reap the consequences there-of (vipāka). They are also infected and influenced by the latent impressions of their past experiences (āśaya). Even if the liberated self is released from all these troubles, it cannot be said that he was always free from them. It is God and God alone who is *eternally* free from all defects. God is the perfect immortal spirit who ever remains untouched by afflictions and actions, and their effects and impression (kleśa-karma-vipākā-śayai-raparāmrṣṭaḥ). He possesses a perfect nature, the like of which is not to be

God is the perfect spirit who is eternal, all-pervading, omnipotent and omniscient.

---

1. Vide *Yoga-sūt.*, *Bhāṣya* and *Vṛtti*, 1. 23-29. 2. 1, 32. 45, 3. 45.

met with anywhere else. He has also the fullest possible knowledge of all facts and is, therefore, capable of maintaining the whole world by His mere wish or thought. He is the Supreme Ruler of the world, and has infinite knowledge, unlimited power and wisest desires, which distinguish Him from all other selves.

The proofs of God's existence :

The existence of God is proved by the following arguments :

(1) The testimony of the scriptures.

The Vedas, the Upaniṣads and other important scriptures speak of the existence of God as the Supreme Self who is also the ultimate reality and the final goal of the world. Therefore, God exists in the way in which the scriptures testify to His existence.

(2) The law of continuity as applied to degrees of knowledge and power.

According to the law of continuity, whatever has degrees must have a lower and an upper *limit*. There are, for instance, different magnitudes, small and great. An atom is the smallest magnitude, while ākāśa or space is the greatest magnitude. Similarly, there are different degrees of knowledge and power. So there must be a person who possesses *perfect* knowledge and *perfect* power. Such a supreme person is God, the highest. There cannot be any self who is equal to God in power and knowledge, for in that case, there will be conflict and clash of desires and purposes between them, and a consequent chaos in the world.

(3) The association and dissociation of puruṣa and prakṛti.

The creation of the world is due to the association of purusa with prakṛti and its dissolution to the dissociation of the one from the other. Puruṣa and prakṛti being two independent principles cannot be said to be naturally related or associated. Nor are they naturally dissociated, for that would make their relation inexplicable. So there must be an intelligent cause which effects their association and dissociation according to the unseen moral deserts (adṛṣṭa) of individual selves. No individual self can guide and control its adṛṣṭa or destiny, because it has no clear understanding about it. Therefore, there must be a perfect and an omniscient Being who brings about the association or dissociation between puruṣa and prakṛti according as the adṛṣṭa of the individual selves require the creation or the destruction of a world. This Being is God, without whose guidance prakṛti cannot produce just that order of the world which is suited to the moral education and final emancipation of individual selves.

Devotion to God is the best means for concentration and restraint of mind.

Devotion to God is not only a part of the practice of yoga but the best means for the attainment of concentration and restraint of mind (samādhi-yoga). The reason is that God is not only an object of meditation (dhyāna), like other objects, but is the Supreme Lord who, by His grace purges away the sins and evils in the life of His devotee and makes the attainment of yoga easier for him. One who is sincerely devoted to God and is resigned unto Him cannot but meditate on Him at all times and see Him in all the walks of life. On such a devoted person God bestows his choicest gifts, *viz.* purity of the heart and enlightment of the intellect. God removes all the serious impediments and obstacles in the path of His devotee, such as the kleśas or afflictions of the mind, and places him under conditions most favourable for the attainment of yoga. But while the grace of God can work wonders in our life, we, on our part, must make ourselves deserving recipients of it through love and charity, truthfulness and purity, constant meditation of and complete resignation to God.

V. Conclusion

To an unsympathetic critic the Yoga may appear to be not so much system of philosophy as a school of mysticism and magic. The Yoga conception of the self as a transcendent subject which is quite distinct from the body, the mind and the ego, is far removed from the commonsense and the ordinary psychological concepts of it. As compared with these, the spiritual conception of the self in the Yoga is apt to be regarded as unintelligible and mysterious. Similarly, the supernormal powers associated with the different stages in the practice of Yoga can hardly be reconciled with the known laws of the physical or the psychical science. So these may appear to be reminiscent of some primitive religion of magic. But it is to be observed that the Yoga scheme of self-realization has a solid foundation in the Sāṅkhya metaphysics which proves the reality of the self as a metaphysical and eternal principle of consciousness. If one believes in the transcendent spirit, one cannot but admit that there are deeper levels of consciousness than the empirical one, and wider possibilities and higher potencies than those of the physical and the sensuous. Glimpses of this deeper reality of our individual life have been caught not only by the seers and saints of different countries, but also by some great philosphers like Plato and Aristotle, Spinoza and Leibniz, Kant anud Hegel. The Society for Psychical Research and the modern school of psycho-analysis have of late contributed much towards our knowledge about the dark regions of the psychical life hidden from the ordinary view. The Yoga goes further in the same direction when it formulates certain practical methods of purification and self-control for the realization of the true self of man. Both from a theoretical and a practical standpoint, it occupies a better position than the Sāṅkhya in so far as it admits the existence of God and relies mostly on actual experiences to carry conviction to its followers. What is necessary for an appreciation of this philosophy is a sympathetic understanding of it and a sincere endeavour to realize its truths. We find one such appreciation of it by Miss Coster when she says : "I·am certain that there is a region beyond that painted drop-scene which forms for so many the boundary of this life ; and that it is penetrable and susceptible of exploration by those who are sufficiently determined.[1] The aim of yoga is to explore this region of genuine super-physical experience and to reveal the reality of man and the world—'the real Self, the Ātman as eternally pure, enlightened and free, as the only true, unchanging happiness.'[2]

---

1. *Yoga and Western Psychology,* pp. 246-47.
2. Cf. Prabhavānanda and Isherwood, *How to Know God : The Yoga Aphorism of Patanjali,* p. 18.

THE MĪMĀṀSĀ PHILOSOPHY

A SELECT BIBLIOGRAPHY

Jaimini ... *Mīmāṁsā-sūtra* (with Sabara's *Bhāsya*), Banaras.

Kumārila Bhaṭṭa ... *Śloka-vārtika* with Nyāyaratnākara (Chowkhamba, 1898)

Gangānāth Jhā ... *Mīmāṁsā-sūtra of Jaimini* (Eng.trans., Oriental Inst., Baroda, 1933, 1934, 1936).

" ... *Śloka-vārtika* (Eng.trans., Asiatic Soc., Calcutta, 1909)

" ... *Prabhākara School of Pūrva Mīmāṁsā* (B.H.U.), Banaras, 1918).

Pārthasārathi ... *Śastra-dīpikā*, Tarkapāda, (Nirṇaya Sāgar, Bombay, 1915).

Śālikanātha ... *Prakaraṇa-pañcikā* (Chowkhamba, 1903).

Paśupatināth Śāstrī ... *Introduction to the Pūrva Mīmāṁsā* (A.N. Bhattacharya, Calcutta, 1923).

A.B. Keith ... *The Karma Mīmāṁsā* (Oxford U. Press, London, 1921).

S. Radhakrishnan ... *Indian Philosophy*, Vol. II., Ch. VI.

" ... *History of Philosophy — Eastern and Western*, Vol. I, Ch. XII.

CHAPTER IX

THE MĪMĀṀSĀ PHILOSOPHY

I. Introduction

The Mīmāṁsā developed out of the ritualistic aspects of Vedic culture.

We have noticed in the *General Introduction* that the Pūrva Mīmāṁsā School or the Mīmāṁsā School, as it is more usually called, is the outcome of the ritualistic side of the Vedic culture just as the Vedānta (sometimes called also Uttara Mīmāṁsā) is the development of its speculative side. The object of the Mīmāṁsā School is to help and support ritualism chiefly in two ways, namely, (a) by giving a methodology of interpretation with the help of which the complicated Vedic injunctions regarding rituals may be understood, harmonized and followed without difficulty, and (b) by supplying a philosophical justification of the beliefs on which ritualism depends. We are concerned here with the second or the philosophical aspect of the Mīmāṁsā.

Its double achievement: Methodology and Philosophy.

As a philosophy, the Mīmāṁsā tries to uphold Vedic ritualism.

The faith underlying Vedic ritualism consists of different elements such as brief in the existence of a soul which survives death and enjoys the fruits of rituals in heaven, the belief in some power or potency which preserves, the effects of the rituals performed, the belief in the infallibility of the Vedas on which rituals stand, the belief that the world is real and our life and actions performed here are not mere dreams. The Buddhists, Jainas and Cārvākas challenge the authority of the Vedas. The reality of the world and the existence of the soul are denied by some Buddhists. Some Upaniṣads disparage the idea that 'heaven' is the goal of man and rituals are the best possible human activities. The Mīmāṁsā tries to meet all such criticisms and upholds the original faith underlying ritualism.

Literature.

Jaimini's *Sūtra*, in twelve elaborate chapters, laid the foundation of the Pūrva Mīmāṁsā. Śabarasvāmī wrote the major commentary or *Bhāṣya* on this work. He is followed by a long line of commentators and independent writers. The two most important among them are Kumārila Bhaṭṭa and Prabhākara (nicknamed 'Guru'), who founded the two schools of Mīmāṁsā named after them, and thus the Mīmāṁsā philosophy gradually developed. Etymologically, the word Mīmāṁsā means 'solution of some problem by reflection and critical examination.' As its subject-matter was karma or rituals, the Mīmāṁsā is also sometimes called Karma or Dharma Mīmāṁsā.

The philosophy of the Mīmāṁsā School may be conveniently discussed under three heads, namely, Theory of Knowledge, Metaphysics, and Ethics and Theology.

II. The Mīmāṁsā Theory of Knowledge

Mīmāṁsā's contribution to the theory of knowledge.

In its attempt to justify the authority of the Vedas, the Mīmāṁsā came to discuss very elaborately the nature of knowledge, the nature and criterion of truth as well as of falsity, the different sources of valid knowledge (pramāṇas) and other cognate problems. The epistemology of the Mīmāṁsā deals with some very interesting problems. Other schools, specially the Vedānta, freely draw upon the Mīmāṁsā in epistemological matters. We shall notice here very briefly some of the peculiar and important things.

1. The Nature and Sources of Knowledge

The Mīmāṁsā, like most other schools, admits two kinds of knowledge, immediate and mediate. Valid knowledge is one which yields some new information about something, is not contradicted by any other knowledge and is not generated by defective conditions (such as defective sense-organ in the cases of perceptual knowledge, fallacious premises in the cases of inference, etc.)[1]

The meaning of knowledge.

The object of immediate knowledge must be something existing (sat). Only when such an object is related to sense (one of the five external senses and the internal sense, manas), there arises in the soul an immediate knowledge about it. When an object is related to sense, at first there arises a bare awareness of the object. We simply know *that* the object *is*, but have not yet understood *what* it is. This primary, indeterminate, immediate knowledge is called nirvikalpaka pratyakṣa or ālocana-jñāna. When at the next stage we interpret the meaning of this object in the light of our past knowledge and come to understand what it is, that is, what class it belongs to, what quality, activity and name it possesses, we have a determinate (savikalpaka) perception, which is expressed by judgments like 'This is a man,' 'This has a stick,' 'This is white,' 'This is moving,' 'This is Ram.'[2]

Immediate knowledge : its two stages of development—indeterminate and determinate perceptions.

Perception, thus completed in two stages, gives us a real knowledge of the world composed of different objects. Though at the first stage the objects are not known explicitly, all that we know about them at the second stage is implicitly known even at first. In understanding the object at the second stage, the mind only interprets, in the light of past experience, what is given at first, it does not ascribe to it any imaginary predicate. For

The objects known in perception are real and possess diverse characters.

1. Vide *Śāstra-dīpikā* on Jaimini's *Sūtra*, 1.1.5.

2. *Ibid.*, and *Śloka vārtika* on 1.1.4.

if we did not perceive at first a man, a white one, etc., how could we judge later that it was a man, it was white, etc., and that it was not a cow and not black, etc. Hence it must be admitted that perception, in spite of containing an element of interpretation, is not necessarily imaginary and illusory as some Bauddhas and some Vedāntins hold. Neither is it true that what we are immediately aware of, before the mind interprets, is a purely unique particular (svalakṣaṇa) without any distinguishing class character (as those Bauddhas hold), or is pure existence without any differentiating property (as those Vedāntins say). The diverse objects of the world with their different characteristics are given to the mind at the very first moment when we become aware of them.[1]

2. Non-perceptual Sources of Knowledge

Prābhākaras admit five sources of knowledge, while Bhāttas admit six.

In addition to perception, there are five other valid sources of knowledge, admitted by the Mīmāṁsā, namely, inference (anumā-na), comparison (upamāna), authority or testimony (śabda), postulation (arthāpatti) and non-perception (anupalabdhi). The last one is admitted only by the school of Kumārila Bhaṭṭa and not by that of Prabhākara. The Mīmāṁsā theory of inference is more or less similar to that of the Nyāya and need not be mentioned here. We shall discuss the other four non-perceptual sources of knowledge.

(i) Comparison (upamāna)

The Mīmāṁsā conceives upamāna in a way different from the Nyāya.

It has been previously seen that the Nyāya admits comparison as a unique source of knowledge. But the Mīmāṁsā, though accepting comparison as an independent source, accepts it in quite a different sense. According to it, knowledge arises from comparison when, on perceiving a present object to be like

1. Vide *Prakaraṇa-pañcikā*, pp. 54-55.

an object perceived in the past, we come to know that the *remembered object is like* the perceived one. Some examples will make this clear. On seeing a rat one perceives that it is like a mouse perceived in the past, and thence he gets the knowledge that the remembered mouse is like the perceived rat. This knowledge, namely 'that mouse, perceived in the past, is like this rat,' is obtained from comparison, or from the knowledge of a similarity of the rat to the mouse. Similarly one who has been a cow previously at home goes to a forest and finds a gavaya (nilgai) and perceives its similarity to the cow at home. He may thence obtain by comparison (*i.e.* by the knowledge of this similarity) the further knowledge that the cow at home is like the gavaya.[1]

Knowledge of similarity about an absent object is obtained by comparison.

Such knowledge cannot be classed under perception. For, the object (the mouse of the cow) known to be similar is not perceived *then.* It does not come under memory, because though the *object* was perceived in the past, its *similarity* to the present object was *not then* known, and, therefore, this similarity cannot be said to be simply remembered. It is not also an inference. From a knowledge like 'this *gavaya* is like the cow at home' we cannot infer 'the cow at home is like this *gavaya*,' unless we have another premise like 'all things are similar to other things which are similar to them.'[2] And such a universal premise containing an invariable concomitance between two terms *is not really used* in the above case where one arrives at the knowledge of the absent cow's similarity to the present

Such knowledge cannot be placed under perception, memory inference or testimony.

1. The Mīmāṁsā view of upamāna is fully discussed in *Śloka vārtika*, *Śāstra-dīpikā* (1.1.5) and *Prakaraṇa-Pañcikā* and briefly in *Sabara-bhāṣya* on 1.1.5.

2. Vide *Śāstra-dīpikā*, 1.1.5.

gavaya, from the perception of the gavaya being similar to the cow. Again, such knowledge does not obviously arise from verbal testimony or authority. Hence it is given an independent place.

Hence it is given a separate place.

The Nyāya holds that on learning from an authority that a gavaya is like a cow, a person goes to a forest, perceives some animal like the cow and thence he has by upamāna or comparison the knowledge that such an animal is a gavaya. Against this Nyāya view it is pointed out by Mīmāṁsaka writes that the knowledge that the particular animal perceived is like the cow is derived from perception and the knowledge that such an animal looking like the cow is a gavaya is obtained through recollection of what was previously learned from some authority. Lastly, the knowledge that *this* particular animal is a gavaya, is a mere inference from the last knowledge. Hence what the Nyāya considers to be derived from a new source, namely comparison, is not really so.[1]

Why the Nyāya view of upamāna is untenable.

It may be noted here that though the account given above is the one generally accepted by later Mīmāṁsakas, Śabarasvāmi[2] seems to understand upamāna, as, what is called in Western logic analogical argument. The existence of another self is proved, he remarks, by an argument like this. "Just as you feel the existence of your own self, similarly by analogy you can believe that others also feel the existence of their own selves." Such an argument he calls upamāna. Śabara's definition of upamāna as "knowledge of an unperceived object as being similar to some known object," is not

Śabara seems to treat upamāna as analogical argument in general.

1. Vide *Prakarana-pañcikā*. For critical discussion of 'upamāna' *vide* D.M. Datta, *The Six Ways of Knowing*, Bk. II.
2. Vide his *Bhāṣya* on *Jaim. sūt.*, 1.1.5.

incompatible with the suggestion that he takes upamāna as analogical argument.

It should also be remembered that 'similarity' (sadrsya), which is the object of upamana is regarded by the Mīmāṁsā as an independent category of reality. It is pointed out that similarity cannot be called a quality (guṇa), because a quality cannot be possessed by another *quality* ; but 'similarity' is possessed by qualities even. It cannot be treated as a universal (sāmā nya or jāti). Because a universal means something which is exactly *identical* in many individuals (*e.g.* cowness in cows). Similarity does not mean any completely identical character.

Similarity is not a quality, nor a universal. It is a separate category.

(ii) Authority or Testimony (śabda)

The Mīmāṁsā pays the greatest attention to this source of knowledge, because it has to justify the authority of the Vedas.

An intelligible sentence yields knowledge except when it is known to be the statement of an unreliable person (anāpta-vākya). This is known as verbal testimony or simply testimony (śabda) or authority. There are two kinds of authority—personal (pauruṣeya) and impersonal (apauruṣeya). The first consists in the written or spoken testimony of some person. The second denotes the authority of the Vedas. Again, authority may either give information as to the existence of objects (siddhārtha-vākya) or give directions for the performance of some action (vidhāyaka-vākya). The Mīmāṁsā is interested primarily in the impersonal authority of the Vedas and that again, because the Vedas give directions for performing the sacrificial rites. The

Two kinds of authority : Personal and impersonal.

Again authority is either a source of information or a source of command.

The Vedas are valued by the Mimāṁsā as the impersonal source of commandments.

Vedas are looked upon as the Book of Commandments; and therein lies thier value. The Mīmāṁsā even holds that as the sole use of the Vedas lies in directing rituals, any part of them which does not contain such *direction* but gives information about the *existence* of anything is useless, unless it can be shown at least to serve the purpose of persuading persons to follow the injunctions for performing rituals.[1] The attempt is constantly made, therefore, to show all existential sentences (regarding the soul, immortality, etc.) as indirectly connected with some commandment, by way of persuading people to perform some ritual or dissuading them from forbidden activity. This attitude of the Mīmāṁsā reminds us of modern Pragmatism which holds that every type of knowledge — ordinary, scientific or philosophical—is valuable only in so far as it leads to some practical activity. The Mīmāṁsā philosophy may be called ritualistic pragmatism, for according to it the value of Vedic knowledge is for ritualistic activity.

The ritualistic pragmatism of the Mīmāṁsā.

According to most of the pro-Vedic schools, the authority of the Vedas lies in their being the words of God. But the Mīmāṁsā which does not believe in any Creator or Destroyer of the world, believes that the Vedas, like the world, are eternal.[2] They are not the work of any person, human or divine. Hence the authority of the Vedas is said to be impersonal. Elaborate arguments are advanced to support this view. If the Vedas had any author, his name would have been known and remembered; for, the Vedic lore has been passed down by an unbroken series of successive generations of teachers and learners from unknown

The Vedas are not the work of *any* person; they are *eternal*.

Arguments to prove this view.

1. Vide *Jaim. sūt.*, 1.2.1. and 1.2.7. and *Sabara-bhāsya* thereon.
2. *Ibid.*, Adhikaranas, 6-8, Chap. I.

antiquity. But no such name is remembered. Even those (among the ancient Indian thinkers) who believe that the Vedas are not eternal, but produced, are not unanimous as to their origin. Some ascribe them to God, some to Hiranyagarbha, some to Prajāpati. The fact is that they think vaguely, on the analogy of ordinary books, that the Vedas also must have some author, but do not know precisely who the author is. The names of certain persons are of course cited along with the Vedic hymns. But they are the seers (ṛṣis) to whom the hymns were revealed, or the expositors or the founders of the different Vedic schools (sampradāyas). So the Vedas are not the works of any persons.

But are not the Vedas composed of words and are not words produced and non-eternal ? In reply to this question, the Mīmāṁsakas propound the theory that words (śabdas) are not really the perceived sounds (dhvanis). The sounds produced by the speaker and perceived by the hearer are only the revealers of the words which are not themselves produced. Words are really the letters which are partless and uncaused. A letter, like 'k', is pronounced (and revealed) by different persons at different places and times in different ways. Though these letter-sounds vary, we recognise that the *same* letter is pronounced by all of them. This identity of the letter shows that it is not produced at any time and place, but transcends them. So the words as letters may be regarded as eternal, that is, as having existence, but being uncaused.

Another argument in support of the theory that the Vedas are not the works of any person is that they enjoin some ritual duties and declare their fruits (like attainment of heaven). The connection between the actions and such fruits is not such as can be said to have been observed by any person (like the connection between the taking of a prescribed medicine and the cure of a disease). So no person can be said to be the author of the Vedas. It is not also reasonable to hold that the author may be a cunning deceiver (as the Cārvākas suggest). For had it been so, no one would care to study such deceptive works and hand them down to posterity.[1]

The Vedas are infallible.

The infallibility of the authority of the Vedas rests on the fact that they are not vitiated by any defects to which the work of imperfect persons is subject.

The statement of a reliable person is also a source of valid knowledge.

But in addition to the impersonal Vedic authority, the testimony of a reliable person (āpta) also is accepted by the Bhāṭṭas[2] as a valid source of knowledge. There is, however, a special value attached to Vedic authority, because the knowledge of the commandments (dharma) which we have from it is not to be obtained from any other source, such as perception and inference. While the knowledge that personal authority may impart to us can be sometimes obtained otherwise by perception, inference, etc. and is itself based on such previous knowledge, the knowledge derived from the Vedas is neither obtainable otherwise nor dependent on any previous knowledge, the Vedas being eternal. But the Prābhākaras,[3] like the Vaiśeṣikas, hold that the statement of a non-Vedic authority yields knowledge through inference based on the reliability of the authority.

But the knowledge of duty is obtainable only from the Vedas.

Knowledge from authority is not dependent on inference.

In reply to those who try to reduce all knowledge derived from testimony to inference on the ground that the validity of such knowledge is ascertained by inference based on the reliability of authority, the Mīmāṁsā makes

1. Vide *Śāstradīpikā*, Śabda-nityatā-dhikaranam (pp. 138 f.) and *Prakaraṇa-pañcikā*, Śabda-pariccheda (pp. 87 f.)
2. Vide *Śāstradīpikā*, Śabda-pariccheda (p. 72).
3. Vide *Prakaraṇa-pañcikā* (p.95).

an important reply. It asserts that the validity of every knowledge is assured by the conditions which generate that knowledge, so that the knowledge imparted by authority, like every other knowledge, carries with itself such assurance of its own truth. We shall see later on the full reasons in support of this view.

Every knowledge by itself claims truth.

(iii) Postulation (arthāpatti)

Postulation[1] (arthāpatti) is the necessary supposition of an unperceived fact which *alone* can explain a phenomenon that demands explanation. When a given phenomenon is such that we cannot understand it in any way without supposing some other fact, we have to postulate this other fact by way of explaining the phenomenon. This process of explaining an otherwise inexplicable phenomenon by the affirmation of the explaining fact is called arthāpatti.[2] Thus when a man, who is growing fat, is observed to fast during the day, we find an apparent contradiction between his growing fatness and his fasting. We cannot in any way reconcile these two facts, namely, fatness and fasting, unless we admit that the man eats at night. That the man must eat at night explains the complex whole of apparently conflicting facts, namely, fasting attended with increasing fatness.

Postulation is the necessary supposition of an unperceived fact to explain some conflicting phenomena.

---

1. It is difficult to find an exact word in English for 'arthāpatti'. Postulation in the Kantian sense has a close similarity to 'arthāpatti'. A demand for explanation underlies the use of this method, and 'postulate' in Latin means 'demand'.

2. Vide *Sabara-bhāsya*, 1.1.5. *Śloka vārtika*, *Śāstra-dipikā* and *Prakarana-pañcikā* on Arthāpatti. For critical discussion, *vide* D.M. Datta, *The Six Ways of Knowing*, Bk. V.

Knowledge obtained in this way is distinctive because it is not reducible to perception or inference : and it is not, of course, a case of testimony or comparison. Such knowledge cannot be explained as perception since we do not see the man eat at night. Nor is it a case of 'inference', because there is no invariable concomitance (vyāpti) between fatness and eating at night, so that we cannot say that whenever there is fatness there is eating at night, as we can say that wherever there is smoke there is fire.

Knowledge so obtained does not come under perception or inference.

Though we are not ordinarily aware of it, we employ this method of arthāpatti very often in daily life. Some examples will make this clear. When we call on a friend and do not find him at home, though we are sure that he is alive, we say : "He must be somewhere outside home," This last supposition is made by us because this alone can explain how a man who is alive cannot be at home. This method is also largely used by us in the interpretation of language. When some words are omitted in a sentence, we suppose those words without which the meaning implied by the context cannot be explained. On reading or hearing a sentence like 'shut up,' we supply (by arthāpatti) the words 'your lips,' because without them the meaning is incomplete. Similarly, when the primary meaning of a word does not suit the context, we suppose a secondary or figurative meaning which alone can explain the sentence. For example, when we are told, 'Industry is the *key* to success' we suppose that the meaning of 'key' here must be 'means' and not a real key.

The use of this method of knowledge is very frequent in life.

Mīmāṁsakas distinguish between two kinds of postulation that which is employed to explain something which is perceived (dṛṣṭārthāpatti), such as fatness in a man who is fasting by day, and that which is used to explain the meanings of words heard (srutā rthāpatti), such as those cited above.

Two kinds of postulation distinguished by Mīmāṁsakas.

It will be found that arthāpatti resembles a hypothesis as understood in Western logic. It appears to be like an explanatory hypothesis. But the difference is that it lacks the tentative or provisional character of a hypothesis. What is known by arthāpatti is not simply hypothetically supposed or entertained, but is *believed* in as the *only* possible *explanation.* As arthāpatti arises out of a *demand for explanation,* it is different from a syllogistic inference the object of which is to *conclude* from given facts, and not to *explain* given facts. Arthāpatti is a search for *grounds*, whereas an inference is a serarch for *consequents*.

The distinction between postulation and hypothesis.

The distinction between postulation and deduction.

(iv) Anupalabdhi or non-perception

According to the Bhāṭṭa Mīmāṁsā and the Advaita Vedānta, non-perception (anupalabdhi) is the source of our immediate cognition of the non-existence of an object. The question here is : How do I know the non-existence, say, of a jar on the table before me ? It cannot be said that I perceive it with my senses, because non-existence is a negative fact which cannot stimulate any sense as a positive fact like the table can. The Bhāṭṭas and the Advaitins hold, therefore, that the non-existence of the jar on the table is known from the absence of its cognition, that is, from its non-perception (anupalabdhi). I judge that

Non-perception yields an immediate knowledge of non-existence.

Such knowledge can be obtained neither from perception,

the jar does not exist on the table because it is *not perceived.* It cannot be said that the non-existence of the jar is

nor from inference,

inferred from its non-perception. For, such an inference is possible, if we already possess the knowledge of a universal relation between non-perception and non-existence that is, if we know that when an object is not perceived it does not exist. Thus it would be begging the question or assumption of the very thing which was sought to be proved by inference. Nor can we explain the knowledge of the jar's non-existence by comparison or testimony, since it is not due to any knowledge of similarity or of words and sentences. Hence to explain the direct knowledge of the jar's non-existence we have to recognize non-perception (anupalabdhi) as a separate and an independent source of knowledge.[1]

but from appropriate non-perception.

It should, however, be remarked here that all non-perception does not mean the non-existence of what is not perceived. We do not see a table in the dark, nor do we perceive any such supersensible entities as atoms, ether, virtue, vice. Yet we do not judge them to be non-existent. If a thing should have been perceived under certain circumstances, *then* only its non-perception under those circumstances would give the knowledge of its non-existence. It is such appropriate non-perception (Yogyā nupalabdhi) that is the source of our knowledge of non-existence.

3. The Validity of Knowledge

In the presence of sufficient conditions knowledge arises with a belief in its truth.

Whenever there are *sufficient* conditions for the generation of a particular kind of knowledge (and, therefore, no grounds for doubt or disbelief are known), there arises at once that kind of knowledge containing an element of belief in the object known. For example, when our normal eyes light on

1. Vide *Śloka-vārtika, Śāstra-dīpikā* and *Vedānta-paribhāṣā* on Anupalabdhi. For further critical discussion, vide *The Six Ways of Knowing*, Bk. III.

an object conveniently situated in broad daylight, there is visual perception ; when we hear some one speak a meaningful sentence, we have knowledge from his testimony. When there are sufficient premises, inference takes place. That we act on such knowledge in everyday life as soon as we have it, without any attempt to test its validity by argument, shows that we believe in it as soon as it arises ; and the fact that such knowledge leads to successful activity and not to any contradiction shows further that such knowledge is valid. When, however, the conditions required for the generation of that kind of knowledge are known to be defective or wanting (if, for example, the eyes are jaundiced, light is insufficient, premises are doubtful or words are meaningless, etc.) no such knowledge arises ; neither, therefore, does any belief airse, so long as the grounds for doubt and disbelief do not disappear. From these facts two conclusions are drawn by the Mīmāṁsā : (a) The validity of knowledge *arises* fromthe very conditions that give rise to that knowledge, and not from any extra conditions (prāmāṇyam svataḥ utpadyate), (b) The validity of a knowledge is also *believed* in or known as soon as the knowledge arises ; belief does not await the verification of the knowledge by some other knowledge, say, an inference (prāmāṇyam svataḥ jñāyate ca). This Mīmāṁsā view, in its double aspect, is known as the theory of intrinsic validity (svataḥ- prāmānya vāda).[1]

The conditions of knowledge generate its validity and belief in the validity.

Truth is self-evident, according to this view. Whenever any knowledge arises, it carries with it an assurance about its own truth. Sometimes another knowledge may point out that this assurance is misleading, or that the conditions of the knowledge are defective. In such a case we infer from the existence of defective conditions the falsity of the knowledge. Thus the falsity of a knowledge is ascertained by inference, while truth is self-evident. To put the whole position simply, belief is normal, disbelief is an exception.

Truth is self-evident.

But falsity is known by inference.

1. *Śloka-vārtika*, 2.1.1 and *Sarva-darśana.*, on Jaimini system.

As perception, inference and any other knowledge arise, we *implicitly accept them,* believe in them without further argument, unless we are compelled by some contrary evidence to doubt their validity or to infer their falsity. On this unsuspecting faith in our knowledge our life runs smoothly.

If truth were to be ascertained by inference, there would be an infinite regress.

Against the Nyāya theory that validity is generated by some extra conditions (such as soundness of organs), over and above the ordinary conditions which generate a knowledge, the Mīmāṁsā points out that those extra conditions really form a part of the normal conditions of that knowledge ; without them there would be no belief and, therefore, no knowledge at all. Against the Nyāya view that the validity of every knowledge is ascertained by inference, the Mīmāṁsā points out that this would lead us to an infinite regress and activity would be impossible. If any knowledge, say, a perception, before being acted upon were to be verified by an inference, then by the same Nyāya rule *that* inference also would have to be verified by another inference and so on ; and there would have been no end to this process of verification and life would have been impossible. As soon as we perceive a tiger we run away, as soon as we infer the approach of a car from its horn we guard our steps ; if we are to wait for verifying our knowledge with the never-ending series of inferences, we would have to wait for ever before we could act on any knowledge. It is true that when there is any positive cause for doubt regarding any knowledge, we take the help of verifying inference ; but that only does the negative work of removing the obstacles that stand in the way of knowledge. After the obstacles are removed, knowledge arises out of its own usual conditions, if present there, and along with it arise its validity and belief in its validity. If that verifying inference is unable to remove doubt, then that knowledge does not arise at all.

Belief in authority, personal or impersonal, Vedic or non-Vedic, arises in a similar way. On hearing a meaningful sentence we at once believe in what it says unless there

The truth of the Vedas, therefore, is self-evident.

are reasons for doubt or disbelief. Therefore, authority of the eternal, impersonal Vedas also stands on its own legs. Its validity is self-evident and not dependent on inference. Arguments are necessary for the negative, work of clearing the mind of doubts. This being done, the Vedas themselves reveal their own meanings and belief invariably accompanies the understanding of these meanings. To secure this belief all that the Mīmāṁsā does is to refute the possible grounds on which the infallibility of the Vedas may be doubted, and thus to prepare the mind for the immediate acceptance of what is known from the Vedas.

4. What is error ?

If truth is self-evident and every knowledge claims truth, how does error arise ? The problem of error has been discussed threadbare by every Indian School. The Prābhā karas[1] hold that every knowledge is true, that nothing false ever appears in any error like the mistaking of a rope for a serpent. Even in a so-called case of serpent, we have a mixture of two different kinds of knowledge, the perception of a long tortuous thing and the memory of a serpent perceived in the cast, and each of these is true. Only owing to lapse of memory we forget that the serpent is a thing perceived in the past ; and the distinction between the perceived and remembered objects is not observed : we behave towards the rope as we should towards a serpent. It is this *behaviour* which is faulty. The cognitive defect here is a lapse of memory (smṛti-pramoṣa) or its effect, non-discrimination (vivekāgraha). This is *negative* and is surely not the same thing as error, which means not merely a want of knowledge but a positive mental state. This Prābhākara theory of error is technically known as akhyāti vāda or denial of illusory appearance. The Bhāṭṭas do not accept this theory.[2] They point out that mere non-discrimination cannot explain

Illusory appearance is denied by Prābhākaras.

---

1. Vide *Prakarana-pañcikā*, pp. 32-38.
2. *Śāstra-dīpikā*, 1.1.5.

error. We cannot deny that sometimes the illusory object *appears* positively before us. No one can deny that if the eye-ball is pressed while looking at the moon, two moons positively appear before us. The serpent illusion is also similar. In explanation of error, the Bhāṭṭas point out that when we perceive a snake in a rope and judge "This is a serpent," both the subject and the predicate are real. The existing rope is brought under the serpent-class which also exists in the world. Error consists, however, in relating these two really existing but separate things in the subject-predicate way. *Error always attaches to such wrong relation* (saṁsarga), and *not to the objects* related which are always real. Even in the moon illusion two real parts of space perceived are attributed to the real moon perceived, and by such wrong relation the one moon appears to be in two places. Such wrong judgement makes one behave in a way which is the reverse of the right one. This Bhāṭṭa theory of error is, therefore, known as viparīta-khyāti-vāda or the view that error is reversal of right behaviour (akāryasya kāryatayā bhānam).

It is admitted by Bhāṭṭas, but explained as due to wrong relation of real objects.

Thus we find that the Prābhākaras exempt all knowledge from error, but the Bhāṭṭas admit that error may affect some cognitive *relations* of objects, though the objects themselves are always correctly perceived. But according to both, error chiefly affects our *activity* rather than knowledge. Moreover, error is rather an exceptional case of the falsification of the normal claim that every knowledge makes for truth. On the acceptance of this claim alone our everyday life becomes possible. Therefore the falsification of the truth-claim in some cases does not affect the normal acceptance of it.

Error is an abnormal or exceptional phenomenon.

III. Mīmāṁsā Metaphysics

1. General Outlook

The Mīmāṁsā belives in the reality of the perceived world, and of other objects.

Depending on the validity of sense-perception the Mīmāṁsā believes in the reality of the world with all its diverse objects. It rejects, therefore, the Buddhistic theory of voidness and momentariness, as well as the Advaita theory of the unreality of the phenomenal world. In addition to objects perceived it comes to believe, through other sources of knowledge, in souls, heaven, hell and deities to whom sacrifice is to be performed, according to the Vedic commandments. The souls are permanent, eternal substances, and so also are the material elements by the combination of which the world is made. The law of karma is thought sufficient to guide the formation of objects. The world is composed of (a) living bodies wherein the souls reap the consequences of their past deeds (bhogāyatana), (b) the sensory and motor organs, *i.e.* the indriyas, which are instruments for suffering or enjoying those consequences (bhoga-sādhana), and (c) the objects which constitute the fruits to be suffered or enjoyed (bhogya-viṣaya). No necessity is felt for admitting the existence of God. Some Mīmāṁsakas[1] believe like the Vaiśeṣikas in the atomic theory. But the difference is that, according to the Mīmāṁsā, atoms do not require, for their arrangement in the world, an efficient cause like God. The autonomous law of karma independently regulates the atoms. There is neither creation nor total destruction. *The world is eternally there.*[2] This Mīmāṁsā view is unique in Indian Philosophy.

There are souls, which are eternal spiritual substances.

The world is always there, neither created nor destroyed, but regulated by karma.

---

1. Not all (vide *Śloka-vārtika*, Chap. on Inference, verse 183, and Mānameyodaya 2.13). For arguments in support of atomism, vide Prābhākara-vijaya.
2. Vide *Śloka-vārtika*, pp. 672 f.

The Mīmāṁsakas mostly follow the Vaiśeṣika conception of Padārthas and their sub-classes. The important points on which they differ from the Vaiśeṣikas may be noted here. The Prābhākaras do not admit non-existence as a separate reality, but consider it to be but an aspect of its locus. All Mīmāṁsakas recognize Śakti (potency) as an important causal factor, some accepting it as a new padārtha, others as a quality inherent in a cause. Some reject Viśeṣa and Samavāya, and admit only the remaining five padārthas. Some admit Sound (Śabda) as an eternal substance, the audible sounds being regarded as its manifestations. In these deviations even the writers of the same school sometimes differ among themselves.

The Mīmāṁsā philosophy is pluralism and realism, but not empiricism.

The Mīmāṁsā metaphysics is then pluralistic and realistic. It is not empiricism, because it believes in the non-empirical Vedic source of knowledge which is thought even to be more dependable than sense experience[1] and also because it believes in many realities like potential energy, the unseen moral principle, heaven, hell, etc., which cannot be known through sense-experience.

2. *The Theory of Potential Energy (śakti and apūrva)*

There is a power in every cause. It produces the effect when it is not obstructed.

In connection with the question of causation the Mīmāṁsā formulates the theory of potential energy (śakti[2]. A seed possesses in it an imperceptible power (śakti) with the help of which it can produce the sprout ; when this power is obstructed or destroyed (as, for example, by the frying of the seed), it fails to produce that effect. Similarly, there is the power of burning in fire, the power of expressing meaning and inducing activity in a word, the power of illumination in light and so on. The necessity of admitting such unperceived potency in the cause is that it explains why in some cases

1. In fact Kumārila observes (in *Śloka-vārtika*, verse 72, 11.2) that the fact that the Vedas contradict ordinary empirical knowledge is a proof of their superior authority.

2. Vide *Śastra-dīpikā* p.80, and *Prakaraṇa-pañcikā*, p. 146.

though the cause (*i.e.* seed or fire) is there, the effect (*i.e.* sprout or burning) does not take place. The explanation is that in such cases though the cause-substance is there, its causal potency has been destroyed or over powered temporarily, as the case may be, by some obstructing conditions obtaining there.

Nyāya criticism answered.

The Nyāya realists reject this theory. They say that even without admitting an imperceptible potency in causes the above difficulty may be solved by holding that a cause produces the effect in the absence of obstructions and does not produce in is their presence. The Mīmāṁsā meets this objection by saying that as we have to admit, even according to the Nyāya, something else in addition to the cause (namely, absence of obstruction), for the production of the effect, the Nyāya suggestion is no improvement. If you must suppose something, why not admit a positive something in the very substance (say, seed) which is taken by all as the cause (say, of the sprout), rather than an additional negative condition having a causal power. It would be reasonable, therefore, to suppose in the cause-substance a positive power (śakti) to explain the positive effect, and to suppose the non-functioning of this power (owing to its destruction or suppression) to explain the negative fact of non-happening of the effect.

The theory of apūrva or the soul's potency for enjoyment of the fruits of rituals.

One important application of this theory of potency made by the Mīmāṁsā is for the solution of the problem how an action lika a sacrifice performed now bears fruit after a long time (say, after this life, in Heaven) when the action has ceased. It is held that the ritual performed here generates in the soul of the performer an unperceived potency (*i.e.,* power for generating the fruit of the action) called apūrva, which remains in the soul and bears fruit when circumstances are favourable.[1] It will be found that the theory of apūrva is a limited hypothesis which tries to explain a part of the general problem

1. Vide *Śāstra-dīpikā*, p.80; *Prakaraṇa-pañcikā*, pp. 184-95; *Sabara-bhāṣya*, 2.1.5.

of conservation of the fruits of all actions, ritualistic and non-ritualistic, which the more universal law of karma seeks to explain.

3. The Mīmāṁsā Conception of Soul

The conception of soul in the Mīmāṁsā is more or less like that of other realistic and pluralistic schools such as the Nyāya-Vaiśeṣika.[1] The soul is an eternal, infinite substance, which is related to a real body in a real world and it survives death to be able to reap the consequences of its action performed here. Consciousness is not the essence of the soul, but an adventitious quality which arises when some conditions are present. In dreamless sleep and in the state of liberation the soul has no consciousness, because its conditions, such as relation of sense to object, are absent. There are as many souls as there are individuals. The souls are subject to bondage and can also obtain liberation. In all these respects the grounds, on which the Mīmāṁsā views are based, resemble those of the other schools mentioned previously and we need not repeat them here.

The soul is an eternal, infinite substance which has the capacity for consciousness.

Regarding the knowledge of the soul, however, there is something worth mentioning. The Bhāṭṭa School holds that the self is not known whenever any object is known : it is known occasionally. When we reflect on the self, we know it as the *object* of self-consciousness (ahaṁ-vitti). But the Prābhākara School objects to this view on the ground that the very conception of self-consciousness is untenable, because the self cannot be both subject and object of the same act of knowledge any more than food can be both the cook and the cooked. The functions of the subject and the object are mutually incompatible (karma-kartṛ-virodha) and

How is the self known ?

'As the *object* of self-consciousness'—say the Bhāṭṭas.

1. Vide *Śloka-vārtika,* Ātma-vāda ; *Śāstra-dīpikā,* Ātma-vāda, p.119 et seq.; *Prakaraṇa-pañcikā*, Prakaraṇa 8.

cannot be attributed to the same thing at the same time. In every act of knowing an object, however, the self is revealed as the *subject* by that very knowledge. It is thus that we can speak of the self as the knower in judgments like "I know this pot." If I myself did not appear as the subject in every knowledge, the distinction between my knowledge and another man's knowledge would have been impossible.[1] The Bhāṭṭas reply to this that if the self were revealed whenever an object were known, we would have invariably had then a judgement like "I know this pot." But this is not always the case. This shows that self-consciousness does not always accompany the consciousness of an object ; but it only occasionally takes place and is, therefore, something different from the consciousness of objects. As for the opposition between subjectivity and objectivity, it is more verbal than real. If there were any real opposition, then the Vedic injunction "Know the self," and everyday judgements like "I know myself" would have been meaningless. Besides, if the self were never the object of any knowledge, how could we remember the existence of the self in the past ? Here the *past* self cannot be said to be the *subject* or knower of the *present* memory-knowledge ; it can only be the object of the present self that knows it.[2] This shows that the self can become the object of knowledge.

'As the *subject* of every knowledge'— say the Prābhākaras.

The Bhātta reply to the Prābhākaras.

Closely connected with this question is another, namely, 'How is knowledge known?' The Prābhākaras hold that in every knowledge of an object, such as expressed by the judgment '*I know* this *pot*,' three factors are present namely, 'I' or the knower (jñātā), the object known (jñeya) and the knowledge itself (jñāna). All these *three* are simultaneously revealed (triputrījñāna). Whenever knowledge arises, it reveals itself, its object and the subject. Knowledge

How is knowledge known ?

The Prābhākaras hold that knowledge reveals itself as well as its subject and object.

1. *Prakarana-pañcikā*, p. 148.
2. *Śāstra-dīpikā*, pp. 122-23.

is self-revealing (svayamprakāśa) and is the revealer of its subject and object as well. The Bhāṭṭas hold, on the contrary, that knowledge by its very nature is such that it cannot be the object of itself, just as the finger-tip cannot touch itself. But how then do we at all come to know that we have the knowledge of a certain object ? The Bhāṭṭas reply that whenever we perceive an object it appears to be either unfamiliar or familiar. If it appears to be familiar or previously known (jñāta), then from this character of familiarity or knownness (jñātatā) which the object presents to us, we *infer* that we had a knowledge of that object. Knowledge is thus known indirectly by inference on the ground of the familiarity or knownness observed in the object.

The Bhāṭṭas hold that knowledge is inferred from the knownness of its object.

IV. Mīmāṁsā Religion and Ethics

1. The Place of the Vedas in Religion

The Mīmāṁsā does not believe in a creator of the world. In its anxiety to secure the supreme place for the eternal Vedas, the Mīmāṁsā could not believe in God whose authority would be superior to, or at least on a par with, that of the Vedas. According to the Mīmāṁsā, the Vedas embody not so much eternal truths as eternal injunctions or laws which enjoin the performance of the sacrificial rites. Religion or Dharma thus becomes identical with the Vedic injunctions (codanā-lakṣaṇo'rtho dharmaḥ). The Vedas supply the criterion of what is right, and what is wrong. A good life is a life led in obedience to the Vedic commandments.

Religion is based on the Vedic commandments.

2. The Conception of Duty

The sacrifies performed in the Vedic times were calculated to please, by oblations and hymns, different deities (the Fire-god, the Sun-god, the Rain-god and others) either to win some favour or avert some ill. Though the Mīmāṁsā is a continuation of this Vedic cult, the ceremonial details of the rituals absorb its interest, rather than the gods themselves who gradually recede and fade into mere grammatical datives. A deity comes to be described not by

A ritual must be performed because it is enjoined by the Vedas, and not with any other motive.

its moral or intellectual qualities, but as 'that which is signified, in a sacrificial injunction, by the fourth case-ending' (the sign of a dative, to which something is given). In short, a deity is necessary merely as that in whose *name* an oblation is to be offered at a sacrifice. But the primary object of performing a sacrifice, says an eminent Mīmāṁsaka, is not worship : it is not to please any deity. Nor is it purification of the soul or moral improvement.[1] A ritual is to be performed just because the *Vedas command us* to perform them. Some of these rituals, it is true, are to be performed in order to enjoy Heaven hereafter or to obtain worldly benefits such as rainfall. But there are some (*e.g.* nitya and naimittika karmas) which must be performed *just* because they are enjoined by the Vedas. Here the Mīmāṁsā ethics reaches, through ritualism, the highest point of its glory, namely the conception of duty for duty's sake. Like Kant, the Mīmāṁsā believes that an obligatory action is to be performed *not because* it will benefit the performer but because we *ought* to perform it. Like him again the Mīmāṁsā believes that though an obligatory duty is not to be done with any interested motive, yet the Universe is so constituted that a person who performs his duty does not ultimately go unrewarded. The difference is that while for this purpose the Mīmāṁsā postulates in the universe the impersonal moral law of karma, Kant postulates God. Again, whereas the source of obligation for Kant is the higher self (which commands to the lower, 'thou oughtest to do what good'), for the Mīmāṁsakas it is the impersonal Vedic authority which categorically enjoins duty.

Duty for duty's sake.

Kant and Mīmāṁsā : agreement and difference.

3. The Highest Good

The highest good in the early Mīmāṁsā conception appears to have been the attainment of Heaven or a state in which there is unalloyed bliss. Heaven is regarded as the usual end of rituals.[2] The Mīmāṁsaka writers gradually fall in with the other Indian thinkers and accept liberation from bondage to the flesh as the highest good (niḥśreyasa). They realize that the performance of actions, good or bad, if dictated by any desire

Heaven is the highest good, according to early Mīmāṁsā.

1. Vide *Prakarana-pañcikā*, pp. 185-86.
2. 'svargakāmo yajeta.'

for enjoyment of objects, causes repeated birth. When one understands that worldly pleasures are all mingled with pain, and becomes disgusted with life in the world, one tries to control one's passions, desists, from forbidden actions, as well as actions with motives of future enjoyment. Thus the chance of future birth and bondage is removed. By the disinterested performance of obligatory duties and knowledge of the self, the karmas accumulated in the past are also gradually worn out. After this life such a person, being free from all karma-ties, is never born again. He is thus liberated. As bondage is the fettering of the soul to the world through the body including the sense, the motor-organs and manas, liberation is the total destruction of such bondage through the stoppage of rebirth.[1]

Liberation replaces Heaven later on.

We have seen already that, according to the Mīmāṁsā, consciousness and other mental states are not inherent in the soul. They arise only when the soul is related to objects through the body and the organs. The liberated soul, being dissociated from the body and, therefore, from all the organs including manas, cannot have any consciousness : nor can it, therefore, enjoy bliss. Liberation is then desirable not as a state of bliss, but as the total cessation of painful experience. It is a state where the soul remains in its own intrinsic nature, beyond pleasure and pain.[2] The soul in its intrinsic state (svastha) can be defined only as substance having existence and a potentiality for consciousness—though no actual consciousness. Some later Bhāṭṭas hold, however, like the Advaitins that liberation is an experience of joy [3].

Liberation is an unconscious state, free from pleasure and pain.

4. *Is Mīmāṁsā Atheistic ?*

Should the Mīmāṁsā be called atheistic ? Though the reply to this question would seem to be in the affirmative in the light of the traditional conception of the Mīmāṁsā philosophy we have described above, doubts are raised by such a competent authority as Max Müller.[4] Bearing in mind that of all

Some Scholars think that the Mīmāṁsā is not atheistic.

1. Vide *Prakarana-pañcikā*, Prakarana 8, pp. 154-60.
2. Vide *Śāstra-dīpikā*, pp. 125-31.
3. Vide *Mānamayodaya*, 2.26
4. Vide The *Six Systems of Indian Philosophy*, Ch. V. Dr. Paśupatināth Sāstrī also advocates this view in his *Introduction* to *Pūrva Mīmāṁsā* . Vide also *Mānamayodaya*, 2.14.

schools the Mīmāṁsā claims to follow the Vedas most faithfully, he finds it difficult to believe that it could reject the Vedic belief in God. The arguments adduced by the Mīmāṁsakas against the conception of a creator of the universe mean, according to Max Müller, that if God were supposed to be the creator, He would be liable to the charges of cruelty, partiality, etc. But the rejection of a creator-God, he contends, is not necessarily the rejection of God. Even some forms of pantheism like those of the Advaita Vedānta and Spinoza, Max Müller contends, do not accept the reality of creation ; and it is unfair to call them atheistic, just because they do not conform to the customary conception of God.

But this view is difficult to support.

If the Mīmāṁsā is to be judged by the Vedic ancestry, of which it is so proud, then Max Müller is perhaps right. But judged by what the Mīmāṁsā itself does and says, his contention cannot be fully accepted. When we find that the early Mīmāṁsakas are silent about. God and later ones reject the proofs for the existence of God, like the Jainas, without replacing them by any other, we have no positive proof that the early Vedic faith was still alive in them. The different Vedic deities of course still form necessary parts of the sacrifies performed. Depending on this evidence one might say at best that the Mīmāṁsā believes in polytheism. But even such a view is rendered doubtful by the facts that these deities are not regarded as objects of worship,[1] nor even believed to have any existence anywhere except in the Vedic hymns (mantras) that describe them.[2] While the Vedic hymns are inspired by the living presence of the deity in the place of worship, the Mīmāṁsakas wonders how the deity can be simultaneously present in different places

The Mīmāṁsā rejects proofs of God's existence.

1. Yāgādinām devatārādhanahetutve pramāṇābhāvāt, *Prakaraṇa - pañcikā*, p. 185.

2. Vide Jhā. *Śloka-vārtika*. Eng. Tr., Introduction.

where he is invoked.[1] So polytheism of the ordinary kind cannot also be attributed to the Mīmāṁsā without some qualification. The deities of the Mīmāṁsaka are immortal entities. They are not existing persons, belonging to the space-time world. But they are not the products of our imagination either; they are eternal and self-manifesting entities described by the eternal, self-revealing Vedas. There may be some grandeur and even purity in such a conception of deities, but one would miss here the living faith of the Vedas. It would not be fair, then, to judge the Mīmāṁsā simply by its Vedic ancestry. Inherited elements of a faith, like inherited limbs, become atrophied by disuse. The Vedic conception of God had no active place in the Mīmāṁsā scheme of life, as it had in the Vedānta one, and it is natural that it should gradually fade away. The Mīmāṁsā is one of the many examples in human history of how an overemphasized means becomes its own end, and how gods are sacrificed for temples, prophets and books. In its great anxiety to maintain the supremacy of the Vedas, the Mīmāṁsā relegates God to an ambiguous position. It is here that the Vedānta comes to differ from it, utilising its faith in the Vedas to develop a still greater faith in God, as we shall see in the next chapter.

It loses the living faith in deities found in the Vedas.

1. Vide *Prakaraṇa-pañcikā*, p. 186.

THE VEDĀNTA PHILOSOPHY

A SELECT BIBLIOGRAPHY

V. L. Śāstrī ... *One Hundred and Eight Upaniṣads* (Nirnaya Sagar, Bombay, 1932).

Nikhilānanda ... The Upanishads (abridged, Eng.trans., Harper, N. Y., 1962).

R. D. Ranade ... *A Constructive Survey of Upaniṣadic Philosophy* (Oriental Book Agency, Poona, 1926).

Deussen ... *The Philosophy of the Upaniṣads* (T. & T. Clark, Edinburgh, 1908).

Śaṅkara ... *Brahma-sūtra-bhāṣya* (Nirnaya Sagar, 1934).

Rāmānuja ... *Brahma-Sūtra-bhāṣya* (R. Venkateśvar Co., Madras, 1936-40).

G. Thibaut ... *The Vedānta Sūtra*, with the Commentaries of Śaṅkara and Rāmānuja (Eng. trans., S. B. E. Series, Oxford, 1890, 1896 and 1904).

S. Radhakrishnan ... *Indian Philosophy*, Vol. II, Chs. VII-IX.

Kokileśvar Śastrī ... *Introduction to Adwaita Philosophy* (Calcutta University, 1924).

V.S. Ghate ... *The Vedānta* (Bhandarkar Institute, Poona, 1926).

M. Hiriyanna ... *Outlines of Indian Philosophy* (G. Allen & Unwin, 1932), Chs. XIII-XIV.

T. M. P. Mahadevan ... *The Philosophy of Advaita* (Luzac & Co., London, 1938).

CHAPTER X

THE VEDĀNTA PHILOSOPHY

I. Introduction

1. *Origin and Development of the Vedānta*

The Vedānta may be regarded as the end of the Vedas in different senses :

'Vedānta' literally means 'the end of the Vedas.' Primarily the word stood for the Upaniṣad though afterwards its denotation widened to include all thoughts developed out of the Upaniṣads. The Upaniṣads may be regarded as the end of the Vedas in different senses : (1) First, the Upaniṣads were the last literary products of the Vedic period. Three kinds of literature of this period can be broadly distinguished : the earliest being the Vedic hymns or mantras compiled in the different Saṁhitās (Ṛk, Yajus, Sāma and Atharva), the next being the Brāhmaṇas, treatises guiding and encouraging the Vedic rituals and the last, the Upaniṣads which discuss philosophical problems. All these three were treated as revealed texts (śruits) and sometimes also called the Vedas, in the wider sense of this term. (2) Secondly, in respect of study also, the Upaniṣads come last. As a rule, a man studied the Saṁhitās first ; the Brāhmaṇas were required next for guiding him when he entered life and had to perform the rituals enjoined on a householder ; and last of all the Upaniṣads (some of which are also known as āraṇyakas or forest-treatises) were needed to help him when he retired from the world, led a secluded life in forests and tried to understand the meaning of life and contemplate the mystery

(1) as the last literary products of the Vedic period.

(2) as studied after the other Vedic literature.

(3) as the culmination of the Vedic culture.

of the universe. (3) Thirdly, the end Upaniṣads may be regarded as the end of the Vedas also in the sense that they mark the culmination of the Vedic speculation. In the Upaniṣads themselves we are told that even after the study of the Vedas with other branches of learning a man's education is not complete till he receives instructions in the Upaniṣads.[1]

The literature of the Vedānta.

'Upaniṣad' means 'what destroys ignorance and gets man near to God,' or 'what gets man near to the teacher (upa-ni-sad)'.[2] The last meaning tallies with the fact that the Upaniṣadic doctrines were esoteric, *i.e.* they were very secretly taught only to the select pupils seated close to (upāsanna)[3] the teacher. The Upaniṣads were regarded as the inner or secret meanings (rahasya) of the Vedas, hence their teachings were sometimes called Vedopaniṣad[4] or the mystery of the Vedas. The Upaniṣads were many[5] in number and developed in the different Vedic schools (sākhās) at different times and places. The problems discussed and solutions offered presented differences in spite of a unity of general outlook. The need was felt, therefore, in course of time for systematizing the different teaching so as to bring out the harmony underlying them. Bādarāyaṇa's *Brahma-sūtra* also known variously as *Vedānta sūtra Śārīraka-sūtra* or *Śārīraka-mīmāṁsā, Uttara-mīmāṁsā,* undertakes this task. It discusses in four chapters : *(a)* the coherence (samanvaya) of the Upaniṣadic teachings, *(b)* their non-contradiction (avirodha) in relation to established theories and logical rules, *(c)* the means of

1. *Vide Chāndogya*, Chaps. 6 and 7.

2. *Vide Śaṅkara's* Introduction to *Kaṭha, Taittirīya, Bṛhadāraṇyaka.*

3. The verb 'upasad' ('go near') is repeatedly used in the Upaṇisads to describe the pupil's approaching the teacher for instruction.

4. *Vide Taittirīya, 1. 11.*

5. Vide Dasgupta, *History of Indian Philosophy,* Vol. I, p. 28, for a list of 112 Upaṇisads.

realization (sādhana), and *(d)* the fruit (phala) achieved. His sūtras, being brief, were liable to different interpretations. Various commentaries thus came to be written to elaborate the doctrines of the Vedānta in their own light. Each tried to justify its position as the only one consistent with the revealed texts (śrutis) and the sūtras. The author of each of these chief commentaries (bhāṣya) became the founder of a particular school of the Vedānta. Thus we have the schools of Śaṅkara, Rāmānuja, Madhva, Vallabha, Nimbārka and many others.[1] Each school of the Vedānta consists not simply of the philosopher who theoretically accept its views but also of a large number of monks and lay followers who try to mould their lives accordingly. It is in this way that the Vedānta in its different forms still persists in the lives of millions. After the chief commentaries, the literature of the Vedānta developed through the innumerable sub-commentaries, glosses and independent treatises written by the leading thinkers of each school to support its view and refute those of the other schools. The total output of Vedānta literature thus became very large, though only a small fraction of it has been printed as yet.

The schools of the Vedānta.

The practical followers of the Vedānta.

The most common question on which the schools of the Vedānta are divided is : What is the nature of the relation between the self (jīva) and God (Brahman) ? Some, like Madhva, hold that the self and God are two totally different entities ; their view is called dualism (dvaita). Some others,

The chief problem on which the schools of the Vedānta differ.

1. For a short comparative account of some of these schools, *vide* P. Nagaraja Rao's *The Schools of Vedānta* (Bhāratīya Vidyā Bhavan, Bombay) and Ghate's *The Vedānta.*

like Śaṅkara, hold that the two are absolutely identical ; this view is known as monism (advaita). Some others, like Rāmānuja, again hold that the two are related like part and whole ; this view may be briefly called qualified monism (viśiṣṭādvaita). There were many other views, each specifying a particular type of identity (abheda), difference (bheda) or identity-in-difference (bhedābheda) between the self and God, too many to be mentioned here. But the best known among the Vedānta schools are those of Śaṅkara and Rāmānuja which will be discussed here.

The three periods of the Vedānta.

Three stages in the development of the Vedānta may be distinguished in the light of what has been said above : (1) The creative stage represented by the revealed texts (śrutis) or the Vedic literature, chiefly consisting of the Upaniṣads. The fundamental ideas of the Vedānta take shape here mostly in the poetic visions and mystic intuitions of the enlightened seers. (2) The stage of systematization represented by the Brahma-sūtras which gather, arrange and justify the ideas of the previous stage. (3) The stage of elaboration represented by all works beginning from the chief commentaries downwards in which the ideas and arguments are cast into the proper philosophical forms, appeal being made not simply to earlier authority but also to independent reasoning. Though it is possible to consider separately the philosophical speculations of each of these periods, in consideration of space we shall discuss them together. Orthodox Indian writers themselves generally look uopn the entire current of thought, spread over the succesive stages, as one flow, inseparable at source, but developing and ramifying in its onward course. Let us have a bird's-eye view of the development of the Vedānta through the Vedas and Upaniṣads.

2. *How the Vedānta Developed through the Vedas and the Upaniṣads*

The Vedic conception of gods and nature.

Of the three Vedas, Ṛk, Yajus and Sāma, the first is the basic work, the second two contain Ṛk hymns (mantras) in different arrangements to suit their application to sacrifices. The hymns of the Ṛg-veda mostly consist of praises of the different deities—Agni, Mitra, Varuṇa, Indra, and so on. They describe the mighty and noble deeds of the various deities, and pray for their help and favour. Sacrifices offered to the gods consisted in pouring oblations of clarified butter and other things into the sacrificial fire along with which the hymns in their praise were recited and sung. These deities were conceived as the realities underlying and governing the different phenomena of nature, such as fire, sun, wind, rain and others, on which life, agriculture and prosperity depended. Nature, though peopled with different gods, was conceived as subject to some basic law (called Ṛta) by which the whole world, objects of nature as well as living beings, was regulated.

The belief in the moral nature of the universe.

Its function was not only the preservation of order and regularity in planets and other objects, but also the regulation of justice.

The Vedic faith in gods. Is it polytheism?

Belief in many gods is called polytheism. The Vedas are, therefore, often said to be polytheistic. But there is a peculiarity in Vedic thought that makes this view doubtful. Each of many gods, when praised, is extolled by the hymn as the supreme God, the Creator of the universe and the lord of all gods. Max Müller thinks, therefore, that polytheism is not an appropriate name for such a belief, and he coins a new word 'henotheism' to signify this. But whether the Vedic faith is really polytheism or henotheism depends largely on the explanation of this phenomenon. It is polytheism. If the raising of each god to the supreme

Max Müller's view : Henotheism.

position be not the indication of real belief in the supremacy, but only a wilful exaggeration, a poetic hyperbole. But if the Vedic poets really believed what they said, henotheism would be a better name. The latter view is rendered more than probable by the fact that in the Ṛg-veda we come across passages where it is explicitly stated that the different gods are only manifestations of one underlying reality. "The one reality is called by the wise in different ways : Agni, Yama, Mātariśvā" (Ekaṁ sad viprā bahudhā vadanti..........).[1] It was possible, therefore, to look upon each deity as the Supreme.

Is henotheism a transition ?

According to many writers, there is a development noticeable in Vedic thought and they believe that the idea of God gradually developed from polytheism through henotheism, ultimately to monotheism, *i.e.* belief in one God. This hypothesis may be true. But henotheism is not a mere transition phenomenon ; even in the most developed form, Indian monotheism retains the belief that though God is one, He has various manifestations in the many gods, any one of which may by worshipped as a form of the Supreme Deity. Even to-day we have in India the divergent cults — Śaivism, Vaiṣṇavism and the like—flourishing side by side and almost every one of them is at bottom based on a philosophy of one Supreme God—perhaps even one all-inclusive reality. Indian monotheism in its living forms, from the Vedic age till now, has believed *rather in the unity of the gods in God, than the denial of gods for God.* Hence Indian monotheism has a peculiarity which distinguishes it from the Christian or the Mahomedan. This is a persistent feature of orthodox Indian faith throughout, not a mere passing phase of the Vedic times.

The persistent feature of Indian monotheism.

1. *Ṛg-veda,* 1. 164. 46 (*vide* also 10. 114. 4, 10. 129, 10. 82, *et passim*

Belief in the unity of all gods which we find in the Ṛg-veda is only a part of a greater thought which also we find there in a clear form, namely, the unity of all existence. In the famous Puruṣasūkta which is even now daily recited by every devout Brāhmin, the Vedic seer visualizes, perhaps for the first time in human history, the organic unity of the whole universe. Some stanzas are quoted below :

The unity of all existence.

Illustrated in the Hymn to Man.

> The Man had a thousand heads, a thousand eyes, a thousand feet : he covered the earth on all sides and stretched ten fingers' length beyond it.
>
> The Man was all that is and all that will be : ruling over immortality, he was all that grows by food.
>
> Such was his greatness ; and the Man was greater still: this whole world is a fourth of him, three-fourths of him are immortal in the sky.
>
> For with three-fourths the Man went on high ; but a fourth of him remained here, and then spread on all sides, over the living and the lifeless world.[1]

All existence—earth, heavens, planets, gods, living and non-living objects—is conceived here as the parts of one great person (Puruṣa), who *pervades* the world, but also remains beyond it. In Him all that is, has been and will be, are united. We have in this hymn the poetic insight not only into the universe as one organic whole, but also into the Supreme Reality which is both immanent and transcendent; God pervades the world, yet He is not exhausted thereby; He remains also beyond it. In terms of Western theology, this conception is panentheism—(pan—all, en—in, theos–God), not pantheism; all is not equal to God, but all is *in* God, who is greater than all. One

The transcendence and immanence of God.

1. *Ṛg-veda*, 10. 90 (Peterson's trans).

flash of the seer's imagination, in this hymn, reveals a variety of ideas that inspired the Vedic mind : monism, panentheism and organic conception of the world.

The impersonal Absolute.

In another hymn (commonly known as the Nāsadīyasūkta), we are introduced further to the Vedic conception of the Impersonal Absolute. The reality underlying all existence—the primal one from which everything originates—cannot be described, it says, either as non-exixtent or as existent (na asat, no sat). Here we have perhaps the first flash of a conception of the Indeterminate Absolute, which is the reality underlying all things, but is in itself indescribable.

The hymn thus begins :

There was then neither what is, nor what is not, there was no sky; nor the heaven which is beyond.

It concludes :

He from whom this creation arose, whether he made it or did not make it ; the highest seer in the highest heaven, he forsooth knows, or does even he not know?[2]

The relation between the personal and the impersonal ideas of God.

As for the relation between the conception of Ultimate Reality as a Person and the conception of it as an Indeterminate Absolute, we may note that even in the description of Reality as Person, there is also a mention of its transcendent aspect, which is not describable in terms of the objects of the world and, therefore, indeterminate. They are thus conceived as the two aspects of the same Reality.

---

1. Sa bhūmiṁ viśvato vṛtvā atyatiṣṭhad daśāṅgulam. Pado'sys viśvā bhūtāni, tripādasya amṛtam divi. *Ibid.*
2. *Ṛg-veda*, 10, 129 (Max Müller's trans).

Though many of the important elements of the Vedānta are to be found thus in the Ṛg-veda, they are presented in a poetic way. The method by which the sages arrive at these views is not mentioned, neither the arguments which support them. Philosophy proper must be based on explicit reasoning and argument chiefly. There is therefore, no regular philosophy, strictly speaking, in the Vedas. The first attempt at philosophical speculation is to be found in the Upaniṣads, where problems about self, God and the world are clearly put and discussed. But even here the philosophical method of arriving at conclusions, rigorously supported by arguments, is only partly evidence. Some of the Upaniṣads are written in verses and they contain, like the Ṛg-veda, inspired utterances on philosophical matters. So also are some other Upaniṣads, though written in prose. The only approach to philosophical method is to be found in the few Upaniṣads, where through dialogues—questions and answers—attempt is made to lead the sceptical pupil, step by step, to some conclusion. But in spite of the lack of strict argumentative form, the Upaniṣads have a profound charm and appeal. This is due to the joint effect of the loftiness of ideas, the depth of insight, the mysterious appeal to all that is good and sublime in man and the irresistible force with which the views are asserted as though they are born of a direct vision of truth. A famous German philosopher, Schopenhauer, impressed by the Upaniṣads, declared : *"In the whole there is no study so beneficial and so elevating as that of the Upaniṣads. It has been the solace of my life, it will be the solace of my death."*

Philosophy based on arguments is absent in the Vedas.

It is found first in the Upaniṣads in a rudimentary form.

The problems of the Upaniṣads, to mention only some of the more frequent ones, are : What is the Reality from which all things orginate, by which all live and into which all dissolve when destroyed ? What is that by knowing which everything can be known ? What is that by knowing which the unknown becomes known ? What is that

The problems of the Upaniṣads.

by knowing which one can attain immortality? What is Brahman? What is Ātman? As the very nature of these questions implies, the Upaniṣadic mind was already steeped in the belief that there is an all-pervasive reality underlying all things which arise from, exist in and return to it; that there is some reality by *knowing* which *immortality can be attained.*

The belief in an all-pervasive reality called Brahman or Ātman.

The name given to this Reality is sometimes Brahman (God), sometimes Ātman (Self), sometimes simply Sat (Being). "At first there was the Ātman alone," say the *Aitareya* (1.1.) and the *Bṛhadāraṇyaka* (1.4.1). "All this is Ātman", says the *Chāndogya* (7.25.2), "Ātman being known. ....everything is known," says the *Bṛhadāraṇyaka* again (4.5.6.). Similarly we find, "There was only Being (Sat) at the beginning, it was one without a second." (*Chānd.*, 6.2.1.). Again, "All this is Brahman" (*Muṇḍaka*, 2.2.11. and *Chānd.*, 3.14.1.). Brahman and Ātman are used synonymously in these different contexts. We are also told explicitly in some places that "This self is the Brahman" (*Bṛhad.*, 2.5.19.), "I am Brahman" (*Ibid.*, 1.4.10.).[1]

Interest is shifted from gods to the Self.

The Upaniṣads shift the centre of interest from the Vedic gods to the Self of man. They analyse the Self, distinguish between its outer husk and its inner reality. The body, the senses, the manas, the intellect and pleasures arising out of them are all tested and found to be passing. Changeful modes, not the permanent essence of the Self. These are merely the sheaths (koṣas), the outer covers, so to say, which conceal an inner, permanent reality, which cannot be identified with any of these, though all

The real self behind the outer sheaths.

1. The texts translated here are respectively : 'Om ātmā vā idam eke eva agre āsīt.' 'Ātmā eva idaṁ agre āsīt." 'Ātmā eva idaṁ sarvam,' 'Ātmani khalu are dṛṣṭe śrute mate vijñāta idaṁ sarvaṁ viditam.' Sad eva saumya idam agre āsīt, ekam eva advitīyam.' 'Brahma eva idaṁ viśvam.' 'Sarvaṁ khalu idaṁ brahma.' 'Ayam ātmā brahma.' 'Ahaṁ brahma asmi.'

of these are grounded in it and are its manifestations. The Real Self is pure consciousness, every particular consciousness of objects being its limited manifestation. Not being limited by any object, this pure consciousness is also infinite. The Real Self is called Ātman. As infinite, conscious reality (satyam, jñanam, anantam) the self of man is identical with the Self of all beings (sarva-bhūtātmā) and therefore with God or Brahman. In the *kaṭha* we are told : "This Self is concealed in all things, and does not, therefore, appear to be there. But it is perceived by the keen-sighted with the help of a sharp, penetrating intellect" (3.12).

It is the same as the reality underlying all things.

All attempt is made to help man discover this his Real Self. Realization of the Self (ātmavidyā or ātmajñāna) is regarded as the highest of all knowledge (parā-vidyā), all other knowledge and learning being inferior to it (aparā-vidyā). The method of self-realization lies through the control of the lower self, its deep-rooted interests and impulses, and through study, reasoning and repeated meditation (śravaṇa, manana, nididhyāsana) till the forces of past habits and thoughts are completely overcome by a firm belief in the truths learnt. It is a difficult path which can be followed only if one is strong and wise enough to reject what is pleasant (preyas) for what is good (śreyas).

Self-realization is the highest knowledge.

The Vedic belief in sacrifice is shaken by the Upaniṣads which declare that with these one cannot achieve the highest goal of immortality. The *Muṇḍaka* says that these sacrifices are like weak rafts (*i.e.*, they are unable to take one across the sea of worldly misery) and those fools that take these as the superior means, suffer again the pangs of old

Rituals are inadequate.

age and death.[1] A ritual can at best secure a temporary place in Heaven, and when the merit (puṇya) earned by it is exhausted there is again birth into this world. A deeper significance is attached to sacrifice, when the worshipping self and the gods worshipped are realized to be the same. The ceremonies of offering oblations to gods thus come to be looked upon as mere external affairs fit for the ignorant who do not understand the mystery of the universe. Sacrifice to the Self or Brahman is regarded as superior to sacrifice to gods. It is only through the realization of the Self or Brahman that rebirth can be stopped and along with it all misery. One who truly realizes his unity with the Immortal Brahman, realizes immortality.

Knowledge of the self or God is the means of attaining the highest good.

The Upaniṣads conceive Brahman not only as the pure ground of all reality and consciousness, but also as the ultimate source of all joy. Worldly pleasures are only the distorted fragments of that joy, just as worldly objects are limited manifestation of that Reality.[2] One who can dive into the deepest recess of his Self, not only realizes his identity with Brahman but gets to the heart of Infinite joy. The proof of the Self's being the source of all joy (says Yājñavalkya to his wife Maitreyī) is that it is the dearest thing to man. One loves another person or thing because he identifies himself with that person or thing, regards him or it as his own self. Nothing is dear for its own sake, says Yājñavalkya. The wife is not dear because she is wife, the husband is not dear because of being a husband, the son is not dear because of being a son, wealth is not dear for its

Brahman is the ultimate source of all joy.

All is dear because of the Self.

1. *Muṇḍaka*. 1. 2. 7.
2. *Bṛhadāraṇyaka*, 4.3.32.

own sake. All is dear because of the Self.[1] That the Self in itself is bliss is shown also by pointing out that when a man falls into dreamless sleep, forgets his relation with the body, the senses, mind and external objects and thus retires into his own intrinsic state, he is at peace, he is untouched by pleasure and pain.

Desire to live is due to the joy that lies in life.

Modern biology tells us that self-preservation is a basic instinct in all living beings. But why is self or life so dear ? The answer is given by the Upaniṣads. Life is so dear because there is joy. Who would like to live if there was not joy?[2] The joy that we have in daily life, however disturbed and meagre it might be, sustains our desire to live. Greater joy is not obtained by running further away from the Self, after worldly objects. Desires for objects are the fetters that bind us to the world, to the painful vicious circle—birth, death and rebirth. The forces of desires take us away from the self and condition our existence in the way we hanker after. The more we give up our hankerings for objects and try to realize our identity with the true Self (Ātman) or God (Brahman), the more do we realize true happiness. To feel at one with the Self is to be one with the Infinite God, the Immortal, the Infinite Joy. Nothing then remains unattained, nothing left to be desired. The *Kaṭha* declares, therefore, that a mortal attains immortality and unity with Brahman even here, in this very life, when his heart is

Self-realization is the greatest joy.

---

1. *Ibid.*, 4. 5. 6.
2. *Tait.*, 2. 7.

free from all desires.[1]

Creation of the world out of Brahman or Ātman.

If Brahman or Ātman is the Reality underlying the whole universe then the question may arise as to the exact relation between Brahman and the world. The accounts or creation given in the different Upaniṣads do not exactly tally. But all appear to be unanimous in holding that Ā tman (or Brahman or Sat) is both the creator and the material cause of the world. And in most of these accounts the starting point of creation is described somewhat like this ; At first there was the self. It thought, 'I am one, I will be many,' 'I will create the worlds.' Description of the subsequent steps by which things are created varies, some stating that out of Ātman first arises the subtlest element 'Ākāśa,' thence gradually all the grosser ones; others give different accounts.

The denial of multiplicity.

From these statements creation would appear to be real and God (*i.e.*, The Absolute Soul) a real creator. But in many places we are told that there is no multiplicity here (neha nānā asti kiñcana)[2], that one who sees the many here is doomed to death ('mṛtyoḥ as mṛtyum āpnoti ya iha nāneva paśyati').[3] In explanation of the unity of all things, which appear to be many, examples like these are cited : Just as different articles made of gold are all really one, gold is the only real substance in them and the different names and forms (nāma-rūpa) which make them appear as many, are merely matters of verbal distinction, similarly in all objects there is the same Reality, and their

1. *Kaṭha*, 6. 14.

2. *Kaṭha*, 4. 11 : *Bṛhad.*, 4. 4. 19.

3. *Bṛhad.*, 4. 4. 19.

differences are merely verbal.[1] The objects of the world are denied separate, individual existences. Brahman (or Ātman) is also described in many passages not as Creator, but as a Reality which is indescribable, being not only unspeakable but even unthinkable . Brahman cannot be an object of worship even. Thus the *Kena* declares : "That (Brahman) is other than what is known and beyond the unknown. What is not expressed by speech and by which speech itself is expressed, know that to be Brahman, and not what one worships as Brahman."[2]

Is Creation then real ?

These two different kinds of statements about the world and God naturally present a puzzle. Is god really the creator of the world and the world also therefore real ? Or, is there really no creation and is the world of objects a mere appearance ? Is God a determinate knowable reality which can be described by suitable attributes or is God indeterminate and unknowable? What is the real view of the Upaniṣads? Subsequent Vedānta treatises take up these problems for solution. As already stated, the *Brahmasūtra* of Bādarāyaṇa attempts to systematize and ascertain the real views of the revealed texts. But its brief statements themselves admit of different meanings. Subsequent writers who commented on the *Brahma-sūtra* give their own interpretations to the Upaniṣads and the sūtras very clearly and elaborately. Of the different rival schools that came into existence in this way, that of Śaṅkarācārya is the leading one. In fact what ordinarily passes now-a-days as the Vedānta, and sometimes even as Indian philosophy to outsiders, is really the Advaita Vedānta of the Śaṅkara

The different views leading to different schools of Vedānta.

1. *Chand.*, 6. 1.

2. *Kena*, 1. 4-5.

school. Next comes, in point of popularity, the Vi śiṣṭādvaita school of Rāmānujācārya. These two main and more widely known schools of the Vedānta are being treated below.

3. The Unanimous Views of the main schools of the Vedānta

The unanimous Vedānta conception of the world.

Following Bādarāyaṇa, both Śaṅkara and Rāmānuja reject theories which explain the world (1) either as the product of material elements which by themselves combine together to form objects, (2) or as the transformation of an unconscious nature that spontaneously evolves all objects, (3) or as the product of two kinds of independent reality, such as matter and god, one of which is the material, the other the efficient cause which creates the world out of the first. Both agree that an unconscious cause cannot produce the world, and both hold that even the dualistic conception of two ultimately independent realities, one conscious and another unconscious, producing the world by interaction, is unsatisfactory. Both take their stand on the Upaniṣadic view that 'All is Brahman' (sarvam khalu idam Brahma), and matter and mind are not independent realities but grounded in the same Brahman, Both are, therefore, monists or believers in one Absolute, Independent Reality which pervades the world of multiple objects and selves.

Śaṅkara and Rāmānuja are both monists.

Both follow Bādarāyaṇa and reject other views.

Bādarāyaṇa, whom both Śaṅkara and Rāmānuja follow, discuss at length the unsatisfactory nature of other alternative theories of the world. Ŗefutation of other views is based both on idependent reasoning and the testimony of earlier scriptures. We may briefly sum up here the independent arguments by which the cheif theories are refuted.[1]

The Śāṅkhya theory that unconscious primal matter (prakṛti), composed of the three guṇas (sattva, rajas and tamas), gives rise to the world without the guidance of any conscious agent is not satisfactory, because the world is a harmonious system of nicely adjusted objects which cannot be believed to be the accidental product of any unconscious cause. As the Sāṅkhya itself admits, this world consisting of bodies, senses, motor organs and other objects is made just to fit the diverse souls born into it in accordance with their past deeds. But how can an unconscious nature carry out such a complicated plan? In admitting that there is a purpose in the world, but denying at the same time the existence of a conscious creator, the Sāṅkhya commits itself to an absurd position. Unconscious teleology is unintelligible. Adaptation of means to ends is not possible without conscious guidance. The spontaneous flow of milk form the cow for the sake of a calf is cited by the Sāṅkhya as an example of unconscious but purposive act. But it is forgotten that the cow is a living, conscious being and milk flows impelled by her love for the calf. No undisputed example of an unconscious object performing a complicated purposeful act can be cited. The souls (puruṣas) that the Sāṅkhya admits are said to be inactive and, therefore, they also cannot help the evolution of the world.

Refutation of the Sāṅkhya view of creation.

The evolution of an ordered world is not possible without conscious guidance.

The Vaiśeṣika theory that the world is caused by the combination of atoms is similarly untenable because these unconscious atoms cannot produce this wonderful by adjusted world.

The refutation of the Vaiśesika view.

1. *Vide Sec.* 2. Chap. II of the *Brahma-sūt.* and the *Bhāṣyas* of Śaṅkara and Rāmānuja thereon.

For the regulation of the atoms in the formation of the world, the moral law of Adṛṣṭa is, of course, admitted by the Vaiśeṣika. But this law is also unconscious and the difficulty is not removed. Besides, how atoms at first begin to move in order to create the world is not explicable. If movement were the inherent nature of the atoms, they would never cease to move and the dissolution (pralaya) of objects, as the Vaiśeṣika admits, would never occur. Souls are of course admitted, but they are not admitted to have any intrinsic consciousness. Consciouness arises after the souls are associated with bodies and the organs of knowledge ; and these do not exist *before* creation. Hence atoms cannot receive any conscious guidance even from souls.

Unconscious atoms cannot produce this world.

Against those Bauddha thinkers who explain the objects of the world as aggregates of different momentary elements, it is pointed out that momentary things cannot possess any causality. Because to produce an effect the cause must first arise and then act and, therefore, stay for more than one moment, which is against the doctrine of momentariness. Even if the separate momentary elements be somehow produced, no aggregate can be caused, for no substances are admitted (by these Bauddhas) which can bring together the elements and produce the desired objects. As consciousness itself is admitted to be the effect of the aggregation of the different elements, it cannot exist before aggregation, and the difficulty of unconscious cause, seen before, arises here also.

Refutation of the Bauddha view.

Against those Bauddhas who hold the view of subjectvie idealism (vījñānavāda) and declare that the world, like a dream, is only an illusory product of the imagination, the following important objections are pressed by Śaṅkara following Bādarāyaṇa. *(a)* The existence of external objects cannot be denied because they are

Bauddha idealism which denies the external world, is untenable.

perceived to exist by all persons. To deny the existence of a pot, cloth or pillar while it is being perceived, is like denying the flavour of the food while it is being eaten : it is a falsification of immediate experience by sheer force. *(b)* If immediate experience is disbelieved, then even the reality of mental states cannot be believed in. *(c)* To say that ideas of the mind illusorily appear as *external objects* is meaningless unless at least something external is admitted to be real. Otherwise, it would be as good as to say that a certain man looks *like* the child of a barren woman. *(d)* Unless different perceived objects like pot and cloth are admitted, the idea of a pot cannot be distinguished from that of a cloth, since, as consciousness, they are identical. *(e)* There is a vital difference between dream-objects and perceived objects : the former are contradicted by waking experience, while the latter are not. External objects perceived during waking experience cannot be said to be unreal so long as they are not felt to be contradicted. So subjective idealism, and along with it also nihilism (śūnya-vāda), fail to explain the world satisfactorily.

Bauddha nihilism is, therefore, untenable too.

Even a deistic theory (held by the Śaivas, pāśupatas, Kāpālikas and Kālāmukhas)[1] which holds that God is the efficient cause and matter is the material cause of the world is not accepted. The chief objection raised is that as such a view is based not on the Vedas, but on independent reasoning and ordinary human experience, it should tally with what we observe in life ; but it does not do so. So far as our experience goes, a spirit can act upon matter only through a body, consisting of organs of perception and movement. Again his activity is caused by some motive, such as attainment of pleasure and removal of pain. But God is said to be devoid of body as well as passions and desires. In the light of empirical experience we fail, therefore, to understand the manner as well as the motive of God's creation of the world.

Deistic theories of creation are not tenable.

1. For this fourfold classification of non-Vedic deistic schools *vide* Rāmānuja's *Bhāṣyas* on 2.2. 35 which quotes *Śaivāgama*.

The unanimous Vedānta conception of God.

We have seen that God is conceived even as early as the Vedas in two aspects : God pervades the world, but He is not exhausted in the world. He is also beyond it. God is both immanent and transcendent. These two aspects of God persist throughout the Upaniṣads[1] and the later Vedānta, though the meanings of transcendence and immanence are not the same in all thinkers. It is usual to call the theory of the presence of God in all things 'pantheism', and Vedānta is commonly described by this name. Pantheism etymologically means all-God-theory. But if all is God, the question remains open whether God is the mere totality of all objects of the world, or the totality of things and something more. When such distinction is made, the word 'pantheism' is generally confind to the first view, whereas 'panentheism' (a word coined by a German philosopher, Krause) is used for the second. To avoid the ambiguity of the word 'pantheism' and to remind ourselves of the fact that God in Vedānta is not simply immanent, but also transcendent, we should call the Vedānta theory of God panentheism, rather than pantheism.

The wider and narrower meanings of 'God.'

It is necessary to mention here that in the Upaniṣads, and later Vedānta literature, the word, Brahman, is used for the Highest Principle or Absolute Reality, *as well as* for the creator of the world, the object of worship. The word, Īśvara, is also sometimes used in later literature to denote the second aspect. In English 'Absolute' is sometimes used for the first, and 'God' for the second. But 'God' is also used in a wider sense for both the aspects (*e.g.* in Spinoza, Hegel, Whitehead). In his *Evolution of Theology in the Greek Philosophy* (p.32, Vol. I) Edward Caird even defines "the idea of God as an absolute power or principle." We have used the word, God, here, along with Brahman, in the wider sense (for both God of religion and Absolute of Philosophy) and the context in each case will show the precise meaning. The use of two names is apt to suggest two corresponding

1. *Cf.* "Dve vāva brahmaṇorūpe, etc." *Bṛhadāraṇyaka*, 2. 3. 1.

realities and obscure the truth of *one* reality having two aspects.

Belief in God starts from an acceptance of scriptural testimony.

Another point of agreement among Vedāntins is that all of them believe that the knowledge of the existence of God is, at the first instance, obtained not by reasoning but from the testimony of the revealed scriptures. It is admitted, of course, that on the perfection of religious life the presence of God can be realized by the devout souls. But to start with, we have to depend on indirect knowledge of God through the undoubted testimony of the scriptures. Scarcely any attempt is made, therefore, in the Vedānta, as in the Nyāya and other theistic systems, to adduce purely logical proofs for the existence of God. Arguments are confined generally to showing the inadequacy of all theories of God, not based on scriptures, and to the justification of the scriptural views. This attitude of the Vedānta appears to be dogmatic and is sometimes made the object of criticism.

No independent argument can prove God.

Testimony of Kant, Lotze and others on this.

It should be noted, however, that even many Western philosophers (like Kant, Lotze and others) have ever and anon rejected theistic proofs as inadequate. Lotze makes it clear that unless we start with some faith in God, the rational proofs are of little avail. As he puts it : "Therefore, all proofs that God exists are pleas put forward in justification of our faith." This faith according to him springs from "the obscure impulse which drives us to pass in our thought—as we cannot help passing—from the world given in sense to a world not given in sense, but above and behind sense."[1] According to the Vedānta also an initial

1. Lotze, *Outlines of a Philosophy of Religion*, pp. 8-10.

faith is necessary for religious life and thought. This faith, though starting from a personal feeling of inadequacy and disquiet and a longing for something higher, remains a mere blind groping in the dark till it is enlightened by the teachings of the scriptures that embody the sages' direct realization of God. Reasoning is necessary for the understanding of the teachings, for removing doubts and realizing their cogency. By itself reasoning is an empty form or method of thinking which can work only when materials are supplied. The scriptures supply to reason the matter for speculation, argumentation and meditation. This kind of dependence of reason on matter supplied from a non-rational source is nothing peculiar to theology. Even the greatest discoveries in science can be traced back to some non-rational origin like intuitive flashes of truth in imagination which reasoning afterwards attempts to justify, by further observation, experiment, proof and elaboration. "Dialectic," says Bergson,[1] "is necessary to put intuition to the proof." Though all Vedāntins primarily depend on the scriptures for belief in God, they make full use of reasoning in the justification and elaboration of that belief. They learn from the Upaniṣads that God is the Infinite Conscious, All-inclusive Reality, the Creator of the universe as well as its Preserver and Destroyer. Each one tries in his own way to develop what he thinks to be the most consistent theory of God.

Reasoning is necessary to justify faith already present.

The sūtras of Bādarāyaṇa have for their subject-matter God and are, therefore, named *Brahmasūtra*. But they are written for man, the embodied soul, and, therefore, called also *Śārīraka-sūtra*. Man, therefore, occupies a central place in the Vedānta. It is for his enlightenment and his salvation that the Vedānta undertakes philosophical discussion. But what is the real nature of man ? The Upaniṣads teach us that man has no existence independent of God. Both Śaṅkara and Rāmānuja accept this view. But they interpret the self's dependence on God in different ways.

Man's position is central in Vedānta.

1. *Creative Evolution*, p. 251, Eng. Tr. by a. Mitchell.

II. The Monism of Śaṅkara (Advaita)

1. *Śaṅkara's Conception of the World*

Śaṅkara's problem : how to reconcile the Upaniṣadic accounts of creation with the denial of plurality ?

Śaṅkara finds it difficult to reconcile the Upaniṣadic statements about creation, taken in the literal sense, with those denying the world of multiplicity. Considered in the light of the general trend and spirit running throughout the Upaniṣads, the stories of creation seem, to him, to be out of joint. Description of Brahman as really devoid of all assignable marks becomes unintelligible if His creatorship is real. The teachings about the disappearance of all multiplicity on the realization of Brahman cannot also be understood. If the world were real how could it disappear ? The dawn of the knowledge of Reality can dispel only the unreal appearing as real, not what is really real. This idea furnishes Śaṅkara with the clue to the mystery of the world. If the world is a mere appearance, *like* an object in dream or illusion, then the present appearance of the world and its disappearance on the knowledge of Reality become intelligible. This reconciliation is suggested by the Upaniṣads themselves. Even in the Ṛg-veda[1] the one Indra (God) is said to appear in many forms through powers creating illusion (māyā). The *Bṛhadāraṇyaka* also accepts this.[2] The *Śvetāśvatara* clearly states that the origin (prakṛti) of the world lies in the magical power (māyā) of God.[3]

Reconciliation lies in understanding creation as a magic show.

---

1. Ṛk., 6. 47. 18.

2. 'Indro māyābhiḥ puru-rūpa iyate.' Vide Bṛhad., 2.5.19 and Śaṅkara thereon.

3. 'Māyām tu prakṛtim vidyāt, Māyinam tu Maheśvaram.' Vide Śvet., 4. 10. and Śaṅkara thereon.

Māyā as a power of God is indistinguishable from Him, just as the burning power of fire is from the fire itself. It is by this that God, the Great Magician, conjures up the world-show with all its wonderful objects. The appearance of this world is taken as real by the ignorant, but the wise who can see through it finds nothing but God, the one Reality behind this illusory show.

Māyā, the magical power of creation, is indistinguishable from God.

If we try to understand the process by which ordinary illusions in life take place, we find that an illusion, say, of snake in a rope, is due to our *ignorance* of what really is there behind the appearance, *i.e.* ignorance of the substratum or ground (adhiṣṭhāna), in this case, the rope. If we could know the rope as the rope, there would be no illusion about it. But mere ignorance of the rope cannot give rise to the illusion. For, otherwise, even a person who has never known what a rope is would always see serpents in things. The ignorance creating an illusion does not simply conceal from our view the real nature of the ground, the rope, but positively distorts it, *i.e.* makes it appear as something else. Concealment (āvaraṇa) of reality and distortion (vikṣepa) of it into something else in our mind are then the two functions of an illusion-producing ignorance (avidyā or ajñāna).

Creation understood in the light of an ordinary illusion.

Ignorance with its double function of concealment and distortion.

When an illusion is produced in us by some one else, for example, when a magician makes one coin appear as many to us, it is an illusion for us, the perceivers, and not for the conjurer. From our standpoint, then, illusion is the product of our ignorance, which prevents us from seeing the real nature of the thing and which makes us see something else in its place. If any spectator can persist to see the one coin as it is, the magician's wand will create no illusion for him. For the

The magician's show deceives only the ignorant, but not himself.

magician, the illusion is only a conjuring will, by which his spectators are deceived, and not himself.

The conception of māyā as a magic power and producer of the world-show.

In the light of such cases, māyā, the cause of the world appearance, may also be understood from two standpoints. For God, māyā is only the will to create the appearance. It does not affect God, does not deceive Him.[1] For ignorant people like us, who are deceived by it and see the many objects here instead of one Brahman or God, māyā is on illusion-producing ignorance. In this aspect māyā is also called, therefore, 'ajñāna' or 'avidyā' (synonyms for 'ignorance') and is conceived as having the double function of concealing the real nature of Brahman, the ground of the world, and making Him appear as something else, namely the world. In so far as māyā *positively* produces some illusory appearance it is called positive ignorance (bhāva-rūpam ajñanam); and in so far as no beginning can be assigned to the world, māyā is also said to be beginningless (anādi). But, for those wise few who are not deceived by the world-show, but who perceive in it nothing but God, there is no illusion nor, therefore, illusion-producing māyā. God to them is not, therefore, the wielder of māyā at all.

Śaṅkara's interpretation of māyā.

Rāmānuja, following the *Śvetāśvatara*, speaks also of māyā, but he means thereby either God's wonderful power of *real* creation or the *eternal*, unconscious, primal matter which is in Brahman and which is *really* transformed into the world. Śaṅkara also speaks of māyā as the power of God, but this creative power, according to him, is not a permanent character of God, as Rāmānuja thinks, but only a free will which can, therefore, be given up at will. The wise who are not deceived by the world-appearance need not conceive God at all as the bearer of this illusion-producing power. Besides, even when conceived as a power, māyā is not a distinct entity in Brahman, but inseparable and indistinguishable from it as the burning power is from fire, or will is from the mind that wills. Even when Śaṅkara identifies māyā with prakṛti,

1. *Brahma-sūtra* 2.1.9. and Śaṅkara thereon.

he means nothing more by it than that this creative power is the source or origin (prakṛti) of world-appearance, to those who perceive this appearance. The difference between Rāmānuja and Śaṅkara, then, is that while, according to Rāmānuja, the matter or prakṛti which is an integral part of God really undergoes modification, Śaṅkara holds that God does not undergo any real change, change is only apparent, not real.

Illusory modification of any substance, as of the rope into the snake is called *vivarta*, and real modification, as of milk into curd, is called *pariṇāma*. Śaṅkara's theory of creation, as described above, is, therefore, known as *vivarta vāda* and is distinguished from the Sāṅkhya theory of evolution (by the real modification of prakṛti) which is called *pariṇāma-vāda*. Rāmānuja's theory also is a kind of pariṇāma-vāda, because he admits that the unconscious element in God really changes into the world. Vivarta-vāda and pariṇāma-vāda both agree, however, in holding that the effect is already contained somehow in its material cause and, therefore, both come under satkārya-vāda or the theory that the effect (kārya) is existent (sat) in the material cause, and is not a new thing. The process of the imaginary attribution to where it does not exist is called adhyāsa. In modern psychological terminology a process of this kind is called projection. In all illusion there is such projection (adhyāsa), the serpent is projected (adhyasta) by imagination on the rope, and the world on Brahman.

Śaṅkara does not believe in real change.

Pariṇāma-vāda and Vivarta-vāda are the two forms of Sat-kārya-vāda.

The Upaniṣadic accounts of creation, then, are to be understood in the sense of the evolution of the world out of Brahman through its power of māyā. This māyā, Śaṅkara admits, is described in some scriptures also as avyakta or even prakṛti having three elements of sattva, rajas and tamas. But this should not be mistaken to be the prakṛti of Sāṅkhya, an independent reality.[1] It is a power of God, and absolutely dependent on God.

Māyā is sometimes called prakṛti.

1. *Vide Śaṅkara on Brahma-sūt.*, 1. 4. 3. and on *Śvetāśvatara*, 4. 5. and 4. 11.

Vedānta works, like the Upaniṣads, are not always unanimous regarding the exact process by which, and the order in which, the world's objects arise out of Brahman through māyā. According to a well-known account, at first there arise out of Ātman or Brahman the five subtle elements, in the order—ākāśa (ether), vāyu (air), agni (fire), ap (water), kṣiti (earth). These five are again mixed up together in five different ways to give rise to the five gross elements of those names. Gross ākāśa is produced by the combination of the five subtle elements in the proportion,

The evolution of the material elements out of Brahman.

The subtle elements and the gross ones.

$\frac{1}{2}$ ākāśa + $\frac{1}{8}$ air + $\frac{1}{8}$ fire + $\frac{1}{8}$ water + $\frac{1}{8}$ earth. Similarly, each of the other four gross elements is produced by the combination of the subtle elements in the proportion of half of that element and one-eighth of each of the other four. This process is known as combination of the five (pañcī karaṇa). The subtle body of man is made of the subtle elements, and the gross body, as well as all gross objects of nature, is produced out of the gross elements which arise by the mixture of the five subtle ones. Śaṅkara accepts this account of creation; but he understands the entire process in the light of his theory of vivarta (or adhyāsa).

In addition to the advantages of consistent interpretation of scriptures, the theory of vivarta, Śaṅkara points out, gives also a more rational explanation of creation. If God is the creator of the world and creates the world out of any other substance like matter, then in addition to God, another reality is to be admitted and God ceases to be the all-inclusive, only reality; His infinity is lost. But if that matter be conceived as something real and *within* God, and the world be conceived as a real transformation of it, we have to face a dilemma.[1] Either matter is a part of God, or identical with the whole

The merits of Śaṅkara's view of creation.

1. *Brahma-sūt.*, 2. 1. 26-28.

of God. If the first alternative is accepted (as Rāmānuja does), then we are landed into the absurdity that God, a spiritual substance, is composed of parts like material substances, and is consequently also liable to destruction, like such objects. If the second alternative (namely that primal matter is the whole of God) be accepted then, by the transformation of matter, God is wholly reduced to the world and there is no God left after creation. Whether God changes partly or wholly, if change be real, then God is not a permanent, unchanging reality. He then ceases to be God. These difficulties are avoided by vivarta-vāda according to which change is apparent.

Authority and reason.

These difficulties are felt also by Rāmānuja. But he thinks that the mystery of creation is beyond human intellect and we are to accept the account of creation given in the scriptures. As for difficulties, once we admit that God is ommipotent, omniscient and has wonderful powers, nothing should be thought impossible for him.[1] Though Śaṅkara also believes that without the help of the revealed scriptures the mystery cannot be solved simply by the unaided human reasoning (kevalena tarkeṇa),[2] he points out that the scriptures themselves have told us how the many can illusorily appear out of the one. Following the light shed by the scriptures we can employ our reasoning and understand, even in the likeness of our ordinary experiences of illusion, the mystery of creation so far as it is humanly possible.

(i) The Rational Foundation of Śaṅkara's Theory of the World

If we put together the *arguments* used by Śaṅkara to support the theory of apparent change (vivarta) and the cognate concepts of nescience (māyā and avidyā) and of projection or super-imposition by imagination (adhyāsa),

1. *Vide Sri bhāṣya* on 2. 1. 26-28 and 1. 1. 3.
2. *Vide* Śaṅkara on *Brahma-sūt.*, 2. 1. 27.

we find that they constitute a strong rational foundation of the Advaita theory. Those who do not believe in any revealed scripture or in any mystic intuition, but try to understand the real nature of the world in the light of common experience and reasoning based thereon, will also value these arguments, if only for their great logical and philosophical merit. The followers of Śaṅkara have multiplied such arguments in independent treaties in some of which (*e.g. Tattvapradīpikā or Citsukhī, Advaita-Siddhi, Khaṇḍana-Khaṇḍakhādya*) logical skill and dialectical subtlety attain heights scarcely reached by the most profound treaties of this kind in the West. While the Vedānta was based on intuitive experience, embodied in the revealed texts, it did not ignore the fact that so long as the reasoning faculty of man is not fully satisfied and the things are not explained by reasoning in the light of common experience, there is no possibility of his accepting the intuitions of others however high. To give the beginner an idea of this aspect of Advaita philosophy we shall briefly mention below how Śaṅkara tries to reach his theory of the world by subjecting common experience to rational criticism and logical construction :—

The arguments showing that the effect is non-different from the cause.

(a) If the relation between any effect and its material cause is carefully examined it is found that the effect is nothing more than the cause. Perception cannot show in a pot made of clay anything other than clay, nor in a ring made of gold anything other than gold. An effect is, again, inseparable from its material cause ; the effect cannot exist without it. We cannot separate the pot from the clay, nor the ring from the gold. It is not reasonable, therefore, to think that the effect is a new thing which is now produced, but was absent before. In substance it was always there in its material cause. In fact we cannot even *think* of a non-existent entity coming into existence. We can only think of a substance changing from one form into another. If something non-existent could ever be brought into existence, there would be no reason why we could not press oil out of sand (where it is non-existent),

and why we have to select only a particular material, namely oilseed, to produce the particular effect, oil. The activity of an efficient cause, the oilman, the potter or the goldsmith, cannot produce any new substance, it only manifests the form of the substance concealed by its previous state. The effect must thus be admitted to be non-different (ananya) from the cause, and to be existing in it from before.[1]

Śāṅkhya theory of pariṇāma, real change, is not wholly consistent with its grounds.

On these grounds Śaṅkara admits the theory of Satkārya-vāda which, we have seen, is also accepted by the Sāṅkhya. But he finds that the Sāṅkhya does not realize the full implication of Satkārya-vāda. For, it holds that though the effect exists previously in its material cause, there is a real change (pariṇāma) of the material into the effect, since the material assumes a new form. Now this view amounts to the confession that this form which did not exist previously comes into existence. The doctrine of Satkārya-vāda, that *nothing* which did not exist previously can come into existence, thus breaks down. If the grounds on which that doctrine stands, are sound, then we must be prepared to accept all that logically follows from it, and cannot hold any view which implies any violation of this doctrine, rationally established.

Change of form does not imply change in reality.

But how can we, it may be asked, deny the perceived fact that the effect does have a new form? Śaṅkara does not deny the perception but only questions the interpretation, the logical significance, of it. Is the Sāṅkhya right in holding that change in form *means* a change in reality ? It would be right, only if a form had a reality of its own. But closer consideration shows that the form is but a state of the material or substance, and cannot be separated from the latter even in thought. Whatever status in reality a form may possess is in virtue of its substance. We have

1. Vide Śaṅkara on *Brahma-sūt.*, 2. 1. 14-20; Chānd., 6. 2; Tait., 2. 6.; Bṛhad, 1. 2. 1; Gītā, 2. 16.

no reason, therefore, to interpret the perception of a change in form as a change of reality. On the contrary, it is found that in spite of changes in form a substance is recognized by us as the identical entity. Devadatta, sitting, standing or lying is recognized as the identical person. How could this be, if change in form implied change in reality?[1]

Form or quality not distinct from substance.

Moreover, if the form or, for the matter of that, any quality were granted any distinct reality, we would fail to explain the relation between the quality and its substance. For, two *distinct* realities cannot be conceived to be related without the help of a third entity to connect them. Now, as soon as we think of this third entitiy (which must be distinct from the two terms it attempts to relate) we have to think of a fourth relating entity, and also a fifth, which would relate the third with each of the first two terms respectively. Similarly, these fourth and fifth entities would require other similar media for relating them to the terms they themselves want to relate, and so on. There would then be an *infinite regress* (anavasthā). We can thus never come to the end of our supposition and there will never be a complete explanation of the relation between the quality and its substance. In other words, the supposition of any distinction in reality between any quality and its substance would be logically indefensible. So a form cannot be treated as a distinct reality, and no change in form can be logically accepted as a real change, unless there is change in substance.

Change is rationally untenable; it is an appearance.

But we have seen that no causation involves any change in substance. Hence causation does not imply any real change. Moreover, as every change is a process of causation, there cannot be any change in reality. This amounts to the position that though we *perceive* changes we cannot rationally accept them as real. We have therefore to understand them in the same way as we do, when we perceive an illusory object. We *do* perceive a rainbow, a

1. Śaṅkara on *Brahma-sūt.*, 2. 1. 18.

blue sky, movement of the sun and many other things which we cannot believe as real because reasoning proves them to be unreal. Such a perceived but unreal phenomenon is called an appearance and distinguished from reality. On the same ground we must call change also an appearance, and distinguish it from reality. We can thus reach, on purely logical grounds supported by common observation, the theory of, *vivarta* or apparent change, as a rational doctrine required for the explanation of the world. The acceptance of this theory also leads us to think that our perception of change is nothing more than a supposition or mental projection of change on reality. This is but Śaṅkara's conception of adhyāsa. Again, a wrong supposition of this kind implies that we are deluded by a sort of ignorance which makes us perceive things where they do not really exist. This is but Śaṅkara's conception of ajñāna, avidyā or māyā, which he regards as the cause of the appearance of the world.

Existence alone common to all objects.

(b) But it may be asked, supposing that the world, with its changing objects is an appearance, what is the substance or reality which appears to us in various forms as objects ? Ordinarily we call anything which is the bearer of some qualities a substance. A pot or a ring is a substance in that sense. But we have seen that the qualities of a pot have no reality apart from the pot, and also that the pot itself has no reality apart from its cause, the clay, which is the real substance of which the pot is only one form of manifestation. But as clay itself is liable to modification and may cease to be clay, even it cannot be called a real substance ; it is only a form of manifestation, though more abiding than a pot, of some other substance which persists through all the modifications of clay, and is also present in what clay itself comes from and in what it is changed into, after its destruction. If all so-called substances[1] are thus liable to modification (vikāra), then the substance underlying all

1. Modern Physics shows that even the so-called elementary substances of Chemistry, are not immutable; that being made of electrons and protons, differently organized, these elements can be transmuted into other forms.

objects of the world would be that which persists through all forms of objects. And we observe that *existence* (not of any specific form but existence pure and simple) is what is common to all forms of objects. Existence is revealed in the perception of every object, whatever be its nature. It can, therefore, be called the substance, the material cause or the underlying reality behind the world of objects.

It is also common to all mental state.

But when we examine the changing states within our minds what we also find there is that every state, every idea, whatever its object, exists. Even an illusory idea[1] Which lacks an external object exists as an idea (avagati). A state of deep dreamless sleep or of swoon, also exists, though no object of consciousness is present there.[2] Existence is thus found to be the one undeniable reality presisting through all states, internal and external.[3] It can, therefore, be accepted as *the* substance, and material cause of which all determinate objects and mental states are the diverse manifestations.

Pure existence is the common reality behind all forms, external and internal.

We find then that pure existence which is the common cause of the entire world is itself formless, though appearing in various forms ; partless, though divisible into different forms ; it is infinite, though it appears in all finite forms. Śaṅkara thus reaches the conception of an infinite, indeterminate (nirviśeṣa) existence as the essence or material cause of the world. He calls this Absolute or Brahman.

Existence is self revealing consciousness as well.

(c) But is this Absolute existence conscious or unconscious ? Ordinarily we think that external objects are unconscious and the internal states of our mind are conscious. But what is the criterion of consciousness ? A mental state is conscious, because its existence is self-

1. Śaṅkara on *Brahma-sūt.*, 2. 1. 14
2. Śaṅkara on *Chānd.*, 6. 2. 1.
3. Cf. Mc Taggart's *The Nature of Existence*, for a similar modern theory.

revealing. But when we perceive the external world its existence also reveals itself. The power of appearing (bhā ti) is common to both internal and external forms of existence; and it can, therefore, be argued that existence which is common to the internal and the external world must possess the power of revealing itself. Therefore, it is more reasonable to hold that Absolute existence is of the nature of self- revealing consciousness. In fact, a little reflection shows that self-revelation may even be taken as the differentia that distinguishes existence from non-existence. What is non-existent (*e.g.,* the son of a barren woman) cannot even appear or reveal itself for a moment.

Two objections met.

But two objections may be raised against this view. Are there not objects which exist but do not appear before us, and are there not also illusory objects which lack existence and yet appear to be there ? As to the first, the reply is that the non-perception or the non-appearance of some existing objects may be explained by supposing the existence of some obstruction to revelation, just as the non-appearance of the sun, which is capable of self-revelation, is explained as being due to obstruction of light by clouds (or as the non-revival, at a particular time, of some ideas existing in the mind, is explained by some obstruction to recollection.[1] As to the second objection, the reply is that even in illusion there is existence underlying the illusory appearance, and that is what appears before us. Existence is thus co-extensive with the power of self revelation, that is consciousness.

Consciousness present in every appearance of existence.

(d) This conclusion is also strengthened by another consideration. Wherever there is appearance of existence there is awareness invariably present. Even an external object, say clay, which appears to us is presented by an awareness of clay (mṛt-buddhi). When we perceive clay becoming a pot, our clay-consciousness turns into pot-consciousness (ghaṭa buddhi).[2] An imaginary object is just

1. *Vide Śaṅkara* on *Bṛhad.*, 1. 2. 1.
2. *Vide Śaṅkara* on *Chānd.*, 6. 2. 2.

the idea of the object, and so also is an illusory object. So we find that awareness prevades all forms of existence known to us.

The world originates from Brahman, Absolute Existence, by apparent change.

By a series of arguments like these Śaṅkara reaches logically what he accepts on the authority of the revealed texts, namely that the world originates from Brahman, which is Absolute Existence and Consciousness and that Brahman has the power of manifesting itself in diverse apparent forms, without really undergoing any modification.

Brahman, or Existence, as such, is uncontradictable, and therefore supremely real.

Though Brahman (or Existence-consciousness) appears in all our experiences, or in all that appears to exist, the forms vary. Moreover, one form of experience (*e.g.* illusion or dream) is contradicted by another form of it (*e.g.*, normal waking experience). The contradicted form is thus regarded as less real than the contradicting one. But in spite of such contradictions among the different forms, existence (or consciousness) *as such* remains uncontradicted. When we disbelieve an illusory serpent we only deny that the existence there is of the form of a serpent, but do not deny that there is some existence. Again, even when we deny a dream object, we do not deny that the experience or idea existed. And when we think of a time or place where nothing exists, we are *thinking* of the *existence* of at least that time or place. So existence, in some form or other, is as wide as thought, and we cannot conceive of the absence or denial of existence. This universal, pure existence (or consciousness) is thus the only thing whose contradiction is unthinkable. Śaṅkara calls it, therefore, supreme reality (Pāramārthika sattā). He thus logically arrives also at his conception of reality as that which persists uncontradicted through all forms of existence in all places and times.

About any definite or particular form of existence which may appear in our experience, we can never be certain that it will not be supplanted by a contradictory experience arising in future. So the theoretical or logical possibility of its being contradicted is always there. This is another reason why Śaṅkara holds that such an object, or the world as the totality of such objects, does not enjoy the status of uncontradictable or supreme reality. On account of the above reasons, he sometimes defines reality as that which persists (through all forms of existence) and unreality as that which does not do so. Persistence or pervasion (anuvṛtti) is the criterion of the real, particularity or exclusion (vyabhicāra) that of the unreal.[1]

Persistence is the mark of reality and exclusion that of unreality.

It is in the light of this logic that we can understand the somewhat puzzling assertion of Śaṅkara that a pot and a cloth which exclude each other, also contradict and falsify each other. There are two kinds of contradiction that Śaṅkara has in mind, experiential and logical. The perception of an existence as a snake is contradicted by a stronger or better perception of it as a rope. Actual experience is here corrected by another actual experience. We have here experiential contradiction. This is what is ordinarily and almost universally regarded as the mark of unreality. Śaṅkara also admits this. But he (like some thinkers of the West, *e.g.* Zeno, Kant and Bradley) also recognizes a kind of logical contradiction which consists in actual experience being proved inconsistent by thought, or one thought being contradicted by another thought. We have seen previously how change, which is actually perceived, is shown by Śaṅkara as unreal because it is found inconsistent by logical thinking. In a similar manner it is shown that though the perception of a pot is not experientially contradicted by that of a cloth, both are found

The two kinds of contradiction, experiential and logical.

1. Śaṅkara on *Chānd.*, 6. 2, 2. *Brahma-sūt.*, 2. 1. 11. and *Gītā*, 2. 16.

logically inconsistent with the nature of reality. The experience of the truly real (*viz.* pure existence), we saw, is not only not actually contradicted, but also logically uncontradictable, since the contradiction of it is unthinkable. The experience of a particular, *e.g.* the experience of existence as a pot or as a cloth, does not, however, possess such uncontradictable nature. On the contrary, the very fact that existence is experienceable in different forms keeps the door open to the possibility that what is experienced to have one particular form now *may be* experienced to have a different form later (just as what was experienced as a snake is experienced later as a rope). This theoretical possibility of change in perception, and of consequent precarious, in respect of its reality. We can never be absolutely certain that what appears now as pot will not appear otherwise later. We see, therefore, how different particular forms of existence, like pot and cloth, weaken and undermine each other's claim to indubitable reality. If, however, these claimed only pure existence, and not existence of particular forms, their claims would not have been mutually exclusive. Each would enjoy uncontradictable reality as pure existence. The rival claims of particulars *as particular* existents thus prevent them from having the position of indubitable reality such as pure existence enjoys.

A particular, excluding another particular, is logically open to contradiction.

(*e*) By assessing the claims to existence made by all changing and particular objects of the world Śaṅkara discovers a dual nature in them. These objects cannot be called real in so far as they are particular and changing ; but they are not surely utterly unreal like the son of a barren woman, since existence *as such* shines even through their appearance, and is present in them. In view of this they can be described as neither real, nor unreal. They are indescribable (anirvacanīya).The world of appearance as a whole, and the power of ignorance (māyā or avidyā) which conjures up such a puzzling world, are also indescribable in this sense.

A particular presents a dual, and indescribable nature.

(ii) The Advaita Theory of Error

Mīmāṁsa explanation of error is untenable.

As Śaṅkara tries to explain the appearance of the world in the light of illusory perception, he and his followers discuss the nature of perceptual error very elaborately, particularly because the explanations of such error offered by other schools make Advaita view of the world inconclusive. The Mīmāṁsakas altogether deny the possibility of error in perception, holding like some Western realists, that all knowledge, at least of the immediate kind, is true. If this view is correct, the Advaita position would be altogether unfounded. The Advaitins have, therefore, to examine this view. Now, the Mīmāṁsakas argue, as we have seen, that the so-called case of illusion, *e.g.* of a snake in a rope, is really not *one* simple kind of knowledge, but a *mixture* of perception and memory, and non-discrimination between the two. Against this, the Advaitins urge the following chief points. The judgement expressing an illusory perception, this is a snake, shows that there is here a single piece of knowledge. It may be true that the perception of the thing present ('this' awakens the memory of a snake perceived in the past, but if this memory did not combine with the perception to constitute *one* state of cognition, but simply lay undiscriminated in the mind alongside of the perception, there would have been two judgement like, 'I perceive this' and 'I remember a snake,' or 'This is' and 'That snake was.' The judgement 'This is a snake' shows on the other hand, that snake-hood is predicated of 'This' or the present object ; and there is, therefore, a positive identification, and not merely non-recognition of difference, between the two elements, the perceived and the remembered. In fact, without such identification, or the belief that the present object is a snake, the reaction (such as fear and running away) which follows such knowledge would remain unexplained. Perceptual error cannot, therefore, be denied.

It fails to account for the undeniable unity of the erroneous judgement.

While admitting this the Nyāya-Vaiśeṣika school tries to explain perceptual error in a realistic way by showing that it is only an extraordinary case of perception, in which the memory idea, for example, of a snake perceived in the past is so vividly aroused in the mind (by the perception of the similarity of the snake in the rope) that it amounts to an immediate awareness. So, what really existed in the past (*e.g.* the snake previously perceived in another place) is presented to the mind now through the instrumentality of a vivid idea. Illusion does not, therefore, show, as the Advaitins think, the possibility of the perception of an eternally unreal thing ; no unreal object can ever be perceived. The present perception of the world cannot be explained, therefore, like an illusion, without supposing a real world perceived at least in the past ; and the unreality of the world at all times can never be proved.

The Nyāya-Vaiśeṣika theory also unsatisfactory.

The Advaitins reject this view on the following chief gounds. The perception, at the present place and time, of an object which existed at some other place and time is absurd. However vivid the memory-idea may be it will be an idea of a *that* (thing perceived there in the past) and never of a *this* (object present here and now). So the quality of *presence* belonging to the illusory object remains unexplained. To hold that a memory-idea can really dislocate a real object from its own time and place transport it to a different time and place is equally absurd. In any case it has to be admitted that what does not really exist here and now can appear as present, and that it is also due to our ignorance of the thing (the rope) existing here and now. Construing these facts into a consistent theory, the Advaitins hold that in illusion ignorance conceals the form of the existing object (rope) and constructs instead, the appearance of another object. The non-perception of the existing form is produced by different factors such as defective sense organ, insufficient light. The perception of similarity, and the revival of memory-idea caused by it,

It cannot explain how the illusory object can be immediately presented.

help ignorance to *create* the positive appearance of an object (the snake). This apparent object must be admitted to be *present as an appearance*, here and now. It is then a temporary creation (sṛṣṭi) of ignorance.

The temporary creation of an immediate object must be admitted.

This creation is neither describable as real, since it is contradicted by later perception (of the rope), nor as unreal because it *appears,* though for a moment, unlike what is unreal (*e.g.* the child of a barren mother) which can never appear to *be* there. So it is called, by the Advaitin, an indescribable creation (anirvacanīya sṛṣṭi), and his theory of illusion is called the theory of the appearance of the indescribable (anirvacanīya-khyāti-vāda). This view may appear as an admission of the mysterious. But every illusion does present a mystery, and fling a challenge to the unsuspecting realist and the naturalist. Even the Nyāya-Vaiśeṣika realist has to admit this ; and he calls it, therefore, an *extraordinary* (alaukika) case of perception.

The explanation of the world-appearance, in the light of an ordinary illusion, as the creation of an ignorance, with the power of concealing and distorting reality, is, therefore, well-grounded. The question may still be asked, however, as to how the present world can appear unless there were the experience of a similar one in the past. But this would not present any difficulty, since the Advaita, like many other Indian schools, does believe that the present world is only one of a beginningless series of previous world and the present birth is similarly preceded by a beginningless series of previous births. Śaṅkara describes, therefore, the process of illusory superimposition (adhyāsa) as the appearance of what was previously experienced, in a subsequent locus.[1] He means that through ignorance we superimpose on pure being (Brahman) the diverse forms of objects experienced in past lives. But even

The possibility of the immediate appearance of what is not really present, makes the Advaita explanation of the world plausible.

1. Introduction to *Br.-Sūt.*

if this hypothesis of a beginningless series is not admitted, the possibility of the appearance of existence in some other form can be maintained simply on the strength of an illusory experience. In every case of illusion the possibility of the appearance of some form of existence in place of another form of it is demonstrated—a fact which clearly shows that what *does not really exist now* can appear as such. The appearance of the unreal as real is thus shown to be possible by every illusion.

The Advaita view is neither nihilism nor subjectivism.

The Advaita view of error should not be confused with that of the nihilistic Bauddha, who holds that the utterly unreal appears as the world, or with that of the subjectivist Bauddha who holds that mental ideas appear as the external world. Because unlike them Śaṅkara and his followers clearly state that there is always the background of pure existence (Brahman) behind every appearance, and that this ground is neither unreal nor a mere subjective idea, but existence itself.

Though the world of normal waking experience is explained in the light of illusion and as the product of an ignorance like the latter, the Advaitin, we have already seen, observes a distinction between these two kinds of appearance. They distinguish, therefore, also the ignorance responsible for the normal world by calling it the root ignorance (mūlāvidyā), from that causing a temporary illusion by calling this latter similar ignorance (tulāvidyā).

The peculiar realism of Advaita.

Objectivity is granted by the Advaitin to both the normal world and the illusory object, by admitting creation in both cases. In this the Advaitin is more realistic than ordinary realist. Where he differs from them is that according to him objectivity does not imply reality, nor does unreality imply subjectivity (a position which some contemporary American neo-realists like Holt also admit). On the contrary, on the strength of arguments already mentioned every *object* which is particular and changeful is shown by him to have a contradictory nature, and therefore, to be not real in the sense in which pure existence is.

(iii) Criticism of Śaṅkara's Philosophy of the World

The charge that Śaṅkara explains the world away.

Many kinds of objections have been raised against Śaṅkara's theory of the world. The chief one is that Śaṅkara does not explain the world, but explains it away; that philosophy has for its business the explanation of the world, and if it explains the world away as unreal, it only cuts away the ground on which it stands. But such criticism is rather rash. It is true that the task of philosophy is to explain the world, that is, the sum total of experienced facts. But it does not mean that philosophy is committed, from the beginning, to the view that the world of common sense must be totally accepted as real. It must examine common experience and common view of the world, but only to judge their natures and interrelations in the light of reason, and find out what would be the most consistent view of the world. But it is found, on examination, as shown by Śaṅkara, that all experiences cannot claim to be equally reliable, nor all common views about the world free from contradiction. One kind of experience actually contradicts and supplants another and claims greater reality. Again some experiences and beliefs, in their particular forms, are found to be in conflict with possible future experience. Philosophy must, therefore, rationally discriminate between belief and belief, experience and experience, and critically assign to each its proper place. On such rational grounds Śaṅkara grades and classifies common experience. As we saw, he, first of all, distinguishes

The world presents different kinds of experience which Śaṅkara critically discriminates on the basis of contradiction.

all objects of possible and actual experience from utter unreality, like the child of the barren mother. The former again are classed under three heads : (1) those that only appear momentarily in illusions and dreams, but are contradicted by normal waking experience, (2) those that appear in normal waking experience—the particular and changing objects, which form the basis of our ordinary life and practice, but which are still not acceptable to reason as completely real (because they exhibit contradiction or are open to future contradiction), and (3) pure existence which reveals itself through all experience, and is neither contradicted nor contradictable.

The three aspects of the world, possessing different grades of existence.

If 'world' is the name of all these kinds of experienced facts, surely it will be irrational to say that the world, as a whole, and in every aspect of it, is real. The first kind of facts possesses only ephemeral existence (prātibhāsika sattā or apparent existence); the second empirical or virtual existence, the sort of existence necessary for ordinary life and practice (vyāvahārika sattā or practical existence) and the third absolute existence (pāramārthika sattā or supreme existence). The world is thus not a homogeneous conception; and if, in spite of this, one insists on being told what such a world (as a whole) is, the fairest reply can only be, what Śaṅkara gives, namely that it is indescribable (anirvacanīya) either as real or as unreal. But if the word, world, is confined only to the second aspect, it would be again fair to say, that the world is real only for practical purpose, more real than the first and less real than the third kind of existence. But if the word is taken in the third sense, Śaṅkara would emphatically assert that the world is eternally real. As he puts it : "As the cause, Brahman, does not lack existence at any time, past, present or future, so does the world not lack existence in any of the three periods of time."[1] Again, "All particular modes of existence with different names and forms are real as existence, but unreal as particulars."[2]

It will be quite clear now that Śaṅkara does not deny the world even in the second or practical aspect, like a subjective idealist who reduces it to a *mere idea* of the perceiving individual, and who does not allow it an extramental existence. This will be further evident from the way in which he refutes the subjectivism of the Vijñānavādin.[3] Here he asserts that the objects of normal waking experience are not on a par with dream-objects, since dream experience is contradicted by waking experience, which, therefore, is relatively more real; that external objects like pillars, pots, etc., which are immediately felt to be outside the mind cannot be reduced to the status of mere ideas in the mind, and that while the former are perceived by all, the latter only by the individual in whose mind they are. He also makes it clear that though he explains the world on the analogy of a dream he does not deny the difference between the contradicted dream-experience and the contradicting waking experience on which the world is based, nor does he overlook the fact that these two experiences are differently caused.[4] The ignorance responsible for the first is of an individual and temporary nature, and that at the root of the second is public and relatively permanent. The first is sometimes called avidyā (individual ignorance), the second māyā (general ignorance), though these two terms are also sometimes used synonymously in the sense of illusion-producing ignorance in general.

Śaṅkara does not wholly deny the world.

1. Vide *Br.-Sūt.* 2. 1. 16.
2. Vide *Chānd.*, 6. 3. 2.
3. *Br.-Sūt.* 2. 2. 28.
4. *Ibid.*, 2. 2. 29.

2. *Śaṅkara's Conception of God*

From the empirical standpoint God is the omniscient and omnipotent creator, possessed of qualities.

God, according to Śaṅkara, can be conceived from two different points of view. If we look at God from the ordinary practical standpoint (vyāvahārikadṛṣṭi) from which the world is believed to be real, God may be regarded as the cause, the Creator, the Sustainer, the Destroyer of the world and, therefore, also as an Omnipotent and Omniscient Being. He then appears as possessed of all these qualities (saguṇa). God in this aspect is called Saguṇa Brahman or Īśvara in Śaṅkara's philosophy. He is the object of worship.

But this view of God does not reveal His essence.

But the world, as we have seen, is conceived by Śaṅkara as an appearance which rests on our ignorance. Description of God as the Creator of the world is true only from the practical point of view, so long as the world-appearance is regarded as real. Creatorship of the world is not God's essence (svarūpa-lakṣaṇa); it is the description of what is merely accidental (taṭastha-lakṣaṇa) and does not touch His essence.

Let us try to understand with the help of an ordinary example the distinction that Śaṅkara wants to make here. A shepherd appears on the stage in the *role* of a king, wages war, conquers a country and rules it.[1] Now, the description of the actor as a shepherd gives what he is from the *real point of view*. It is an *essential* description of him (svarūpalakṣaṇa). But the description of him as a king, ruler and conqueror, is applied to him only from the *point of view* of the stage and his *role* there; it is merely a description of what is accidental to the person (taṭastha-lakṣaṇa) and does not touch his essence.

1. Vide Śaṅkara on *Brahma-sūt.*, 2. 1. 18. for the analogy of the actor (nata).

Similarly, the description of God as conscious, real, infinite (satyam, jñānam, anantam Brahma)[1] is an attempt to describe His essence (svarūpa) whereas the description of Him as Creator, Sustainer and Destroyer of the world, or by any other characteristic connected with the world, is a mere accidental description and it holds good only from the point of view of the world (vyāvahārikadṛṣṭi). As we can regard the actor on the stage from a point of view other than that of the stage, so we can look at God also from a non-worldly point of view (pāramārthikadṛṣṭi) and try to dissociate Him from the characters which we ascribe to Him from the point of view of the world. God in this aspect of what He really is, without any reference to the world, is called by Śaṅkara Paraṁbrahma or the Supreme God.

From the transcendental standpoint God is consciousness, real and infinite.

For understanding this higher aspect of God as He is really in Himself (without relation to the world) along with the lower aspect, Śaṅkara constantly draws on the analogy of the magician (māyāvī)[2] as suggested in the *Śvetā śvatara*. The magician is a juggler only to those who are deceived by his trick and who fancy that they perceive the objects conjured up. But to the discerning few who see through the trick and have no illusion, the juggler fails to be a juggler. Similarly, those who believe in the world-show think of God through this show and call Him its Creator, etc. But for those wise few who know that the world is a mere show, there is neither any real world nor any real Creator.

The analogy of the magician.

This is the only way, thinks Śaṅkara, in which we can understand in the light of common experience how God can be both in the world and yet beyond it—understand, that is to say, the immanence and the transcendence of God, which are taught by the Upaniṣads.

Śaṅkara tries to reconcile the immanence and the transcendence of God.

1. *Tait.*, 2. 1.
2. *Vide* his com. on *Br.-Sūt.* 2. 1. 9.

The world, so long as it appears, is in God, the only Reality, just as the snake conjured out of the rope is nowhere else except in the rope. But God is not really touched by the imperfections of the world just as the rope is not affected by any illusory characters of the snake, or even as the actor is not affected by the loss and gain of kingdom on the stage.

This reconciliation is difficult for Rāmānuja.

Rāmānuja, we shall see, finds difficulty in reconciling the immanence of God with His transcendence. He tries to explain in different ways how God can be said to be in the world and yet remain unaffected by the world's imperfections. This difficulty, however, is not peculiar to Rāmānuja alone. It is present in most Western forms of theism also which, like Rāmānuja's look upon creation as real.

God is an object of worship only when viewed from the lower standpoint.

God as the object of worship is based essentially on a belief in the distinction between the worshipping self and the God worshipped. The reality of the limited self like that of a worldly object is based on ignorance—on the failure to realize that God is the only Reality. Besides, God is worshipped because God is thought of as the creator and controller of the world. So worship and the God worshipped are bound with our lower standpoint (vyāvahārika dṛṣṭi) from which the world appears as real and God appears as endowed with the many qualities in relation to the world. It is this Saguṇa Brahma or Īśvara who can be regarded as an object of worship.

God from the transcendental standpoint is devoid of all qualities and distinctions.

Brahman from the higher or transcendental point of view (pāramārthika-dṛṣṭi) cannot be described by qualities which relate to the world or to the ego. Brahman in this aspect is devoid of all distinctions, external as well as internal (sajātīya, vijātīya and svagata bhedas). Here, therefore, Śaṅkara differs from Rāmānuja who, we shall see, believes that God is possessed of at least internal distinction (svagata bheda), because within Him there are the really distinct conscious and unconscious realities. Brahman, in this absolutely transcendent aspect, says Śaṅkara, cannot be described at all and it is, therefore, called indeterminate or characterless or nirguṇa. The description of Brahman even as infinite, real, consciousness, though more accurate than accidental descriptions, cannot directly convey the idea of Brahman. It only serves to direct the mind towards Brahman by denying of it finiteness, unreality and unconsciousness.[1]

To predicate a quality is to limit God.

Every quality predicated of any subject is a sort of limitation imposed on it. This follows from the logical principle of obversion. If S is P, then it is not non-P and, therefore, non-P is excluded from S, which becomes then limited to that extent. A great Western philosopher, Spinoza, recognizes this and lays down the dictum, 'Every determination is negation.' He also thinks, therefore, that God, the ultimate substance, is indeterminate and cannot be described by any positive qualification. The Upaniṣads recognize this principle and deny of God all predicates, even worshipability.[2] This conception is developed by Śaṅkara who calls Brahman, in this transcendent aspect, nirguṇa or attributeless.

God, from the real standpoint, is indeterminate.

Māyā is attributable to God only from the lower standpoint, not from the higher.

We have said previously that the world-appearance is due to māyā. God regarded as the Creator of the world is, therefore, described as the wielder of māyā. Ignorant people like us believe that the world is real and that, therefore, God is really *qualified by māyā,* i.e. possessed of the power of creating the world (māyā-viśiṣṭa). But really creativity is not an essential character of God, it is only an apparent accidental predicate (upādhi) that we illusorily ascribe to God. God is only

1. *Vide Śaṅkara's* com. on *Tait.*, 2. 1.
2. Vide Kena, 1. 5.

apparently associated with creativity (māyopahita). God is immanent (saguṇa) and God as transcendent reality, (nirguṇa) are not two, any more than the man on the stage and that man outside the stage are two. The first is only the apparent aspect of the second. The first is relative to the world, the second is irrelative or absolute.

The distinction of points of view is made in daily life.

Distinction between standpoints is always made by us in life and is nothing new or queer in Advaita philosophy as it may appear to some. In daily life, we say that a currency note is really paper, but *conventionally* it is money; a photograph is *really* paper but *appears* as a man ; the image in a mirror appears as a real object, but is not *really* so; and so on. This ordinary kind of distinction between the apparent and the real is philosophically utilized by Vedā nta for explaining the relation of God to the world. Thus the vyāvahārika and the pāramārthika—empirical (conventional or practical) and the transcendental (absolute or irrelative)—which the Vedānta distinguishes are neither uncommon nor unintelligible. It is only the extension of a common distinction.

The view of God as immanent leads to that of God as transcendent.

Though God as Creator is only apparent, yet His importance and value should not be ignored. It is only through the lower standpoint that we can gradually mount up to the higher. Advaita Vedānta, like the Upaniṣads, believes in the gradual revelation of truth in stages through which spiritual progress takes place. The unreflecting man who regards the world as a self- sufficient reality feels no urge to look beyond it and search for its cause or ground. When he comes to realize somehow the insufficiency of the world and looks for something which sustains the world from behind, he comes to discover God as the Creator and Sustainer of the world. He feels admiration and reverence and begins to pray to the Creator. God thus becomes the object of worship. With the further

Gradual revelation of Truth.

advancement of thought, so the Advaita thinks, the man may discover that God, whom he reached through the world, is really the only reality, the world is only an appearance. Thus at the first level, the world alone is real ; at the second, both the world and God ; at the last, only God. The first is atheism. The second represents theism as we find in Rāmā nuja and others. The last is the Absolute monism of Śaṅkara. Śaṅkara recognizes that the last level has to be reached only gradually through the second. He, therefore, believes in the utility of worshipping God (as Saguṇa Brahma). For, this purifies the heart and prepares one for gradually reaching the highest view, and without it no God, immanent or transcendent, would ever be found. Śaṅkara gives a place even to the worship of the many deities, because it redeems the spiritually backward at least from utter atheism, and it serves as a stage on the way to the highest truth.

(i) The Rational Basis of Śaṅkara's Theory of God.

Śaṅkara's conception of God is logically deducible from his theory of Existence and Appearance.

The different ideas about God, as explained above, are based primarily on the interpretation of the scriptures. But they can also be logically deduced from the conclusions established in the previous section by the critical analysis of ordinary experience and by reasoning based thereon. We saw there how Śaṅkara demonstrates by argument that (1) pure existence is the ground and material of all particular and changing forms of existence constituting the world, (2) that particular objects being open to contradiction cannot be taken as absolutely real, (3) that only pure existence is beyond actual and possible contradiction and, therefore, the only Absolute Reality, and (4) that pure existence is pure consciousness as well. It will be found, therefore, that this Absolute Existence-Consciousness is nothing other than God, described by the Upaniṣads as Brahman, real, conscious and infinite. Now the two aspects of God, the immanent and the transcendent, can also be logically deduced. The idea of God, as pure existence is reached, we saw, through the world of particular objects, by a logical enquiry into its nature and reality. Till such critical examination takes place, the world of normal waking experience passes as the only reality. Our ordinary practical life is based on such an unsuspecting acceptance of this world. But when on examination one comes to realize pure existence as the universal ground of the world, one perceives such existence in every phenomenon. In other words, God or Brahman is found manifested through every particular form of existence. Although the world appears to him in all its multiplicity, God is thought to be its sole ground and substance. But when it is realized that though pure existence appears in many forms, yet these latter cannot be accepted by reason as real, one has to think that the cause of the world has the inscrutable power of manifesting itself as many without undergoing any real modification. This metaphysical idea, put in terms of theology, is nothing but the conception of God as the Creator of the world and possessed of a magical creative power, māyā. This is also the conception of Īśvara or Saguṇa-Brahman, Brahman endowed with the attributes of omnipotence (the power of causing all things) and omniscience (consciousness revealing all forms of existence). Again, as all objects perish only to merge in *existence* of some other form, objects can be conceived as being withdrawn into their ground, that is existence. God can thus be described as also the Destroyer or that into which the world's objects lose their particular forms.

Saguṇa Brahman regarded as ground of appearance.

But on still deeper thought it is realized that relation of the unreal to the real cannot be itself real. The attributes ascribed to God to express His relation to the apparent world cannot, therefore, be taken as real. Thus emerges the idea of God in His transcendent and truly real aspect of Parabrahman, the Supreme Reality, above all multiplicity and devoid of

Nirguṇa Brahman or Existence in itself.

all really ascribable attributes, the Nirguṇa Brahman or Indeterminate Absolute. Śaṅkara's conception of Brahman in its twofold aspect and all ideas connected therewith are, therefore, found to be logically deducible also from a critical view of ordinary experience.

This view is not atheism, but super theism.

Like Spinoza's conception of God, as substance, Śaṅkara's conception of God, as Parabrahman or Nirguṇa, Brahman, differs from the God or Religion, that is, God conceived as an object of worship, distinct from the worshipper and endowed with the highest attributes. It is no wonder, therefore, that like Spinoza, Śaṅkara also is sometimes accused of atheism. This charge stands or falls according as God is taken in this narrow sense or in the wider one, we have previously discussed. If God connotes, among other things, the Supreme Reality, Śaṅkara's theory is not surely atheism, but rather the logical perfection of the theistic faith. Indeed, whereas atheism believes only in the world and not at all in God, and ordinary theism believes in both, the world and God, Śaṅkara believes only in God. For him God is the only Reality. Rather than denying God, he makes the most of God. This view also marks the highest extension of the ordinary religious emotion towards God. For it points to the stage where love of God becomes absolute, suffering neither the ego nor the world. If this type of faith is to be distinguished from ordinary theism (or believe in personal God), the word for it should be, not atheism, but rather '*super*-theism'.

Three stage of the evolution of the world out of God and Māyā, metaphorically conceived.

In connection with the process of creation, we saw, that the Advaitin imagines the gradual evolution of the world out of Brahman through Māyā, by a process of apparent change of the subtle to the gross. Three stages are sometimes distinguished[1] in this process of evolution in analogy with the development of a seed into a plant, namely, the undifferentiated seed stage or causal

1. Vide *Vedāntasāra* of Sadānanda.

stage, the subtly differentiated germinating stage and the fully differentiated plant stage. Brahman, the unchanging reality, cannot, of course, be said to be undergoing evolution. All change and, therefore, evolution belong to the sphere of Māyā. It is Māyā, the creative power which at first remains unmanifested, then becomes differentiated into subtle objects, and then into the gross ones. Brahman conceived as the possessor of the undifferentiated Māyā is named Īśvara, and described as omniscient and omnipotent. It is the conception of God existing prior to actual creation, but possessed of the power of creation. Brahman possessed of subtly differentiated Māyā is called Hiraṇyagarbha (also Sūtrātmā and Prāṇa). God in this aspect would be the totality of *all* subtle objects. Brahman possessed of Māyā differentiated further into gross or perceptible objects is called Vaiśvānara (also Virāṭ). This aspect of God is the totality of all gross objects, the entire manifested world, including all individuals (jīvas). Sometimes this gradual process of evolution is compared to the three states of the individual, namely, deep sleep, dream and wakefulness. Īśvara is God in deep slumber. Hiraṇyagarbha is God in dreaming state, and Vaiśvānara is God fully awake. It should be remembered that whereas ordinarily Īśvara implies the entire immanent aspect of God, that is Brahman associated with, Māyā in all stages, the world is used in the present context in a narrower sense, and confined only to the first stage.

The four aspects of Brahman.

Counting these three immanent aspects of God in relation to creation along with the transcendent aspect beyond all such relation, we have the four possible aspects of Brahman, namely, Pure Consciousness-Existence (Parabrahman). Īśvara, Hiraṇyagarbha and Vaiśvānara. Though these are generally taken as the successive stages of manifestation, it is equally possible to think of them as simultaneously existing. For, Pure Consciousness never ceases even when it *seems* to evolve, nor do the subtle manifestations (*e.g.* buddhi, manas, prāṇas, senses and motor organs) cease when the gross ones comes into existence.

The Philosophy of creation distinguished from mythology.

Śaṅkara does not seem to attach any serious importance to the different alternative accounts of the order of creation, and metaphors in support thereof, though he tries to explain all of them as they occur in the different scriptures, without any attempt to justify some and reject the rest. There are two problems that appear in the human mind as to the world. One of them is : What is the ultimate ground, substance or reality *logically presupposed by* the world ? The other is : *Why or how the* world originates from what is accepted as the ultimate ? The solution of the first is the primary business of philosophy. Śaṅkara, Spinoza, Green, Bradley and most other great philosophers of the world address themselves to this problem. They start from the world of experienced facts, analyse it critically and try to find out what is logically presupposed by it. Reasoning or logic is the cheif instrument here. We saw already how Śaṅkara thus discovers pure existence and consciousness as the only and ultimate reality. The solution of the second problem is the business of mythology which starts with God (or some other ultimate) and gives an imaginary account of why and how the world is created. Imagination is the chief instrument here, and no logical rigour can be expected in its work. The mythological explanation of the world has always been a pastime for the human mind in all lands, as all the scriptures and legends of the world would show. Sometimes it is found intermingled also with philosophical speculation. But all great philosophers have fought shy of mythological explanation. The hackneyed criticism against Spinoza that his substance is like a lion's den to which there are many steps but out of which there are none, points to this fact, though it misunderstands the primary business of the philosopher. Green[1] and Bradley[2] plainly confess that the why and how of creation cannot be explained by philosophy. Similarly, Śaṅkara does not take the stories and motives of creation, described in different

1. Prolegomena to Ethics, p. 93.
2. Appearance and Reality. p. 453.

scriptures, with the same seriousness with which he tries to establish the reality of Brahman, the ultimate ground of the world, or expose the contradictory character of all changing and particular finite modes of existence. The accounts of creation are true, for him, only from the lower point of view.

3. Śaṅkara's Conception of the Self, Bondage and Liberation

We have found already that Śaṅkara believes in unqualified monism. All distinctions between objects and objects, the subject and the object, the self and God are the illusory creation of māyā. He holds fast to the conception of identity without any real difference and tries to follow it out logically in every respect. He accepts, therefore, without any reservation, the identity of the Soul and God, that is repeatedly taught in the Upaniṣads.

The self is absolutely identical with Brahman.

Man is apparently composed of the body and the soul. But the body which we perceive is, like every other material object, merely an illusory appearance. When this is realized, the reality that remains is the soul which is nothing other than God. The saying, 'That thou art', means that there is an unqualified identity between the soul, that underlies the apparently finite man, and God. It is true that if we take the word 'thou' in the sense of the empirical individual limited and conditioned by its body, and the word 'that' as the reality beyond the world, there cannot be an identity between the 'thou' and 'that'. We have to understand, therefore, the word 'thou' to imply pure consciousness underlying man and 'that' to imply also pure consciousness which forms the essence of God. Between these two, complete identity exists and is taught by the Vedānta. An identity judgement like 'This is that Devadatta' (which we pass on seeing Devadatta for a second

The body is not real.

The meaning of 'That thou art.'

time) makes the above point clear. The conditions which the man had the previous day cannot be exactly identical with those he has the second day. Therefore, there cannot be any identity between the man qualified by one set of conditions with the man qualified by another set. What we mean, therefore, must be that the man, viewed apart from the different conditions, is the same. Similar is the case with the identity taught between the Self and God. The Self, viewed apart from the conditions that differentiate it from pure consciousness, is identical with God viewed apart from the attibutes that differentiate Him from pure consciousness. Such identity judgement is not tautological and superfluous, because it serves the purpose of pointing out that what are illusorily taken as different are really one. The identity that is taught between man and God is a *real* identity between terms which *appear* as different. Being identical with God, the soul is in reality what God also really is. It is the supreme Brahman—the self-luminous, infinite, consciousness. The soul appears as the limited, finite self because of its association with the body which is a product of ignorance.

Identity judgement is neither tautological nor impossible.

The body is not composed simply of what we perceive through the senses. In addition to the gross perceptible body, there is also a subtle one, composed of the senses, the motor organs (these two groups together being called indriyas), vital elements (prāṇas) and the internal mechanism of knowledge (antaḥkaraṇa). While the gross body perishes on death, the subtle body does not, and it migrates with the soul to the next gross body. Both of these bodies are the products of māyā.

The gross body and the subtle body are the products of *māyā*.

Owing to ignorance, the beginning of which cannot be assigned, the soul erroneously associates itself with the body, gross and subtle. This is called bondage. In this state it forgets that it is really Brahman. It behaves like a finite, limited, miserable being which runs after transitory worldly objects and is pleased to get

Bondage is the soul's association with the body through ignorance.

them, sorry to miss them. It identifies itself with a finite body and mind (antaḥkaraṇa) and thinks 'I am stout,' 'I am lame,' 'I am ignorant.' Thus arises the conception of the self as the 'Ego' or 'I'. This limited ego opposes itself to the rest of existence, which is thought to be different from it. The ego is not, therefore, the real self, but is only an apparent limitation of it.

The ego (aham) is not the self (ātman).

Consciousness of the self also becomes limited by the conditions of the body. The senses and antaḥkaraṇa (the internal organ of knowledge) become the instruments through which limited consciousness of objects takes place. Such empirical, finite knowledge is of two kinds, immediate and mediate. Immediate knowledge of external objects arises when, through any sense, the antaḥkaraṇa flows out to the object and is modified into the form of the object. In addition to immediate knowledge (pratyakṣa), the Advaitins admit five different kinds of mediate knowledge, namely, inference (anumāna), testimony (śabda), comparison (upamāna), postulation (arthāpatti) and non-cognition (anupalabdhi). The Advaitins agree, in the main, with the Bhāṭṭa school of Mīmāṁsa regarding these sources of knowledge. As the Bhāṭṭa views have been already stated we need not repeat them here.[1]

The consciousness of the self in bondage is limited.

When a man is awake, he thinks himself identified with the gross body, as well as with the internal and external organs. When he falls asleep and dreams, he is still conscious of objects that arise from memory-impressions, and, therefore, the feeling of his limitation as a subject or knower opposed to objects still persists there. When he has deep, dreamless sleep, he ceases to have any ideas of objects. In the absence of objects, he ceases to be a knower as well. The polarity of subject and object, the opposition between the knower and the known, vanishes altogether. He no longer feels that he is

Waking experience, dream and dreamless sleep—the three levels of ordinary consciousness.

1. For a critical discussion of the Advaita theory of knowledge *vide* D. M. Datta, *The Six Ways of Knowing*.

confined to and limited by the body. But yet consciousness does not cease in dreamless sleep ; for otherwise how could we remember at all on awaking from sleep that we had such a state ? How could we report 'I had peaceful sleep, had no dreams,' if we were unconscious then?

The study of dreamless sleep gives us a glimpse of what the self really is when dissociated from its feeling of identity with the body. The soul in its intrinsic state is not a finite, miserable being. It does not separate itself from the rest of existence and does not limit itself by a feeling of the 'I' (aham) opposed to a 'thou' or 'this' or 'that'. It is also free from all worries that arise from hankerings after objects. The self, really, then is unlimited consciousness and bliss.

The Rational Basis of Śaṅkara's Conception of Self :

The different meanings of self.

The conception of self set forth above is chiefly based on revealed tests. But it is also independently reached by the Advaitin through different lines of argument based on the logical analysis of ordinary experience. We may briefly indicate them here. It should be clearly mentioned at the outset that Śaṅkara does never think that the existence of the self (ātman) need be proved by any argument. The self is self-manifest in everyone. "Everyone believes that he exists, and never thinks 'I am not'.[1] But there are so many different kinds of meaning, attached to 'I' or 'Self' that it requires a good deal of analysis and reasoning to find out what the self really is.

Analysis of the meanings of 'I' shows pure consciousness to be the essence of the self.

One method of enquiry is the analysis of language. The word 'I' seems sometimes to imply the body (*e.g.* 'I am fat'), sometimes a sense (*e.g.* 'I am blind'), sometimes a motor organ (*e.g.* 'I am lame'), sometimes a mental faculty (*e.g.* 'I am dull'), sometimes consciousness (*e.g.* 'I know'). Which of these should be taken to be the real essence of the self ? To determine this we have to remember the true criterion of reality. The reality or the essence of a thing is, as we saw previously, that which persists through all its states.[2] The

1. *Brahma-sūtra.*, 1. 1. 1.
2. *Vide* Śaṅkara on *Br.-Sūt.* 2. 1. 11. (Eka-rūpeṇa hi avasthito yo'rthaḥ sa paramārthaḥ) and on *Gita*. 2. 16. (Yadviṣayā buddhir na vyabhicarati tat sat, yadvisayā vyabhicarati tadasat).

essence or the reality behind the world of objects was found, in this way, to be pure existence because while other things about the world change and perish, this always reveals itself in every state. In a similar way it is found that what is common to the body, sense, mind, etc., with which the self identifies itself from time to time, is consciousness. The identification of the self with any of these means some form of consciousness or other that is the consciousness of the self as the body ('I am fat') as a sense ('I am blind') and the like. Consciousness is, therefore, the essence of the self in whichever from it may appear. But it is not consciousness of any particular form, but simple consciousness common to all its forms. Such consciousness is also pure existence since existence persists through all forms of consciousness. The different particular and changing forms of consciousness can be shown, from their contradictory natures, to be mere appearances, in the same way as the different forms of existence were shown to be so before.

'My consciousness,' does not really imply distinction between self and consciousness.

This conclusion is further supported by the linguistic expressions 'my body,' 'my sense,' 'my intellect,' etc. which show that the self can alienate itself from these (body, sense, etc.) and treat them as external objects distinct from itself. These cannot, therefore, be regarded as the real essence of the self. It is true, one also sometimes says 'my consciousness'. But such an expression cannot be taken literally, as implying a distinction between the self (as possessor) and consciousness (as possessed). For, if the self tries to distinguish itself from consciousness, it only assumes the form of distinguishing consciousness. Consciousness thus proves imseparable and indistinguishable from the self. So 'my consciounsness' must be taken in a metaphorical sense. The possessive case here does not really imply distinction, but rather identity or apposition (as in 'The city of London'). By comparing and analysing the different meanings of the self expressed by 'I' and 'mind' we discover thus pure consciousness as the real essence of the self.

If again we compare the three states, namely of waking, dreaming and sleeping without dreams which the human self experiences daily, we can reach the same conception. The essence of the self must remain in all these or the self would cease to be. But what do we find common to all these states ? In the first state there is consciousness of external objects ; in the second also there is consciousness, but of internal objects present only to the dreamer. In the third state no objects appear, but there is no cessation of consciousness, for otherwise the subsequent memory of that state, as one of peace and freedom from worries, would not be possible. The persistent factor then is consciousness, but not necessarily of any object. This shows again that the essence of self is pure consciousness without necessary relation to object.

Comparison of waking, dreaming and dreamless sleep states again shows pure consciousness to be the essence of the self.

But two more points of special importance also emerge out of this consideration. The first one is that consciousness, the essence of the self, is not dependent on objects. There is no reason, therefore, to think that consciousness is produced by the relation of the self to objects through some proper medium. We have to revise then our ordinary theory of knowledge. If the self is self-existing and self-revealing consciousness, and every object also is, as we saw before, a form of self-revealing existence-consciousness, the only way we can understand the non-cognition of an existing object is that there is some obstacle which conceals the object. The relation of the self to the object through sense, etc. is required then only to remove this obstruction, just as the removal of the obstacle of a cover is required for the perception of a self-revealing light.

Consciousness not produced by objects.

The other point is that the self in its intrinsic nature, isolated from all objects, as it is dreamless sleep, is found to have blissful or peaceful existence. Consciousness in that state is bliss.

Pure consciousness is bliss.

When in the light of this discovery we scan the other two states we can understand that even there some joy or bliss does exist though in distorted or mutilated forms. The fleeting pleasures which we have in wakeful life and in dream can be understood as the fragmentary manifestation of the joy or bliss which forms the essence of the self. This explanation is further supported by the fact that man derives pleasure by *owning* property, etc., that is, by *identifying* them with his self. The self can thus be explained as the ultimate source of all joy. This joy is ordinarily finite and short-lived because the self limits itself by identifying itself with finite and fleeting objects. Sorrow is related to want and joy to fulness. When the self can realize what it really is, namely, pure consciousness which is infinite (being free from all particularity), it is one with the essence or self of the universe. It is then above want and attains infinite bliss.

Brahman, pure consciousness, the ground of both the self and the external world.

It is also found from the above arguments, that pure existence without any specific limitation is common to the self and to the world outside, that consciousness is also present in both, though it is patent in the former and concealed in the latter. The reality underlying the world is, therefore, indentical with that underlying the self. Had the self and the world not a common basis, knowledge of the latter by the former would not be possible ; and far less possible would be the identification of the self with external objects. In other words, Brahman, the infinite existence-consciousness is the only reality that constitutes the self and the external world. Brahman is also found to be bliss or joy, since the state of dreamless sleep exhibits the intrinsic nature of the self, pure objectless consciousness, to be identical with bliss. The finite appearance of the self as the ego, 'I' in different contexts must, therefore, be due to ignorance (avidyā) which makes it identify itself now with the body and then with a sense or any other finite existence.

Māyā or Avidyā, the principle of limitation and multiplication of the One Brahman into many selves.

How infinite, formless consciousness, which is the self's essence, can assume particular forms is a problem which we already came across in another form, namely, how pure existence can appear as particular objects. As no particular and changing phenomenon can be regarded as real we have to face here the same insoluble puzzle ; namely, the appearance, in experience of what is unreal to thought. In admitting this unintelligible fact of experience logical thought has to acknowledge a mysterious or inscrutable power by which the Infinite Self can apparently limit itself into the finite. So Māyā is admitted by the Advaitin as the principle of apparent limitation and multiplication in this as in every other sphere. But this Māyā may be conceived in a collective as well as in a distributive way. We can imagine Brahman, the Infinite Pure Consciousness-Existence-Bliss limiting itself by an all-overpowering Māyā and appearing as the universe of finite objects and selves. Or we can think of each individual self as labouring under a power of ignorance and seeing, in place of the One Brahman, the universe of many objects and selves. These would be but thinking of the same situation from two different points of view, the cosmic and the individual. When such distinction is made the word, Māyā, is restricted, as we said before, to the first or collective aspect of the power of ignorance and avidyā to the individual aspect.

The metaphor of reflection, pratibimba.

The individual (jīva) can then be imagined mataphorically as but the reflection (pratibimba) of the Infinite Consciousness on the finite mirror of ignorance (avidyā) and compared to one of the many reflections of the moon cast on different receptacles of water. Just as there the reflection varies with the nature of the reflecting water, appearing clear or dirty, moving or motionless, according as the water is of one nature or another, similarly does the human self, the reflection of the Infinite, vary with the nature of the avidyā. We saw previously that the human body, gross and subtle, is the product of ignorance, and the mind (the antaḥkaraṇa) is one of the elements composing the subtle body. The mind is thus a product of avidyā. Now, the mind may be more or less cultured ; it may be ignorant, impure, swayed by passion or enlightened, pure and dispassionate. These differences can be said to constitute differences in the avidyās of the individuals. The analogy of reflection would thus explain how the same Brahman can appear as different kinds of individual selves, without really becoming different and only being reflected in different kinds of minds constituted by different avidyās. This conception would also point to the possibility of attaining to a better and better realization of the Brahman in us by purifying the mind more and more. The possibility of a more tranquil state is also shown by our daily experience of dreamless sleep, wherein the self, dissociated from objects, enjoys temporary peace.

The alternative metaphor of the limitation of space by imaginary boundaries.

The attempt to understand the appearance of individual souls on the analogy of images, is called the theory of reflection (pratibimbavāda). One great disadvantage of this metaphor is that it reduces the souls to mere images, and liberation, which according to it would consist in breaking the mirror of ignorance, would also mean the total cessation of the illusory individuals. To secure a status of greater reality for the individual, there is an alternative metaphor preferred by some Advaitins, namely the imaginary division of Space, which really remains one and undivided, into different particular spaces. Just as the same space is conceived to exist every where and yet it is conventionally divided, for practical convenience, into the space of the pot, that of the room, that of a town and so on, similarly though Brahman is the one and all-pervasive Reality, it is supposed, through ignorance, to be limited and divided into different objects and souls. Really, however, there is no distinction between objects and objects, souls and souls, since all are at bottom the same pure existence. What is illusory here (in this alternative imagery) is only the limitation, the finitude imposed on Reality by ignorance. Every soul, even when supposed to be finite, is really nothing other than Brahman. Liberation consists only in breaking the illusory barriers, and what was limited by them, namely existence, is then left unaffected. This alternative explanation is known as the theory of limitation (avacchedaka-vāda).

The attempt of Śaṅkara and his followers is to show how the intrinsic, pure condition of the self can be regained. The fact that the blissful state of dreamless sleep is not permanent and man once more returns to his finite, limited, embodied consciousness on waking up, shows that there remain even in dreamless sleep, in a latent form, the forces of karma or avidyā which draw man into the world. Unless these forces, accumulated from the past, can be completely stopped, there is no hope of liberation from the miserable existence which the self has in this world.

Vedānta helps man to destroy ignorance completely.

The study of the Vedānta helps man conquer these deep-rooted effects of long-standing ignorance. But the study of the truth taught by the Vedānta would have no effect unless the mind is previously prepared. This initial preparation according to Śaṅkara, is not the study of the *Mīmāṁsā sūtra*, as Rāmānuja thinks. The Mīmāṁsā, which teaches the performance of sacrifies to the various gods, rests on the wrong conception of a distinction between the worshipper and the worshipped. Its spirits is, therefore , antagonistic to the absolute monism taught by the Vedānta. Far from preparing the mind for the reception of the monistic truth, it only helps to perpetuate the illusion of distinctions and plurality from which man already suffers.

Preparation, necessary for the study of Vedānta, is not the study of any ritualistic work.

The preparation necessary for undertaking the study of the Vedānta is fourfold, according to Śaṅkara.[1] One should, first, be able to discriminate between what is eternal and what is not eternal (nityānityavastu-viveka). He should, secondly, be able to give up all desires for enjoyment of objects here and hereafter (ihāmutrārtha-bhogavirāga). Thirdly, he should control his mind and his senses and develop qualities like detachment, patience, power of concentration (śamadamādisādhanasampat). Lastly, he should have an ardent desire for liberation (mumukṣutva).

But the fourfold culture of the mind alone makes one a fit student of Vedānta.

With such preparation of the intellect, emotion and will one should begin to study the Vedānta with a teacher who has himself realized Brahman. This study consists of the threefold process : listening to the teacher's instructions (śravaṇa), understanding the instructions through reasoning until all doubts are removed and conviction is generated (manana), and repeated meditation on the truths thus accepted (nididhyāsana).

Study, reasoning and contemplation are necessary for the realization of truth.

The forces of deep-rooted beliefs of the past do not disappear so soon as the truths of the Vedānta are learned. Only repeated meditation on the truths and life led accordingly can gradually root them out. When wrong beliefs thus becomes removed and belief in the truths of the Vedānta becomes permanent, the seeker after liberation is told by the teacher 'Thou art Bahman.' He begins then to contemplate this truth steadfastly till at last he has an immediate realization of the truth in the form 'I am Brahman.' This the illusory distinction between the self and Brahman at last disappears and bondage, too, along with it. Liberation (mukti) is thus attained.

Realization of the identity between the self and Brahman is liberation from bondage.

1. Vide Śaṅkara's *Bhāṣya* on *Br. Sutra*, 1. 1. 1.

Liberation is possible even while the soul is associated with the body.

Even on the attainment of liberation the body may continue because it is the product of karmas which has already borne their effects (prārabdha-karma). But the liberated sould does never again identity itself with the body. The world still appears before him, but he is not deceived by it. He does not feel any desire for the world's objects. He is, therefore, not affected by the world's misery. He is in the world and yet out of it. This conception of Śaṅkara has become well known in later Vedā nta as Jīvanmukti[1] (the liberation of one while one is alive). It is the state of perfection attained here. Like Buddha, the Sāṅkhya , the jaina and some other Indian thinkers, Śaṅkara believes that perfection can be reached even here in this life. It is not a mere extra mundane prospect, like heaven, to be attained hereafter in an unperceived future. It is true that the seeker after liberation is asked to begin with some faith in the testimony of the scriptures regarding the utility of the spiritual discipline he is required to follow. But his faith is fully justified and more than repaid by the end it secures in the very life.

Three kinds of karma can be distinguished. Karmas gathered in past lives admit of a twofold division, those that have borne their effects (prārabdha-karma) and those that still lie accumulated (sañcita-karma). In addition to these two kinds, there are karmas which are being gathered here in this life (sañcīyamāna). Knowledge of reality destroys the second kind and prevents the third and thus makes rebirth impossible. But the first kind which has already borne effects cannot be prevented. Hence the present body, the effect of such karma, runs its natural

1. *Vide* Śaṅkara's *Bhāsya* on *Sūt*. 1.1.4.; "siddham jīvato'pi viduṣaḥaśarī ratvam" also on *Kaṭha*., 6. 14 : "Atha martyo amṛto bhavatyatra brahma samaśnute."

course and ceases when the force of the karma causing it becomes automatically exhausted, just as the wheel of a potter which has been already turned comes to a stop only when the momentum imparted to it becomes exhausted. When the body, gross and subtle, perishes, the jīvan-mukta is said to attain the disembodied state of liberation (videha-mukti).

It is not a new product.

Liberation is not the production of anything new, nor is it the purification of any old state ; it is the realization of what is always there, even in the stage of bondage, though not known then. For, liberation is nothing but the identity of the self and Brahman, which is always real, though not always recognized. The attainment of liberation is, therefore, compared by the Advaitins to the finding of the necklace on the neck by one who forgot its existence there and searched for it hither and thither. As bondage is due to an illusion, liberation is only the removal of this illusion.

Liberation is positive bliss.

Liberation is not merely the absence of all misery that arises from the illusory sense of distinction between the self and God. It is conceived by the Advaitin, after Upaniṣads, as a state of positive bliss (ānanda), because Brahman is bliss and liberation is identity with Brahman.

It is not incompatible with work without attachment.

Though the liberated soul, being perfect, has no end to achieve, it can work still without any fear of further bondage. Śaṅkara, following the *Gītā,* holds that work fetters a man only when it is performed with attachment. But one who has obtained perfect knowledge and perfect satisfaction, is free from attachment. He can work without any hope of gain and is not, therefore, affected by success or

The value of disinterested work for both the wise and the ignorant.

failure. Śaṅkara attaches great importance to disinterested work. For one who has not yet obtained perfect knowledge, such work is necessary for self-purification (ātma-śuddhi), because it is not through inactivity but through the performance of selfless action that one can gradually free oneself from the yoke of the ego and its petty interests. Even for one who has obtained perfect knowledge or liberation, selfless activity is necessary for the good of those who are still in bondage.[1]

The life of the liberated should be a worthy ideal of society.

The liberated man is the ideal of society and his life should be worthy of imitation by the people at large. Inactivity or activity that would mislead them should, therefore, be avoided by the perfect.[2] Social service is not, therefore, thought by Śaṅkara to be incompatible with the perfect life, but rather desirable. In his own life of intense social service Śaṅkara follows this ideal. This ideal is also advocated by some eminent modern Vedāntists like Svāmī Vivekānanda[3] and Lokamānya B. G. Tilak.[4]

Does the Vedānta disregard the distinction between right and wrong ?

The critics of Advaita Vedānta have often urged that if Brahman be the only reality and all distinctions false, the distinction between right and wrong also would be false. Such a philosophy is, therefore, fruitful of dangerous consequences for society. This objection is due to the confusion of the lower and the higher standpoint. From the empirical standpoint, the distinction

---

1. *Vide* Śaṅkara's *Bhāsya* on the *Bhagavadgītā*, 4. 14. 3. 20. 26. and *passim*.

2. *Ibid*.

3. *Vide* his *Practical Vedānta*.

4. Vide his *Gītārahasya* (a Marathi treatise on the *Gītā*) on the above verses and Introduction, sec. 12.

between right and wrong, like other distinctions, is quite valid. For one who has not yet attained liberation, any action which directly or indirectly leads him towards the realization of his unity with Brahman, is good and that which hampers such realization, directly or indirectly, is bad. Truthfulness, charity, benevolence, self-control and the like would be found to fall under the first category even according to this criterion, whereas falsehood, selfishness, injury to others would come under the second. One who has attained perfect knowledge and liberation would look back upon these moral distinctions as being relative to the lower standpoint and, therefore, not absolutely valid. But neither would he perform a bad action in so far as the motive of every bad action is based on the ignorant identification of the self with the body, the senses and the like, in a word, on the lack of the sense of unity between the Self and Brahman.[1]

Śaṅkara's philosophy is not detrimental to practical life.

A Pragmatic critic, for whom practical utility is the highest value, often complains that Śaṅkara indulges in visionary speculation which reduces the world to an empty show, deprives life of all zest and causes failure in the struggle for existence. The reply to such a charge is that if man chooses to live the unreflecting life of an animal, or of the primitive man, he need not go beyond the world of practical reality. But if he is to use his reason and think of the nature and meaning of this world he is irresistibly led by logical necessity to realize, as we saw, the contradictory and unreal nature of it and search for its real ground. Reason demands again that he should reshape his life on a rational basis in the light or what it discovers to be the

1. For a fuller discussion *vide* Radhakrishnan, *Ind. Phil.*, Vol. II. pp. 612-34. and speeches of Vivekānanda quoted by James in *Pragmatism*, pp. 152 f.

highest reality. As an child grows into a adult he has to remodel life gradually in accordance with his changing outlook. The playthings which were once valued more than things precious to the adult, yield place to the latter.

It places life on a more rational and stable basis.

Remodelling life to suit a truer conception of reality and value causes no harm to practical life, but, on the contrary, places life on a more rational, real and permanent footing. It surely deprives life of its zest in the sense that it controls the passions and impulses which push the animal, the child, and the primitive man blindly from behind. But it gradually replaces these blind forces by conscious and rational ideals which can create for life an enthusiasm of a higher and a more abiding kind.

It also imparts to life a greater survival value.

As to the question of survival in the struggle for existence it should be borne in mind that what constitutes fitness for survival in the plant world, is not the same in the animal world, and it is all the more different in the human world. Social qualities like love, unity, self-sacrifice and rational conduct possess greater survival value than egoism, jealousy, selfishness and blind passionate conduct. And no view of the world and life can supply a better foundation for such superior qualities than the one which inspires man with the beliefs in the unity of all men, all creation and all existences. Such is the view, we have found, of Śaṅkara. It is a misunderstanding, then, to suspect it of baneful effect on practical life. The moral and spiritual discipline which he recommends, aims at the actual realization, in immediate experience, of the unity of existence or the presence of Brahman in all things, the unity which reasoning convinces us to be real by its irresistible logic, but which our present actual experience of difference and multiplicity tries to set aside.

Conclusion.

In conclusion, we should observe that the Vedānta of Śaṅkara, in its different aspects, is an attempt to follow out of the Upaniṣadic idea of the unity of all existence to its logical conclusion. With all its defects and excellence, it stands in the history of human thought as the most consistent system of monism. As William James puts it (in appreciation of Śaṅkara's Vedānta as presented by Svāmī Vivekānanda in America): "The paragon of all monistic system is the Vedānta Philosophy of Hindostan."[1] It is true that such a system fails to appeal to those who turn to philosophy for the justification of their imperfect ideas of worldly distinctions and worldly values. Like the teachings of early Buddhism and Jainism, the monistic philosophy of Śaṅkara is only for the strong-hearted who can follow logic dauntless and face conclusions, however, subversive of ordinary ideas of reality and value. But, for those few who have the heart for it, Advaita monism is not without recompense and is not even without emotional satisfaction. As James puts it: "*An Absolute One, and I that one,*—surely we have here a religion which, emotionally considered, has a high pragmatic value ; it imparts a perfect sumptuosity of security."[2] "We all have some ear for this monistic music : it elevates and reassures."[3]

III. The Qualified Monism of Rāmānuja (Viśiṣṭādvaita)

1. Rāmānuja's Conception of the World

Rāmānuja accepts the Upaniṣadic account of creation literally.

Rāmānuja takes the Upaniṣadic accounts of creation, stated previously, in a literal sense. He holds that God, who is omnipotent, creates the manifold world out of Himself by a gracious act of will. Within

1. *Vide* James, *Pragmatism*, p 151.
2. *Loc. cit.*, p. 153.
3. *Loc. cit.*, p. 154.

the All-inclusive God (Brahman) there are both unconscious matter (acit) and the finite spirits (cit). The first is the source of the material objects and as such called prakṛti (*i.e.*, root or origin) after the *Śvetāśvatara-Upaniṣads*,[1] the Purāṇas and Smṛtis whose authority Rāmānuja highly values. This prakṛti is admitted, as in the Sāṅkhya, to be an uncreated (aja), eternal reality. But unlike the Sāṅkhya, Rāmānuja believes that it is a part of God and controlled by God just as the human body is controlled from within by the human soul. During the state of dissolution (pralaya) this primal unconscious nature of prakṛti remains in a latent, subtle (sūkṣma) and undifferentiated (avibhakta) form. God creates out of this the world of diverse objects in accordance with the deeds of the souls in the world prior to the last dissolution. Impelled by the omnipotent will of God the undifferentiated subtle matter gradually becomes transformed into three kinds of subtle elements—fire, water and earth. These differentiated elements manifest also the three kinds of qualities known as sattva, rajas and tamas. Gradually the three subtle elements become mixed up together and give rise to all gross objects which we perceive in the material world.[2] In every object in the world there is a mixture of three elements. This process of triplication is known as trivṛtkaraṇa.

The world is created by God from matter which exists in Him.

Three subtle elements are first created and then mixed up together to form gross elements.

---

1. Svet., 4.5 (ajām ekāṁ lohita-śukla-kṛṇām, etc.) and 4. 10 (māyāṁtu prakṛtiṁvidyāt, mayinaṁ tu Maheśvaram; tasyāvayavabhūtaistu byāptaṁ sarvam idaṁ jagat). Also vide *Brahma-sūt.*, 1. 4. 8. and Rāmānuja's *Bhasya* thereon.

2. Vide *Śribhāsya, Vedāntasāra and Vedāntadipa* on 1.4. 8-10, 1.1.3. and 2.1.15 (note that the guṇas are conceived here, after the *Gitā*, as qualities and as *produced* by prakṛti, not as the essence thereof).

Creation is a real act of God.

Rāmānuja holds, therefore, the creation is a fact and the created world is as real as Brahman. Regarding the Upaniṣadic texts which deny the multiplicity of objects and assert the unity of all things, Rāmānuja holds that these texts do not mean to deny the reality of the many objects, but only teach that in all of them there is the same Brahman, on which all are dependent for existence, just as all gold articles are dependent on gold. What the Upaniṣads deny is the independence of objects, but not their dependent existence (apṛthaksthiṭi).[1]

Māyā means the wonderful power of real creation that is in God.

It is true, Rāmānuja admits, that God has been described (in the *Śvetāśvatara*) as wielder of a magical power (māyā), but this only means that the inscrutable power by which God creates the world is as wonderful as that of a magician. The world 'māyā' stands for God's power of creating wonderful objects (vicitrārtha-sargakari śakti). It also stands sometimes for prakṛti to signify her wonderful creativity.[2]

Rāmānuja holds that all knowledge is true.

Rāmānuja denies, therefore, that creation and the created world are illusory. To strengthen this position he further holds that all knowledge is true (yathā rthaṁ sarva-vijñānam)[3] and that there is no illusory object any where. Even in the case of the so-called illusory snake in the rope, he points out that the three elements (fire, water, earth) by the mixture of which a snake is made, are also the elements by the mixture of which a rope is made, so that even in a rope there is something of a snake and this common element *really existing* in a rope is perceived when we take it for snake. No unreal object is perceived then. The constituent elements of every object being in every other thing every so-called illusion can be similarly explained away. This theory of Rāmānuja resembles in

1. *Śribhāsya,* 1.1.1. (p. 101, R. V. Co. ed.).
2. *Ibid.*, p. 88.
3. *Ibid.*, p. 83.

essential respects the view of some modern realists like Boodin, who hold that all immediate experience of objects is true on the strength of the quantum theory of Schrödinger, according to which each of the electrons, which compose material objects, pervades the whole world, so that "Everything is immanent in everything else."[1]

(i) Rāmānuja's Criticism of the Advaita Theory of Māyā

The difficulties of the advaita theory of Ignorance.

Rāmānuja, who lived long after Śaṅkara had the opportunity of criticizing severely the views of Śaṅkara as well as of his followers, in the course of his commentary of the *Brahma-sūtra*. We are indebted to him for exposing many of the obscure points of the Advaita school. Though the charges raised by Rāmānuja have been replied to by the Advaitins, they have great value for understanding more clearly both Rāmānuja and Śaṅkara. We shall mention here Rāmānuja's chief objections against the Advaita theory of Māyā or ajñana and also show briefly how they can be met from the standpoint of Śaṅkara.

(1) Where does Ignorance exist ?

Where does the Ignorance (ajñana), that is said to produce the world, exist ? It cannot be said to exist in an individual self (jīva), because individuality is itself produced by Ignorance and the cause cannot depend on its effect. Neither can Ignorance be said to be in Brahman, because then it ceases to be omniscient.

These difficulties are based on some misconceptions.

The reply to this, in defence of Śaṅkara, would be that even if Ignorance be said to be in the individual self, the difficulty arises only if we regard the one as *preceding* the other. But if we regard ignorance and individuality as but the two interdependent aspects of the same fact, as a circle

1. *Vide* J. E. Boodin's paper on 'Functional Realism,' *The Philosophical Review,* March, 1934.

and its circumstance, or a triangle and its sides, or fatherhood and sonship, the difficulty does not arise. But if, on the other hand, Brahman be regarded as the locus of Ignorance, even then the difficulty can be removed by removing a misunderstanding on which it is based. Māyā in Brahman is Ignorance only in the sense of the power of producing ignorance and illusion in inviduals ; it does not affect Brahman any more than the magician's power of creating an illusion affects his own knowledge.

(2) If Ignorance conceals Brahman, then its self-revealing nature is destroyed.

It is said that māyā or ajñāna conceals the real nature of Brahman is admitted to be essentially self-revealing. If Māyā conceals Brahman it means that His self revealing nature is destroyed by it and Brahman ceases to be.

The reply to this is that ignorance conceals Brahman in the sense of preventing the ignorant individual from realizing His real nature, most as a patch of cloud conceals the sun by preventing a person from perceiving the sun. So Ignorance does no more destroy the nature of Brahman than the cloud destroys the self-manifesting nature of the sun. Self-manifestation means manifestation of itself in the absence of obstacles—and not in spite of obstacles. The sun does not cease to be self-revealing because the blind cannot see it.

(3) Ignorance is said to be neither real nor unreal, but indescribable.

What is the nature of the Ignorance ? Sometimes the Advaitins say that māyā is indescribable (anirvacanīya), it is neither real nor unreal. This is absurd. Because our experience shows that things are either real or unreal. How can there be a third category besides these two contradictories ?

The real meaning of 'indescribable' (anirvacaniya).

The reply to this is that māyā, as well as every illusory object, is said to be indescribable owing to a genuine difficulty. In so far as it *appears to be* something, an illusion or illusory object cannot be said to be unreal like a square circle or the son of a barren woman which never even appears to exist. Again in so far as it is sublated or contradicted afterwards by some experience, it cannot be said to be absolutely real like Ātman or Brahman whose reality is never contradicted. Māyā and every illusory object have this nature, and compel us to recognize this nature as something unique and indescribable in terms of ordinary reality or unreality. To say that māyā is indescribable is only to describe a fact, namely our *inability* to bring it under any ordinary category, and it does not mean any violation of the law of contradiction. In fact, as 'real' means here the 'absolutely real' and 'unreal' 'the absolutely unreal', they do not constitute a pair of contradictories any more than two words like 'extremely cold' and 'extremely hot' do.

(4) How can ignorance be positive ?

Again sometimes, māyā or avidyā is said by the Advaitins to be positive ignorance (bhāva-rūpam ajñānam). This is also meaningless. Ignorance means want of knowledge, and how can it be positive then?

The reply in defence would be that as the illusion-producing ignorance is not merely an absence of the knowledge of the ground of illusion, but *positively* makes this ground appear as some other object, it is properly described as positive in this sense.

(5) How can Ignorance be destroyed ?

Granting that māyā is something positive, how can it be destroyed by the knowledge of Brahman? Nothing that positively exists can be removed from existence by knowledge.

The reply is that if the word 'positive' be understood in the sense given above, this misunderstanding would not arise. In our daily experience of illusory objects, like the serpent in a rope, we find that the object positively appears to be there and yet it vanishes when we have a clear knowledge of the ground of the illusion, *viz.* the rope.

2. *Rāmānuja's Conception of God*

God is the Absolute Reality, possessed of matter and finite souls.

God, according to Rāmānuja, is the Absolute Reality possessed of two integral parts, matter and the finite spirits. Brahman is the only reality in the universe in the sense that outside or independent of God there is no other reality. But God contains within Himself the material objects as well as the finite souls which are real. The Absolute One contains the many. This monism of Rāmānuja is known, therefore, as Viśiṣṭādvaita which means the Unity (advaita) of Brahman possessed (viśiṣṭa) of real parts (the conscious and the unconscious). It is not a distinctionless unity. Three types of distinction (bheda) are generally distinguished by the Vedāntins. The distinction that anything—say, a cow—has from things of other classes, such as horses, asses, is called heterogeneous distinction (vijātīya-bheda). The distinction that one cow has from another cow (*i.e.* an object of the same class) is called a homogeneous distinction (sajātīya-bheda). In addition to these two kinds of external distinctions, there is a third kind, *i.e.* internal distinction (svagata-bheda), which exists within an object, between its different parts, such as between the tail and the legs of the same cow. In the light of this threefold classification of distinctions, Rāmānuja holds that Brahman is devoid of the two kinds of external distinctions (vijātīya and sajātīya), because there is nothing besides God, either similar or dissimilar to Him. But God is possessed of internal distinctions (svagata-bheda), as there are within Him different conscious and unconscious substances which can be mutually distinguished.

God has all good qualities.

God is possessed of an infinite number of infinitely good qualities such as omnipotence, omniscience, benevolence. Therefore, God is not characterless (nirguṇa), or indeterminate, but possessed of qualities (saguṇa). When the Upaniṣads deny qualities of Brahman, they really mean that God is free from all bad qualities, or imperfections.[1] God really creates the world, sustains it and withdraws it. Even when the world is withdrawn and its objects are destroyed, there remains in God matter in an undifferentiated, homogeneous state, as well as the souls, because both are eternal. Objects

1. 'Nirguṇa-vādāśca parasya brahmaṇo heya-guṇāsam bandhād upapadyante.'—*Śribhāṣya,* 1.1.1. (p. 103, R. V. Co. ed.).

made by the modification of matter undergo change, growth and decay, but matter out of which they are created always remains there. Similarly the spirits always remain, though their bodies may change or perish. In the state of dissolution, when objects are absent, Brahman remains with pure matter and bodiless souls in an unmanifested form (avyakta). This may be called the causal state of Brahman (kārṇa-brahman). When again objects are created, God becomes manifested as the world of objects and embodied souls. This second manifested form of God may be called its effect-state (kārya-brahma). Those texts of the Upaniṣads which deny the existence of objects and describe God negatively as being beyond thought, speech, etc. really indicate the unmanifested state or Brahman.[1]

God as the unmanifested cause.

God as the manifested effect.

If matter and spirit are parts of God, as Rāmānuja repeatedly asserts, then does not God really undergo modification with the change of matter ? Does He not become also subject to the miseries from which the spirits suffer ? Are not then all the imperfections and defects which we find in the world, really in God ? In the face of these difficulties Rāmānuja seems to give up sometimes the imagery of parts and whole and employ other similies. Sometimes he takes recourse to the analogy of the body and the soul. God is the soul of which the material objects and spirits compose the body. Just as the soul controls the body from within, so God controls matter and spirits. He is thus conceived as the Antaryāmin or regulator of the universe from within. With the help of this analogy Rāmānuja tries to explain away the charge of God's being subject to misery and imperfection. The soul, he says, is not affected by the bodily changes and imperfections ; similarly God is not affected by the changes in the universe ; He remains beyond them or transcends them. Sometimes again Rāmānuja tries to prove God's immunity by the analogy of the kind and his subjects. The ruler, in spite of having a body, is not affected by the pleasures and pain suffered by the subjects owing to their obeying or disobeying the ruler's laws.[2]

Rāmānuja's difficulties regarding the relation of God to matter and spirits.

1. *Ibid.*, 1.1.1.1.2., 2.1.15.
2. *Ibid.*, 2.1.14.

These different explanations of Rāmānuja show that we cannot understand every aspect of the relation between God and the world with the help any *one* analogy. We can only try to understand each aspect in the light of one particular type of experience. In fact *no* metaphor claims to resemble the thing compared in *every* respect, and it is extremely difficult to find the ordinary region of experience anything bearing even partial resemblance to God, a unique reality, which can be directly known in religious experience or indirectly from the testimony of those who have realized God. So Rāmānuja stresses so much the authority of scriptures rather than inferences regarding God, the inadequacy of which he tries to expose with the zeal of a sceptic.

Rāmānuja's view of God is theism.

Rāmānuja's conception of God is a kind of theism. Theism, in this narrow sense, means belief in God who is both immanent and transcendent,[1] and is also a Person, *i.e.*, a self-conscious being possessed of will. We have seen that all these characters are present in Rāmānuja's conception of God.

God is the object of worship and the goal of our religious aspiration. It is by pleasing God through prayer that we can obtain salvation through His mercy.

3. Rāmānuja's Conception of the Self, Bondage and Liberation

Between self and God there is identity as well as difference.

Rāmānuja holds that the identity between God and man taught by the Upaniṣads is not really an unqualified one. It is unthinkable that man who is finite can be identical with God in every respect. Man is not different from God in the sense that God pervades and controls man as well as every other thing in the universe. Just as the existence of a part is inseparable from the whole, that of a mode or quality from its substance, or a living body from the soul which

1. Vide Ward. *The Realm of Ends*, p. 224.

controls its life from within, similarly the existence of man is inseparable from God. Identity cannot be asserted, it is true, between two altogether different terms ; but it is also meaningless to assert any identity between exactly identical terms; because it would be a needless tautology. Identity can be asserted between two forms of the same substance. The statement, *'This is that Devadatta'* asserts, for example, identity between the person seen at present and the person seen in the past. The person can be understood as the same in spite of different positions, since the position are occupied at different times. The Upaniṣadic dictum 'that thou art,' (Tat tvam asi) should be understood in a similar way. 'That' stands for God, the omniscient, imnipotent creator of the universe. 'Thou' stands for God existing in the form of man, the embodied soul (acid-viśiṣṭa-jīva-śarīrakam). The identity asserted here is, therefore, between God with certain qualification and God with certain other qualification—identity of the same substance though possessed of different qualities (viśiṣṭasya aikyam). Rāmānuja's philosophy is thus truly called Viśiṣṭā dvaita or the identity of the qualified.[1]

The meaning of "That thou art."

Qualified monism.

Rāmānuja's conception of the relation between the self and God cannot be easily brought under any well-known logical category (such as identity, difference and identity-in-difference). While refuting Śaṅkara's view that this relation is one of identity (abheda) he emphasizes so much the difference between the self and God that the reader would be quite justified to suppose that according to Rāmānuja the relation is one of difference (bheda).[2] This supposition is further confirmed when one reads his commentary on Bādarāyaṇa's sūtra (2.1.22) which points out that Brahmana is other than the embodied self. But the impression is reversed when one reads his commentary on the sūtra (2.1.15) teaching the nondifference (ananyatva) of the world (including the Jīvas) from its cause, Brahman. He thus seems to support two contradictory views.

---

1. Vide *Śrībhāsya* 1.1.1. "Prakāradvaya-viśiṣṭaika-vastu-pratipādanena sāmānādhikaraṇvaṁ ca siddham"(pp. 94-95 of R.V. Co. ed).

2. Vide *Srībhāṣya*, 1.1.1., *passim.*

This conflict disappears, however, on reading his commentary on the sūtra (2.3.42) purporting that the individual self is a part of Bahman. For, Rāmānuja clearly says there that if the self is regarded as a part of Brahman we can reconcile the two opposite kinds of teaching of the revealed texts and of the aforesaid sūtras, namely that there is difference (bheda), and that there is also identity (abheda) between the two. In short, as there are both difference and identity (bhedābheda) between the part and the whole, so also is there a similar relation between the self and God.

It is reasonable to conclude then that according to Rāmānuja, in different respects, there are different kinds of relations between the self and God. In so far as the self is finite and subject to imperfection, and God is just the opposite in nature, there is difference ; in so far as the self is inseparable from God who is its inner substance (ātmā) there is identity (abheda) or ananyatva or tādātmya)[1]; but as the self is part of God, both identity and difference are tenable. This is the final impression created by Rāmānuja's writings on many competent readers, among whom there is no less an authority than Mādhavācārya, who says in the *Śarvadarśana-saṅgraha* that Rāmānuja believes in all kinds of relations, bheda, abheda, and bhedābheda, in different respects. Sadānanda[2] also describes him as a bhedābheda-vādin.

But unfortunately even this well-founded conclusion regarding Rāmānuja's view receives a rude shock from his rather surprising statements here and there in which he launches a wholesale attack on all the three kinds of philosophers who advocate respectively identity (abheda), difference (bheda) and identity-in-difference (bhedābheda).[3] The reader is thus swept away even from the last foothold and is left puzzled.

One can understand why Rāmānuja should reject unqualified identity (abheda) or difference (bheda) ; but it is difficult to see why he criticizes even the theory of identity-in-difference (bhedābheda) if he himself advocates the view that both difference and identity, as taught by the scriptures, are real. The fact seems to be that in criticizing the advocates of bhedābheda he has two cl1asses

1. All these words are used by Rāmānuja.
2. *Vide* his *Advaita-brahma-siddhi* (p. 270, Calcutta University ed.) :- "bhedābhedavādino rāmānujāh.........."
3. E. g. *Sribhāsya* 1.1.1. (p. 96) 1. 1.4.

of them in mind : (1) those who hold that the self is nothing but Brahman *imagined* as limited by some extraneous or accidental adjunct (upādhi)—just as the space of the room is nothing but the all-pervasive space imagined as limited by the room; and (2) those who hold that the self is but a mode of Brahman who has *really* assumed a finite form.[1] In respect of the former, Rāmānuja's objection is that as they hold that the self is really Brahman (the distinguishing limiting adjunct being imaginary), the imperfections of the self would also really belong to Brahman. In respect of the latter, he points out that as Brahman according to them is really reduced to a finite self, He really becomes subject to all the imperfections of the latter. But these objections are obviated, he further points out, by his own theory according to which the conscious souls (cit) and unconscious matter (acit), though possessing different natures (svarūpa) from the all-inclusive Brahman, are eternally and inseparably related to Him as parts to their whole, effects to their material cause, arrtibutes to their substance.

What Rāmānuja tries then to make out is that Brahman never *becomes* in any way a self, just as the whole never *becomes* a part, or a substance never *becomes* an attribute. Brahman is eternally Brahman, and the selves within Him eternally exist as such. But how then can Rāmānuja speak of Brahman as the cause of the Jīva (or of matter) if the latter does not *arise* from the former ? It would appear that by calling Brahman the cause he does not mean the immediate unconditional *antecedent* but only the *material* or the substance. God as the ultimate whole of existence (sat) in the substance *eternally* underlying all finites. The whole does not precede the parts, nor do parts succeed the whole. Brahman always exists as a whole possessed of parts and never *becomes*, parts, and therefore, does not *become* subject to the imperfections of the parts.

Though it is doubtful whether this analogy of the part and the whole saves Brahman from all imperfections, it would be clear from the above that Rāmānuja's objection is not so much against the relation of identity-in-difference as such (which he himself advocates under sūtra 2.3.42) but against the particular formulations of it. Identity-in-difference means, for him, identity of the *one-substance* existing in two real forms ('ekameva vastu dvirūpam prati yate'[2] ; 'prakāra-dvayāvasthitatvāt sāmānādhikarṇyasya'.[3]

1. *Ibid.*, p. 97.
2. *Ibid.*, p. 150.
3. *Ibid.*, p. 94.

What he rejects are (1) identity of the one substance *appearing* as two owing to misconception, and (2) identity of the one which has *become* really *two*. Between the whole and the part there is identity-in-difference, not of any of these last two kinds, but of the first kind. The whole really possesses different parts from which it is always different as a whole, but the same identical whole is also in every part, though it does not become reduced to many (in which case the whole would be divided and cease to be a whole).

It will also be found that in upholding the unity of the substance, and making it the foundation, and in treating multiplicity only as a dependent character of the one, Rāmānuja's emphasis is on the aspect of identity rather than on that of difference, though he treats both as real.

This view also enables us to distinguish the position of Rāmānuja from that of Nimbārka, for example, who too believes in a kind of identity-in-difference (bhedābheda). As Ghate rightly points out, "Thus we see that the doctrine of Nimbārka has very much in common with that of Rāmānuja, both regard the difference as well as the non-difference as real. But, for Nimbārka, difference and non-difference are on the same level, they co-exist and have the same importance ; while for Rāmānuja, non-difference is the principal; it is qualified by difference, which is thus subordinate to it."[1] This also explains why Rāmānuja's philosophy can be called qualified monism, rather than qualified dualism or monism-dualism (dvaitādvaita).

The extremely puzzling statements of Rāmānuja, regarding his attitude to identity, difference, and identity-in-difference tempt some writers to avoid the attempt to bring his view under any of these usual categories of relation ; and lead them to hold that Rāmānuja's conception of the relation between self and God, is a category by itself ; it is inseparability ('apṛthaksthiti'). But this is merely giving up the game of logical understanding. For, inseparability of existence is itself a general relation, admitting of various formulations. Even Śaṅkara's conception of the relation between the effect and the cause (ananyatva) can come under this. Logical thought wants

1. V. S. Ghate. The *Vedānta,* p. 32.

to understand what this relation means in terms of identity and difference ; or, failing this, why this relation defies such affiliation. We have seen above that it is possible to interpret Rāmānuja's conception as one of identity-in-difference of a specific kind, and that he himself accepts this in some places. It may be noted that a later theistic school following Caitanya frankly holds that the relation between self and God is an inconceivable kind of identity in difference (acintya bhedābheda) not amenable to further analysis.

Man, according to Rāmānuja, has a real body and a soul. The body is made of matter which is a part of God. It is obviously finite. The soul is, of course, not made; it is eternally existing. It is also a part of God, and cannot, therefore, be infinite. The all-pervasive nature of the soul which the Upaniṣads describe cannot, therefore, be taken, in the literal sense. The real sense of the prevasiveness of the soul is that the soul is so subtle (sū kṣma) that it can penetrate into every unconscious material substance.[1] Having denied that the soul is infinite, Rāmājuna has to hold that it is infinitely small (aṇu). For, if the soul has neither of these two extreme dimensions, it must be admitted to have the medium one, which things composed by the combination of parts (such as tables and chairs) have ; and then like such objects the soul also would be liable to destruction. The consciousness of the soul is not accidental to it, it is not dependent on its connection with the body. Consciousness is not the essence, but an eternal *quality*, of the soul and it remains under all conditions.[2] In dreamless sleep and even in the state of liberation, when the soul is altogether disembodied, the soul remains conscious of itself as 'I am'. The soul is, therefore, identified by Rāmānuja with what we mean by the word 'I' or the 'ego' (aham).[3]

The human body and soul are both finite.

The soul is eternal but infinitely small.

Consciousness is the *essential* quality of the soul.

---

1. "vyāpī, ati-sūkṣmatayā sarvācetanānatḥ-praveśana-svabhāvaḥ." *Śrībhāṣya* 1.1.1.

2. Contrast Sāṅkhya and Advaita which hold that consciousness is same as self. Rāmānuja school names consciousness as dharmabhūtajñana (—an attribute in relation to self and God).

3. "Svarūpeṇa eva ahamarthaḥ ātmā ;" "muktau api ahamarthaḥ prakāśate," *loc. cit.*

The bondage of the soul to the body is due to its karma.

The bondage of the soul is due to karma.

As the effect of its karma, the soul is associated with the particular kind of body it deserves. Being embodied, its consciousness is limited by the conditions of the organs of knowledge, and the body it possesses. Though the soul is infinity small, it illumines or renders conscious every part of the body in which it is, just as a small light illumines the entire room in which it is. It identifies itself with the body and regards it as itself. Egoism (ahaṅkāra) is a name for this identification of the self with the not-self. Avidyā or ignorance consists in this base propensity.[1] Karma also is sometimes identified by Rāmānuja with this ignorance.

The liberation of the soul is sought through work.

The attainment of liberation must be sought through work and knowledge, because they pave the way for devotion. By work (karma) Rāmānuja means here the different obligatory rituals enjoined by the Vedas on persons according to their respective castes and stations in life (varṇāśrama). These should be performed life-long as bounded duties without any desire for reward, like heaven. Disinterested performance of such duties destroys the accumulated effects of the past deeds which stand in the way of knowledge. For the correct performance of these rituals it is necessary to study the Mīmāṁsa philosophy. Rāmānuja regards, therefore, the study of the Mīmāṁsa as a necessary pre-requisite to the study of the Vedānta. By the study of the Mīmāṁsa and performance of the duties in its light, one comes to realize also that the sacrificial rites cannot lead to any permanent good and cannot help man to attain salvation. This persuades him to study the Vedānta. The Vedānta reveals to him the real nature of the Universe. He comes to know that God is the creator,

The necessity of performing rituals for destroying karmas.

The necessity of the knowledge of Vedānta.

1. "Śarīragocarā ca ahambuddhir avidyaiva ;" anātmani dehe ahambhāvakaraṇa-hetutvena ahaṅkāraḥ," *Ibid.*

sustainer and controller of all beings, and that his soul is not identical with the body, but is really a part of God who controls it from within. He further learns that liberation can be attained not by 'study and reasoning', but only if God is pleased to choose him for liberation.

The knowledge of God matures into constant remembrance or devotion.

The study of the Vedānta produces only book learning and does not bring about liberation. It is true, as the Upaniṣads say, that liberation is brought about by knowledge. But that real knowledge is not a verbal knowledge of scriptures; for then everyone who reads them would be liberated at once. Real knowledge is a steady, constant remembrance of God (dhruvā smṛti). This is variously described as meditation (dhyāna), prayer (upā sanā), devotion (bhākti).[1] Constant meditation on God as the dearest object of love, should be practised continuously along with the performance of the obligatory rituals which remove the obstacles to knowledge. Intense remembrance of God, or devotion thus practised, ultimately matures into an immediate knowledge (darśana or sākṣātkā ra) of God. This is, therefore, the final means to liberation. This brings about the destruction of all ignorance and karmas by which the body is caused. Therefore, the soul that realizes God is liberated from the body for ever, without any chance of rebirth. We should remember, however, that liberation cannot be attained simply by human efforts. God, pleased by devotion, helps the devotee to attain perfect knowledge by removing obstacles. God lifts from bondage and misery the man who flings himself at the mercy of God and constantly remembers Him as the only object of love. Such complete self-surrender is called *prapatti*.

Constant remembrance turns into immediate knowledge of God.

God's help is necessary for liberation.

---

1. "Ato...dhyānopāsanādhi-vācyam jñānam" ; "vedanam upāsanamsyāt"; "upāsana-paryāyatvāt bhakti-śabdasya", *Śribhāṣya*, 1.1.1.

Liberation is not the soul's becoming identical with God. The liberated soul having pure consciousness, untainted by any imperfection, becomes, in this respect, similar to God (brahmaprakāra). This similarity of nature is what is meant by the Upaniṣads which say that the liberated soul attains unity with God.[1]

The liberated soul is *like* God, *not identical* with God.

We saw previously that according to the unqualified monism of Śaṅkara, the highest good lies in a complete denial of the separate self and the realization of its unity with God. The religious sentiment of the monist attains full satisfaction by total self-effacement which leaves nothing but God, the sole, self-shining Reality. But for the theist, like Rāmānuja, this is a dismal prospect. The highest satisfaction of the religious emotion demands no doubt self-purification and self-surrender, but not complete self-effacement. The highest good for the devotee is the pure and constant contemplation of the infinite glory of God, and the liberated one needs his self if only for, the enjoyment of this highest bliss. Free from ignorance and bondage of every kind, the liberated soul enjoys, in perfect love and wisdom, infinite joy born of complete communion with God.[2]

Conclusion.

---

1. "Jñānaikāratayā Brahma-prakārtā ucyate," *Śrībhāṣya*, p. 71 (R. V.& Co. edition).

2. *Ibid.*, 4th Pāda of the 4th Adhyāya, *passim*.

INDEX